T0340385

Sustainable Urban Tourism in Sub-Saharan Africa

This book investigates urban tourism development in sub-Saharan Africa, highlighting the challenges and risks involved, but also showcasing the potential benefits.

While much is written about Africa's rural environments, it seems little has been written about the tourism potential of the vast natural, cultural and historical resources in the continent's urban areas. Yet these opportunities also come with considerable environmental, social and political challenges. This book interrogates the interactions between urban risks, tourism and sustainable development in sub-Saharan African urban spaces. It addresses the underlying issues of governance, power, ownership, collaboration, justice, community empowerment and policies that influence tourism decision-making at local, national and regional levels. Interrogating the intricate relationships between tourism stakeholders, this book ultimately reflects on how urban risk can be mitigated, and how sustainable urban tourism can be harnessed for development.

The important insights in this book will be of interest to researchers and practitioners across Tourism, Geography, Urban Development and African Studies.

Llewellyn Leonard is a Professor at the Department of Environmental Science, School of Ecological and Human Sustainability at the University of South Africa (UNISA). He has a Ph.D. from Kings College, University of London, and is a human geographer and environmental sociologist. His research interests include environmental justice, governance, democracy and human rights, civil-society-state-industry relations, urban risks, sustainable development, risk society and political economy/ecology.

Regis Musavengane (Ph.D.) is a political ecologist and tourism and conservation geographer. He is a faculty member at the Midlands State University, Zimbabwe, Department of Tourism and Hospitality, and a Research Fellow at the School of Ecological and Human Sustainability, Department of Environmental Sciences at the University of South Africa (UNISA). He holds a Ph.D. in Geography and Environmental Studies from University of the Witwatersrand, Johannesburg, South Africa. His research interests include collaborative management of natural resources, community-based tourism, land reform for community development and inclusive tourism systems for both urban and rural spaces.

Pius Siakwah (Ph.D.) is a development and resources geographer and a Research Fellow at the Institute of African Studies (IAS), University of Ghana. He holds a Ph.D. in Geography from Trinity College Dublin (TCD), Ireland. He has keen interest in political economy, natural resources, renewable energies ans sustainability, development geographies, governance, livelihoods, network theories and tourism and development.

Routledge Studies in Cities and Development

The series features innovative and original research on cities in the Global South, aiming to explore urban settings through the lens of international development. The series particularly promotes comparative and interdisciplinary research targeted at a global readership.

In terms of theory and method, rather than basing itself on any one orthodoxy, the series draws on a broad toolkit taken from across social sciences and built environment studies, emphasizing comparison, the analysis of the structure and processes, and the application of qualitative and quantitative methods.

The series welcomes submissions from established and junior authors on cutting-edge and high-level research on key topics that feature in global news and public debate.

Sustainable Urban Tourism in Sub-Saharan Africa

Risk and Resilience

Edited by Llewellyn Leonard, Regis Musavengane and Pius Siakwah

Routledge
Taylor & Francis Group

LONDON AND NEW YORK

First published 2021
by Routledge
2 Park Square, Milton Park, Abingdon, Oxon OX14 4RN

and by Routledge
52 Vanderbilt Avenue, New York, NY 10017

Routledge is an imprint of the Taylor & Francis Group, an informa business

British Library Cataloguing-in-Publication Data
A catalogue record for this book is available from the British Library

Library of Congress Cataloging-in-Publication Data

Names: Leonard, Llewellyn, editor. | Musavengane, Regis, editor. | Siakwah, Pius, editor.

Title: Sustainable urban tourism in sub-Saharan Africa : risk and resilience / edited by Llewellyn Leonard, Regis Musavengane and Pius Siakwah.

Description: New York : Routledge, 2021. | Series: Routledge studies in cities and development | Includes bibliographical references and index.
Identifiers: LCCN 2020035058 (print) | LCCN 2020035059 (ebook) | ISBN 9780367904142 (hardback) | ISBN 9781003024293 (ebook)

Subjects: LCSH: Urban ecology (Sociology)--Africa, Sub-Saharan. | Cities and towns--Growth--Environmental aspects. | Ecotourism--Africa, Sub-Saharan.

Classification: LCC HT243.A43 S87 2021 (print) | LCC HT243.A43 (ebook) | DDC 307.760967--dc23

LC record available at https://lccn.loc.gov/2020035058
LC ebook record available at https://lccn.loc.gov/2020035059

ISBN: 978-0-367-90414-2 (hbk)
ISBN: 978-1-003-02429-3 (ebk)

Typeset in Times New Roman
by SPi Global, India

Contents

Tables

Figures

Contributors

Robin Nunkoo is an Associate Professor in the Faculty of Law and Management at the University of Mauritius; a Visiting Senior Research Fellow at the University of Johannesburg, South Africa; an Adjunct Professor at Griffith Institute for Tourism, Griffith University, Australia; and a Visiting Researcher in the Department of Marketing, Copenhagen Business School, University of Copenhagen, Denmark. He is an Editor in a number of A-rated journals, extensively published and cited. http://orcid.org/0000-0002-3583-9717

Brij Maharaj is a Senior Professor of Geography at the University of KwaZulu-Natal in Durban, South Africa. He has received widespread recognition for his research on urban politics, mega-events, segregation, local economic development, xenophobia and human rights, migration and diasporas, religion, philanthropy and development, and has published over 150 scholarly papers and co-edited 5 book collections. http://orcid.org/0000-0003-1266-2231

Wilma Sichombo Nchito is a Senior Lecturer in the Department of Geography and Environmental Studies in the School of Natural Sciences at the University of Zambia. She is an urban geographer, specialised in planning in transition. http://orcid.org/0000-0001-7089-9777

Euphemia Mwale holds a B.A. Ed and MSc in Environment and Natural Resources Management from the University of Zambia. Has been teaching Geography at the secondary-school level for over 10 years.

Ayanda Dladla holds a master's degree from the University of Johannesburg, School of Tourism and Hospitality. He has always been interested in researching on sustainable tourism with a focus on pro-poor tourism and social change.

Clément Longondjo Etambakonga is an Adjunct Professor at Rennes School of Business, France. He holds a Ph.D. in Management from Rennes Business School. He researches on corporate social responsibility, responsible business, business ethics, sustainable development and waste management and recycling in post-conflict context. https://orcid.org/0000-0002-8688-3769

Dieudonné Trinto Mugangu is a freelance consultant for biodiversity, climate change and land degradation covering several African countries for several institutions, including the World Bank, the United Nations Environment

Programme (UNEP), UNDP, GEF, the United States Agency for International Development (USAID), the World Wide Fund for Nature (WWF) and the Central Africa Regional Programme for the Environment (CARPE). He holds a Ph.D. in Wildlife Ecology from the University of Maine.

Eromose E. Ebhuoma is a Postdoctoral Research Fellow at the Department of Environmental Sciences, College of Agriculture and Environmental Sciences, University of South Africa. His research interest lies in climate change vulnerability and adaptation; climate services; local and indigenous knowledge systems; political ecology; community development and environmental sustainability. http://orcid.org/0000-0002-3446-3463

Francini van Staden is a Directorate of Environmental Sustainability based at the Department of Environmental Affairs & Development Planning, Western Cape Government. She holds an MBA in Sustainability Management. Her research focuses on the nexus of socioeconomic and environmental systems, and the influences arising from this nexus on the theory and practice of environmental management. http://orcid.org/0000-0001-9457-4942

Raphael Ane Atanga is a Postdoctoral Research Fellow at the University of Johannesburg. He holds a Ph.D. from the Faculty of Environmental Sciences at the Technische Universität Dresden (Germany). His research interests are in the intersection of resilience, disaster risk management, stakeholder analysis, sustainable development and tourism in West Africa. https://orcid.org/0000-0002-5372-6599

Tembi Tichaawa is the Academic Head of the Tourism Department and an Associate Professor in Tourism at the School of Tourism and Hospitality, University of Johannesburg. He holds a Ph.D. in Geography and Environmental Management from the University of KwaZulu-Natal. He conducts research on a range of developmental issues linked to tourism, hospitality and events management with specific focus on the developing context. https://orcid.org/0000-0002-1913-3730

Felix Kwabena Donkor is a Postdoctoral Research Fellow at the College of Agriculture and Environmental Sciences (UNISA), South Africa. His research interests include sustainable rural livelihoods, indigenous knowledge systems, environmental governance and sustainable development. http://orcid.org/0000-0001-8353-8313

Kevin Mearns is a Professor at the College of Agriculture and Environmental Sciences, University of South Africa. His research interests include sustainable tourism, environmental management, ecology and ecotourism. http://orcid.org/0000-0001-5874-3542

Prudence Khumalo is a Professor in the Department of Public Administration, University of South Africa. His research interests include development management, policy and human settlements management. http://orcid.org/0000-0001-5316-2941

Michael Dyssel lectures in the Department of Geography, Environmental Studies and Tourism at the University of the Western Cape, Bellville, South Africa. His research and teaching interests include urban-ecological challenges, conservation, communities and resource-use challenges, environmental management and the impacts of tourism. https://orcid.org/0000-0003-2492-645X

Zibanai Zhou is a Lecturer and current Head of Tourism & Hospitality Management Department at the Midlands State University, Zimbabwe. His research interests include tourism management, destination marketing, event tourism and community-based tourism development. http://orcid.org/0000-0002-7918-2200.

Erisher Woyo is a Senior Lecturer at Sol Plaatje University. He holds a Ph.D. in Tourism Management from the North-West University, Potchefstroom Campus, South Africa. His research interests include information technology, destination branding, destination competitiveness and destination attractiveness; and more importantly, the intersection of ICT with higher education. https://orcid.org/0000-0002-0776-6645

Acknowledgements

The editors of this book would like to thank all contributors from diverse backgrounds who contributed to this volume. It was not an easy call; the complex issues intertwining development, risk and livelihoods are always challenging to address. Moreover, despite the unexpected 2020 coronavirus challenges, the authors thrived to complete their chapters – some wrote their chapters in self-isolation and others in quarantine centres. Thumbs up to you all. You raise the flag of Africa higher, you are true heroes and heroines, and we salute you. The chapters provided by the contributors demonstrated the strong linkages between urban risk and tourism development in the sub-Saharan African region and pointed out strategies needed to develop inclusive and sustainable urban spaces. We also acknowledge the input made by the 3 anonymous reviewers who provided insightful comments to our book proposal. In the same vein, we appreciate Taylor & Francis team, who guided the effort from the start to its completion, in particular, Rosie Anderson and Elizabeth Cox.

All chapters were peer reviewed by 2 external reviewers; we would like to thank the external review experts for their valuable comments and suggestions, which made this volume a possibility. Reviewers at the following institutions are acknowledged: University of the Witwatersrand (South Africa); University of Johannesburg (South Africa); University of Cape Town (South Africa); Central University of Technology (South Africa); Chinhoyi University of Technology (Zimbabwe); University of South Africa; Northwest University (South Africa); Midlands State University (Zimbabwe); University of Ghana; Namibia University of Science and Technology (Namibia); Sol Platje University (South Africa); University of Coventry (United Kingdom); and the World Bank.

Finally, we thank our families and friends for their love and support. Llewellyn would like to thank Jessica, Udhav and Tulsi Rasa Leonard for providing sustenance for spiritual enlightenment to continue his work towards pursuing for a more just society. He would also like to thank his co-authors for their dedication and for sharing this journey with him. What began as an informal discussion on urban risks and tourism quickly resulted in spearheading this book publication. Regis would like to thank his wife, Rutendo Rhoda Musavengane, his son, Christian Tapiwanashe, and daughter, Chantelle Ruvimbo Musavengane, for the social support and understanding that the work dad is doing for building a better Africa. Pius thanks his family and the Institute of African Studies (IAS), University of Ghana for their support during working on this project.

Preface

Africa is known for its pristine destinations, mainly associated with rich fauna and flora. This explains the existence of vast material, written and visual on rural environments or nature-based destinations. However, little has been written on urban tourism within an African context except South Africa with some remarkable work on slum tourism. The link between urban risks, urban tourism and sustainable development has also been limitedly explored in the academia and under-researched in the Global South, especially on the African continent. This book provides theoretical and empirical evidence on the interactions between urban risks, tourism and sustainable development in sub-Saharan African urban spaces. At the backdrop of vast natural, cultural and historical resources in African urban areas are numerous environmental, social and political challenges. The book, therefore, provides in-depth analysis of the linkages between tourism and urban risk in African cities, towns and townships. This book is a toolkit of the urban tourism development on the African continent, valuable to tourism, geography and social science students and practitioners. The discussion on tourism and urban risk provides a platform to interrogate possible efficient development approaches on tourism in urban spaces. This volume showcases the many facets of urban tourism through examining broad and localized empirical studies and conceptual frameworks. It addresses the underlying issues of governance, power, ownership, collaboration, justice, community empowerment and policies that influence tourism decision-making at local, national and regional levels. It further contributes to understanding the intricate relationships between tourism stakeholders across the social, class, racial and national strands.

1 Urban risk and tourism in Africa

An overview

Llewellyn Leonard, Regis Musavengane, and Pius Siakwah

1 Introduction

African cities, and particularly urban spaces in sub-Saharan Africa (SSA), are pivots of socioeconomic development with ever-increasing potential for tourism development, despite the plethora of challenges these urban spaces experience. Urbanisation is a multifaceted concept (Musavengane et al., 2020); it is not only about population growth in towns and cities, but also the extent to which this growth is accompanied by structural shifts in the economic, employment, social, environmental and political spheres (UN-Habitat, 2016; Awumbila, 2014). Urban areas are settlements with large and high population densities and built infrastructures (Satterthwaite, 2017). They have been experiencing significant population and structural changes. According to the United Nations Development Program (UNDP) (2015), the global population in urban areas is expected to double, with an estimated 1 in 3 persons residing in cities and over 3 billion persons living in slums by 2050. In 2014, 880 million urban residents were estimated to live in slums, an increase of 11% since 2000 (UNDP, 2015). Regionally, SSA urban areas currently contain approximately 472 million people, with the global share of African urban residents projected to grow from 11% in 2010 to 20% by 2050 (Saghir & Santoro, 2018). Similarly, in SSA, nearly 60% of people live in slums (UN-Habitat, 2016). Although urbanisation levels in many large mainland countries have reduced since the 1970s due to Structural Adjustment Programmes (SAPs) impacting urban economies and livelihoods, some countries continued to urbanise fairly rapidly due to the global commodity boom around 2003–2014 (Potts, 2013, 2017). A sharp rise in urban population over the next 30 years is expected in Asia and Africa (Neiderud, 2015).

With this urban transition in mind, the poor and the vulnerable travelling to these urban areas generally settle in lower-income and hazardous areas, as healthy environments are beyond their reach economically and socially. As Agyeman et al. (2003) note, customarily low-income areas become targets for social and environmental injustices. As the poor move into those spaces with little or no provision of social services, it also exposes and increases their vulnerability. Poverty is becoming increasingly urbanised, and the urban poor are susceptible to various urban risks, such as societal and health risks (UN Habitat, 2016). Unplanned urban growth can contribute to urban social, political and environmental risks

(Asian Development Bank, 2013), and there is a need for effective planning to mitigate (and alleviate) risks that affect tourism development (Fraser et al., 2017), as the sector is not immune to urbanisation challenges.

2 Contextualising urbanisation, urban risk and tourism

Despite the obvious interlocks between urban risks and tourism development, academic research in this arena has been limited (Siakwah et al., 2020), with urban tourism in many southern African cities seeming largely invisible to the scholarly gaze (Visser, 2019). An understanding of current and future trends in sustainable tourism is thus critical, and it has to be complemented with an appraisal of urban risks (Musavengane et al., 2020). Some of the urban risks that pose challenges to urban tourism development (and as understood in this book) include population pressures, inadequate social services, (in)security, xeno-phobia, limited economic opportunities and inequalities, crime, environmental challenges, governance and strained resources (Dodman et al., 2017; Falt, 2016; Smith, 2001). The United Nations' 2030 Sustainable Development Goal (SDG) 11, "making cities and human settlements inclusive, safe, resilient and sustainable," partly informs this book to interrogate the relationship between urban risk and tourism development in SSA. The manner in which a region or space is perceived is of major importance to its success or failure as a tourist destination (Becken et al., 2017). Therefore, this book aims to assess challenges pertaining to sustainable urban tourism in SSA and how its urban spaces could potentially become more resilient in the face of urban risk; this includes building resilient, inclusive cities. Although understandings about urban resilience are ambiguous, they are generally viewed as a means to increase the ability of urban systems to prevent varied range of shocks and stressors (Nop & Thornton, 2019), and thereby withstand and recover from unexpected urban risks through proper urban planning and management (Asian Development Bank, 2013). The foundations of tourism resilience lie in the acknowledgement that the social and environmental issues are an intertwined, social-ecological entity and that tourism resilience complements sustainability, with the urban tourism environment continually experiencing change (Cheer & Lew, 2017). In SSA, the Sustainable Development Goals (SDGs) present some form of an integrated development approach (albeit challenged) to risk management, vulnerability reduction and poverty eradication (Fraser et al., 2017) and thereby aim to promote urban resilience. Sustainable urban tourism has the potential to mitigate urban poverty and urbanisation-related risks (Musavengane et al., 2020; Rogerson, 2002; Rogerson & Visser, 2007; Robinson, 2006). Fraser et al. (2017) highlight the multiple ways in which risk and urban development coevolve in Africa by broadening the understanding of the nature, scale and distribution of urban risks, and examine relationships between daily activities and disaster risks across scales. Nevertheless, little seems to be known about the relationship between urban risk, tourism and resilience, and it is not clear what factors contribute to, or hinder inclusive and sustainable tourism in African cities. Understanding the link between urban risk and tourism can help mitigate the negative effects of urban risks pertaining to tourism operations through good governance practices (Musavengane et al., 2020).

There are various ways that urban risks can negatively impact urban tourism development. For example, urban risks can manifest in the form of exclusionary development practices, where the poor are ejected from urban spaces, with no provision of basic social services for the development of hotels and facilities for tourism promotion (Siakwah et al., 2020). Satterthwaite (2017) noted how urbanisation in SSA is underpinned by rapid population growth without the necessary governance structures to meet responsibilities and manage change. These challenges in urban settings negatively affect tourism development (UN-Habitat, 2016) through unjustified displacement or limited investments in spaces, which the poor previously occupied. Falt (2016) posited that the displacement of the urban poor through forced eviction is underpinned by multiple rationalities such as neoliberal market-oriented policies and the social desire for clean and beautiful surroundings. Urban revanchism elucidates how urban politics are driven by market-logics and anti-poor attitudes, and aesthetics construct and reconstruct (new) patterns of socio-spatial segregation globally (Falt, 2016, p. 466; Smith, 2001). Leonard (2018) observed that neoliberalism has not necessarily been economically successful but has actually increased inequality. Thus, market-driven and social desires that are not developmentally sensitive to diverse interests and groups can lead to exclusionary outcomes.

Linked to governance, some urban areas in Africa are facing infrastructural crises with negative implications, where a substantial proportion of the populace live in those areas (Satterthwaite, 2017). Simiyu et al. (2019) highlight the importance of social services provisions in reducing urban risks in informal settlements in Kenya. Urban infrastructure deficit, partly driven by exclusionary neoliberal policies, poses risk to sustainable tourism development (Musavengane et al., 2020). In Zimbabwe, infrastructure such as roads, drainage and hospitals are dilapidated and pose a threat to sustainable tourism development (Manjengwa et al., 2016). Thus, following Goldman (2011) and Watson (2014), Falt (2016) postulates that a spatial rationality based on land speculation is rife in the urban spaces. Spatial rationality highlights socially produced knowledge bases that emphasise (1) the benefits of spatial order; (2) the links between the physical environment, human well-being and morality; and (3) different strategies for development of the 'social whole' (Falt, 2016:483). These points, driven by neoliberal policies, can lead to artificial increases in land prizes and exclusion of the poor from urban spaces for tourism promotion. Land speculation and dispossession drive speculative urbanism, and this captures shifts in urban governance, where it has become a core government business to create world-tourism cities (Goldman, 2011, Watson, 2009). In Bangalore, India, Goldman (2011) reported shifts in urban governance where speculation in land values have forced the poor from those lands that are later developed into hotels and other uses for tourism promotion (Falt, 2016).

Urban inequalities and unemployment are urban risks that pose challenges to urban tourism development. Excluding the poor in tourism development poses a risk to tourism itself, as local residents do not gain from the economic benefits derived from tourism or participate in tourism activities to increase its profitability. Poverty can be a driver of crime, and crime, in whatever form, is a risk to tourism development (Allen, 1999; Boakye, 2012; Holcomb & Pizam, 2006; Levantis & Gani, 2000), with security an imperative determinant of a destination's attractiveness (Sonmez & Graefe, 1998). Neoliberal tourism development in the urban space exhibits exclusionary tendencies that drive the urban poor into poverty and social vices. Neoliberal economic policy has led to a speedy growth of tourism activities in its numerous magnitudes, and these activities are often in opposition to the interests of the wider social benefits (Pavlovic & Knezevic, 2017). These types of neoliberal tourism strategies often perceive the urban poor and their informal activities as incompatible with neoliberal goals of increasing profit.

These strategies were implemented for the African Cup of Nations in Ghana in 2008 and the World Cup in South Africa in 2010, when some poor spaces were cleared to improve the areas for tourists. These urban tourism development strategies resulted in evictions, restrictions and the relocation of poorer urban groups that did not economically benefit from the events in favour of powerful actors (Lindell et al., 2010). In South Africa, transitioning to democracy has therefore not assisted in addressing many of the urban risks' challenges experienced by vulnerable citizens who are exposed to inequalities and unemployment due to the state's neoliberal policy agenda (Leonard, 2017). Instead, the neoliberal states' engagement in macroeconomic policies has increased urban risks for vulnerable citizens, excluded from decision-making (thus, resulting in poor housing, unemployment, crime, xenophobia and a lack of water, waste and sanitation facilities) (McKinley & Veriava, 2004).

Similarly, Manjengwa et al. (2016) stated that economic crisis, unemployment and urban poverty is prevalent in African countries such as Zimbabwe due to economic turmoil, which is driven by structural adjustment and propelled by political sanctions. Poverty manifests in the form of urban slums, limited access to productive assets, poor health, poor education and poor social capital capacity (Chronic Poverty Research Centre [CPRC], 2005). Urban unemployment and poverty are risks to tourism promotion as the poor, especially the youth, can be lured into crimes that can also make the tourism destinations unattractive. The poor also have no resources to spend on domestic tourism promotion. Thus, tourism development can be a product of the neoliberal phase of the development of modern capitalism (Lindell et al., 2010). Nonetheless, unbridled neoliberalism, that is not inclusive will also undo tourism promotion.

Environmental challenges (for example, climate change causing extreme heat or flooding, waste and air pollution, and industrial risks such as explosions) influence a destination image and risk perceptions, and thus, shape tourism development. Depietri and McPhearson (2019) observe how climate change, in terms of heatwaves and flooding, are affecting urban spaces and increasing urban risks. Ecological challenges such as flooding and the destruction of historical sites are risks to urban tourism development. For instance, Accra, Ghana, which had a population of 4.3 million people in 2016, is faced with challenges, including flooding (Atanga, 2016; Songsore et al., 2009). The expansion of cities and the population implies that wetlands and watercourses are converted into residential land use, while open drains are filled with waste that disrupts the flow of water and thus causes waterborne diseases (Atanga, 2016).

Urban centres can be incubators for new epidemics, and zoonotic diseases can spread rapidly and become global threats (Neiderud, 2015), as witnessed with the spread of the coronavirus (COVID-19) in the central city of Wuhan, China, which has had implications for local, national and global tourism (Lee, 2020). Environmental and societal changes also tend to increase urban risks, such as the loss of shorelines and heritage sites (Addo et al., 2008), and these have negative implications for tourism development, for example, in coastal urban cities (Becken et al., 2017). This is evident in the instance of the Castles (Cape Coast and Elmina) and Forts along the coast of Ghana, which are under threat from climate change and human activities (Siakwah, 2018). Urban industrial emissions and transport pollution can also have implications for urban tourism due to the air pollution they create. For example, Becken et al. (2017) observed that inbound tourist arrivals, especially from the West into China, have been declining in recent years, possibly in response to increasing levels of urban air pollution. Cognitive and affective destination image and cognitive and affective risk perceptions influence tourists' intentions to visit a specific destination. While China's cognitive image attributes are generally perceived as positive, potential travellers express negative views about travel risks in China, with a specific emphasis on air quality.

In order to understand the link between urban risk, tourism and resilience, it is important to explore how the tourism field has developed. Tourism is naively regarded as a 'new' phenomena by some tourist researchers and readers (Leigh, 2013). This can be attributed to a lack of historical analysis of tourism development by researchers within this field (Butler, 2015). Walton (2005: 6) noted that "a problem in tourism studies has been a prevailing present-mindedness and superficiality, refusing deep, grounded or sustained historical analysis". Early tourism research was more aligned with development and planning issues (Saarinen et al., 2017) and geography. It can be traced to the 17th century, where it was more prevalent in Europe and North America (Carlson, 1980; Wolfe, 1964). Being aligned to development and planning issues, the tourism research topics that dominated included land use, destination or location issues and the tourism economy (Duffield, 1984; Joerg, 1935; Jones, 1933). A focus on urban tourism was necessitated by the need to have seaside health resorts. Most notable are the Romans, some two millennia ago, as they developed an interest in pleasure resorts, including spas and seaside communities (Patmore, 1968; Graburn, 1995).

3 Urban risk and tourism in sub-Saharan Africa: The state of knowledge

In SSA, researchers have focused much on rural-based tourism due to the high concentration of natural resources in the rural spaces in the region. A perusal of top tourism journals, including the *Annals of Tourism, Tourism Management, Tourism Management Perspectives, Journal of Travel Research, Tourism Geographies* and *Current Issues in Tourism and Tourism Analysis* reveals an overemphasis on nature-based tourism in SSA since the years 1990-2020. Journals with a focus on Africa, such as the *African Journal of Hospitality and Tourism Leisure* also shows the domination of nature-based tourism. In essence, an overemphasis on rural-based tourism resulted in the neglect of African cities as possible tourism spaces. This is evident as only a handful of books, reports and articles have been published on urban tourism in SSA. African cities have seemingly been thought of as business and political hubs. The UN-Habitat's '*State of the world's cities 2010-2011 – Cities for all: Bridging the urban divide*' pointed out that cities play a significant role in reducing poverty, particularly where pro-poor policies are well-formulated and implemented (UN-Habitat, 2010). They can also reduce transaction costs such as infrastructure and services, and well-knitted hubs that promote social networking. The proximity of cities makes tourism an important element for urban development. Tourism brings vitality and dynamism to cities; however, it also brings new patterns and changes to their urban landscape. Therefore, the tourism industry has to be innovative so as to provide significant revenue and benefit to its residents, whilst reducing urban risks that may affect tourists and the host populace (United Nations World Tourism Organisation [UNWTO], 2012). It is also important to discuss the challenges that cities in the SSA region may encounter. These may include: issues related to the sustainable and responsible management of he increasing number of tourists arriving in cities; the role of urban tourism in poverty alleviation; managing host-tourist relations; practical steps taken to reduce the impact on the environment; and the promotion of benefits related to greener tourism.

In October 2019, Scopus TITLE-ABS-KEY (urban AND tourism) revealed a total of 6223 documents, and TITLE-ABS-KEY (urban AND risk AND tourism), revealed 350 documents. Not all 350 documents related directly to tourism; only handful did. A further scan of these documents showed that urban risk tourism-related articles focused on themes such as the nexus between climate change and cities (Pandy & Rogerson, 2019); the linkages between cities, tourism and diseases (Fang et al., 2019); eco-friendly tourism (Zhang & Zhang, 2019), tourism and sustainability (Mata, 2018); and disaster risk reduction and tourism (Agustan & Kausar; 2019). From papers identified in the Scopus database, themes dominating the urban tourism discourse in sub-Saharan Africa include economic development (Rogerson, 2016), inclusive tourism, sustainable tourism, pro-poor tourism (Musavengane et al., 2019; Ashley & Roe, 2002), responsible tourism (Musavengane, 2019), green tourism and township (slum) tourism. The increasing population living in slums outlined earlier explains the growing interest in slum tourism research in the SSA region (Fenzel, 2018; Hoogendoorn & Giddy, 2017; Rogerson & Booyens, 2019), especially in South Africa. However, most of these studies tend to be on the neoliberal trajectory, where the emphasis is placed on economic gains whilst neglecting the relations between urban risk, tourism and resilience.

A perusal of the articles pertaining to the above-mentioned themes shows that there is a greater need for building strong resilience in African urban spaces in light of the urban shocks and stressors involved. What is evident is that rapid and unplanned urbanisation is the leading driver of urban risk. Lew (2014) noted that major disasters and crises have been the areas researchers in resilience tourism have concentrated on. This denotes the narrow application of resilience thinking in tourism (Hall et al., 2018). Studies that have applied resilience thinking in tourism focused more on climate change (Becken, 2013; Prayag, 2018), natural resources management (Musavengane, 2019), terrorism, floods and economic instability (Luthe & Wyss, 2014). The resilience of the urban poor heavily depends on the quality of governance systems and institutions (Asian Development Bank, 2013; Siakwah et al., 2020). Regardless of the fragmented pieces of literature on resilience in tourism, there is a need to discuss the types of resilience that matter in urban tourism in light of urban risks associated with African cities. In doing so, this book further adds to the growing body of knowledge on positive tourism in Africa (Filep et al., 2016). Positive tourism is a way of understanding the total and specific value of tourism to host communities, economies and other elements of the tourism system (Mkono, 2019). There is however an increasing amount of tourism research on Africa being conducted by Western researchers or temporary residents in the West for education purposes (Mkono, 2019). The fact that different tourism scholars originate mainly from Western Europe, North America, Australia and New Zealand has led to the general perception that tourism research is Eurocentric (Dangi & Jamal, 2016). Thus, this book highlights the voices of African scholars contributing to African discourse and knowledge on urban risk, tourism and resilience.

4 The knowledge gap on urban risk and urban tourism

Despite some of the above-mentioned urban risks and implications for urban tourism development, including a growing interest in urban tourism research, there is a paucity of literature on the relationship between urban risk, tourism and resilience (Agustan & Kausar, Ritchie, 2008; Musavengane et al., 2020). Although there are some studies on risks associated with tourism, most studies do not explicitly discuss the relation between urban risk and tourism (Boakye, 2012; Booyens, 2010). Urban risk, including resilience, is mainly discussed in development and disaster management studies, and is often not linked to tourism. Literature that seems to point to the relation between risks (not urban risk, per se) and tourism is fragmented. This can be attributed to the shortage of experts and researchers in this specialised area of urban tourism. Generally, tourism research also appears to lack the respect it should command (Butler, 2015). It is often regarded as a discipline that is not independent, but rather a field of interest to researchers from various disciplines, which includes geography, political science, sociology, anthropology, history, business, urban planning, architecture and engineering (Tribe, 1997).

Hence, there is a need for this volume to start a conversation about the linkages between urban risk and tourism. This can be achieved by hearing from experts from different disciplines who have diverse knowledge pertaining to urban risk, tourism and resilience. The contributors to this book hail from various disciplines such as tourism geography, environmental sociology, urban development, chemical engineering, planning and development, waste management, climatology, sports management and peace-building. Whilst most African tourism literature emanates from South Africa (Rogerson & Visser, 2014), this book gives voice to a diversity of African scholars who aim to better contextualise challenges relating to sustainable urban tourism across sub-Saharan Africa. Furthermore, whilst global tourism literature is dominated largely by Western scholars (Kirilenko & Stepchenkova, 2018), Rogerson and Visser highlight that African urban tourism research provides unique features and highlights challenges regarding Northern concepts about urban tourism (including urban risks, tourism and resilience). This book provides invaluable discussions about urban risk and resilience in the tourism discourse sphere, largely from practitioners from the continent.

5 Structure of the book

This book explores four main themes. Theme 1, *"Urban tourism and environmental pollution risks"*, examines the link between urban tourism and pollution and its implications for sustainability. It inspects how tourism may contribute to urban pollution, and how vulnerable communities affected by urban pollution use tourism to address the environmental and socioeconomic impacts created by capitalist political economies. It further interrogates how urban challenges such as environmental degradation and waste impact tourism development. In Chapter 2, Llewellyn Leonard and Robin Nunkoo examine 'toxic tourism' as a new form of alternative urban tourism and environmental justice in the South Durban Industrial Basin, South Africa. In Chapter 3, Wilma Sichombo Nchito and Euphemia Mwale evaluate the linkages between waste management in the hospitality industry and urban risk in Livingstone City, Zambia. In Chapter 4, Pius Siakwah analyses the political economy of unplanned urban sprawl, waste and tourism development in Ghana. In Chapter 5, Llewellyn Leonard and Ayanda Dladla examine an assessment of environmental risk management and township tourism development based in Alexandra Township, Johannesburg, South Africa.

Theme 2, *"Peace tourism, battlefields and war risks"*, acknowledges the unequal and unsustainable tourism development, which can create conflict and divisions within sub-Saharan African urban cities at the same time contribute to building peace amongst social actors. This theme explores the complexity of (peace) tourism and building amity in African cities. In Chapter 6, Brij Maharaj explores mega sport events and urban risks, specifically examining the relations between FIFA 2010, the African bid and xenophobic violence. In Chapter 7, using the case of Zimbabwe, Regis Musavengane evaluates the intersection between election risks and urban tourism in SSA cities with the aim to explore peace through tourism. In Chapter 8, Clément Longondjo Etambakonga and Dieudonné Trinto Mugangu evaluate the role of responsible tourism in peace-building and social inclusion in war-risk cities in Goma, Democratic Republic of Congo.

Theme 3, *"Tourism, climate change and flood risks"*, examines how climate change impacts African tourism businesses, and how tourism businesses could adapt to a changing environment. Climate change is altering the nature of environments globally, and the operation and sustainability of tourism depends on the nature and scale of climate change. This theme, thus explores the nexus between African cities, climate change and urban tourism risk. The theme begins with Chapter 9, where Eromose Ebhuoma and Llewellyn Leonard, using the case of Nigeria, discuss factors influencing tourism accommodations' lack of preparedness for flooding. In Chapter 10, Francini van Staden's dual case study in Mombasa and Cape Town examines climate change impacts and adaptation strategies for tourism hotspots. In Chapter 11, Raphael Ane Atanga and Tembi Tichaawa examine the risk of flood impacts on tourism in coastal cities of West Africa, using a case study of Accra, Ghana. In Chapter 12, Felix Donkor and Kevin Mearns explore the nexus of climate change and urban tourism in South Africa.

Lastly, Theme 4, "*Inclusive urban tourism and enclaves*", explores inclusive sustainable urban tourism and ways to enhance local sustainable tourism development for all, within a cosmopolitan African urban tourism space. Although tourism is a fast-growing sector that contributes to livelihoods, it can be exclusionary for certain sectors of the population such as vulnerable groups and informal settlers in urban spaces, as highlighted earlier. This theme delves into the exclusionary tendencies of the tourism sector in the urban space and offers ways to overcome these. The theme starts with Chapter 13, where Prudence Khumalo examines human settlements and tourism development in Kenya, with emphasis on prospects for tackling urban risks in informal settlements. In Chapter 14, Michael Dyssel examines conservation tourism challenges and opportunities on the Cape Flats in South Africa. In Chapter 15, Zibanai Zhou focuses on resilience, inclusiveness and challenges of cosmopolitan cities' heritage tourism in Harare, Zimbabwe. In Chapter 16, Erisher Woyo delves into prospects and challenges of sustainable urban tourism in Windhoek, particularly linkages between poverty, inequality and urban risks. The concluding Chapter 17 navigates the future of urban tourism amidst environmental, political and social risks.

This book builds upon previous books on urban tourism (see Page & Hall 2003; and Rogerson & Visser, 2007). However, they seem to lack details from a sub-Saharan African perspective, and do not uniquely converge and analyse urban risk and tourism issues. This book will be of importance in the tourism political economy and ecology fields, and specifically add value to the urban tourism content. The chapters will be of interest to a global scholarly audience of tourism geographers, students and lecturers, tourism managers and policymakers, professional tourism and urban risk practitioners and city planners. This volume can also be used as a main course textbook or a supplementary book, and includes a variety of rich cases from sub-Saharan Africa. This volume raises important insights in dealing with a range of developmental policy and planning issues in sub-Saharan Africa relating to urban risks, tourism and resilience. It outlines the implications of urban risks on sustainable tourism and suggests future research directions.

References

Addo, K.A., Walkden, M. & Mills, J.P. (2008). Detection, measurement and prediction of shoreline recession in Accra, Ghana. *ISPRS Journal of Photogrammetry and Remote Sensing* 63: 543–558.

Agustan, A. & Kausar, D.R.K. (2019). Towards a framework for disaster risk reduction in Indonesia's urban tourism industry based on spatial information. *Geographia Technica* 14: 32-38. DOI: 10.21163/GT_2019. 141.16

Agyeman, J., Bullard, R. & Evans, B. (2003) *Just Sustainabilities: Development in an Unequal World*, United Kingdom, Earthscan Publications.

Allen, J. (1999). Crime against international tourists. *NSW Bureau of Crime Statistics and Research* 43: 1–8.

Ashley, C. & Roe, D. (2002). Making tourism work for the poor: Strategies and challenges in southern Africa. *Development Southern Africa* 19(1): 61-82. DOI:10.1080/03768350220123855

Asian Development Bank (2013). *Moving from risk to resilience*. Pacific Studies Series, Philippines.

Atanga, R.A. (2016). Flood risk management strategies and resilience, PhD Thesis–Technische Universität Dresden.

Awumbila, M. (2014). Linkages between urbanization, rural-urban migration, and poverty outcomes in Africa. *World Migration Report* 2015: 1–31.

Becken, S. (2013). Developing a framework for assessing resilience of tourism sub-systems to climatic factors. *Annals of Tourism Research* 43: 506–528.

Becken, S., Jin, X., Zhang, C. & Gao, J. (2017). Urban air pollution in China: Destination image and risk perceptions. *Journal of Sustainable Tourism* 25(1): 130–147. DOI:10.1080/09669582.2016.1177067

Boakye, K.A. (2012). Tourists' views on safety and vulnerability. *Tourism Management* 33: 327–333.

Booyens, I. (2010). Rethinking township tourism. *Development Southern Africa* 27(2): 273–287. https://doi.org/10.1080/03768351003740795.

Butler, R.W. (2015). The evolution of tourism and tourism research. *Tourism Recreation Research* 40(1):16-27. DOI:10.1080/02508281.2015.1007632

Carlson, A. W. (1980). Geographical research on international and domestic tourism. *Journal of Cultural Geography* 1: 149–160.

Cheer, J. & Lew, A. (2017) Sustainable tourism development: towards resilience in tourism. *Interaction* 45(1): 10–15

CPRC (Chronic Poverty Research Centre). (2005). *The Chronic Poverty Research Report 2004–2005*. CPRC, Institute for Development Policy and Management, University of Manchester, Manchester, UK.

Dangi T.B. & Jamal T. (2016). *An Integrated Approach to "Sustainable Community-Based Tourism"*, Department of Recreation, Park and Tourism Sciences, Texas.

Depietri, Y. & McPhearson, T. (2019). Changing urban risk: 140 years of climatic hazards in New York City. *Climatic Change* https://doi.org/10.1007/s10584-018-2194-2.

Dodman, D., Leck, H., Rusca, M. & Colenbrander, S. (2017). African Urbanisation and Urbanism. *International Journal of Disaster Risk Reduction* 26: 7–15.

Duffield, B.S. (1984). The study of tourism in Britain – a geographical perspective. *GeoJournal* 9(1): 27–35. DOI:10.1007/BF00518315.

Falt, L. (2016). From shacks to skyscrapers. *Urban Forum* 27: 465–486.

Fang, Z., Zhang, J., Guo, W. & Lou, X. (2019). Assemblages of culturable airborne fungi in a typical urban, tourism-driven center of southeast China. *Aerosol and Air Quality Research* 19(4): 820–831. DOI:10.4209/aaqr.2018.02.0042.

Fenzel, F. (2018). On the question of using the concept 'Slum tourism' for urban tourism in stigmatised neighbourhoods in inner-city Johannesburg. *Urban Forum* 29(1): 51–62. DOI:10.1007/s12132-017-9314-3.

Filep, S., Laing, J. & Csikszentmihalyi, M. (2016). (eds). *Positive tourism*. New York: Taylor and Francis.

Fraser, A., Leck, H., Parnell, S. & Pelling, M. (2017). Africa's urban risk and resilience. *International Journal of Disaster Risk Reduction* 26: 1–6.

Goldman, M. (2011). Speculative urbanism and the making of the next world city. *International Journal of Urban and Regional Research* 35(3): 555–581.

Graburn, N. (1995). The past in the present in Japan: Nostalgia and neo-traditionalism in contemporary Japanese domestic tourism. In R.W. Butler & D.G. Pearce (Eds.), *Change in tourism people, places processes* (pp. 47–70). London: Routledge.

Hall, C.M., Prayag, G. & Amore, A. (2018). *Tourism and resilience: Individual, organizational and destination perspectives*. Bristol, UK: Channel View Publications.

Holcomb, J. & Pizam, A. (2006). Do incidents of theft at tourist destinations have a negative effect on tourists' decisions to travel to affected destinations? In, Y. Mansfeld and A. Pizam (eds.), *Tourism security and safety: From theory to practice*, New York: Butterworth-Heinemann.

Hoogendoorn, G. & Giddy, J.K. (2017). "Does This Look Like a Slum?" Walking Tours in the Johannesburg Inner City. *Urban Forum* 28(3): 315–328.

Jones, S.B. (1933). Mining and tourist towns in the Canadian Rockies. *Economic Geography* 9: 368-378.

Joerg, W.L.G. (1935). Geography and national land planning. *Geographical Review* 25: 177–208.

Kirilenko, P. & Stepchenkova, S. (2018) Tourism research from its inception to present day: Subject area, geography, and gender distributions. *PLoS ONE*, 13(11). https://doi.org/10.1371/journal.pone.0206820.

Lee, Y. (2020). Coronavirus outbreak has turned Asia's best performing currency into one of the worst, CNBC, 6 February.

Leigh, J. (2013). 'Peak Oil' confronts society and tourism: A futuristic view. In J. Leigh, C. Webster, and S. Ivanov (Eds.), *Future tourism political, social and economic challenges* (pp. 7–20). London: Routledge.

Leonard, L. (2017). Governance, participation and mining development. *Politikon* 44(2): 327–345.

Leonard, L. (2018). Converging political ecology and environmental justice disciplines for more effective civil society actions against macro-economic risks: the case of South Africa. *Journal of Environment and Sustainable Development* 17: 1–18.

Levantis, T. & Gani, A. (2000). Tourism demand and the nuisance of crime. *International Journal of Social Economics* 27(1): 959–967.

Lew, A.A. (2014). Scale, change and resilience in community tourism planning. *Tourism Geographies* 16:1, 14-22, DOI: 10.1080/14616688.2013.864325.

Lindell, I. Hedman, M. & Nathan-Verboomen, K. (2010). The World Cup 2010 and the urban poor 'World class cities' for all? Nordic Africa Institute Policy Notes 2010(5). https://www.files.ethz.ch/isn/121748/2010_5.pdf.

Luthe, T. & Wyss, R. (2014). Assessing and planning resilience in tourism. *Tourism Management* 44: 161–163.

Manjengwa, J., Matema, C. & Tirivanhu, D. (2016). Understanding urban poverty in two high-density suburbs of Harare, Zimbabwe. *Development Southern Africa* 33(1): 23–38. DOI: 10.1080/0376835X.2015.1116376.

Mata, J. (2018). Intelligence and innovation for city tourism sustainability. The future of tourism: Innovation and sustainability (pp. 213-232) DOI:10.1007/978-3-319-89941-1_11.

McKinley, D. & Veriava, A. (2004). *From Swaart Gevaar to Rooi Gevaar: The 'Story' of State Repression in the South African Transition*, Centre for Civil Society, University of KwaZulu-Natal.

Mkono, M. (2019). Positive tourism in Africa: resisting Afro-pessimism. In M. Mkono (Ed.), *Positive Tourism in Africa* (pp. 1-7). London, Routledge.

Musavengane, R. (2019). Small hotels and responsible tourism practice: Hoteliers' perspectives. *Journal of Cleaner Production* 220: 786-799. DOI.10.1016/j.jclepro.2019.02.143.

Musavengane, R., Siakwah, P. & Leonard, L. (2019). "Does the poor matter" in pro-poor driven sub-Saharan African cities? towards progressive and inclusive pro-poor tourism. *International Journal of Tourism Cities*, 5 (3), 392-411, DOI. 10.1108/IJTC-05-2019-0057.

Musavengane, R., Siakwah, P. & Leonard, L. (2020). The nexus between tourism and urban risk: Towards inclusive, safe, resilient and sustainable outdoor tourism in African cities. *Journal of Outdoor Recreation and Tourism* 29(100254): 1–13. https://doi.org/10.1016/j.jort.2019.100254.

Neiderud, C. (2015). How urbanization affects the epidemiology of emerging infectious diseases. *Infection Ecology & Epidemiology* 5(1). DOI: 10.3402/iee.v5.27060.

Nop, S. & Thornton, A. (2019) Urban resilience building in modern development. *Ecology and Society* 24(2): 23.

Page, S. & Hall, C.M. (2003). *Managing Urban Tourism. Upper Saddle River*, New Jersey: Prentice Hall.

Pandy, W.R. & Rogerson, C.M. (2019). Urban tourism and climate change: Risk perceptions of business tourism stakeholders in Johannesburg, South Africa. *Urbani Izziv* 30: 225-243.

Patmore, J. (1968). The Spa towns of England and Wales. In G. Beckinsale (Ed.), *Problems of urbanisation* (pp. 168–194). London: Methuen.

Pavlovic, D. & Knezevic, M. (2017). Is Contemporary Tourism Only a Neoliberal Manipulation? *Acta Economica Et Turistica* 3(1): 59–66.

Potts, D. (2013). Rural-Urban and Urban-Rural Migration Flows as Indicators of Economic Opportunity in Sub-Saharan Africa: What Do the Data Tell Us? Migrating out of poverty Research Programme Consortium, University of Sussex, Working Paper 9.

Potts, D. (2017) Urban data and definitions in sub-Saharan Africa. *Urban Studies* 55(5), 965–986.

Prayag, G. (2018). Symbiotic relationship or not? Understanding resilience and crisis management in tourism. *Tourism Management Perspectives* 25: 133–135.

Ritchie, B. (2008). Tourism Disaster Planning and Management: From Response and Recovery to Reduction and Readiness. *Current Issues in Tourism* 11(4): 315-348.

Robinson, J. (2006). *Ordinary cities*. London: Routledge.

Rogerson, C. & Visser, G. (2007). *Urban tourism in the developing world*. New Jersey: Transaction Publishers.

Rogerson, C. & Visser, G. (2014). Decade of Progress in African Urban Tourism Scholarship. *Urban Forum* 25: 407–417.

Rogerson, C.M. (2002). Urban tourism in the developing world: The case of Johannesburg. *Development Southern Africa* 19(1): 169–190. DOI: 10.1080/03768350220123927.

Rogerson, C.M. (2016). Climate change, tourism and local economic development in South Africa. *Local Economy* 31(1-2): 322-331.

Rogerson, C.M. & Booyens, I. (2019). Re-creating slum tourism: Perspectives from South Africa. *Urbani izziv* 30: 52-63, DOI: 10.5379/urbani-izziv-en-2019-30-supplement-004.

Saarinen, J., Rogerson, C. & Hall, C.M. (2017). Geographies of tourism development and Planning. *Tourism Geographies* 19(3): 307-317, DOI:10.1080/14616688.2017.1307442.

Saghir, J. & Santoro, J. (2018). *Urbanisation in sub-Saharan Africa: meeting challenges by bridging stakeholders.* Centre for Strategic and International Studies, https://www.csis.org/analysis/urbanization-sub-saharan-africa. [Accessed 29 May 2019].

Satterthwaite, D. (2017). The impact of urban development on risk in Sub-Saharan Africa's cities with a focus on small and intermediate urban centers. *International Journal of Disaster Risk Reduction* 26: 16–23.

Siakwah, P. (2018). Tourism geographies and spatial distribution of tourist sites in Ghana. *African Journal of Hospitality, Tourism and Leisure* 7(1): 1–19.

Siakwah, P., Musavengane, R. & Leonard, L. (2020) Tourism Governance and Attainment of the Sustainable Development Goals in Africa. *Tourism Planning & Development*, 17:4, 355-383, DOI: 10.1080/21568316.2019.1600160.

Simiyu, S., Cairncross, S. & Swilling, M. (2019). Understanding Living Conditions and Deprivation in Informal Settlements of Kisumu, Kenya. *Urban Forum* 30: 223–241. https://doi.org/10.1007/s12132-018-9346-3.

Smith, N. (2001). Global social cleansing. *Social Justice* 28(3): 68–74.

Songsore, J., Nabilia, J.S., Yangyuoru, Y., Avle, S., Bosque-Hamilton, K.E., Amponsah, E.P. & Alhassan, P. (2009). Integrated risk disaster and environmental health monitoring: Greater Accra Metropolitan Area, Ghana. In: M. Pelling & B. Wisner (eds.), *Disaster Risk Reduction: Cases from Urban Africa.* Ghana, Accra: Universities Press.

Sonmez, S. & Graefe, A. (1998). Influence of terrorism risk on foreign tourism decisions. *Annals of Tourism Research* 25(1): 112–144.

Tribe, J. (1997). The indiscipline of tourism. *Annals of Tourism Research* 24(3): 638–657.

UNDP (2015). *Sustainable Development Goals.* New York.

UN-Habitat. 2010. State of the world's cities 2010-2011: Bridging the urban divide - Overview and key findings. Online: Accessed 25 January 2020 https://sustainabledevelopment.un.org/index.php?page=view&type=400&nr=1114&menu=35

UN-HABITAT (2016). *Urbanization and development: emerging futures.* World Cities Report, Nairobi, Kenya, 1–147.

United Nations World Tourism Organization (UNWTO). (2012). *Global Report on City Tourism – Cities 2012 Project (AM Report n° six).* The World Tourism Organization (UNWTO), Madrid.

Visser, G. (2019). The challenges of tourism and urban economic (re)development in Southern cities. In: Muller, D. *A Research Agenda for Tourism Geographies*, Edward Elgar Publishing, United Kingdom.

Walton, J.K. (2005). Introduction. In: J.K. Walton (Ed.), *Histories of Tourism: Representation, Identity and Conflict*, sClevedon: Channel View, 1–18.

Watson, V. (2009). Seeing from the South: refocusing urban planning on the globe's central urban issues. *Urban Studies* 46(11): 2259–2275.

Watson, V. (2014). African urban fantasies: dreams or nightmares? *Environment and Urbanization* 26(1): 215–231.

Wolfe, R.J. (1964). Perspectives on outdoor recreation: A bibliographical survey. *Geographical Review* 54: 203–238.

Zhang, J., & Zhang, Y. (2019). Low-carbon tourism system in an urban destination. *Current Issues in Tourism*, doi:10.1080/13683500.2019.1641473.

Theme 1

Urban tourism and environmental pollution risks

2 Examining 'toxic tourism' as a new form of alternative urban tourism and environmental justice

The case of the South Durban Industrial Basin, South Africa

Llewellyn Leonard and Robin Nunkoo

1 Introduction

The concept of tourism and tourism destinations has evolved over the decades, expanding from more natural environments in rural areas to include additional 'manufactured' attributes to attract tourists. The classical tourism destination needed to meet certain criteria, such as having (natural) tourist attractions and accommodations with a degree of market attractiveness (Jovicic, 2019). Alternative tourism normally identifies both the natural environment and the local communities, who make their living in particular environments, as important tourism draws. This satisfies the industry's desire to secure profit; the tourist's longing to partake in an authentic natural experience, and perhaps the environmentalists' yearning to improve deteriorating environmental conditions (Di Chiro, 2000). It is, however, questionable whether the costs and benefits of tourism are equitably distributed among different stakeholders (Musavengane et al., 2019; Jamal & Camargo, 2014). Nevertheless, alternative tourism normally portrays a well-ordered convergence of capitalist political economies with environmental well-being (Di Chiro, 2000). However, another alternative form of tourism is 'toxic tourism'. This normally takes place in urban environments, which emphasises the relationship between the environment and local communities, but also within an environmental justice framework. Although there are various understandings of environmental justice (Agyeman & Evans, 2004), it is generally concerned with exposing the injustice for different socioeconomic groups that are associated with the unequal distribution of goods and services, and it generally aims to create healthy and safe communities (Chitewere, 2010). Environmental justice emphasises human rights and democratic accountability, including recognition of communities and procedural justice (Martin et al., 2016).

Although the literature on toxic tourism has been under-researched, there have been some limited attempts to define the concept. Razee (2009) notes that toxic tourism examines strategies of environmental justice, and tourism in chemically toxic places and neighbourhoods. In another sense, it refers to the (perceived) culturally toxic effects of tourism. Di Chiro (2000) adds that toxic tourism challenges conventional tourism practices and appropriates some of its methods, bringing the visitor in contact with the hidden externalities of industrial society, rather than the imagined purity and virtuousness of the world of modernity. It thus casts a much-altered contention that a harmonious relationship can exist between capitalism and the well-being of humans and the environment. Conversely, toxic tourism can be used, in some cases, as a commercial activity for income generation separate from local communities. For example, Yankovska & Hannam (2013) examined 'dark' and 'toxic' tourism in the Chernobyl exclusion zone in Ukraine, the site of the Chernobyl power station nuclear disaster that occurred on 26 April 1986. An accidental explosion during an experiment resulted in the roof of the reactor detaching and this, in turn, led to a radioactive cloud spreading over Ukraine, Russia, Belarus and most of Europe. The immediate result was significant ecological harm due to the spread of radioactive ions in the environment, 400 times more than the Hiroshima and Nagasaki nuclear bombs. The first tourists arrived in Chernobyl on the back of this industrial disaster in the mid-1990s, with 7 500 visiting the site in 2008 and spending around £130 per day. The Chernobyl exclusion zone exemplifies the darker aspects of the ability of disaster to lure increasing numbers of tourists for profit generation. Unfortunately, the research undertaken for the current study is restricted to interpretations of tour guides and tour agents surrounding toxic and dark tourism, given the immediate need to explore toxic forms of tourism for local communities and the environment.

There are many benefits associated with conducting so-called 'toxic tours' in communities exposed to urban environmental risks. Pezzullo (2007) highlights that where modernity separates people from their communities and democratic practices and principles, toxic tourism generally strives to bring them together. This is because toxic tours can be effective strategies for environmental justice, as they can open discursive spaces and bring together the cultures of tourists and locals because they allow locals to challenge (and be challenged by) the discourse of industrialism. Toxic tours normally create a sense of agency that mobilises individuals for democratic action and provides a means of fostering identification with people, places and arguments. Di Chiro (2000) notes that although the 'reality' exposed in the toxic tourism experience is often disheartening, it may exploit the historical convergence of the tourism industry with the discourses of sustainable development and environmental consciousness. The reality experienced seeks to raise important social, economic and environmental issues that communities that are exposed to injustices face. Toxic tours are educational and political tools that community organisations use to tell these stories and promote personal connections. Thus, although seemingly opposite (landscape) environments, the growing popularity of the ecotourism industry has opened up potentially interesting and innovative political spaces for environmental justice to organise via toxic tours. For the authors, toxic tourism is not only confined to tourism in chemically toxic places and neighbourhoods, but also includes other non-chemically impacted areas that experience environmental injustices (e.g. townships lacking social amenities and resulting in pollution and environmental degradation).

Within this context, this chapter has two aims: it first examines toxic tours as a tool to address environmental injustices created by capitalist political economies in the South Durban Industrial Basin (SDIB), South Africa, and their potential to serve as a platform to address urban risks. Secondly, it explores the potential for toxic tourism to serve as an alternative form of tourism not only to highlight urban industrial risk issues, but also to serve as a new tourism product offering for other tourism sites experiencing environmental degradation, such as township tourism environments. Additionally, despite the growing literature on environmental justice, limited links have been made with tourism (Hales & Jamal, 2015). This paper indirectly contributes to this discourse through its discussion of toxic tourism. Toxic tourism, thus, represents an interpretive lens for analysis, linking environmental justice with tourism. Unfortunately, as noted, the literature and research on toxic tourism is underdeveloped. This paper contributes to this discourse, especially as a case from the global South and, specifically, South Africa. This paper will first explore how toxic tourism may be an alternative form of urban tourism beyond just industrial pollution sites (e.g. townships) to highlight and potentially assist in unravelling developmental challenges. It will present a brief background of environmental injustice in South Durban and the emergence of toxic tourism. The authors will then present the methodology, present the results, engage in a discussion and draw conclusions. Since toxic tourism in South Africa first began in South Durban and is still active, this is used as a case to explore the effectiveness of toxic tours against urban risks, as well as drawing on lessons learnt, including their potential as a new form of alternative tourism.

2 Linking toxic tourism to township tourism for environmental justice

Although communities affected by urban industrial pollution sites have used toxic tourism as a tool for educational and political purposes to bring attention to local environmental injustices, it has not been extended to alternative tourism sites, such as urban townships where environmental injustices are rife. For example, in 2015, the Presidency revealed that approximately 80% of South African municipalities had failed to execute their required duties pertaining to the delivery of basic services, with service-delivery protests worsening since 2008 (Human Science Research Council, 2018). Coupled with such challenges, townships such as Soweto, Alexandra and Langa have become the focus of township tourism development with township tours practiced since the dawn of democracy and conducted by small tourism companies for international visitors (Butler, 2010). In comparison to mainstream tourism, township tourism is increasingly seen as a niche within the tourism industry, an example of pro-poor tourism (National Tourism Sector Strategy, 2011). Leonard and Dladla (in Chapter 5) explore Alexandra township tourism,[1] which is characterised by a high rate of poverty, crime, unemployment and especially environmental pollution challenges. The government has identified Alexandra tourism as a strategy to solve these development challenges. Over the years, the provincial government has been implementing projects to develop Alexandra and promote tourism, such as the Alexandra Renewal

Project and the Alexandra Tourism Development Project to promote Alexandra as a unique tourism destination (Naidoo, 2010; Mabotja, 2012). Despite some improvements in Alexandra (Agupusi, 2007), township tourism still encounters many challenges (Roefs et al., 2003; Mabotja, 2012). The township is still characterised by social and environmental problems such as poor waste and sanitation services and polluted waterways (Dladla, 2020; Petesch, 2013; Smith, 2013). Generally, government's efforts to address the challenge of tourism development in South Africa have not been effective (Visser & Hoogendoorn, 2011). Although protest actions against service delivery across the South African landscape have been widespread, it is questionable if protests in townships have any outcomes in catalysing the government to spearhead the urgent interventions required (Friedman, 2019). Within this context, what is the potential, then, for toxic tourism to serve as a new form of alternative urban tourism in townships to highlight concerns and be used as an educational tool for environmental justice? After all, urban risks and environmental injustices across the South African landscape arise from the same capitalist political economy. Therefore, expanding the current understanding of toxic tourism and its geographic applicability makes much sense. The following sections draw on the case of toxic tourism in South Durban and uncover some lessons that may be learnt.

3 Environmental justice and toxic tourism in South Durban

The SDIB in KwaZulu-Natal is an example of an industrial hub that comprises a mixed use of residential areas situated next to heavy industries (Leonard & Pelling, 2010a), containing 22 000 households and 200 000 residents (Broughton, 2017). South Durban is greatly industrialised and one of the more heavily polluted areas in southern Africa, containing two of South Africa's four oil refineries and Africa's largest chemical storage facility (Wiley et al., 2002). The SDIB currently supports the operation of approximately 600 industries, with principle emissions sources emanating from the Engen and South African Petroleum Refinery (SAPREF), as well as from the Mondi paper manufacturing facility (Duigan & Sivakumar, 2017). The refineries, especially Engen, are located close to two low-income residential communities, Merebank (Indian residents) and Wentworth (Coloured residents). These communities were strategically placed in the SDIB during Apartheid as part of the Group Areas Act.[2] The placement of the refineries immediately adjacent to these communities throws the problems of the industry's impact on public health and the problems of poor environmental and social quality of black communities into sharp focus for many (See Figures 2.1 and 2.2 below). As was the case during apartheid, South Durban communities continue to endure the environmental, health and socioeconomic costs of pollution from surrounding industries, especially the refineries (Niranjan, 2005).

The South Durban Community Environmental Alliance (SDCEA) is a community-based environmental justice organisation that was formed in 1995 during the transition to democracy. It is made up of 19 affiliate community organisations and has, since its inception, been active in holding corporations accountable

Figure 2.1 Merebank residents overlooking the Mondi Paper industrial facility.
Source: First author, 2011.

Figure 2.2 The Engen Refinery bordering Merebank and Wentworth residents.
Source: First author, 2011.

for the pollution impacts that residents face. SDCEA relies on financial support from nonindustrial funders for its existence and operates for the benefit of the local community. The organisation is active in lobbying government as well as in reporting and researching industrial incidents in the community (SDCEA, 2017). According to Reid and D'Sa (2005), SDCEA was formed to link local concerns across racial boundaries to respond systematically to pollution issues, although it has been unable to reach the African Township leaders from Lamontville and Umlazi, given that these townships are strongly government affiliated (Barnett & Scott, 2007). The organisation has also been active since its formation in challenging government to address the inequities of pollution and unsustainable development in the area, and simultaneously, in raising public awareness about environmental justice (Toxic City, n.d.).

The SDCEA has used a variety of methods to address pollution issues in South Durban. Such methods have included engaging in protest actions (Leonard & Pelling, 2010b); engaging in formal, technical and legal processes (Leonard, 2011); taking air samples to gather pollution data to challenge industries and relevant government officials (Mthembu, 2017); and holding workshops to create awareness in the community about pollution (Thousand Currents, 2019). According to Bhengu (2019), the SDCEA also conducts toxic tours in the pollution hotspots in South Durban and the residential areas of Merebank, Wentworth, the Bluff, Clairwood and Jacobs. Although it is not exactly documented when the toxic tours began, according to Kramer-Duffield (2005), their formal beginnings were on the back of funding obtained from the Global Greengrants Fund of $4 000 in 2004 and $5 000 in 2005. One of the accomplishments of these grants was the creation of a 'toxic tour' of South Durban called "From the Cradle to the Grave." This was described as a tour of the industrial areas of South Durban, allowing participants to witness first-hand the potential for disaster looming between industries and the adjacent residential communities. However, considering that the toxic tours in South Durban have been conducted with various participants for almost two decades as a new form of alternative tourism moving beyond the conventional tourism sites, this chapter is also interested in how effective the toxic tours have become an educational tool, as well as towards addressing environmental injustices for residents.

4 Methodology

Fieldwork to examine the effectiveness of the toxic tours in South Durban as an alternative form of urban tourism and as a tool towards addressing environmental injustices for residents was examined as part of a larger study on environmental justice conducted in the region in 2017 and 2019. In 2017, six interviews were conducted. Interviews were held with one researcher, who was dealing with social development issues based at the University of KwaZulu-Natal and who was also a previous resident in the area, and five residents, who worked for the SDCEA on environmental justice issues in South Durban. In 2019, seven interviews were conducted. Two were with local governmental officials: a local government official responsible for social development in the South Durban area, and a local government official who wished to remain anonymous. Two were with researchers: one dealing with health studies, and the other with industrial expansion issues, both at the University of KwaZulu-Natal. Two were with civil-society actors: one within the SDCEA leadership, and one with a local resident, who also was a member of the local Merebank Residents' Association (MRA) community based organisation. And one was from local industry: a representative for a private water company in the area, who was previously a local government employee responsible for issues of air pollution in South Durban. Ethical clearance was obtained for the research and confidentiality of social actors are protected. Interviews were conducted based on purposive sampling and using a snowball technique. Unfortunately, several attempts in 2019 to obtain interviews with key personnel – such as two key local government officials dealing with air quality and waste in the South Durban region, including obtaining interviews from several large-to-medium-scale industries – proved fruitless. One key academic civil-society scientist working in the area was attending to health issues and could not be interviewed. Only selected interviews, based on toxic tourism, are reported upon in this chapter. Grounded theory and open coding were employed for data analysis to identify similar emerging themes across the interviews. This assisted in splitting the data into relevant groups.

5 Results

The value of toxic tourism for environmental justice and its potential as a form of alternative urban tourism

Toxic tours were regarded as an important activity by all informants besides the local government, since they were seen to be educating people about urban risk (i.e. pollution and industrial incidents) and impacts on the environment and surrounding communities. The SDCEA CBO engaged in toxic tours to educate people and create awareness of the impacts on residents and the environment of industrial pollution in South Durban. The aim was to expose surrounding major industries causing pollution, health and environmental impacts in the hope that this would result in some kind of action being taken to address urban risks. According to Informant A (personal interview, 2017), a resident and SDCEA employee, referring to the importance of the toxic tours:

> …from a toxic tour perspective, it's good to show people just exactly what we are doing… to expose [polluting industries] and get the momentum going…. So that toxic tour really… opens people's understanding to see just how much we suffer. There's been numerous accounts of incidents and accidents where tanks have… been burning for more than five days… [and] pollution that comes out of that…

Informant B (personal interview, July 2017), a projects officer at the SDCEA, noted that toxic tours were about potentially attaining justice for vulnerable groups impacted by urban pollution risks, and educating local people about the polluting industries with a hope that such education would result in catalysing some sort of support or further awareness-sharing:

> …the toxic tour… is [about] justice to someone who comes from a vulnerable community…. They [the community] get it [pollution] from all sides…. When I first went on a toxic tour, as much as I am from South Durban, but I got to see exactly… how people suffer and why there is such a high rate of all these… illnesses, all these cancer[s], these leukaemia[s]. Because now you get to see and understand…. I think more people need to go on this tour and that maybe it will give them the drive… to help in whichever way they can. Whether it is just… to spread the word or to highlight these problems…

Beyond the general awareness created by going on a toxic tour, the tours were also used strategically by the SDCEA during important events to create awareness of urban risks in South Durban. Tours were conducted with civil society broadly and for people attending important events, workshops or conferences in the city of Durban. According to Informant C (personal interview, July 2017), a resident and employee at the SDCEA:

> …with the toxic tour, we host a number of different groups. International groups, be it church organisations, be it academics, be it civil society, be it students that are from overseas… civil society from different provinces… it's for us to create that awareness about the issues that are concerning the communities of South Durban…. [During] the 2010 World Cup…it [was] our opportunity to create awareness [and] open this toxic tour to anyone, free of charge, and open it to everyone that is willing to be educated about the issues around South Durban. And, you know, to our surprise, a lot of people were interested in signing up for a toxic tour. We took them for a toxic tour and then people were… informed and educated about the issues…. During [the Conference of Parties] COP17 [in 2011], we were hosting buses and buses. I think we hosted the bigger number… during the COP17…. We had about four full busloads of [people], which seat about 60 people [each]…. And then we had about seven Kombi [van] loads, and we had small vehicles as well… we had about plus-minus 400 and something people…

This suggests that toxic tours are not just important for education and awareness against environmental justice and to potentially and strategically contribute to social change, but such tours also provide an opportunity for an important form of alternative tourism, as noted for the World Cup and COP17, and a new tourism marketing offering that could be usefully promoted by the City of Durban. At the time of this study, the toxic tours were being run solely by the local community organisation (at no charge) and with no support from local government. Due to government engaging in a neoliberal development paradigm and promoting industrial expansion in Durban, toxic tours were seen by government as working against the state's neoliberal agenda, since they exposed the reality of the impacts of industrial development on people and the environment. Government, therefore, did not see toxic tours as beneficial to the city and did not support the initiative. According to a local government official [Informant D], toxic tours were viewed as working against promoting tourism in the city:

> As the city, together with the community, we are trying to brand South Durban as a tourism destination. We have unspoilt beaches, we have very historical links to old railway stations and arts and culture. There's a lot of lovely products there, and over the last 10 or 12 years, we have really worked hard to build it as a tourist destination.... A toxic tour is contrary to what we trying to do. A toxic tour does not grow investment. A toxic tour just badmouths and rubbishes industry... by saying look how horrible they are, this is what they are doing [they are] killing us, which may be true, but it is not going to help the economy, it not going to help the people's livelihood in anyway... as human beings, that is basic Maslow; they [are] just wanting food on the table...

Opposed to government, all other informants noted the importance of toxic tours. However, one informant suggested that toxic tours needed to go beyond just educating people about environmental injustices and that they should result in more practical outcomes. Secondly, toxic tours could additionally be used to promote the rich history of the area. According to Informant E, a former local government employee and now an employee at industry [X] in South Durban, although the toxic tours are useful for education and awareness, they also need to be used as a platform to present the alternatives to the current destructive industrial development system in addition to being used for historical tourism purposes. Unfortunately, government has not seen the potential of toxic tourism to promote the history of the area:

> It [the toxic tour] has the benefit of educating people about the effects of industries and about the history of the area... but we can make them more relevant today... like... promote integration like craft workshops so you can have the toxic tour in this context, how a decision should form [and] the challengers in a modern era, so you bring in creativity... we need to challenge them [government and industry] and move them... so, like promoting clean traffic and mobility... so the same vehicle can be used, but they need some injection.... It [South Durban also] has so much history to it. If you go to Sweden or to Norway, the histories are celebrated; [the] same with New York. They bring the vegetation back to life whereas here we letting it go down. Here we have the history of the transition [and] apartheid. So you can renew it [that history].... So there [are] huge opportunities for social development and for making things happen in a democratic space, but there is not good leadership [in government and industry]."

Despite the lack of support for toxic tourism by local government and the City of Durban, the SDCEA has been promoting such tours to national levels of government with some success. The aim was to educate the decision-makers to bring attention to environmental injustices in South Durban. According to Informant C (personal interview, July 2017):

> The challenges that we are faced with... we are not getting the right people... in the sense of getting decision-makers.... Those are the people that are not available. So that is why... I was so excited, because two weeks [ago]... SDCEA... and Groundwork [national NGO] took a Portfolio Committee for a toxic tour... to say "okay guys, we want to take you for a tour," [or else] none of them would have been interested. They would have said no way, why should we come from Cape Town, Jo'burg, for a toxic tour.... SDCEA and Groundwork have been doing it for [many] years... going to Parliament and requesting them to come down and see these issues, because what we have seen as well from the Portfolio Committee, they are more interested in the priority areas, [like] your Vaal Triangle area.... We fought this... with no success in making government consider or change South Durban to be a priority area, and they are refusing totally.... So hopefully, the one [toxic tour] that we recently had on 28 June 2017, it will bring about change. Because now, whenever, SDCEA and Groundwork goes to Parliament, they will reflect on what those guys have seen, fresh in their minds, so that will possibly bring about change in [the] sense of regulations and laws and bylaws...

However, the toxic tours, including the activities conducted by SDCEA in raising pollution issues in South Durban, have not gone unnoticed by government and industry. According to Informant C, (personal interview, July 2017):

What was so interesting [was during the toxic tours during COP17] we were followed by... [secret service] intelligence because... all these top delegates from all over the world, they were here in the city in Durban, so we were just followed by a different vehicle. Some of the vehicles... didn't even have license plates.... I remember in two different occasions, we had a chopper on top of our heads... a SAPS chopper... they had to bring private vehicles to park at our gates to just see what's our plans were... so this is basically the first [place] that we take people for a toxic tour...

Besides local government, only one civil-society informant was less optimistic about toxic tourism having significant value for expansion and education, as well as awareness for social change against urban risks in South Durban. According to Informant F, a researcher at the University of KwaZulu-Natal who has been working in the area for many years on pollution impacts on health, it was uncertain if the toxic tours had changed people's opinions, and they had failed to attract people who had no knowledge about the area:

> The toxic tours are already for people who are either in the know and who appreciate the problems that are going on already in these poor socioeconomic neighbourhoods. I am not sure that someone who doesn't believe there is a problem there would be convinced there is a problem. You don't need to go to South Durban to know what the problems that's been opposed there. I am aware of how these tours operate, but I am not sure it changes opinions one way or another.

6 Discussion, conclusion and recommendations

Communities situated in chemically toxic industrial sites have been some of the only areas where toxic tourism has been practised. Organisations such as the local SDCEA organised toxic tours to provide indisputable physical evidence that South Durban residents suffer from a disproportionate impact of hazardous pollution from surrounding industries and multinational corporations. However, toxic tourism, although effective for raising awareness about environmental injustices, has not been able to mobilise a significant number of people for direct democratic action, nor has it (yet) created a shift towards effective radical changes to hold local corporations accountable. Nevertheless, the toxic tours bring a level of education and awareness on pollution issues and the environment to both residents and civil society in general, with the SDCEA making headway in educating key national government decision-makers. It is noted that on 2 August 2019, leaders of the Inkatha Freedom Party (IFP) (a South African political party) were reported to have taken a toxic tour of South Durban. The leaders attending the tour included members of Parliament and local councillors. The tour was intended to give those attending firsthand experience within the communities, thus allowing them to make informed decisions on the role that the IFP could play towards ensuring that all people will be able to realise the dream of living healthy and fruitful lives (IFP, 2019). Thus, toxic tours have the potential to draw attention to environmental injustices in South Durban and beyond, and could result in improved regulations and laws to address urban risks.

Secondly, the toxic tours can be an important alternative tourism offering in the city of Durban for people interested in forms of dark and toxic tourism – similar to that witnessed at the Chernobyl exclusion zone in Ukraine, with thousands of tourists visiting the site in 2008. Unfortunately, since industries creating urban risks are currently operational in South Durban (unlike at the Ukrainian Chernobyl site, which is a post-industry operation), the Durban local government has not seen the value of the toxic tours operated by SDCEA. Rather, local government has viewed such toxic tours as anti-tourism initiatives, working against developing tourism in South Durban. Rather than view toxic tours as anti-tourism development initiatives, the Durban city government can use such tours to work *with* local communities to promote the rich history of the area, while tourists going on such tours could provide feedback on improved governance of industrial operations, including how to address the urban risk impact on people and the environment. Thus, such tours can work beyond merely educating tourists and could create a further platform for engagement between civil society, government and industry (and tourists) to address environmental injustices in South Durban.

This chapter suggests that toxic tours can be effective strategies for environmental justice efforts by germinating discursive spaces and bringing together the cultures of tourists and residents – including issues of how residents challenge, and are challenged by, capitalism frameworks. Considering that South Africa is a United Nations member state and party to the 2030 Agenda for Sustainable Development, with its plan of action for the people, planet and prosperity, toxic tours could certainly be a mechanism in a wide range of strategies to enable a more inclusive government approach to realise some of the 2030 targets of the Sustainable Development Goals (SDGs). These include SDG 9, which supports economic development *and* human well-being by promoting inclusive and sustainable industrialisation, as well as SDG 11, which aims to make cities and human settlements inclusive, safe, resilient and sustainable (United Nations, 2019).

From the case of toxic tourism in South Durban, we note that toxic tourism can also provide invaluable lessons for other non-chemical sites exposed to environmental injustices, such as for townships in South Africa (and slums globally). The current scholarly understanding of toxic tourism within the environmental justice literature needs to be extended beyond the narrow confines of conducting toxic tourism in chemically polluted sites to include other areas experiencing environmental injustices and also impacted by capitalism frameworks. For example, due to township socioeconomic and environmental challenges and limitations of protest action against environmental injustices, toxic tourism could be a new political tool and strategy employed by residents to strategically bring attention to social and environmental pollution challenges in the community (as witnessed in South Durban) and to highlight disparities in standards of living and services between the rich and poor. Additionally, it can be used as a new form of alternative tourism to bring economic benefits to the local community and encourage alternative toxic tourism guided activities. Thus, toxic tourism can serve the two-prong approach of bringing attention to environmental injustices in townships and contributing to township tourism development by organising guided tours and incorporating historical and cultural tourism. Toxic tourism then can be an alternative form of tourism integrated into social, environmental and economic life. Social and environmental justice activists must, therefore, engage in joint actions and strategies to expand the applicability of toxic tourism beyond chemically polluted sites for wider societal benefits. Since environmental justice is an inclusive discourse concerned with exposing the injustice for different socioeconomic groups and for creating healthy communities, it would make sense for toxic tourism to be applied across geographic localities.

Notes

1 Township tourism is also known as slum tourism in regions such as Asia and Africa (Costa, 2013)
2 The Apartheid system enacted a nation-wide social policy of separate development. The Population Registration Act in 1950 classified residents into four racial groups, namely black, white, coloured, and Indian. The Group Areas Act in 1950 assigned different regions to different races.

References

Agupusi, P. (2007). Small Business Development and Poverty Alleviation in Alexandra, South Africa. Paper prepared for the second meeting of the Society for the Study of Economic Inequality, ECINEQ Society, Berlin; July 12–14

Agyeman, J., & Evans, B. (2004). Just sustainability: the emerging discourse of environmental justice in Britain? *The Geographical Journal*, 170(2), 155–164.

Barnett, C., & Scott, D., (2007). Space of opposition. *Environment and Planning A* 39(11): 2612–2631

Bhengu, S. (2019) *Toxic tour highlights South Durban pollution hotspots, East Coast Radio*, 3 August. Retrieved from https://www.ecr.co.za/news/news/toxic-tour-highlights-south-durban-pollution-hotspots/ (Accessed 8 August 2019)

Broughton, T. (2017) Legal fight over R4.5bn Logistics Park in Durban, *News24*, 15 September. Retrieved from https://www.news24.com/SouthAfrica/News/legal-fight-over-r45bn-logistics-park-in-durban-20170915 (Accessed 7 December 2019).

Butler, S. (2010). Should I stay or should I go? Negotiating township tours in post-apartheid South Africa. *Journal of Tourism and Cultural Change*, 8(1), 15–29.

Chitewere, T. (2010) Equity in Sustainable Communities: Exploring Tools for Environmental Justice and Political Ecology. *Natural Resources Journal*, 50(2): 315-339

Costa, J. (2013). Slum Tourism as an Economic Activity: is it Ethical? A Theoretical Review. *Indian Journal of Research,* 2(10), pp. 32–34.

Di Chiro, G. (2000). Bearing witness or taking action? Toxic tourism and environmental justice. In R. Hofrichter (Ed.), *Reclaiming the environmental debate: The politics of health in a toxic culture* (pp. 275 – 300). Cambridge, MA: MIT Press

Dladla, A. (2020) *Obstacles in tourism growth: The case of Alexandra Township, Johannesburg,* Master thesis, University of Johannesburg.

Duigan, B., & Sivakumar, V., (2017) Air pollution Studies in Durban, South Africa - A review of CO, O3, PM10 and VOC studies. *Journal of Neutral Atmosphere*, 1:21-32.

Friedman, S. (2019) How portrayal of protest in South Africa denigrates poor people, *News24*, 17 April.

Hales, R., & Jamal, T. (2015) Environmental Justice and Tourism. In: Hall, M.; Gossling, S. and Scott, D. (eds) *The Routledge Handbook of Tourism and Sustainability*, Routledge, New York.

Human Science Research Council (2018) The social costs of violent and destructive service-delivery protests in South Africa. Retrieved from http://www.hsrc.ac.za/en/review/hsrc-review-dec-2018/service-delivery-protests (Accessed 27 March 2020)

Inkatha Freedom Party (2019) IFP leaders to undertake a toxic tour of South Durban, 1 August. Retrieved from http://www.ifp.org.za/ifp-leaders-to-undertake-a-toxic-tour-of-south-durban/ (Accessed 4 August 2019)

Jamal, T., & Camargo, B. (2014) Sustainable tourism, justice and an ethic of care: Toward the just destination. *Journal of Sustainable Tourism*, 22(1): 11-30

Jovicic, D. (2019) From the traditional understanding of tourism destination to the smart tourism destination. *Current Issues in Tourism*, 22:3, 276-282, DOI: 10.1080/13683500.2017.1313203

Kramer-Duffield, M. (2005) Seeking environmental justice in South Africa, *Global Green Grants Fund*. Retrieved from https://www.greengrants.org/2005/09/09/seeking-environmental-justice-in-south-africa/ (Accessed 9 August 2019)

Leonard, L. (2011). Leadership against industrial risks: Environmental justice in Durban, South Africa. *Journal of Asian and African Studies,* 46(2): 113-129. doi:10.1177/0021909610391049

Leonard, L., & Pelling. M. (2010a). Civil Society Response to Industrial Contamination of Groundwater in Durban, South Africa. *Environment and Urbanization,* 22 (2): 579–595.

Leonard, L. & Pelling. M. (2010b). Mobilization and Protests: Environmental Justice in Durban, South Africa. *Journal of Local Environment*, 15(2): 137-151

Mabotja, K. (2012). Tourism plans for Alex: Retrieved from http://www.joburg.org.za/index.php?option=com_content&view=article&id=7818:tourism-lans-for-alex&catid=135:alexandra&Itemid=192#ixzz2vkZ5D2dz (Accessed 12 April 2019)

Martin, R., Sunley, P., Gardiner, B., & Tyler, P. (2016). How regions react to recessions: resilience and the role of economic structure. *Regional Studies*, 50(4), 561-585.

Mthembu, B. (2017) How polluting industries affect people's health within the South Durban community. Retrieve from http://sdcea.co.za/2019/07/15/2077/ (Accessed 8 August 2019).

Musavengane, R., Siakwah, P. & Leonard, L. (2019). "Does the poor matter" in pro-poor driven sub-Saharan African cities? towards progressive and inclusive pro-poor tourism. *International Journal of Tourism Cities*, 5 (3), 392-411, DOI. 10.1108/IJTC-05-2019-0057.

Naidoo, R. (2010). *Alex youth get tourism training:* Retrieved from http://www.joburg.org.za/index.php?option=com_content&view=article&id=6046:ale   x-youth-get-tourism-training&catid=129&Itemid=214 (Accessed 16 April 2014).

National Tourism Sector Strategy (2011) Retrieved from https://www.tourism.gov.za/AboutNDT/Branches1/Knowledge/Documents/National%20Tourism%20Sector%20Strategy.pdf (Accessed 8 December 2019).

Niranjan, I., (2005). *A case study of environmental health in the South Durban Basin.* Masters diss., University of KwaZulu-Natal.

Petesch, C. (2013). *Mandela's First Township Home Shows Lack of Progress.* Available from: http://news.yahoo.com/mandela-39-1st-township-home-shows-lack-progress-64016671.html (Accessed 14 April 2014).

Pezzullo, P.C. (2007.) *Toxic Tourism: Rhetorics of Pollution, Travel, and Environmental Justice.* Tuscaloosa, AL: University of Alabama Press. 320 pp. ISBN: 9780817315504.

Razee, A. (2009) Strategies for Environmental Justice: A Rhetorical Tour of Toxic Tours. *The Review of Communication*, 9(3):232-235

Reid, K., & D'Sa, D. (2005) The double edged sword: Advocacy and lobbying in the environmental sector. *Critical Dialogue* 2(1): 1–39.

Roefs, M., Naidoo, V., Meyer, M. & Makalela, J. (2003). *Alexandra: A Case Study of Services delivery for the Presidential 10 year Review Project*, Review by the Human Sciences Research Council (Democracy and Governance Programme) in Association with Indlovo Link. Retrieved from: https://www.google.com/search?q=Alexandra%3A+A+Case+Study+of+Services+delivery+for+the+Presidential+10+year+Review+Project&rlz=1C1NHXL_enZA812ZA812&oq=Alexandra%3A+A+Case+Study+of+Services+delivery+for+the+Presidential+10+year+Review+Project&aqs=chrome.69i57j69i58.470j0j4&sourceid=chrome&ie=UTF-8 (Accessed 27 March 2020).

Smith, E. (2013) Addicted to drugs in Mandela's old neighbourhood. Global Post, 20 July.

South Durban Community Environmental Alliance (2017) Retrieved from https://sdcea.co.za/about/ (Accessed 15 November 2019)

Thousand Current. (2019) Building community power to address toxic policies. Retrieved from https://thousandcurrents.org/partners/sdcea/ (Accessed 8 August 2019)

Toxic City. (n.d.) Retrieved from https://sdcea.co.za/downloads/ (Accessed 4 August 2019)

United Nations (2019) Sustainable Development Goals: Knowledge Platform. Retrieved from https://sustainabledevelopment.un.org/?menu=1300 (Accessed 7 December 2019)

Visser, G. & Hoogendoorn, G. (2011). Current Path in South African Tourism Research. *Tourism Review International*, 15: 5-20.

Wiley, D., Root, C., & Peek, B. (2002). Contesting the urban industrial environment in South Durban in a period of democratisation and globalisation. In: Freund, B., & Padayachee, V., (eds). *(D)urban vortex.* Pietermaritzburg, South Africa: University of Natal Press, 223–254

Yankovska, G., & Hannam, K. (2013) Dark and toxic tourism in the Chernobyl exclusion zone. *Current Issues in Tourism*, DOI: 10.1080/13683500.2013.820260

3 Waste management and urban risk in Livingstone City, Zambia

The sustainability of the hospitality sector

Wilma Sichombo Nchito and Euphemia Mwale

1 Introduction

Municipalities in African cities continue to struggle with waste management, which is mainly due to the quantities of waste produced, compounded by insufficient and unsustainable methods of waste disposal. Many cities in the Global South rely on dumpsites that have been labelled 'the world's most polluted places' by the International Solid Waste Association (ISWA, 2015) to dispose off most of their waste. Dumpsites are unsustainable options for waste disposal used by most local authorities in developing countries because of the low costs attached to them and risks of pollution. Unlike sanitary landfills that are fully engineered to minimise risks, open dumps are sites where waste is disposed of indiscriminately, with limited measures taken to protect the environment (ISWA, 2015). The problem of waste disposal becomes critical when urbanisation and tourism are intertwined. The tourism industry contributes to waste in a disproportionate manner because it is highly consumptive and yet in most cases, there is no clear understanding of the actual nature and quantities of waste from urban tourism. The additional waste generated by tourists is offloaded into the existing waste stream that is unable to handle waste in an environmentally sustainable manner, causing stress to the environment and health risks to the population. Tourism appears to be a heavy producer of waste that pollutes soils and water bodies, thereby contributing to environmental degradation (Wong, 2004). Municipalities have the responsibility to ensure that urban tourism can take place with minimum risk and, at the same time, deal with the additional waste produced by tourist activities. Cities that host tourists must adequately dispose of the resultant waste or face risks that could inadvertently disrupt the tourism activities on which their economies depend. Using arguments from the sustainable tourism discourse focusing on the natural environment, this chapter advocates the improvement of waste management within the hospitality subsector to reduce urban risk in Livingstone.

The growth of the tourism sector in Zambia cannot be discussed without mentioning the city of Livingstone; neither should it be discussed without referring to waste management. Tourism activities in Livingstone exert pressure on waste management through the extra waste produced by individual tourists and the waste produced as by-products from the services that are provided for tourists.

Unfortunately, waste management strategies in the city have lagged behind global practices. High rates of urbanisation and poor local governance seem to be pivotal to the lack of effective waste management approaches in Zambia. In this chapter, waste management in relation to the hospitality subsector in Livingstone is considered as a way of reducing urban risk and promoting sustainable urban tourism. To ensure the sustainability of tourism activities in Livingstone, a holistic approach that includes the management of waste is needed. In order to devise strategies for efficient waste management, an inventory of waste sources and types should be the first step (Gruber & Obersteiner, 2017). In the absence of such an inventory, the waste management strategies applied will continue to contribute to the deterioration of the environment. In this chapter, the practices in waste generation, recycling and disposal within the hospitality subsector in Livingstone are analysed as indicators of waste management performance. An examination of national policies helps to explain the current trends and, therefore, the legal frameworks are briefly presented in this chapter.

This chapter shows how waste from the hospitality subsector in Livingstone enters the waste stream and contributes to the risks caused by municipal waste. The different types of waste produced by the subsector are analysed, and the deficiencies of the different strategies used to dispose of hospitality waste are highlighted. The fact that the hospitality subsector has not been encouraged to reduce its waste indicates that it contributes to the cumulative quantities of waste disposed of by the local authority (LA). At present, the LA, the Livingstone City Council (LCC), uses an open dumpsite, which is unsustainable and can cause risks that negatively affect urban tourism. The chapter considers hospitality waste in view of sustainable waste management and critically analyses the approaches used to dispose of waste generated by the hospitality subsector in Livingstone. If there is a lack of adherence to the basic practices of sustainable waste management, it is possible for tourism in Livingstone to continue taking place in a safe and secure environment? The presence of both negative and positive practices within the same city indicates that there is a gap in practices based on the size of the hospitality entity. The municipality can use the larger entities as examples of best practice and achieve a reduction in the amount of waste taken to the dumpsite. The presence of recyclers in Livingstone is another opportunity for waste reduction within the subsector. All of these aspects are discussed from the perspective of reducing risks emanating from urban tourism.

The management of waste in the country is guided by a legal framework set out by government institutions. The Zambian Environmental Protection and Pollution Control Act (EPPCA), No. 12 of 1990, is the key legislation for the management of the environment in Zambia (Government of the Republic of Zambia [GRZ], 1990). This legislation seeks to protect the environment and control pollution. The Act created the Environmental Council of Zambia (ECZ) in 1992 (now Zambia Environmental Management Agency [ZEMA]), responsible for the protection of the environment (ECZ, 2004). Other major legislations that support this Act are the National Solid Waste Management Strategy for Zambia of 2004, the amended Environmental Management Act (EMA), No. 10 of 2013 and the Public Health Act (Cap.295) (the National Water, Sanitation and Waste Management Policy is yet to be ratified) (ECZ, 2004). One outstanding feature of the EMA is the Extended Producer Responsibility regulation. This regulation requires the producer of a product to be responsible for the 'life cycle' of the said product. This entails that products that are reusable and recyclable should not be disposed of in the environment but returned to the producer.

Despite having adequate legislation, there are several weaknesses with regard to solid waste management (SWM) in Zambia. These include the lack of effective enforcement in practice due to inadequate revenue and the lack of manpower and logistical support in the institutions charged with the enforcement (ECZ, 2004). The ECZ (2004) further identified duplication of responsibilities, inadequate by-laws and legislation, and slowness in changing relevant policies and providing information on SWM. Both ZEMA and LCC are understaffed and, therefore, they cannot perform all the duties assigned to them efficiently. This results in insufficient monitoring and control of operators in the solid waste sector. The Statutory Instrument (SI) regarding plastics was finally released in 2019 by the Ministry of Water Development, Sanitation and Environmental Protection (GRZ, 2019). However, the SI only covers single-use plastics supplied by supermarkets; other users such as the tourism industry were not included.

2 Sustainability and tourism

Sustainable tourism is defined as "tourism that takes full account of its current and future economic, social and environmental impacts, addressing the needs of visitors, the industry, the environment and host communities" (United Nations World Tourism Organization [UNWTO], 2013, p.17). The direct negative environmental impacts of tourism have been tabulated as impacts on air, water and noise levels (Fletcher et al., 2013). However, the impacts of tourism on both man-made and natural environments vary according to geographical location, season (temporal dimensions) and the nature of the destination (Fletcher et al., 2013). The fact that urban tourism shares environments with other sectors makes it difficult to ascertain specific damage posed on the environment by the tourism sector. Goeldner and Brent-Ritchie (2012) note that a holistic approach is preferred in the analysis of complex 'tourism-environment' scenarios because it factors in all elements that possibility affect tourism operations. Furthermore, the UNWTO (2017) lists waste management as one of the core indicators of sustainable tourism. Therefore, the promotion of waste management infrastructure is part of sustainable tourism (Mihai, 2013). The infrastructure of waste management includes adequate secondary collection facilities such as skip bins, recycling and reuse facilities, and sanitary landfills. Within the Sustainable Development Goals (SDGs), SDG 11 seeks to create inclusive, safe, resilient and sustainable cities (United Nations, [UN], 2015). Urban tourist destinations, should thus, take strides to becoming sustainable by reducing the negative impacts of tourism and travel on water, soil and air. The complex nature of the tourism–environment relationship requires that the two 'coexist' in harmony (Williams, 2009).

2.1 Tourism activities and tourism waste

Tourism plays an important role in the local economies of African countries (Musavengane et al., 2020). To increase potential benefits, nations seek to provide improved services within the hospitality subsector. Zambia is no exception and currently has eight multinational brands, which are Minor Hotel Group, Courtyard, Radisson Blu, Intercontinental, Three Cities, Best Western, Hilton Garden Inn and Protea Hotels (GRZ, 2018). The hospitality subsector is expanding in cities as the tourism industry tries to cater for the increasing numbers of guests. Against this backdrop, there is rapid urbanisation on a global scale. By 2050, it is estimated that 66% of the world's population will live in cities (UN, 2015). As urban populations increase, more environmental challenges such as contamination of water, air and soil will be encountered, which will cause risks to public health and productivity (Fletcher et al., 2013; Vardoulakis et al., 2016). Furthermore, the expansion of the tourism sector will take place in stressed urban environments since climate change continues to pose challenges to these rapidly growing cities. Cities now face increased incidences of disease, water shortages and flooding caused by increased frequency of extreme weather events (Bates et al., 2008). The Millennium Ecosystem Assessment (2005) notes that human activity is placing much strain on the natural functions of the earth. The MEA estimates that 60% of ecosystems in the world have been degraded (MEA, 2005; Nellemann and Corcoran, 2010). It appears that urban tourism is, therefore, taking place in environments that are already fragile. It is for this reason that the sector should make positive contributions to the creation of sustainable human settlements.

The Zambian government recognises the tourism industry as one of the major contributors to the socioeconomic development of the nation (Zambia Development Agency [ZDA], 2013). Hence, Livingstone, a 'tourist capital' of Zambia, is a priority destination for investments (GRZ, 2018). To achieve the desired economic gains from tourism, there has been an increase in the number of entities offering hospitality and aligned services to both domestic and international tourists over the years (Table 3.1). In 2017, Zambia received approximately 915 000 tourists[1] annually with an average length of stay of 3-5 days. Earnings from

Table 3.1 Accommodation types and available bed spaces, 2015 and 2017

	Category	2015	Bed spaces	2017	Bed spaces
1	Hotel	60	5,518	94	12,927
2	Lodges	575	30,595	774	42,838
3	Guesthouses	446	5,657	351	10,231
4	Motels	27	975	46	2,210
5	Apartments	0	0	16	232
6	Backpackers	9	149	20	576
7	Campsite	46	159	62	560
8	Bed & Breakfast	9	66	28	480

Source: GRZ, 2018.

tourist activities are US$465 million per year. The industry is estimated to provide 31 200 jobs, whilst the bed capacity in the country is over 29 000 (GRZ, 2018).

The drive to attain global standards in terms of the hospitality services in Zambia has not always matched the efforts to attain global standards in environmental management. This is despite the increasing importance of environmental management, as several entities clamour for 'eco-friendly' certification. Internationally, there has been a drive to reduce the waste taken to landfills by eliminating disposable complimentary products supplied to guests where possible (Gruber & Obersteiner, 2017). The amount of food waste, which makes up 40% of the total hospitality waste from larger hotels, is also being reduced (Zorpas et al., 2014). Although the contribution of the hospitality subsector to the total waste generated is usually small, the cumulative quantities are large (Styles et al., 2013). The fact that tourists can generate almost twice as much waste per capita than locals is a matter that should concern environmentalists in tourist destinations. Von Bertrab et al. (2009) found that in affluent destinations, a tourist can generate up to 7 kg of waste per day. This is compounded by the seasonal nature of tourism, which entails that more waste is produced during peak seasons, thus placing pressure on the municipal waste management systems and causing potential risk to human health and the environment. Solid waste generation is one of the most adverse environmental impacts created by the hospitality subsector, and smaller entities are often the main culprits (Mensah, 2020). It must be noted that if waste is not properly managed, it can cause irreversible economic, environmental and social impacts such as loss of biodiversity, pollution of ground and surface water, increase in greenhouse gas emissions, land degradation and loss of aesthetic value of tourist sites (Fletcher et al., 2013; Ezeah et al., 2015). For the industry to be profitable and sustainable, there must be an inclusion of components of environmental protection in all areas of the hospitality subsector (Zorpas et al., 2014).

3 Methodological underpinnings

3.1 Study setting

Livingstone District is on the southern extent of the country, bordering Zimbabwe, Botswana and Namibia and covering an area of 695 km². Zambia's fourth largest city is regarded as the tourist capital of Zambia based on the high traffic of tourists due to numerous tourist attractions at the destination. These include the Victoria Falls, or *Mosi-oa-Tunya* (the smoke that thunders), and the Mosi-oa-Tunya National Park, the most economically viable park in Zambia (GRZ, 2020). Other popular attractions include the Livingstone Museum, the Railway Museum, Mukuni Village, Mukuni Big Five Safaris and Mukuni Park Curio Market. Common activities in Livingstone are white water rafting, bungee jumping, quad biking, helicopter flights, gorge swinging and elephant and horseback safaris. Hotels, lodges, guesthouses, apartments and backpackers have been established over the years to cater to increasing visitor numbers in the city.

3.2 Research approach, data collection and analysis

Using a case study approach, a survey of waste management practices in the hospitality subsector in Livingstone was carried out from June to August 2017 to establish the waste management strategies used, and to assess possible environmental impacts. Questionnaires were administered to administrative, housekeeping and food and beverage staff in each establishment. Interviews were also conducted with officials from the LA, two local private waste collectors and one recycler for additional information on waste management. Data were analysed in terms of types of waste produced and risks posed to the general population and to the environment by the various waste management strategies used by the subsector. At the time of the study, the Livingstone Tourism Association (LTA) had 131 accommodation entities on its register. All levels of guest accommodation were sampled to gain an overview of the state of waste management in the hospitality subsector. These levels ranged from a 5-star hotel to low-budget lodges and guesthouses that were not classified by the LTA. Of the 12 hotels (one 5-star, six 3-star and five 2-star hotels), six were purposively sampled. The remaining registered accommodation consisted of 119 lodges and guesthouses dotted around the city. National statistics list lodges and guesthouses separately, but these have not been defined. To achieve as wide a coverage of the city as possible and to incorporate all types of establishments, lodges were categorised into three classes: (a) bed space: large (more than 50 bed spaces), medium (11-50 bed spaces) and small (10 bed spaces and below); (b) location; and (c) facilities offered (Figure 3.1). This study randomly sampled 10 entities from each category. A minimum of 10 establishments were selected from each category of lodges, and the total sample consisted 6 hotels and 30 lodges shown in Figure 3.1.

4 Results and discussion

This section presents the findings of the study carried out in Livingstone that investigated the waste management practices of the hospitality subsector. Disposal of waste from hospitality entities was analysed according to type of waste and method of disposal. This approach highlights the issue of waste separation, which is important if reduction of waste is to be achieved. The study focusses attention on efforts being made by various entities in the hospitality subsector that ordinarily would be overlooked if waste types were not analysed separately. The section also considers the attempts being made to recycle waste and analyses the barriers that are encountered in trying to reduce the waste that is being disposed of at the dumpsite.

4.1 Waste management in Livingstone

The study found that waste in Livingstone is collected by the LA and six private contractors. The LA uses one compactor truck and two trailers that are hitched to tractors. There are two dumpsites in the city, the municipal dumpsite and the dumpsite of the Avani Victoria Falls Resort, both of which are located on the

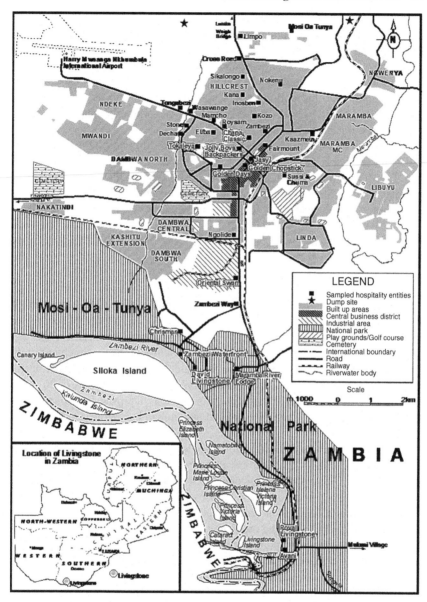

Figure 3.1 Location of sampled hospitality entities in Livingstone.
Source: authors.

northern edge of the city (Figure 3.1). Muller et al. (2017) estimated that the total amount of waste collected in Livingstone in 2017 was 2 200 tonnes. Of the collected waste, it is estimated that 1 431.4 tonnes are potentially recyclable, whereas only 83.4 tonnes are being recycled at the time of their study (Muller et al., 2017). This indicates a gap in the attempts to reduce the amount of waste in the environment since currently, 2 106.1 tonnes of waste goes to the municipal dumpsite per month. The municipal dumpsite is a hazard because mixed waste is allowed to accumulate in heaps on both sides of a 2.5 km gravel road that is close to an intermittent stream. Neither dumpsite is fenced off to keep out people and animals and hence, scavengers are found at both sites. The municipal dumpsite is only manned during working hours, meaning that illegal dumping can take place undeterred after hours. The LA indicated that when the quantity of waste accumulates, it is burnt.

The method of collection of waste is door-to-door from hospitality entities that pay for the service. It was found that 11% of the entities did not pay for waste collection. The official from the LCC admitted that the LA faces challenges in carrying out its mandate due to financial, personnel and machinery constraints. The LA is unable to purchase adequate machinery for waste management in the city. It is noted that:

> 'The funding which the department receives from the government is not enough to address the challenges that are faced in waste management, and the revenue base within the department is weak'. (LCC Official, 2017)

The official from the LCC said that the total number of staff employed in the Waste Management Unit is 50, and those employed in the Waste Collection Unit is 22, with an ideal establishment size of 150 personnel. This critical shortage of personnel hinders the efficient provision of SWM and the management of the municipal dumpsite. This contravenes the guidelines that are stipulated in the Local Government Act and Council By-Laws of 1991 and the EMA of 2011 that the LA must manage the solid waste and municipal dumpsite in a manner that does not cause a threat to the environment and human health or become a public nuisance.

The franchise arrangement was mooted to address some of the challenges that LAs faced in SWM. In Livingstone, private companies such as Waste Master, Zamrex, Kelly Clean and Professional Waste Solutions have been engaged to aid in the collection and disposal of waste among tourist entities. The findings show that there is limited interaction between the private companies and the LA beyond payment to use the municipal dumpsite. The LA cannot monitor the day-to-day collection, transportation and disposal of waste. Collection of waste from hospitality entities is not systematic, and different entities make their own arrangements for the frequency of waste collection. Council workers located at the dumpsite do not have the mechanisms to regulate the various types of waste deposited there. It is clear that the garbage disposal regulatory framework as promulgated in the ZEMA Act of 2013 is not followed by either the LA or the private companies. This situation exposes the city to risks that can emanate from the disposal of undetected hazardous materials.

4.2 Disposal of waste by the hospitality sector

Waste from the hospitality subsector in Livingstone is generated by four major units. These are: (a) accommodation, (b) administrative and office functions, (c)

Table 3.2 Types of waste generated by the hospitality sector in Livingstone

Category	Type of waste produced
Accommodation	Facial tissue, detergents, rags, shampoo, bleach, insecticide bottles, pesticide bottles, cosmetic and soap bottles, old towels, linen, old mosquito nets and used furniture, and non-refillable product containers.
Food and Beverages Services	Food remnants, empty cans, bottles, tins, cans from beverages, tetra packs, styrofoam and cardboard boxes.
Administrative and Office Functions	Paper waste from various office functions, newspapers, magazines, envelopes, travel pamphlets brochures and boxes.
Maintenance of Open Spaces and Grounds	Plant and grass trimmings, shrubs and tree cuttings, decaying leaves, stones and other waste materials from construction materials when renovations are being done.

Source: Field data (2017).

food and beverages, and (d) ground maintenance of open spaces. The findings shown in Table 3.2 are similar to those of Muvara and Korobeinykova (2016) on the types of waste that are generated by the hospitality subsector.

4.2.1 Accommodation waste from toiletries and cleaning agents

When managers from the tourist entities were asked how they disposed of plastic containers from toiletries, pesticides and cleaning agents, 71% said this waste was collected and taken to the dumpsite, whilst 27% indicated that they reused some of the items. A small percentage used the pits on their premises to dispose of such waste. Since a large percentage of waste from toiletries ultimately reaches the dumpsite, the LA should intervene and provide guidelines for the introduction of reusable dispensers to reduce the amount of waste.

4.2.2 Furniture and linen

Most of the hospitality entities disposed of used furniture by donating it to charitable organisations (69%). Others left their old furniture outside their premises for collection (25%), whilst the minority (6%) had it burnt within the premises. The same methods were used to dispose of used linen, with a total of 67% of the hospitality entities donating the linen to charity, 28% taking it to the dumpsite and 6% burning it. Some establishments such as Avani Victoria Falls Resort, Sanctuary Sussi & Chuma and Jollyboys Backpackers placed cards in rooms encouraging guests to assist in the reduction of the environmental impacts by opting to keep the same sheets or towels for more than one night. Apart from reducing the amount of water, detergent and bleach used for laundry, this practice slows down the wear and tear of the linen, thus extending its lifespan. Jaffe (2014), however, found that wording indicating how many other guests responded positively is more successful than notices that simply ask guests to help save the environment.

4.2.3 Food and beverage

Managers from the hospitality entities indicated three different ways in which left-over food was discarded. Food waste was kept in bins on-site and later collected by waste collection companies (72%), was used for compost (19%) or was disposed of in pits within the premises (8%). Although these practices indicate that a large proportion of food waste is taken to the dumpsite, there are examples of good practice among some entities. These are the Royal Livingstone Victoria Falls Zambia Hotel by Anantara, a 5-star hotel, and Avani Victoria Falls Resort, a 3-star hotel (known as the Royal Livingstone and Avani hotels, respectively). The other entity is Tongabezi Lodge, located in the Mosi-oa-Tunya National Park along the banks of the Zambezi River. The disposal method used by Avani is presented in Box 3.1.

No attempts are made to separate cans, plastic bottles and glass bottles. Empty bottles from disposable soft drinks and alcohol were left for collection. Reusing glass bottles, which would be the best practice, was not done by any entity. Most of the beverages are locally sourced and, therefore, the Extended Producer Responsibility regulations should be implemented in Livingstone as a way of reducing such waste. Livingstone Green Initiatives and IB Blocks are recycling companies that use crushed glass from bottles for brick making on a very small scale, but they have not received a positive response from the hospitality subsector.

Box 3.1   Case Study: Avani Hotels

The Avani Hotels is a consortium of two hotels on two premises. Due to their location on a UNESCO World Heritage site (African World Heritage Fund, 2019), certain environmental requirements were made during the development stages and the hotels also have to continuously adhere to strict environmental standards. The hotels combine their waste management and have employed a conservation assistant. Waste paper, food waste and non-salty and acidic left-over food are used to produce vermicompost or vermi-tea (worm tea) using three stacked trays (Figure 3.2). The vermi-tea is then used for fertilizing and watering flowers, vegetables and spices in the hotel garden. Three trays are stacked up. The first tray is filled with waste paper and food remnants and mulch soil and black soil at the base which is then covered. The second tray is known as the 'working tray' and this is where the worms from the decomposing waste drop. The third tray which is also known as the 'collecting or holding tray' collects the liquid produced by the worms. The collected liquid is kept in special buckets and is then utilised in the spice and vegetable garden and in the flowers around the two hotels. This is an example of how food waste produced by the hospitality industry in Livingstone can be reused to reduce risk.

(a)   (b)

Figure 3.2 Non-salty and nonacidic food waste and stacked trays.
Source: Mwale, 2017.

4.2.4 Plastic bags, styrofoam, tetra packs and office waste

The study found that plastic bags, styrofoam and tetra packs from the hospitality entities were disposed of at both dumpsites. The concern is that these products are not biodegradable and thus have negative and long-lasting consequences on the environment. Recycling or reuse of plastic bags, styrofoam and tetra packs can help in resource conservation and in the reduction of greenhouse gas emissions. Most entities (83%) had paper and other office waste collected and taken to the dumpsites. The remaining 9% burnt such waste and 8% used it for composting.

4.2.5 Challenges of waste recycling

Very few hospitality entities in Livingstone practise recycling. Only 14% reported some sort of waste recycling, whilst 3% either took their waste to recyclers or had recyclables collected from their premises. Cardboard boxes were collected by informal collectors who sold them for reuse. Scrap metal and plastic PET bottles were also collected by informal waste pickers. Scrap metal was sold to Kafue Steel Corporation, whilst the plastic water bottles were washed and refilled with water for resale at eating places in markets within the city. This practice places those who unwittingly purchase the water at risk because the safety of the source of the water is not known. Most of the entities (97%) disclosed that they did not take their waste to a recycling company. One participant commented:

> 'There is no recycling company in Livingstone that is capable of utilising waste that is generated by the hospitality subsector.' (Lodge manager, Livingstone, 2017)

This indicates that there is limited awareness of waste recycling. Zambezi Nkuku, a recycling company, embarked on an innovative recycling venture involving the collection of food waste, cardboard and empty bottles from the hospitality entities for compost manure and block-making. Challenges arose when the entities started demanding to be paid for waste collected from their premises because the perception was that the recycler was making a great deal of money. Initially, the recycler paid for the waste but with time, the amounts demanded increased and rendered the venture unviable. Another recycler, IB Blocks, faced similar challenges. The nonavailability of separated waste forced the company to engage workers in collecting empty bottles from hospitality entities and bars in the Central Business District (CBD). Sometimes, these workers collect bottles from the municipal dumpsite, which is very risky because of the presence of scavengers that can be violent. To mould concrete blocks the company uses approximately 40 bags of empty bottles packed in 50 kg sacks on a daily basis. This indicates that there is an opportunity for the recycling of glass bottles in Livingstone.

4.3 Moving towards reduced urban risk for sustainable urban tourism in Zambia

The results presented in this chapter show that a large percentage of waste generated by the hospitality subsector in Livingstone is taken to the dumpsite and inadvertently contributes to the degradation of the environment. We have shown how waste created by the hospitality subsector can become a nuisance if it enters a nonfunctional waste management system. The situation in Livingstone reveals weak governance structures that contribute to poor waste management (Musavengane et al., 2020). Strengthening of municipal governance systems will enhance proper waste management systems, thereby reducing associated risks. Apart from detracting from the aesthetics, waste poses health risks in urban tourism. The probability of leachates entering the nearby stream is high because it lies close to the dumpsite. The practice of burning comingled waste with a high content of food waste can cause respiratory tract diseases such as cancer of the throat, coughs and tuberculosis (ISWA, 2015; Muvara & Korobeinykova, 2016). As these substances burn, they produce dioxins, which cause disease when frequently inhaled (Muvara & Korobeinykova, 2016). There is also the likelihood of an increase in diarrhoeal diseases such as cholera and dysentery because the dumpsites provide a breeding ground for flies, vermin and other potential carriers of communicable diseases (Gruber & Obersteiner, 2017). In addition, if these sites are not covered daily with soil, they become a source of unpleasant odour, dust and litter. The scenarios presented here outline the risks that can threaten urban tourism if the aspect of hospitality waste is not addressed. The hospitality subsector should, therefore, play a responsible part in maintaining the environment to ensure the sustainable development of the city.

Among the various actions that should be embarked upon to avert further risk is the halting of the illegal practice of on-site disposal and burning by some smaller establishments. Replacement of the dumpsites with sanitary landfills should be another goal of the LA, but until this is done, the hospitality subsector should reduce its amounts of waste. Another action should be the compulsory separation of waste. This practice reduces the amounts of waste being deposited at the dumpsite and can reduce risks caused by decomposing biodegradable waste. A large percentage of entities (61%) did not sort waste mainly because they felt it was not necessary since the waste would ultimately comingle at the dumpsite. Some entities reported not having adequate receptacles for waste separation, whilst a small number claimed not to know about the strategy. The LA should seek total elimination of organic waste at its dumpsite, since this can be used for compost. The fact that mixed waste is taken to the dumpsite makes it difficult to recycle. It must also be noted that recycling requires establishments to employ additional staff to separate waste or to tend to the compost, which smaller entities cannot afford to do (Hatem et al., 2010). However, recycling can easily be done by minimal staff if clear waste management policies and processes are established and adequate training is provided. Linkages between recyclers, hospitality entities and the LA need to be strengthened to ensure that adequate support is given to smaller entities, encouraging them to attain best practices in waste management. To ensure the creation of a sustainable urban environment, the hospitality subsector must play a leading role in reducing the waste that is taken to the dumpsite. In the absence of a sanitary landfill, waste reduction and recycling are the most feasible approaches leading to Livingstone becoming a sustainable city and attaining SDG 11.

5 Conclusions

Waste management in the hospitality subsector and its associated risks have not received much attention within the sustainability discourse. Zambia's population is projected to increase to more than double, reaching 39.1 million by the year 2050 (Population Reference Bureau, 2019), and this points to increased risks associated with accumulated waste. High urbanisation exacerbates pressure on the already strained waste management systems in Zambia. The increase in population will require concerted strategies towards waste minimisation in Livingstone, which can be achieved through encouraging recycling and reuse. It is clear that investment in waste management in Livingstone is needed urgently to reduce the risks to the environment. Furthermore, there is need to ensure the implementation of waste management policies and regulations in Livingstone. Waste generally contributes to environmental degradation through groundwater pollution due to leachates from the decomposing waste and littering the environment. Decomposing waste also emits hazardous gases such as methane (Hatem et al., 2010), causing unpleasant odours that attract flies and rodents. In addition, continued burning of waste increases the incidence of respiratory-related diseases. Currently, with the new coronavirus (COVID-19), it is highly recommended to eliminate any possible cause of respiratory-related disease since it increases health risks. The LA and the LTA should sensitise the hospitality subsector on the risks posed by comingled waste that is not disposed of at a sanitary landfill and encourage them to collaborate with the recyclers. Training should be provided on green waste management policies, and entities found not following the practices stipulated should face hefty penalties. The realisation that an outbreak of the disease will negatively affect their businesses should incentivise the hospitality sector to participate in keeping the city clean and risk-free. On a positive note, the presence of good practices in waste management can be used as a catalyst to encourage others to do the same. The smaller hotels and lodges can learn from the Royal Livingstone Victoria Falls Zambia Hotel and the Avani Victoria Falls Resort which present examples of good practices. Sharing of skills across sectors should be encouraged. Multi-stakeholder engagement is, after all, the essence of sustainable tourism (Goeldner & Brent-Ritchie, 2012). To be able to improve the management of tourism waste, an in-depth study on the composition and quantities of waste should be undertaken by the LA as a step towards the planning of waste services (Shamshiry et al., 2011). In terms of waste infrastructure, a destination such as Livingstone should prioritise changing from the use of dumpsites to waste management directed at using waste as a resource if risks are to be minimised.

Note

1 This chapter was written during the COVID-19 pandemic, which caused the tourist numbers to fall to zero as borders closed and airlines stopped flying. The Victoria Falls was closed for a period of two months.

References

Bates, B.C., Kundzewicz, Z.W., Wu, S. & Palutikof, J.P. (Eds.). (2008). *Climate change and water.* Technical Paper VI. Intergovernmental Panel on Climate Change Secretariat, Geneva.

Environmental Council of Zambia. (2004). *National solid waste strategy for Zambia.* Lusaka: ECZ.

Ezeah, C., Fazakerley, J. & Byrne, T. (2015). Tourism waste management in the European Union: Lessons learnt from four popular EU tourist destinations. *American Journal of Climate Change*, 4(05), 431-445. Retrieved January 28 2020 from http://www.scirp.org/journal/ajcc

Fletcher, J., Fyall, A., Gilbert, D. & Wanhill, S. (2013). *Tourism: Principles and practice.* (5th ed.). Edinburgh, UK: Pearson Education.

Goeldner, C.R. & Brent-Ritchie, J.R. (2012). *Tourism: Principles, practices, philosophies.* Hoboken, NJ: John Wiley & Sons.

Government of the Republic of Zambia. (1990). Zambia Environmental Protection and Pollution Control Act, 1990. Retrieved January 28 2020 from http://www.parliament.gov.zm/sites/default/files/documents/acts/Environmental%20Protection%20and%20Pollution%20Control%20Act.pdf

Government of the Republic of Zambia. (2018). *2017 Tourism statistical digest.* Ministry of Tourism and Arts. Lusaka, Zambia: GRZ.

Government of the Republic of Zambia. (2019). *Statutory Instrument No. 65 of 2018 on Extended Producer Responsibility (EPR).* Ministry of Water Development, Sanitation and Environmental Protection. Lusaka, Zambia: GRZ.

Government of the Republic of Zambia. (2020). *Zambia tourism master plan 2018-2038. Ministry of Tourism and Arts.* Lusaka, Zambia: GRZ.

Gruber, I. & Obersteiner, G. (Ed.). (2017). Urban strategies for waste management in tourist cities: Compendium of waste management practices in pilot cities and best practices in touristic cities. European Union Report. Retrieved May 25 2020 from http://

www.urban-waste.eu/wp-content/uploads/2017/02/URBANWASTE-Compendium-of-waste-management-practices.pdf

Hatem, R., Radwan, I., Jones, E. & Minoli, D. (2010). Managing solid waste in small hotels. *Journal of Sustainable Tourism*, 18(2), 175-190. https://doi.org/10.1080/09669580903373946

International Solid Waste Association. (2015). *Wasted health: The tragic case of dumpsites*. ISWA Scientific and Technical Committee Report. Rotterdam, Netherlands: ISWA.

Jaffe, E. (2014). Read about how hotels get you to reuse towels. Everyone's doing it. *Fast Company*, October 10. Retrieved January 28 2020 from https://www.fastcompany.com/3037679/read-about-how-hotels-get-you-to-reuse-towels-everyones-doing-it

Mensah, I. (2020). Waste management practices of small hotels in Accra: An application of the waste management hierarchy model. *Journal of Global Business Insights*, 5(1), 33-46. https://doi.org/10.5038/2640-6489.5.1.1081

Mihai, F.C. (2013). Tourism implications on local waste management: Case study: Neamț County, Romania. *Present Environment and Sustainable Development*, 7(1), 214-221.

Millennium Ecosystem Assessment. (2005). *Ecosystems and human well-being: Synthesis*. Washington, DC: Island Press.

Muller, L., Ciaraldi, E., McNaught, A., Allaire, J. & Ngwenya, A. (2017). *Waste as a resource: Development opportunities within Zambia's waste value chain and management system*. Technical Report. ILO Green Jobs Programme. Geneva: ILO.

Musavengane, R., Siakwah, P. & Llewellyn, L. (2020). The nexus between tourism and urban risk: Towards inclusive, safe, resilient and sustainable outdoor tourism in African cities. *Journal of Outdoor Recreation and Tourism*, 29(2020), 100254. https://doi.org/10.1016/j.jort.2019.100254

Muvara, I. & Korobeinykova, Y. (2016). The analysis of the waste problem in tourist destination on the example of Carpathian Region in Ukraine. *Journal of Ecological Engineering*, 17(2), 43-51. https://doi.org/10.12911/22998993/62285

Nellemann, C. & Corcoran, E. (Eds.). (2010). *Dead planet, living planet: Biodiversity and ecosystem restoration for sustainable development. Rapid assessment* United Nations Environment Programme, Grid-Arendal.

Population Reference Bureau. (2019). *Focus area: Zambia*. Retrieved January 28 2020 from https://www.prb.org/international/geography/zambia.

Shamshiry, E., Nadi, B., Mokhtar, B.M., Komoo, I., Hashim, S.H. & Yahaya, N. (2011). Integrated models for solid waste management in tourism regions: Langkawi Island, Malaysia. *Journal of Environmental and Public Health*, 2011, Article ID 709549-5 pages. https://doi.org/10.1155/2011/709549

Styles, D., Schönberger, H. & Galvez-Martos, J.L. (2013). *JRC scientific and policy report on best environmental management practice in the tourism sector*. European Commission, Joint Research Centre. Luxemburg Publication Office: European Union.

United Nations. (2015). *Transforming our world: The 2030 agenda for sustainable development*. A/RES/70/1. https://sustainabledevelopment.un.org/post2015/transformingourworld/publication

United Nations World Tourism Organization. (2013). *Sustainable tourism for development guidebook*. https://www.e-unwto.org/doi/pdf/10.18111/9789284415496

United Nations World Tourism Organization. (2017). *2016 annual report*. https://sustainabledevelopment.un.org/content/documents/2622annual_report_2016_web_0.pdf

Vardoulakis, S., Dear, K. & Wilkinson, P. (2016). Challenges and opportunities for urban environmental health and sustainability: The HEALTHY-POLIS initiative. *Environmental Health*, 15(1), S30. https://doi.org/10.1186/s12940-016-0096-1

Von Bertrab, A., Hernández, J.D., Macht, A. & Rodríguez, M. (2009). *Public-private partnerships as a means to consolidate integrated solid waste management initiatives in tourism destinations: The case of the Mexican Caribbean.* Retrieved January 28 2020 from http://www.iswa.org/uploads/tx_iswaknowledgebase/3-340paper_long.pdf

Williams, S. (2009). *Tourism geography: A new synthesis.* (2nd ed.). London, UK: Routledge.

Wong, P.P. (2004). *Environmental impacts of tourism.* In: Lew, A.A., Hall, M.C. & Williams, A.M. (Eds.), *A companion to tourism.* Oxford, UK: Blackwell Publishing. pp. 450-461.

Zambia Development Agency. (2013). *Tourism sector profile.* Lusaka: ZDA.

Zorpas, A.A., Voukkali, I. & Loizia, P. (2014). The impact of tourist sector in the waste management plans. *Desalination and Water Treatment, 56*(5), 1141-1149 https://doi.org/10.1080/19443994.2014.934721

4 The political economy of unplanned urban sprawl, waste and tourism development in Ghana

Pius Siakwah

1 Introduction

Tourism contributes globally to development, but urban tourism in most of Africa seems to be challenged by environmental and social risks. This chapter maps out urban sprawl, the political economy of waste and urban tourism development by asking questions such as how to promote both tourism in a dirty environment and top-down policies that encourage garbage collection and promote recycling. We note that because Ghana's urbanisation is developing exponentially and outstripping social services provisions, such as waste management, promoting tourism as part of a broad development strategy is challenged. Uncollected urban waste poses health hazards while private-sector involvement in waste management has been underpinned by corruption. Neoliberal policies that monetise waste management adversely affect communities that cannot pay for those services.

While cities in sub-Saharan Africa are hubs of economic activity (including tourism), urbanisation and population growth generate security and sanitation risks in those spaces as well (Satterthwaite, 2017). The United Nations Development Programme reports that globally, the urban population will double by 2050, with 1 in 3 persons residing in cities, and 3 billion people living in slums.[1] The 2019 Sustainable Development Goals (SDGs) Report on SDG 11, "Make cities inclusive, safe, resilient and sustainable", observed that over a billion people reside in slums globally.[2] Sub-Saharan Africa (SSA) is the world's fastest urbanising region, housing 472 million people, with Africa's share of the global urban population projected to increase from 11.3% in 2010 to 20.2% by 2050.[3] Managing such a huge surge in urban population requires planning and the provision of essential social services, including waste management. These services have implications for tourism development. Rapid urbanisation and sanitation challenges are woes facing African economies (Addo et al., 2015). Urban tourism is poorly developed in Africa, except for South Africa, where township tourism is prevalent (Rogerson, 2015, 2002).

As of 2018, the Ghana Statistical Service (GSS) reports that 55% of Ghana's population is urban. The urbanisation and population growth have been fuelled by colonial and post-independence policies that are centred on urban areas (GSS, 2014b), the high birth rate and migration. Owusu and Yankson (2017) advocate that we should be attentive to demographic, economic, social and environmental processes in analysing Ghana's urban population dynamics. Social services like health and education are better provided in urban areas, while economic opportunities also attract migrants. However, because urban waste is uncollected, tourism development in those areas is increasingly coming under threat (Aziale & Asafo-Adjei, 2013). Difficulties with waste management due to infrastructure and technical inefficiencies threaten the achievement of SDGs that emphasise clean, sustainable cities (Addaney & Oppong, 2015). Burning of electronic waste is a public health emergency in Ghana's urban spaces (Amankwaa et al., 2017). However, Agyei-Mensah and Oteng-Ababio (2012) note that sometimes workers' environmental and health perceptions are downplayed, exposing a lack of convergence between lay and expert knowledge. This complex interface between urbanisation and waste management has implications for tourism development in Ghana.

There are limited studies on urban sprawl, waste management and risks to tourism development. This chapter is aimed at mapping out the urban sprawl, political economy of waste and urban tourism development in Ghana. The government of Ghana's waste management policies are lopsided, with a focus on garbage collection and limited recycling. The growth of urban population comes with mounting demand for the management of waste generated daily (Zhu et al., 2008). For instance, Ampofo et al. (2015: 27) observe that cities like Bolgatanga in Ghana have difficulties in waste management due to urban population surge, high consumption of nonreusable materials, societal attitude in handling waste and under-resourced local authorities. The filth that accumulates in urban spaces in Ghana limits urban tourism. Thus, promotion tourism in Ghana needs citizens' ownership of the sanitation drive, attitudinal change and media education in partnership with municipal, metropolitan and district assemblies (MMDAs) and also private companies.

This chapter relies on a review of policy documents and reports from the Ministry of Tourism, the GSS and published articles to analyse waste and urban tourism development. Document analysis as a qualitative approach is inexpensive and unobtrusive. It is a systematic review of print and electronic documents (Bowen, 2009). Data on tourism, urbanisation and waste in Ghana are analysed and emerging themes on urbanisation and waste management, and their implications for tourism development are discussed. The analytic process involves skimming, reading and interpretation of specific documents to elicit meaning and understanding on urbanisation, waste and tourism development. The data are organised into themes related to the research question through pattern recognition within the data (Bowen, 2009). The data are carefully reviewed and constructed to unpack the themes that are pertinent to the nexus between urbanisation, waste and tourism development in Ghana. The next sections focus on urban sprawl and the political economy of waste management, as well as their implications for urban tourism development.

2 Political economy of urban sprawl

Understanding the political economy of the urban sprawl helps to highlight its implications for waste and tourism development, which are discussed later. Urban areas are spaces with high population concentration (Cobbinah & Niminga-Beka,

2017; Owusu & Yankson, 2017). However, using population as the main criterion to define urbanisation ignores the social, economic and ecological dimensions of the urban space (Korah & Cobbinah, 2016). As Cobbinah and Niminga-Beka (2017) observe, urbanisation is a complex phenomenon driven by diverse factors with differentiated manifestation. For this chapter, I use the term 'urban' for spaces with high population concentration, developed social infrastructure, industrial and service-driven economies and some elevated level of living standards, but with the potential of health, housing, sanitation and slum challenges.

The global population has witnessed a major shift, with more than half living in urban areas in 2008 (Oteng-Ababio et al., 2019) and 55% in 2018, according to World Bank estimates. In Africa, 40% of the population currently lives in cities, with the urban populace increasing to 450 million in 2014 and an estimated 1.3 billion by 2050 (Oteng-Ababio et al., 2019; Turok, 2016; UNDESA/PD, 2012). The rural–urban demographic shift has led to increasing pressure on social services and economic changes. Urban spaces are manifesting vulnerability, insecurity, unsustainability and destruction of sensitive ecological areas (Cobbinah & Niminga-Beka, 2017). These urban space changes have implications for tourism development.

In Ghana, a settlement of 5 000 people or more is described as urban. However, as noted earlier, the population as the main determinant of urbanisation is simplistic and highlights the complexities of the urbanisation processes. Significant changes have occurred in Ghana's population with regards to urban dwellers. Ghana's urbanisation level, which was 51% in 2010, is projected as 57% in 2020, 63% by 2030 and 70% by 2050 (Owusu & Yankson, 2017; GSS, 2014a). From 2000 to 2010, Ghana's urbanisation increased by 7% at a rate of 3.9% per annum (GSS, 2012). This rate is higher (5%) in some cities (GSS, 2014a). The unregulated informal economic activities, poor urban planning and waste management in an ever-increasing urban space (Cobbinah & Korah, 2015) negatively impact tourism, as the sector cannot thrive in the dirt.

Increases in socioeconomic activities and political-administrative changes also facilitate transitioning to and the manifestation of urbanisation (Oteng-Ababio et al., 2019). Urbanisation processes are not recent phenomena, and Ghana has witnessed rapid population concentration in cities (Owusu & Yankson, 2017). The GSS (2014b) notes that over the past 10 years, the urban population growth rate averaged 4.5% per year, while the rural rate is 3.0%, but with an uneven distribution due to locality differences like historical advantage, natural resource availability and government policies. There is, however, concentration in Accra and Kumasi. Unrestrained outward city growth is resulting in slum urban spaces that are out of control.

The World Bank reports that urbanisation has contributed to poverty reduction and the structural transformation of Ghana, reflecting a 21% decline in the agriculture share of employment between 1991 and 2013 due to an expansion in services (Owusu & Yankson, 2017). Other reports note that Ghana experienced rapid unplanned urbanisation, which contributed to poverty reduction even amid the incidence of crime (IDRC, n.d.). Migrants' ingenuity has enabled them to build houses, create jobs in the informal sector and send remittances to their home communities (Awumbila et al., 2014). The question, however, is how sustainable those jobs are – and what the social and ecological costs are of urban tourism development.

Urbanisation in Ghana has led to encroachment on public spaces and ecologically sensitive areas, slum pervasiveness, the informality of economic activities and unauthorised land development (Cobbinah & Niminga-Beka, 2017). These changes in the urban spaces have implications for how the spaces can be attractive to tourists. Inadequate planning of cities at the national scale negatively affects the development of housing, sanitation and drainage (Owusu & Yankson, 2017). Oteng-Ababio et al. (2019), for instance, observe that Wa exhibits synergism in risk accumulation, uncertainties and complexities in urban development by manifesting inefficient potable water and sanitation challenges. Slum development, poor housing and unregulated informal economy lead to improper waste disposal with health and environmental repercussions. Amoako and Inkoom (2018) observed vulnerability and flood hazards in urban informal settlements as rooted political and sociocultural factors and indigenous land management systems that encourage informality.

Formal or informal urban settlements have implications for residential land-use commercialisation, urban functionality and urban poor livelihoods. Cobbinah and Niminga-Beka (2017) note that in Kumasi, 85% of residential land-use is commercialised due to demand increases, high land values and a weak urban planning system, while over 86% of the urban poor cannot afford rents. This forces the poor to ply their trades in on-street spaces, creating chaos on the streets and in central business areas. The chaotic and uncontrolled commercial activities and limited parking spaces and sanitation facilities hinder urban functionality (Cobbinah & Niminga-Beka, 2017). These dysfunctionalities in the urban spaces disorganise socioeconomic activities, including tourism development. The survival of the urban poor and their right to the city are threatened by limited basic service provision. Whereas access to potable drinking water is critical in assessing life quality, the proportion of the urban population in Ghana with access to a pipe-borne water facility is less than two-thirds (GSS, 2014b). Sachet or "pure" water serves as drinking water. However, the plastic generation associated with sachet water has environmental implications. Oteng-Ababio et al. (2019) observe that Ghana's urbanisation is associated with plastic waste, choke gutters, floods and poverty. Promotion of tourism within such a space is impossible.

The relations among crime, poverty and urbanisation is conditioned and shaped by dynamic social, psychological and economic factors. The connections between urbanisation, rural–urban migration and poverty are more nuanced, with some level of increases in poverty in urban spaces (Owusu & Yankson, 2017). The argument that rural–urban migration has limited positive outcomes for migrants is challenged by Awumbila et al. (2014). They note that although migrants live in a harsh environment in urban areas, the majority of them believe their well-being has improved in the cities. But we have to question to whom they are comparing their living standards and how their activities in urban spaces negatively impact other economic activities. This raises the question of how urbanisation and its attendant challenges impact tourism development in Ghana.

While recognising the right of the poor to the city, we are also mindful of how limited the provisions of social and sanitation services are and that throwing plastic waste in the environment has negative implications for their lives, the environment and tourism.

3 Waste management risks and tourism

Waste is an indispensable element of humanity. In recent years, however, waste has become more topical because human beings are generating waste at an alarming rate that places the environment and the very human existence at risk. Solid, plastic and electronic wastes are an eyesore and are harmful to the environment due to their non-biodegradability (Oteng-Ababio, 2012b; Collivignarelli et al., 2004). Ghana has struggled to manage its waste, especially plastic waste, polluting the environment and beaches, and placing development initiatives like tourism in despair.

Although it is difficult to put an exact figure on the volume of waste generated annually in Ghana, the country generates tonnes of waste (especially in the cities or urban areas of Accra and Kumasi). The waste comprises of solid, liquid and electronic material. Accra and Kumasi, with their high urbanisation and consumption, generate a significant amount of Ghana's waste (Ampofo et al., 2015). Aziale and Asafo-Adjei (2013) identify food debris, plastic, paper, bottles/cans and metals as the main waste generated in Tema in the Greater Accra area. Addaney and Oppong's (2015) study in the Awutu Senya East Municipality revealed that 23 tonnes of mainly solid organic waste were generated daily in 2014. Ampofo et al. (2015: 27) observed that in Bolgatanga, between 1993 and 2009, waste generation increased from 46 015 to 101 823 tonnes – an increase of 55%. Amoah and Kosoe (2014) argue that waste remains a big challenge in Ghana, with 810 tonnes of solid waste generated daily in Wa, out of which 216 tonnes are collected. This uncollected and poorly managed waste poses serious environmental and public health hazards and hindrances to socioeconomic development.

Electronic waste is becoming very common in Ghana. Even though most of the electronic waste is not produced internally, Ghana is integrated into the electronic waste system as a dumping ground. As Oteng-Ababio (2012a) observes, e-waste scavenging has been embedded in networked spaces within differentiated circuits that produce geographically uneven development. The final management of e-waste has been a challenge for Ghana, since it is driven by an informal sector with limited technical and financial capabilities. The e-waste does not only pose a health risk to those involved in collecting and recycling, but also to residents within the waste enclaves such as Agbogbloshie in Accra (Amankwaa et al., 2017). These e-waste sites in parts of Accra are unpleasant for development (Oteng-Ababio, 2012b), including tourism.

Several institutions and actors are involved in waste management. Waste collection, disposal and recycling (management) involve MMDAs (coordinating on behalf of the state) and private companies such as Zoomlion (Amoah & Kosoe, 2014). Unfortunately, these MMDAs are ill-resourced to manage this waste (Addaney & Oppong, 2015). Since 2008, Zoomlion has been a leader in Ghana's waste management space (Oduro-Kwarteng, 2011). It involves public–private partnerships, due to the government of Ghana's inability to fulfil its financial obligations to waste companies in a timely manner (Addaney & Oppong, 2015) and poor supervision and corruption in the waste space. There are, however, reported cases of corruption involving Zoomlion and poor execution of waste management, which seems to defeat the initial aim of keeping the environment clean.

Two methods have been used for waste collection in Ghana: (1) central collection containers (CCC), and (2) door-to-door or house-to-house (HtH) collection (Oteng-Ababio et al., 2019; Owusu-Sekyere et al., 2013). The HtH is implemented in middle- or high-income and low-density suburbs; and the CCC is suitable in low-income, high-density and poorly planned suburbs (Amoah & Kosoe, 2014). With the HtH, waste bins are shared between households and private collectors get them weekly or monthly at a fee (Oteng-Ababio et al., 2019; Oteng-Ababio, 2010). The CCC, however, entails households or individuals taking the waste to a common space to be collected by MMDAs or a private company. There are often challenges with fee payment and effective, timely communal collection of the waste.

We maintain that waste management has complex environmental, health, economic and social implications. Choked gutters or uncollected waste pose health risks. Abul (2010) found dumpsites to be in smelly and unsightly conditions, while Addo et al. (2015) observe that 40% of the households in Kumasi complained of stench from dumpsites and the diseases like diarrhoea, intestinal worms and typhoid associated with it. These environmental challenges in the urban spaces of Ghana do not promote tourism development. Waste pollution leads to loss of productive time, resources, income, savings and investments. Social relations are also disrupted as people stay in hospitals or die from waste-related sicknesses. Indiscriminate littering and poor waste collection lead to cholera and malaria, as the waste becomes breeding grounds for these diseases (Zhu et al., 2008; Addaney & Oppong, 2015; Collivignarelli et al., 2004). People and communities lose time, money, productive work and financial savings/investments. Losing financial resources and savings limits their ability to expend, including spending on local tourism. In Ghana, choked drains, gutters and beaches scattered with plastic have inhibited tourism promotion. In addition, environmental challenges affect meeting the health/environment components of the SDGs, while a dirty environment negatively impacts tourism promotion as an economic activity in the cities of Ghana.

4 Urban waste and tourism development

In this section, we continue with our analysis of increasing urbanisation, urban waste management and tourism development in Ghana. Tourism contributes significantly to global socioeconomic development. In 2016, tourism contributed 3.1% directly to global GDP growth and 6 million net additional jobs (WTTC, 2017). It generated US$7.6 trillion (10.2% of global GDP) and 292 million jobs (1 in 10 global jobs). With regards to Africa in 2016, tourism contributed US$66.4 billion directly to GDP (3% of the continent's GDP) and directly generated 2.6%

of total employment (WTTC, 2017). In Ghana, tourism generated US$1.8 billion in 2016 (WTTC, 2017); it accounted for 5% of employment and 4.6% of exports, and contributed 6.7% to GDP in 2014 (Deichmann & Frempong, 2016; WTTC, 2015). International tourists to Ghana were 950 000 in 2015, and it is expected to reach 1.5 million by 2024 (Frimpong-Bonsu, 2015). Boakye et al. (2013) note that tourism stimulates economic growth and reduces poverty by (in)directly infusing new demand for local goods and services. But while the macroeconomic impact of tourism has been remarkable, as indicated above, translating macro-gains into micro-gains has been problematic in Ghana. Tourism sites in Ghana are spatially located across urban and rural areas (Siakwah, 2018), but in most urban spaces in Ghana, environmental risks inhibit tourism development.

Even though there are challenges with tourism governance – as well as social and environmental challenges – in Ghana, this chapter focuses on urban risk driven by waste and the threats it poses to tourism development. Although waste is an integral part of human history, its generation, magnitude and impact are compounded by urban sprawl, population increase and poor waste management. Just like other emerging economies, this poses challenges to Ghana's tourism as a dirty environment does not encourage tourism. Although the total amount of waste generated in Ghana is not readily available, poor waste management infrastructure, poor human attitude and increasing urban waste weaken economic activities such as tourism.

The tourism sector in Ghana is under threat from filth – organic, plastic and electronic. This is an environmental risk that threatens the very existence of the tourism industry. First, tourism thrives on both aesthetic and intrinsic values of the environment. Urbanisation and attendant informal economic activities and waste compromise tourism development potential by impacting the aesthetic and intrinsic values of the surroundings. Miezah et al. (2015) note that Ghana generated over 12 710 tonnes of waste per day. But in terms of collection, Mensah and Larbi (2005) opine that 80% of the waste in Accra and 35% in Kumasi goes uncollected. Other urban spaces in Ghana have more tonnes of waste uncollected. Uncollected urban waste poses health and environmental hazards (Amoah & Kosoe, 2014). It is also obvious that the uncollected waste poses a threat to the environment and, ultimately, tourism.

Second, neoliberalisation of the urban space promotes exclusionary tourism where poor people are evicted for tourism promotion. Furthermore, neoliberal policies that monetise waste management have adverse implications for the urban poor, who cannot afford to pay for their rubbish to be collected. Urban waste is problematic despite their potential for renewable energies (Moya et al., 2017). Elsewhere, Hartmann (2018) identified formalisation and capital intensification of urban waste management systems as a threat to poor livelihoods, because elsewhere, it is argued that tourism governance thrives on inclusive participation and equity (Siakwah et al., 2020; Musavengane et al., 2019; Jamal & Camargo, 2017). Tourism governance is not ahistorical; instead, it is embedded in wider society – spatially and temporally. Thus, a waste management system that does consider the poor as victims, as well as perpetrators of risk to urban tourism development, is bound to fail.

Plastics usage for food packaging has become dominant in Ghana despite its threat to the environment and, ultimately, tourism development. The 'plasticisation'[4] of Ghana's waste has not only led to the long-term impact of plastics on the environment, as they are nonbiodegradable, but their visibility in the surroundings as an eyesore. This is a blot to tourism development, as it reduces the aesthetics of the environment. Plastics have become so dominant in the Ghanaian society and psyche that sometimes the plastic materials used to package goods seem more expensive than the products packaged. For instance, a sachet of water costing of GH¢0.20 (less than a tenth of a dollar) is placed in black plastic bags, which seem more expensive than the water.[5] The visibility of plastics in Ghana's environment is extended to some of its beaches. Plasticisation on beaches does not encourage tourist (re)visits. It is time that Ghana de-plasticises its beaches through recycling or by banning plastic packaging to encourage tourists. Paper or reusable bags can be encouraged in Ghana.

Waste management practices do not take place in a vacuum; they are guided by national, institutional and policy frameworks. Ghana's waste policy highlights the need for systematic collection (Government of Ghana, 2010a). The National Environmental Sanitation Strategy and Action Plan identifies electronic, biodegradable, organic, wastewater, septage discharge and faecal sludges as some of the types of waste polluting beaches and rivers (Government of Ghana, 2010b). This waste negatively impacts the promotion of tourism as most tourists find the beaches and tourist sites unconducive to visit, and for holidays (Government of Ghana, 2010b). It does limit the number of persons visiting those spaces. Achieving sustainable waste management depends on diverse factors and actors – the legal framework, institutions and the private sector (Addaney & Oppong, 2015). Amoah and Kosoe (2014) advocate for comprehensive waste management that combines infrastructure improvement, health promotion and community participation. Policy regimes need clarity on the partnership between the government and the private sector, funding and mainstreaming recycling.

The missing link or risk in urban spaces is how to reduce waste flows through reuse, recycling or alternative economic uses. This blatant omission poses threats to public health and the environment, and it is indicative of the marginalisation of decent waste treatment practices (Oteng-Ababio, 2011). A partnership between MMDAs and private companies has, however, been vital in improving waste management. MMDAs and Zoomlion are responsible for waste collection, transportation and disposal (Amoah & Kosoe, 2014). Recently, the Multimedia Group[6] partnered with the Accra Metropolitan Assembly (AMA) on a campaign labelled '*Joy Clean* Ghana *Campaign*', which raises awareness on keeping a clean environment.[7] It has helped to educate and reprimand individuals, households and small businesses on keeping Accra clean. It can also aid in the promotion of tourism.

Attitudinal change is important for the promotion of a clean environment and tourism. In Ghana, however, it is not uncommon to witness people throwing rubbish indiscriminately in their surroundings. Thus, to keep a clean environment to propel tourism requires an attitudinal change where the citizens recognise the need to dispose of waste properly. Citizens' ownership of the sanitation drive, including a form of citizens police or watchdog to report and punish those who throw garbage around, will keep the environment clean to promote tourism. Driving attitudinal change should, however, start in basic schools where children are exposed to the dangers of indiscriminate littering. Media education in partnership with MMDAs can influence attitudinal change through the democratisation of waste collection and involving citizens in waste policing and management. Addo et al. (2015) advocate for community participation in sanitation improvement programmes, including in recycling and sensitisation on waste-related diseases.

We advocate for waste management practice that moves beyond the national–private sector divide. Since the formal systems have not been effective, incorporating them into informal mechanisms in the waste management value chain can be helpful in tourism promotion as well. Navarrete-Hernandez and Navarrete-Hernandez (2018) advocate for unleashing waste-pickers' potential through supporting recycling cooperatives in Chile. Ghana can adopt a similar approach by making use of existing informal networks to manage some of the waste. As Oteng-Ababio (2012a) observes, for some of the urban poor, waste collection and recycling are a common means for earning a living. Waste scavengers contribute to recovery and recycling through sorting and cleaning (Rockson et al., 2013). MMDAs can improve waste recycling and resource utilisation if they recognise these various actors and stakeholders in the waste management space. Cobbinah et al. (2017) advocate for the need to locate the urbanites in the waste management chain in Ghana. Thus, there is a need for the proper integration of the informal sector and the other actors/structures into the existing (public/private) waste management practices. Urban dwellers can afford to patronise private waste management companies while the MMDAs provide public services for the poor. Eventually, this frees the streets of Ghana of dirt for inclusive tourism promotion.

5 Conclusions

Tourism has been an integral part of Ghana's development, contributing to foreign exchange, employment, income and poverty reduction. Urban tourism development in Ghana has, however, been a challenge due to high urbanisation and waste generated, which does not encourage international and local tourism. This chapter maps out urban sprawl, the political economy of waste and urban tourism development. We argue that the promotion of tourism is impossible in a dirty environment with top-down policies that encourage garbage collection without necessarily finding a balance with informal networks in the waste space and recycling. The rate of urban growth has been far beyond social services provisions such as waste management, thus hindering urban tourism development. Private-sector involvement in waste management is underpinned by corruption, while neoliberal policies that monetise waste management have adverse implications for communities who cannot pay for waste management. Although waste management is central in promoting tourism, there is limited appreciation of the political economy of waste and its impact on the environment, people and sustainable tourism. The promotion of urban tourism requires citizens' ownership of the sanitation drive, media education and the use of informal waste practices to de-plasticise Ghana's environment.

Notes

1 https://unstats.un.org/sdgs/report/2019/goal-11/, accessed 10 June 2020.
2 https://sustainabledevelopment.un.org/sdg11, accessed 13 February 2020.
3 https://www.csis.org/analysis/urbanization-sub-saharan-africa, accessed 13 February 2020.
4 'Plasticisation' is used here as the tendency to overuse plastics for packaging of goods.
5 Discussion with an environmental officer, 3 March 2020, Accra, Ghana.
6 A private media company in Ghana.
7 https://www.myjoyonline.com/news/2019/September-2nd/multimedia-partners-ama-on-joy-cleanghanacampaign.php, accessed 12 February 2020.

References

Abul, S. (2010). Environmental and health impact of solid waste disposal: A Mangwaneni dumpsite in Manzini, Swaziland. *Journal of Sustainable Development in Africa, 12*(7), 64–78.

Addaney, M., & Oppong, R. A. (2015). Critical issues of municipal solid waste management in Ghana. *Journal of Energy and Natural Resource Management, 2*(1), 30–36.

Addo, I. B., Adei, D., & Acheampong, E. O. (2015). Solid waste management and its health implications on the dwellers of Kumasi metropolis, Ghana. *Current Research Journal of Social Sciences, 7*(3), 81–93.

Agyei-Mensah, S., & Oteng-Ababio, M. (2012). Perceptions of health and environmental impacts of e-waste management in Ghana. *International Journal of Environmental Health Research, 22*(6), 500–517.

Amankwaa, E. F., Tsikudo, K. A. A., & Bowman, J. A. (2017). 'Away' is a place: The impact of electronic waste recycling on blood lead levels in Ghana. *Science of the Total Environment, 601*, 1566–1574.

Amoah, S. T., & Kosoe, E. A. (2014). Solid waste management in urban areas of Ghana: Issues and experiences from Wa. *Journal of Environment Pollution and Human Health, 2*(5), 110–117.

Amoako, C., & Inkoom, D. K. B. (2018). The production of flood vulnerability in Accra, Ghana: Re-thinking flooding and informal urbanization. *Urban Studies, 55*(13), 2903–2922.

Ampofo, S., Evans Kumi, E., & Ampadu, B. (2015). Investigating solid waste management in the Bolgatanga Municipality of the Upper East Region, Ghana. *Environment and Pollution, 4*(3), 27–41.

Awumbila, M., Owusu, G., & Teye, J. K. (2014). *Can rural–urban migration into slums reduce poverty? Evidence from Ghana.* Migrating out of poverty. Working Paper 13. Brighton: University of Sussex.

Aziale, L. K., & Asafo-Adjei, E. (2013). Logistic challenges in urban waste management in Ghana: A case of Tema Metropolitan Assembly. *European Journal of Business and Management 5*(32), 116–128.

Boakye, K. A., Otibo, F., & Frempong, F. (2013). Assessing Ghana's contemporary tourism development experience. *Journal of Global Initiatives, 8*(1&2), 133–154.

Bowen, G. A., (2009). Document analysis as a qualitative research method. *Qualitative Research Journal, 9*(2), 27–40.

Cobbinah, P. B., Addaney, M., & Agyeman, K. O. (2017). Locating the role of urbanites in solid waste management in Ghana. *Environmental Development* (24), 9–21.

Cobbinah, P. B., & Korah, P. I. (2015). Religion gnaws urban planning: The geography of places of worship in Kumasi, Ghana. *International Journal of Urban Sustainable Development, 8*(2), 1–17.

Cobbinah, P. B., & Niminga-Beka, R. (2017). Urbanisation in Ghana: Residential land use under siege in Kumasi Central. *Cities* (60), 388–340.

Collivignarelli, C., Sorlini, S., & Vaccari, M. (2004). Solid waste management in developing countries. Proceedings of the ISWA 2004 World Congress, 17–21 October, Rome, Italy.

Deichmann, J. I., & Frempong, F. (2016). International tourism in Ghana: A survey analysis of traveller motivations and perceptions. *Journal of Hospitality and Tourism Management* (29), 176–183.

Frimpong-Bonsu, W. (2015). Diagnostic study of tourism in Ghana. *African Centre for Economic Transformation*, 1–18.

Government of Ghana. (2010a). *Environmental Sanitation Policy*. Accra: Ministry of Local Government and Rural Development.

Government of Ghana. (2010b). *National Environmental Sanitation Strategy and Action Plan (NESSAP)*. Accra: Ministry of Local Government and Rural Development, Environmental Health and Sanitation Directorate.

GSS (2014a). *2010 Population and Housing Census Report: District Analytical Report, Kumasi Metropolitan*. Accra: GSS.

GSS (2014b). *2010 Population and Housing Census Report: Urbanisation*. Accra: GSS.

GSS (Ghana Statistical Service) (2012). *2010 Population and Housing Census: Summary Report of Final Results*. Accra: GSS.

Hartmann, C. (2018). Waste picker livelihoods and inclusive neoliberal municipal solid waste management policies: The case of the La Chureca garbage dump site in Managua, Nicaragua. *Waste Management* (71), 565–577.

IDRC (International Development Research Centre) (n.d.). *Crime and the 'poverty penalty' in urban Ghana*. Ottawa: IDRC.

Jamal, T., & Camargo, B. A. (2017). Tourism governance and policy: Whither justice? *Tourism Management Perspectives, 25*, 205–208.

Korah, P. I., & Cobbinah, P. B. (2016). Juggling through Ghanaian urbanisation: Flood hazard mapping of Kumasi. *GeoJournal, 82*(6), 1195–1212.

Mensah, A., & Larbi, E. (2005). *Solid waste disposal in Ghana. Well Factsheet*, November. Retrieved from www.trend.watsan.net.

Miezah, K., Obiri-Danso, K., Kádár, Z., Fei-Baffoe, B., & Mensah, M. Y. (2015). Municipal solid waste characterization and quantification as a measure towards effective waste management in Ghana. *Waste Management, (46)*, 15–27.

Moya, D., Aldás, C., Lópeza, G., & Kaparaju, P. (2017). Municipal solid waste as a valuable renewable energy resource: A worldwide opportunity of energy recovery by using waste-to-energy technologies. *Energy Procedia, (134)*, 286–295.

Musavengane, R., Siakwah, P. & Leonard, L. (2019). "Does the poor matter" in pro-poor driven sub-Saharan African cities? towards progressive and inclusive pro-poor tourism. *International Journal of Tourism Cities, 5 (3)*, 392-411, DOI. 10.1108/IJTC-05-2019-0057.

Navarrete-Hernandez, P., & Navarrete-Hernandez, N. (2018). Unleashing waste-pickers' potential: Supporting recycling cooperatives in Santiago de Chile. *World Development, (101)*, 293–310.

Oduro-Kwarteng, S. (2011). *Private sector involvement in urban solid waste collection: Performance, capacity, and regulation in five cities in Ghana*. London: Routledge.

Oteng-Ababio, M. (2010). Solid waste management in Ghana: Willingness-to-pay for improved services. *Ghana Journal of Geography* (2), 85–107.

Oteng-Ababio, M. (2011). Missing links in solid waste management in the Greater Accra Metropolitan Area in Ghana. *GeoJournal* (76), 551–560.

Oteng-Ababio, M. (2012a). The role of the informal sector in solid waste management in the Gama, Ghana: Challenges and opportunities. *Tijdschrift voor Economische en Sociale Geografie, 103*(4), 412–425.

Oteng-Ababio M. (2012b). Electronic waste management in Ghana – Issues and practices. Retrieved from http://cdn.intechopen.com/pdfs/38097/InTechElectronic_waste_management_in_ghana_ssues_and_practices.pdf.

Oteng-Ababio, M., Owusu, G., & Asafo, D.M. (2019). Following the footsteps: Urbanisation of Wa Municipality and its synergism in risk accumulation, uncertainties and complexities in urban Ghana. *Jàmbá: Journal of Disaster Risk Studies, 11*(1), 479.

Owusu, G., & Yankson, P. W. K. (2017). Urbanization in Ghana: Retrospect and prospects. In, Aryeetey, E. & Kanbur, R. (eds.), *The economy of Ghana sixty years after independence* (pp. 1–21). Oxford: Oxford University Press.

Owusu-Sekyere, E., Osumanu, I. K., & Yaro, J. A. (2013). Dompoase landfill in the Kumasi Metropolitan Area of Ghana: A 'blessing' or a 'curse'? *International Journal of Current Research, 2*(1), 87–96.

Rockson, G. N. K., Kemausuor, F., Seassey, R., & Yanful, E. (2013). Activities of scavengers and itinerant buyers in Greater Accra, Ghana. *Habitat International, (39)*, 148–155.

Rogerson, C. M. (2002). Urban tourism in the developing world: The case of Johannesburg. *Development Southern Africa, 19*(1), 169–190.

Rogerson, C. M. (2015). Tourism and regional development: The case of South Africa's 'distressed areas'. *Development Southern Africa, (32)*, 277–291.

Satterthwaite, D. (2017). The impact of urban development on risk in sub-Saharan Africa's cities with a focus on small and intermediate urban centres. *International Journal of Disaster Risk Reduction, (26)*, 16–23.

Siakwah, P. (2018). Tourism geographies and spatial distribution of tourist sites in Ghana. *African Journal of Hospitality, Tourism and Leisure, 7*(1), 1–19.

Siakwah, P., Musavengane, R. & Leonard, L. (2020) Tourism Governance and Attainment of the Sustainable Development Goals in Africa. *Tourism Planning & Development*, 17:4, 355-383, DOI: 10.1080/21568316.2019.1600160.

Turok, I. (2016). Getting urbanisation to work in Africa: The role of the urban land–infrastructure–finance nexus. *Area Development and Policy, 1*(1), 30–47.

UNDESA/PD (United Nations Department of Economic and Social Affairs/Population Division) (2012). *World urbanisation prospects: The 2011 revision.* New York: United Nations.

WTTC. (2017). *Travel and tourism economic impact 2017 – World.* London: WTTC.

WTTC (World Travel & Tourism Council). (2015). Travel and tourism economic impact 2015 – Ghana. Retrieved from http://www.wttc.org/site_media/uploads/downloads/ghana2013.pdf, 20.12.2017.

Zhu, D., Asnani, P. H., Zurbrugg, C., Anapolsky, S., & Mani, S. (2008). *Improving municipal solid waste management in India: A sourcebook for policy makers and practitioners.* Washington, D.C.: World Bank.

5 Environmental risk management and township tourism development in Alexandra, Johannesburg, South Africa

Llewellyn Leonard and Ayanda Dladla

1 Introduction

'Township tourism', also known as 'slum tourism', has gained momentum throughout the world, particularly in developing countries (Costa, 2013; Chege & Mwisukha, 2013; Booyens, 2010; Klepsch, 2010). It involves tourists travelling to marginalised urban spaces to learn from and experience the way of life and cultures of the local people (Blakeman, 2015). Under the realm of pro-poor tourism, this type of tourism is also considered to promote an inclusive and environmentally considerate tourism development strategy, where poverty alleviation, job creation and local business development are viewed as important for the benefit of host-community residents (Butler, 2010). According to Moyo (2005), Alexandra is one of the oldest townships in South Africa, with a long history dating back to the early 1900s. Although the township is surrounded by wealthy suburbs such as Sandton (McLennan, 2016), the lives and living standards of Alexandra's residents are characterised by a high rate of poverty, unemployment, hunger, crime, socioeconomic inequality, environmental degradation, a lack of education and skills (Dladla, 2020; Davie, 2008). In post-apartheid South Africa, tourism is considered important for the development of townships (National Tourism Sector Strategy, 2011). Rogerson (2004) notes that the government has identified Alexandra as needing urgent development and branding as a tourism destination. Given that township tourism is found in an area characterised by socioeconomic challenges, the government has identified it as a strategy for poverty relief, skills development and employment generation.

Alexandra has been realising its tourism growth opportunity since 2001, with the Gauteng provincial government investing in the area to grow tourism (Mabotja, 2012; Rogerson, 2012), initiating the Alexandra Renewal Project (ARP) and the Alexandra Tourism Development Project (ATDP) to promote Alexandra as a "must visit" destination in Johannesburg (Mabotja, 2011). However, despite these government interventions and the importance of township tourism in Alexandra, this type of tourism is under threat from urban environmental risks (i.e. waste, water and sanitation pollution). Unfortunately, there is limited literature exploring the implications of urban environmental risks for township tourism development and pro-poor tourism. The link between environmental risk and its implications for township tourism development has not been fully explored or thoroughly researched. It is unclear what the major environmental risk challenges in Alexandra are and how, specifically, these may have an impact on tourism development. This chapter explores how environmental risks have undermined the potential and opportunity to successfully pursue tourism growth in the township. It will first explore literature on some potential environmental risks in Alexandra before engaging in the methodology and then presenting results related to environmental risks and their impact on tourism development. Discussion follows and conclusions are drawn before certain recommendations are made.

1.1 Exploring environmental risks in Alexandra

Alexandra Township has environmental risks that have worsened over the years. Challenges that have contributed to environmental risks have included overpopulation, which contributes to poor sanitation and increases waste generation, as well as inadequate social services in the township (Petesch, 2013; Mabotja, 2012). For example, a previous study conducted by anthropologists in Alexandra revealed a growing number of informal dwellings (over 20 000 households), with approximately 7 000 people living in illegal backyard dwellings (Mawela, 2008). In the period following the apartheid era, the population in the township began to grow at a very rapid rate (Moolman, 2014), contributing to increased waste generation (Mabotja, 2012). Environmental pollution challenges are also worsening, due in part to the Johannesburg City Council failing to take responsibility for the area (Moyo, 2005; Petesch, 2013).

There have been, however, limited government interventions to try to address some of the socioeconomic challenges that have contributed to ecological harm. For example, a government-funded development project, the Urban Renewal Plan (URP), was introduced in Alexandra in 1986 to quickly provide proper accommodations for local people in the township who did not have sanitation facilities (Matthew, 2000). The plan included clearing passageways for service lanes (by removing shacks and evicting illegal dwellers in the Jukskei River informal settlement) to open up spaces for the development of new housing projects (Petesch, 2013). However, this plan failed to improve the situation in the township as the number of shacks began to increase, making it difficult to control the fast and unplanned population growth (Moyo, 2005). The spread of informal dwellings led to the creation of a new settlement known as East Bank along the Jukskei River. Petesch (2013) states that this growth in the population caused overcrowding, which led to severe environmental challenges (as noted above). Smith (2013) notes that the new democratic government had insufficient funding to continue with the developments, leading to the permanent cancellation of the Urban Renewal Plan. In an effort to address the environmental problems in Alexandra, both the ARP and ATDP have significantly contributed by arranging clean-up campaigns, such as the Jukskei River Rehabilitation Programme and Alexandra Environmental Awareness Campaign (Mabotja, 2012). According to Mabotja (2011), these campaigns are held every year by the City of Johannesburg and aim to not only protect and clean up the area, but also to educate people and increase environmental awareness in Alexandra. It is, however, unclear how effective these interventions have been, considering that environmental challenges are still a problem and that they are compounded by a variety of factors resulting in environmental issues, which will be explored below.

2 The relationship between urbanisation, environmental risk management and township tourism

There exists an interplay between urbanisation, environmental risk management and township tourism. Firstly, the population in urban areas is increasing rapidly in African cities as more people move to urban areas for employment and economic opportunities (Musavengane et al., 2020), with the number of African urban residents set to nearly double from 2010 to 2050 (Saghir & Santoro, 2018). Due to the growth of tourism and the existing urban inequality in developing countries, it has been forecast that the development of township (slum) tourism is likely to grow and become a worldwide phenomenon (Chege & Mwisukha, 2013). Due to increasing population pressure in the urban areas, this has contributed to congestion and social vices, as well as to waste, water and sanitation challenges, and has implications for the governance of urban environmental risks (UNDP, 2015). For South Africa, urban risks that pose challenges to tourism, especially in townships, include inadequate waste service delivery provisions, increase in population pressure and sanitation challenges, to name but a few (Musavengane et al., 2020; Breetzke, 2018). However, poor service delivery in townships may also be due to poor governance. For example, poor waste disposal services is due to municipal employees lacking the technical skills required to render effective services; corruption and political appointments; irregular appointment of service providers; and not involving local residents in the planning of service delivery (Maleka et al., 2016). Thus, poor governance leads to unsustainable tourism development in urban spaces and to a high possibility of repelling tourists – as well as to a failure to meet the need for urban renewal and to include the vulnerable in development processes (Musavengane et al., 2020). Unfortunately, littering and illegal dumping of refuse or waste by residents in townships can contribute to problems of waste management by putting a strain on municipalities while such activities also discourage tourism business development opportunities and local business investment. For example, Mamelodi Township in the Tshwane Metropolitan Municipality, Pretoria, is faced with the challenge of residents littering the environment and creating a health hazard. Such behaviour has occurred due to a lack of environmental education and information about waste disposal, lack of concern for waste disposal, insufficient provision of rubbish bins and a dirty environment perpetuating the littering behaviour (Garg & Mashilwane, 2015). There is, thus, a need for coordination between government, local residents, businesses and other relevant stakeholders to enable proper environmental management of risks in townships. The following section will explore the case of Alexandra Township to examine environmental risk challenges and, specifically, how these affect tourism development.

3 Research method and design

Data collection followed a qualitative research approach and was part of a larger study undertaken in Alexandra to explore obstacles to township tourism development. Between June and August 2016, semi-structured interviews were conducted with informants (i.e. government, the private sector, civil society and community-based organisations) in Alexandra and within the city of Johannesburg. A purposive sampling design was used, including a snowballing technique. In all, 21 interviews were conducted. Six were with provincial government agency officials – 4 of them in Johannesburg at the Gauteng Tourism Authority (GTA) and Gauteng Enterprise Propeller (GEP). In Alexandra, 2 interviews were conducted with officials from the Department of Economic Development and Tourism (DEDaT). The remaining 15 interviews were conducted in Alexandra with local residents, among them small and medium-sized enterprise (SME) owners (tour firms, restaurant owners, accommodation services) and residents who worked for community-based tourism organisations (i.e. the Alexandra Tourism Association, Alexandra Heritage Association, Alexandra Heritage Centre and Alexandra Tourism Information Centre). Informants from these community-based tourism organisations were interviewed since they deal directly with tourism in the township. For this chapter, only 13 interviews are used, chosen based on their relevance for this area of focus. Although informants agreed to be quoted, their identities have been withheld. In collecting the data, a digital recorder was used, and the data transcribed. The digital recorder was used only if the informant agreed. They were informed that all data collected would be reported anonymously, and this put the informants at ease. All informants agreed that their interviews be recorded. Secondary data was used to supplement the primary data where necessary. A grounded theory approach was used for data analysis and to identify common themes. Themes were generated through the constant comparison of data. Three main and related environmental themes are discussed here (i.e. competing land use – housing or tourism businesses; the risk of waste on township tourism; environmental risk management and township tourism development). The results are presented below, followed by discussions, conclusions and the proposing of recommendations.

4 Results

4.1 Competing land use: Housing or tourism businesses

The findings revealed that it was difficult for local residents to grow tourism businesses due to lack of land and overcrowding in Alexandra. Local informants were concerned that people with business skills who wanted to enter the tourism industry, including those already employed in the tourism industry and who wanted to improve their businesses, were unable to acquire tourism business premises because of the shortage of land. Informant A (23 July 2016), a local resident and owner of a township food business, argued that the tourism sector was facing this shortage of land because of the increasing number of squatters that have been building illegally across the township, while Informant B (13 June 2016), local resident and tour guide at Alexandra Mulaudzi Tours, added that the government was not addressing this crisis and was neglecting Alexandra in favour of richer suburbs such as Sandton, located less than a kilometre away. As people build shacks everywhere, open public spaces have run out. Overcrowding and increasing waste generation in Alexandra have placed the environment under pressure. Informant C (7 June 2016), destination development officer at the GTA, argued that originally, Alexandra was developed according to its capacity to accommodate approximately 150 000 people, but over the years, the township has grown to reach 750 000 inhabitants. Informant D (23 July 2016), local youth and part-time tour guide, commented that "…as a result of overcrowding and congested shacks taking all the free land spaces in Alexandra, it is increasingly becoming difficult for tour operators and guides to conduct tours around the township".

According to Informant E (1 August 2016), local resident and assistant manager at the Alexandra Heritage Centre, the lack of land and narrow streets have resulted in tour operators discouraging bus tours for visitors in Alexandra, as the buses cannot drive around the streets in the area. Informant F (15 July 2016), local resident and tour operator at Alexandra Cycling Tours, claimed that, as a result of this situation, the community has committed itself to promoting walking and cycling tours. Informant B (13 June 2016) agreed, saying that "…in terms of the business sector, the lack of access to land is a main challenge for business operators". The findings revealed that the free spaces around the public schools and the space along the banks of the Jukskei River have been filled with squatters, which has had a negative impact on the running of tourism businesses. It is then questionable whether walking and cycling tours may be possible and whether proper pathways are available.

4.2 The risk of waste on township tourism

The lack of sanitation facilities, waterborne sewerage and waste collection systems has created a challenge for tourists visiting the township due to the unhygienic and unsightly conditions. Informant G (9 July 2016), resident and owner of a local bed-and-breakfast, noted that most of the environmental problems in Alexandra were caused by human activities due to the irresponsible use of the environment and its resources. Most informants highlighted the irresponsible dumping of waste on the streets and in the Jukskei River, which was causing environmental degradation and impacting tourism development. As noted previously by Manala (2014), "during hot seasons, the dumping of waste in the informal settlements attracts flies …, rendering Alexandra a very unsuitable space for humans". The findings showed that the Jukskei River area faces severe environmental problems, in part due to a lack of adequate access to municipal services, such as sanitation facilities and a functioning waterborne sewerage system. Informants noted that Alexandra has become notorious for the pollution in the Jukskei River, littering and for roads covered in sewerage. This is likely to continue if nothing urgent is done to address these challenges contributing to environmental problems, thus compromising local tourism. Goodwin & Santilli (2009) argue that tourists do not like to experience or be exposed to poor environmental conditions of the host community. Alexandra residents have a tendency to dispose of human and other kinds of waste publicly, regardless of the damage being caused to the environment. This has led to the tourism potential and integrity of the area and river being threatened. As no effective action has been taken to address this problem, the tourism sector will remain impoverished and the township of Alexandra underdeveloped.

For example, Informant A (23 July 2016) noted that shacks were being built everywhere in Alexandra, including areas where waterborne sewerage systems pass close by. This affects the day-to-day operations of tourism businesses, such as bed-and-breakfasts and restaurants, because of the poor maintenance of sanitation facilities. Informant H (23 June 2016), manager for tourism development, DEDaT, stated that "…the sewerage system often gets blocked and the municipality would sometimes face challenges and take more time to address the sewerage problem, and many [tourism] businesses end up being affected". According to Informant F (15 July 2016), as it has increasingly been a challenge for the municipality to provide proper maintenance of the sewerage system, the township is now characterised by streets filled with waste, litter and sewage water emanating from blocked waterborne sewerage systems. This has led to bad smells, which are affecting tourism development and local business operations.

The lack of proper social services affecting tourism development has also led to local residents losing hope that the governing party will improve environmental conditions. This has resulted in local residents protesting and further compromising tourism development in the area, such as potentially destroying tourism initiatives in places such as the Alexandra Heritage Centre, which provides an informative history of Alexandra and great views of the township. As Informant I (30 July 2016) noted how social instability negatively affected tourism:

> "The social ills in the township and lack of government intervention had led people to be dissatisfied. To voice their demands, people often resort to violent protests. As they occupy the streets to have their voices heard, protests often result in vandalism and the community often targets public structures, including burning and destroying tourism facilities. For example… protesters… in 2016 [have] been viewed as a major delay for the official opening of the Alexandra Heritage Centre in Alexandra. Even though the centre is now operational, the ongoing violent protests in Alexandra make it… under threat, as people are not happy that the government misallocates funds to less urgent developments instead of prioritising housing and infrastructure, as those are urgent needs more than anything. All these are affecting tourism growth because it is residents themselves that must protect the public facilities such as the Alexandra Heritage Centre; instead they pose a threat of burning it whenever protesters go into the streets to voice their demands."

The ARP, which was formed in 2001, as a five-year project, has brought some development to the area, even though much still needs to be done in most of the township. Informant J (7 June 2016), tourism manager at the GTA, stated that the main priority during the early stages of the ARP was the provision of housing, followed by infrastructure and sanitation. According to Informant K (23 June 2016), tourism researcher at the GTA, "...about 15 000 households in Alexandra have received new houses, which were provided as part of the [previous] RDP (Reconstruction and Development) initiative". The provision of sanitation and sewage management has also improved over the past 15 years. In addition, streetlights, properly tarred roads and parks were introduced. However, these gains have been eroded due to the increase in shack dwellers noticeable throughout the township.

4.3 Environmental risk management and township tourism development

A lack of coherence amongst residents to protect their environment against degradation, as well as poor environmental governance and law enforcement, have a negative impact on tourism development. Informant E (1 August 2016) stated that the community needs to be made aware that every individual should be involved in the promotion of the tourism industry and that taking care of the environment is fundamental. According to Informant C (7 June 2016), "...the host-community residents should continuously engage themselves in workshops that deal with and promote sustainable [tourism] practices". Informant G (9 July 2016) also noted that the lack of education about environmental awareness was affecting the local community and tourism development:

> "As there is a lack of awareness and education, illiterate parents and children suffer the most impact because they have no knowledge on how to address such a social challenge within their own communities... as long as people are not adequately educated on the issues around the importance of the protection and conservation of the environment and its limited resources, the goal of attaining sustainable [tourism] development might not be seen in reality."

The majority of informants also mentioned the lack of environmental law enforcement by government and the absence of a police presence in Alexandra to promote environmental protection. Government clearly did not regard this as a priority, despite the fact that the abuse of the environment has been visible and negatively impacting tourism. Informant D (23 July 2016) noted the need for environmental pollution and degradation to be a punishable crime under law:

> "The situation relating to environmental problems in Alexandra is also worsened by the provincial government's inability to put in place strict environmental laws and declare the irresponsible use of the environment [such as illegal dumping] as a punishable offense. Introducing environmental laws could work in favour of the township [Alexandra], accompanied by the already-launched various environmental programmes that seek to rehabilitate some of the most environmentally affected settlements in Alexandra. As the situation is now, the issue of irresponsible use of the environment is not taken seriously by police, and residents are not encouraged to report it as a criminal matter to the police stations."

The above suggests that the various environmental training and rehabilitation programmes alone are not sufficient to address the environmental challenges in Alexandra. Instead, such environmental programmes need to be supported by laws and good governance and enforcement, which may assist in prohibiting community members from degrading the environment. This is needed if township tourism is to be developed positively. Nevertheless, there have been some positive interventions to educate residents on environmental issues. For example, the Department of Environmental Affairs was noted to have launched the Alexandra Environmental Awareness Programme and the Alexandra Jukskei River Rehabilitation Programme to improve the environmental conditions in Alexandra, and hence, tourism development. Informant L (9 July 2016), resident and owner of a local business, noted that the main purpose of the Alexandra Environmental Awareness Programme was to teach the local people how to take care of the environment and resources. According to Informant K (23 June 2016):

> "The Alexandra Jukskei River Rehabilitation Programme was launched in Alexandra with an objective to identify the areas with ecological challenges, particularly around the informal settlements along the banks of the Jukskei River, and rehabilitate them. Even though it is a government-led initiative, the local community is often consulted and involved in the decision-making and other discussions that take place."

Informant M (24 June 2016), resident and information officer at the Alexandra Tourism Association, added that the Alexandra Tourism Awareness Programme was another government initiative that conducted responsible and sustainable tourism workshops in Alexandra with local residents. The programme provided information as a way to improve the community's knowledge and understanding with regard to creating, maintaining and promoting a sustainable tourism industry that will benefit them in the long term. The Alexandra Environmental Awareness Programme aims to raise awareness of the importance of protecting the environment by conducting workshops and street campaigns. To successfully achieve the goal of the programme, the Department of Environmental Affairs and the ARP have been actively involved in co-facilitating the workshops. Over the years, the Alexandra Tourism Awareness Programme, with the help of the GTA, has also played a significant role in Alexandra with regard to the raising of environmental awareness. Informant M (24 June 2016) elaborated that "…in improving environmental awareness … over 3 000 trees [were] planted throughout the township through these environmental campaigns since it launched in 2001". In addition, the campaign also encouraged the cleaning of public parks on a weekly basis. Informant C (7 June 2016) stated that, through the workshops, the local community was equipped with knowledge on how to play their part in ensuring that Alexandra becomes an environmentally clean area, which will enable the township to gain the status of a tourism destination. However, despite these interventions, it is not certain what positive impact they have had, considering the continued and increased environmental problems and illegal dumping by residents in the area. It can be concluded that the educational interventions being conducted cannot alone solve the environmental challenges of Alexandra and improve tourism without adequate provision of basic services, proper enforcement of environmental regulations and better cooperation between government, local residents, tourism businesses and community-based organisations. All interventions must work in synergy and not operate in isolation.

5 Discussion and conclusion

The study identified the prevailing environmental risks hindering tourism development in Alexandra. The findings revealed that the free spaces around the public schools and the space along the banks of the Jukskei River have been filled with squatters due to overcrowding, which has had a negative impact on the running of tourism businesses. The lack of sanitation facilities, waterborne sewerage and waste collection systems have created a further challenge for tourism visits to the township due to unhygienic and unsightly conditions. The findings showed that the Jukskei River area faces severe environmental problems, in part because of a lack of adequate access to municipal services such as sanitation facilities, and a functioning waterborne sewerage system. Alexandra residents have a tendency to dispose of human and other kinds of waste publicly, regardless of the damage being caused to the environment or the implications for tourism development in the township. This has led to the tourism potential and integrity of the area and river being threatened. As no effective action has been taken to address this problem, the tourism sector will remain impoverished and the township of Alexandra underdeveloped. It was noted that, because of these environmental risks and social ills, bus tours in the township were not possible. However, the environmental challenges also question the ability of local businesses to conduct walking and cycling tours if proper pathways and good environmental conditions are not available. Due to a lack of proper social services impacting tourism development, local residents have been losing faith in the governing party's ability to improve environmental conditions. This has resulted in local residents protesting and further compromising tourism development in the area by destroying tourism initiatives in places such as the Alexandra Heritage Centre.

Although there have been positive government interventions, such as educational awareness programmes for residents on the importance of environmental protection for tourism, the findings of this study show that these have not been so effective. The work done by the various environmental programmes under the ARP are not fully addressing the issues at hand. These programmes include the Alexandra Environmental Awareness Programme, the Alexandra Jukskei River Rehabilitation Programme, the Alexandra Environmental Clean-up Campaign and the Alexandra Tourism Awareness Programme. The findings of the study revealed that some work has been done, such as conducting environmental awareness campaigns, hosting responsible tourism workshops and providing training to local community members to empower them with the necessary knowledge to understand the importance of protecting the environment and its resources for tourism. Yet, despite these interventions, Alexandra continues to be environmentally degraded as residents still dump waste in the township, thereby compromising tourism development. This has been compounded (as above) by the lack of land for tourism businesses due to increasing shack settlements and overcrowding, and the lack of sanitation, sewage and waste collection services that negatively affect tourism, compounded by poor governance and enforcement. This highlights that the various environmental training and rehabilitation programmes alone are not sufficient to address the environmental challenges in Alexandra. Instead, such environmental programmes need to be supported by laws and good governance and enforcement, including service provision, which will assist in prohibiting community members from degrading the environment. This is needed if township tourism is to be developed positively.

The results signal an urgent need for joint coordination between government, residents, industry and civil society to work collectively if problems of environmental risks in Alexandra Township are to be tackled and for improved tourism development. This is important considering that the United Nations Sustainable Development Goal 11: Make cities inclusive, safe, resilient and sustainable – target for 2030 emphasises that "rapid urbanization challenges, such as the safe removal and management of solid waste within cities, can be overcome in ways that allow them to continue to thrive and grow, while improving resource use and reducing pollution and poverty. One such example is an increase in municipal waste collection. There needs to be a future in which cities provide opportunities for all…" Such an approach can be one avenue that will allow township tourism in Alexandra to thrive by ensuring sustainable working environments. What will also be required is a governance approach that engages more openly and directly with a variety of social actors (Meadowcroft & Steurer, 2018) and thereby organising recursive feedback between a diversity of social actors (Wieland, 2010). Thus, for sustainable tourism to occur, there is a need for government to robustly ensure support for and integration of local residents' views into local tourism development frameworks and to ensure wide-ranging benefits (Musavengane et al., 2020). Good governance can also ensure that Alexandra becomes a resilient tourism destination and increases inbound tourists. Fabry & Zeghni (2019) note that a resilient destination can build and achieve resilience and ensure a new trajectory for renewed attractiveness. This requires planning, anticipation and collective responsiveness.

The following recommendations are made to address environmental risks and to improve township tourism development:

- It is important that the government work on improving service delivery in Alexandra Township, especially for the collection of waste. A good waste management service can work only if government includes a wide variety of stakeholders and ensures a coordinated effort. This will involve moving towards the participation of Alexandra residents, private waste contractors and other relevant social actors to assist in identifying appropriate solutions that are context-specific for Alexandra Township.
- The provincial and local government must continue to support local environmental programmes in order to raise environmental awareness and rehabilitate environmentally degraded areas in Alexandra. New residents in the

township should also be inculcated in such programmes. However, these efforts must go hand-in-hand with the provision of proper services in the township and government intervention. An important point to reemphasise is that a coherent and synergistic approach is required by government to address the development challenges in Alexandra.

• As tourism development needs planning, local developments in Alexandra must be studied and guided in terms of location suitability and reserving land for future developments. In other words, tourism must be developed to remain environmentally, socially and culturally considerate so as to minimise environmental impacts and issues associated with overcrowding and the illegal erection of structures.

• Residents must also not wait for government intervention – they need to be proactive. They have a responsibility to ensure that the environment is safe and clean and to establish internal protocols amongst residents (e.g. through setting up community forums to meet regularly and take action on environmental and tourism development in the township). These community forums can also work in partnership with local law enforcement to report illegal dumping of waste and criminal activities. These will have the potential to improve tourism development in the area. According to Sharpley (2009), the community has more ownership and control over its environment and its resources than the government and NGOs; therefore, it should conserve and protect it from misuse or exploitation.

References

Blakeman, S. (2015). Explorations in Slum Tourism: A New Perspective to the Contemporary Understanding. Master's Thesis, Aalborg University: Aalborg.

Booyens, I. (2010). Rethinking township tourism. *Development Southern Africa*, 27 (2), 273–287

Breetzke, G. (2018). The concentration of urban crime in space by race: evidence from South Africa. *Urban Geography*, 39(8), 1195–1220.

Butler, S. (2010). Should I stay or should I go? Negotiating township tours in post-apartheid South Africa. *Journal of Tourism and Cultural Change*, 8(1), 15–29.

Chege, P. & Mwisukha, A. (2013). Benefits of slum tourism in Kibera slum in Nairobi, Kenya, *International Journal of Arts and Commerce*, 2(4), 94–102.

Costa, J. (2013). Slum tourism as an economic activity: is it ethical? A theoretical review. *Indian Journal of Research*, 2(10), 32–34.

Davie, L. (2008). Alex, as told by its residents: Retrieved from http://www.joburg.org. za/index.php?option=com_content&task=view&id=2947&Ite mid=266 (Accessed 14 April 2014).

Dladla, A. (2020). *Obstacles in tourism growth: the case of Alexandra Township, Johannesburg*, Master's thesis, University of Johannesburg.

Fabry, N. & Zeghni, S. (2019). Resilience, tourist destinations and governance: an analytical framework. In Cholat, F., Gwiazdzinski, L., Tritz, C. & Tuppen, J. *Tourismes et adaptations*, Elya Editions, 96–108.

Garg, A. & Mashilwane, C. (2015). Waste disposal pattern of Mamelodi Township in Tshwane Metropolitan Municipality. *Environmental Economics*, 6(2), 91–98

Goodwin, H. & Santilli, R. (2009). Community-based tourism: a success? *Responsible Tourism* ICRT Occasional Paper 11, 1–37.

Klepsch, L (2010). *A critical analysis of slum tours: comparing the existing offer in South Africa, Brazil, India and Kenya*, The Institute of Environmental Management and Regional Development, Amsterdam: University of Amsterdam.

Mabotja, K. (2011). *New projects under way in Alex:* Retrieved from http://www.joburg. org.za/index.php?option=com_content&view=article&id=6337:new-projects-under-way-in-alex&catid=135:alexandra&Itemid=192 (Accessed 10 April 2014).

Mabotja, K. (2012). *Tourism plans for Alex:* Retrieved from http://www.joburg.org. za/index.php?option=com_content&view=article&id=7818:tourism-plans-for-alex&catid=135:alexandra&Itemid=192#ixzz2vkZ5D2dz (Accessed 02 April 2014).

Maleka, M., Motsima, T., Matang, R. & Lekgothoane, P (2016) Comparing residents' perceptions in townships and suburbs regarding service delivery by municipality under administration, *Problems and Perspectives in Management*, 14(3), 137–144

Manala, L. (2014). *Old Alex residents saddened by Jukskei River pollution.* Retrieved From: http://alexnews.co.za/25161/old-alex-residents-saddened-by-jukskei-river-pollution/ (Accessed 02 August 2016).

Matthew, N. (2000). Greater Johannesburg Metropolitan Council: impact of poverty: Available from: http://ceroi.net/reports/johannesburg/csoe/html/nonjava/poverty/impact.htm (Accessed 02 April 2014).

Mawela, A. (2008). *The level of environmental education awareness regarding water pollution-related diseases by learners who live in the Stjwetla informal settlement adjustment to the Jukskei River in Alexandra.* Masters Dissertation, Johannesburg: University of South Africa.

McLennan, D. (2016) The spatial patterning of exposure to inequality and its social consequences in South Africa: work in progress. In World Social Science Report (2016). *Challenging inequality: Pathways to a Just World.* France: UNESCO Publishing

Meadowcroft, J. & Steurer, R. (2018) Assessment practices in the policy and politics cycles: a contribution to reflexive governance for sustainable development? *Journal of Environmental Policy & Planning*, 20:6, 734–751, DOI: 10.1080/1523908X.2013.829750

Moolman, J. (2014). Alexandra Township. Retrieved from: https://www.google.co.za/search?q=alexandra+township+in+johannesburg+map&tb m (Accessed 20 April 2014).

Moyo, A. (2005). *Local Economic Development in Alexandra: A Case Study of Women in the Informal Sector. Master's research report*, Johannesburg: University of the Witwatersrand

Musavengane, R., Siakwah, P. & Leonard, L. (2020). The nexus between tourism and urban risk: Towards inclusive, safe, resilient and sustainable outdoor tourism in African cities. *Journal of Outdoor Recreation and Tourism*, 29, 100254, https://doi.org/10.1016/j.jort.2019.100254

National Tourism Sector Strategy. (2011). Retrieved from https://www.tourism.gov.za/AboutNDT/Branches1/Knowledge/Documents/National%20Tourism%20Sector%20Strategy.pdf (Accessed 8 December 2019).

Petesch, C. (2013). *Mandela's first township home shows lack of progress.* Retrieved from: http://news.yahoo.com/mandela-39-1st-township-home-shows-lack-progress-64016671.html (Accessed 14 April 2014).

Rogerson, M. (2004). Urban tourism and economic regeneration: the example of Johannesburg. In Rogerson, C. & Visser, G. (eds), *Tourism and Development Issues in Contemporary South Africa,* Pretoria, Africa Institute of South Africa, 466–487.

Rogerson, M. (2012). Urban Tourism, Economic Regeneration, and Inclusion: Evidence from South Africa. *Local Economy,* 28(2), 188–202.

Saghir, J. & Santoro, J. (2018) Urbanisation in sub-Saharan Africa: Meeting challenges by bridging stakeholders. Centre for strategic and international studies. Retrieved from: https://www.csis.org/analysis/urbanization-sub-saharan-africa (Accessed 29th May 2019)

Sharpley, R. (2009). *Tourism Development and the Environment: Beyond Sustainability?* New York: Earthscan.

Smith, C. (2013). *Addicted to drugs in Mandela's old neighborhood:* Retrieved from: http://www.globalpost.com/dispatch/news/regions/africa/south-africa/130718/south-africa-nelson-mandela-alexandra-drugs-poverty (Accessed 14 April 2014).

UNDP (2015) *Sustainable Development Goals*, US, New York

Wieland, S. (2010) Reflexive governance: a way forward for coordinated natural resource policy? In: Bäckstrand, K., Khan, J., Kronsell, A. and Lövbrand, E. *Environmental Politics and Deliberative Democracy Examining the Promise of New Modes of Governance,* United Kingdom, Edward Elgar.

Theme 2

Peace tourism, battlefields and war risks

6 Mega sports events and urban risks

2010 FIFA World Cup, the African bid and xenophobic violence

Brij Maharaj

1 Introduction

Tourism is a burgeoning field of research in Africa (Rogerson & Visser, 2014). However, most of it is largely absent in published scholarship (Visser, 2019), which reflects the uneven division of academic labour and resources between the Global North and South; hence the intellectual dominance of the former. Major research themes include pro-poor tourism (Musavengane et al., 2019; Folarin & Adeniyi, 2020); sustainable and responsible tourism (Dube, 2020; Mutana & Mukwada, 2020); tourism and climate change (Rogerson, 2016; Hoogendoorn & Fitchett, 2018); and tourism and disaster risk management (Novelli et.al, 2018). More recently, some scholarly interest in urban risks and tourism focused on the African continent (Musavengane et al., 2020). Urban risks like crime, political conflicts and violence have serious negative impacts on tourism. Mega sports events, like most large-scale projects, present urban risks, especially in terms of economic viability and post-tournament sustainability, some of which are not easily predictable. The outbreak of the coronavirus (COVID-19) and the subsequent global spread of it in the first quarter of 2020 emerged as a major risk in Tokyo for the 2020 Summer Olympics, officially the Games of the XXXII Olympiad and commonly known as Tokyo 2020, which was initially scheduled from 24 July to 9 August 2020. This risk was certainly not on the horizon on 7 September 2013 when the International Olympic Committee awarded the Games of the XXXII Olympiad to Tokyo. As the COVID-19 spread rapidly across the globe, the organisers were forced to postpone Tokyo 2020 for a year, and it was rescheduled to commence on 23 July 2021 (Panja & Rich, 2020).

The scholarly interest in the urban risks of mega sports events has focused on safety, security, and especially on threats of terrorist attacks (Giulianotti & Klauser, 2010; Spaaij, 2016; Ludvigsen & Millward, 2020). During the 1972 Summer Olympics in Munich, the Palestinian terrorist group Black September kidnapped and subsequently killed 11 Israeli athletes and 1 West-German policeman. Since then, the risk of terrorism has been very high on the mega sports event agenda (Silke & Filippidou, 2019). After South Africa won the 2010 FIFA World Cup (FIFA 2010) bid, the main urban risks identified in scholarly literature were crime and safety (Donaldson & Ferreira, 2007; Blumberg, De Frey, Frean & Mendelson, 2010; George & Swart, 2012), and health and disease (Blumberg et al., 2010). Following the initial bid, the FIFA 2010 extravaganza was touted widely as a great African mega event that, while located in South Africa, would bring economic and social benefits across the continent. Even the United Nations (UN) endorsed the view that FIFA 2010 "underline[d] African renaissance" and that the event would "contribute to the confidence and pride of many persons and states in Africa" (SA2010 2010: 2).

However, when South Africa won the FIFA 2010 bid on 15 May 2004, no one could predict an unforeseen risk – the May 2008 xenophobic attacks on undocumented migrants from Africa in major urban centres like Johannesburg, Cape Town and Durban. The violent attacks on and threats against this community continued sporadically before, during and immediately after the FIFA 2010 tournament. This is the crux of this chapter, which reveals that the South African government response to the risk of xenophobic attacks was inconsistent, often reflected denial that it was a problem and conflated it with general crime. This denialism was attributed to a sense of embarrassment that the victims were foreign nationals from Africa. Furthermore, xenophobic attitudes appeared to be entrenched at all levels of government. The South African Cities Network contended that "xenophobia poses a direct risk to our cities' growth and development aspirations" (Ngobese, 2015).

The data sources for this chapter include published and unpublished information such as the World Cup bid book, government documents, nongovernmental organisation (NGO) reports and online and print media. In essence, this chapter also addresses the scholarly vacuum linking mega sports events like FIFA 2010 to xenophobia as an urban risk that needs urgent attention. A focus on the urban risk of violence against foreign migrants is important because it constitutes a "significant national security threat for South Africa, both in terms of domestic stability and international reputation" (Polzer & Takabvirwa, 2010: 3). Yet, comprehensive analysis of FIFA 2010 did not consider xenophobia as an urban risk, although it was acknowledged that it posed a potential threat for the 2006 FIFA World Cup in Germany (Pillay, Tomlinson & Bass, 2009).

This chapter is divided in three sections. The first section focuses on the rhetorical reference to the "African" bid and critique of that. It reveals a subliminal disconnection from the African continent and emerging prejudices. The May 2008 xenophobic violence is the theme of the second section. The South African government was basically in denial about the xenophobic attacks, and there were subtle suggestions that FIFA was considering other options (a 'Plan B') for the 2010 tournament because of risks. The final section analyses the xenophobic threats associated with FIFA 2010 and the aftermaths of that. The responses of political and civil-society organisations to the xenophobic violence and threats, which range from public condemnation to tacit support, is also assessed.

2 "African" World Cup

In 1997, the executive committee of the South African Football Association resolved to submit a bid to host the 2006 World Cup in South Africa. FIFA president Sepp Blatter expressed support for an African tournament in 2006, because he won the bitterly contested FIFA presidential election at the congress in Paris on 8 June 1998 on the basis of the support he received from the African delegates who made up 25% of the voters (Alegi, 2010). South Africa lost the 2006 bid by one vote to Germany amidst a lot of controversy. There was huge disappointment and disillusionment, perhaps best exemplified by President Thabo Mbeki in his television address to the nation: "This is a tragic day for Africa. The disappointment we're experiencing today is a setback to our efforts at gaining the recognition Africa needs in the international sporting community" (Alegi, 2001: 12). Based on the 2006 World Cup bid experience, FIFA was forced to agree to rotate the World Cup among the six continental soccer federations, and Blatter made a commitment that 2010 would be Africa's turn (*The Guardian*, 3/08/2000). In 2004, South Africa submitted a bid for the 2010 World Cup tournament alongside Morocco and Egypt. South Africa was favoured for three reasons: it had hosted international sports events such as the cricket and rugby world cup competitions successfully; it had a well-established infrastructure; and it held the trump card of making it possible for FIFA officials to meet world icon Nelson Mandela (Alegi, 2010). In support of the second bid in 2004, President Mbeki argued that 2010 would be an "African" event:

> "We want, on behalf of our continent, to stage an event that will send ripples of confidence from the Cape to Cairo – an event that will create social and economic opportunities throughout Africa. We want to ensure that one day, historians will reflect upon the 2010 World Cup as a moment when Africa stood tall and resolutely turned the tide on centuries of poverty and conflict. We want to show that Africa's time has come."[1]

After South Africa's successful bid was announced, President Thabo Mbeki promised that 2010 would deliver an "African cup" that would extend to all Africans on and beyond the continent:

> "When we say this is an African Cup, that includes all the other countries and also those who competed against us – Libya, Tunisia, Morocco, Egypt – we want to see them as partners and participants in the World Cup. Other Africans in the Caribbean, United States and Brazil – We want them also to feel part of the African Cup. For this, South Africa will be a home for all Africa."[2]

The official slogan of FIFA 2010 was "*Ke Nako*. Celebrate Africa's Humanity". It was launched in Durban on 25 November 2007. Speaking at the launch, the chairperson of the 2010 FIFA World Cup Organising Committee, Irvin

Khoza, explained the *Ke Nako* symbolism that resonated with hope for the African continent:

> "*Ke Nako* means simply 'it's time'. And, indeed, Africa's time has come to use the 2010 FIFA World Cup to change perceptions of Africa and reposition the continent in a positive light with South Africa as the theatre and Africa the stage... In the development of this slogan – our 2010 message – we were also inspired by the outpouring of excitement and joy that we witnessed from villages and cities across the continent when President Blatter announced the name 'South Africa' on 15 May 2004."[3]

This theme was echoed by the minister of transport, S'bu Ndebele, in his address to the African Renaissance Conference in Durban in May 2010:

> "The 2010 World Cup will forever demonstrate Africa's capacity to deliver world-class events... The World Cup is indeed an opportunity for Africa to take charge. An African World Cup in 2010 is also an opportunity for Africans to reexamine where we are in the project of moving Africa from where it is to where it should be ... [and] ... what we should change regarding the course of Africa's development."
>
> (Ndebele, 2010)

Even the UN endorsed the view that FIFA 2010 "underline[d] African renaissance" and that the event would also "contribute to the confidence and pride of many persons and states in Africa".[4] However, during a celebratory sitting of the South African Parliament after the tournament, the country's subliminal disconnection from the African continent was very evident. The focus was on *South Africa's* (emphasis added) achievement and success, contrary to the doomsday soothsayers:

> "Six years ago, when we won the rights to host the tournament, the task seemed too huge. Many wondered if an African country could make a success of the biggest sporting event in the world. Indeed, others even suggested that there should be a Plan B as they could not believe we were capable of pulling off such a massive project. Working together as South Africans, we have proved that we are a nation of winners".
>
> (Hansard, 2010: 2)

In an article in *City Press,* Professor Pumla Gqola from the University of the Witwatersrand argued that reference to "Africa's World Cup" was rhetorical, meaningless, "condescending and opportunistic" and a superficial connection that simply did not exist:

> "No matter whose lips utter it, "Africa's World Cup" sounds like a sad attempt at a connection that is just not there. Maybe we think that if we say it enough, we will start to believe that it describes a reality rather than wishful thinking. I

suppose saying this is a continental initiative makes the average South African feel better about our shameful relationship with the continent. This way we can stand side by side with Africans from elsewhere without casting them as menacing presences, or their countries as places ripe for South African corporations to expand into.... Against the backdrop of a very conflicted relationship with our kin on the continent, why do we think claims of "Africa's World Cup" are not condescending and opportunistic at the same time?"

(Gqola, 2010: 27).

Although hyped as an "African World Cup" that was "celebrating Africa's humanity", less than 2% of ticket holders were from the continent (Grant Thornton, 2010). This was attributed to three factors: high cost; difficulties in obtaining a South African visa; and online purchases only. Given that less than 6% of Africa was connected to the internet in 2010 and that very few Africans have credit cards, internet sales were doomed to fail. Even in South Africa, sales only picked up after the number of cheap tickets (R140) were increased and across-the-counter sales were introduced on 5 April 2010. However, such sales were restricted to South Africans and "legal residents of the country" (Cape Argus, 21 May 2008: 3)

This precondition was xenophobic as it excluded a significant proportion of undocumented migrants from the African continent in the country.

3 May 2008 xenophobic attacks

The rise of xenophobia has been associated with an escalation in the number of undocumented migrants in South Africa since 1994. This has been attributed to political changes in the country and serious social, economic and political problems on the subcontinent. Since 1994, high levels of xenophobia have been evident in South Africa, with sporadic attacks on foreigners and looting of their premises (Table 6.1). Until May 2008, xenophobic violence was not viewed as an urban risk to FIFA 2010.

May 2008 saw a very serious outbreak of violence. It started in the township of Alexandra in Johannesburg and subsequently spread to other major informal settlements in the country for almost two weeks (Table 6.2). At least 62 people lost their lives, about 40 000 foreign nationals left the country and 50 000 foreign nationals were internally displaced (Human Rights Watch, 2009).

The South African government response to violent attacks on foreigners was delayed, with the army deployed on 21 May 2008 to quell the violence. The state argued persistently that the violence was not xenophobic but rather criminal. This was perhaps best encapsulated in President Mbeki's delayed response in his address to the nation on 25 May 2008:

"I heard it said insistently that my people have turned or become xenophobic ... I wondered what the accusers knew about my people which I did not know. And this I must also say – none in our society has any right to encourage or incite xenophobia by trying to explain naked criminal activity by cloaking it in the garb of xenophobia (Mbeki, 2008: 1)."

Table 6.1 Xenophobic Attacks 1994–2007

Date	Place	Incident
December 1994	Alexandra Township *(Gauteng)*	There is a public backlash against African non-nationals in Alexandra Township. The homes and property of foreign nationals are destroyed and demands are made for their expulsion.
Sept 1998	Johannesburg *(Gauteng)*	Three African non-nationals (2 Senegalese and 1 Mozambican) are violently attacked and thrown from a train. Refugees are blamed for the levels of unemployment, crime and AIDS in South Africa.
October 2000	Zandspruit *(Gauteng)*	Local residents clash with Zimbabweans living in the township.
August 2005	Bothaville *(Free State)*	Zimbabwean and Somali refugees are targeted and physically assaulted.
December 2005	Olievenhoutbosch *(Gauteng)*	African non-nationals living in the Choba informal settlement in Olievenhoutbosch Township are violently expelled from their shacks, shops and businesses.
July 2006	Knysna *(Western Cape)*	Somali small business owners in a township outside Knysna are targeted and expelled from the area. The following month sees between 20 and 30 deaths of Somalians in townships surrounding Cape Town.
February 2007	Motherwell *(Eastern Cape)*	Violence triggered by the accidental shooting of a young South African man (by a Somali shop-owner) results in the looting of over 100 Somali-owned shops in a 24-hour period.
May 2007	Ipeleleng *(North West)*	Shops owned by Bangladeshi, Somali, Pakistani and Ethiopian nationals are attacked, looted and in some cases burnt.
September 2007	Delmas *(Mpumalanga)*	A protest over lack of service delivery turns xenophobic. Shops owned by foreign nationals are looted and burnt, forcing 40 African non-nationals to take refuge in mosques. One death and 2 injuries are reported.
October 2007	Mooiplaas *(Gauteng)*	Two deaths result from a clash between locals and their Zimbabwean neighbours. Eighteen migrants are seriously injured, and 111 shops are looted.

Source: Adapted from Nyar, 2011: 9–10; Misago, Landau & Monson, 2009: 21.

Table 6.2 A Timeline of May 2008 Xenophobic Attacks

11 May

A mob invades a disused factory outside Alexandra said to be inhabited by Zimbabweans, then chases the occupants into the township itself, looting and burning shacks. Two people are killed.

12 May

A third person is killed in Alexandra as the violence continues.

13 May

Thousands of foreigners flee their homes in Alexandra, abandoning many of their possessions, and take refuge in police stations and elsewhere.

14 May

Peace is restored to Alexandra, but there is rioting in Diepsloot.

15 May

The violence spreads to the inner city of Johannesburg. Five people are killed in Cleveland.

16 May

Residents disperse threatening mobs in several parts of Soweto.

17 May

The violence spreads to various parts of Ekhuruleni, including Thokoza, Thembisa, Boksburg and some of the shack settlements around Reiger Park such as Ramaphosa and Jerusalem.

18 May

A Mozambican national, Ernesto Alfabeto Nhamuave, is burnt alive in the public square of the Ramaphosa informal settlement.

19 May

Images of Nhamuave's burning body are published on the front pages of newspapers around the globe and are viewed on international television channels.
The official death toll rises to 22.

20 May

The violence in central Johannesburg and Ekhuruleni continues. A man is killed in Boksburg. Police announce that they have charged more than 200 people since the start of the troubles with crimes ranging from disturbance of the peace to murder.

21 May

Violence is reported in other parts of the country for the first time, specifically in parts of KwaZulu-Natal and Mpumalanga. President Thabo Mbeki calls in the army to assist in bringing about peace. The death toll now stands at 42.

23 May

The violence spreads further. There are now reports of looting and attacks on people in several shack settlements on the outskirts of Cape Town. There is also looting in the small coastal town of Knysna.

25 May

Two weeks after the violence began, President Thabo Mbeki finally addresses the nation on television and condemns the violence. African National Congress (ANC) president Jacob Zuma addresses a large crowd at Bakerton and is heckled when he condemns the violence.

26 May

Safety and security minister Charles Nqakula claims that the violence has been contained. He says that 1 384 arrests have been made and that 56 people died. The figure later rises to 62.

Source: Steinberg, 2008: 2.

Given its clandestine nature, there are many fallacies about undocumented migrants in South Africa. This has fuelled a xenophobic attitude towards fellow African migrants that has sometimes been called 'Afrophobia' (Amusan & Mchunu, 2017). An immediate problem was that migrants were seen to threaten the jobs of locals and undermine market-related wages in an economy with a high unemployment rate. Anti-foreigner sentiment developed because of the failure of the ANC government to meet the great expectations of the poverty-stricken masses. The "enemy" was no longer the apartheid state, but foreigners who were exploiting opportunities intended for locals (Maharaj, 2009).

There were persistent allegations that the South African government, politicians and public officials were complicit in promoting xenophobic tendencies and practices (Maharaj, 2018). In Durban, the then city manager, Dr Michael Sutcliffe, gave instructions to "clean" the city in preparation for FIFA 2010. That resulted in the eviction of refugees and foreign nationals from the Albert Park area (Desai & Goolam, 2010). There were also reports that South African businessmen in the townships were mobilising attacks on foreign operations because of a perception of unfair competition. More sinisterly, young, ambitious, aspiring leaders connected to political parties were leading the attacks on foreigners in order to rise to prominence in their localities and increase their power and influence (Misago et al., 2009). The May 2008 attacks occurred 2 years before FIFA 2010. Given that the preparations for the tournament were in full swing, the delays and lack of coordination at the different tiers of government in responding to the xenophobic violence were alarming. There were suggestions that the event should be moved to another country. This viewpoint was best encapsulated by community scholar Oliver Meth based at the Centre for Civil Society at the University of KwaZulu-Natal:

> "The high levels of crime, violence and attacks by black South Africans against foreign African migrants and displacing thousands and violating their human rights has made the country an unworthy host. The South African government demonstrated an inability or reluctance to protect foreigners and contain the situation."

Some of the foreigners killed were skilled artisans and professionals working on FIFA 2010 projects. For example, an engineer from Zimbabwe who was working on the Gautrain project was murdered in Germiston. Two Mozambican artisans working in renovating the Soccer City stadium were murdered in Alexandra (Meth, 2008).

Danny Jordaan, chief executive officer of the South Africa 2010 Local Organising Committee, condemned the violence against foreign nationals from the continent and acknowledged the negative consequences, but insisted that South Africans are not xenophobic:

> "We can see the focus of attention on our country for completely different reasons, both of them tragic. Our standpoint is that this World Cup must

be a celebration of Africa's humanity. Africa has too often been a continent of division, of wars, of humiliation. And certainly, we condemn any situation that continues to inflict on African people humiliation, suffering, war and diseases. So our position is crystal clear, and we ask that every action must be taken to stop inflicting on displaced people further displacement. It's something that will pass... South Africans are not xenophobic."

(British Broadcasting Corporation, 2008)

While FIFA did not get involved in the internal and domestic affairs of host nations, FIFA spokeswoman Delia Fisher stated that the federation was worried about the xenophobic attacks on foreign Africans and the loss of life and injuries. However, FIFA believed in the "unifying" power of sport: "We are obviously concerned about this issue and hope that the FIFA World Cup and its unifying power will help to overcome these divisions" (Cape Argus, 2008). This view was reinforced by FIFA president, Sepp Blatter, who told a media briefing that they had noted the latest developments in South Africa with concern. He dispelled persistent rumours that the World Cup would be moved to another country:

"We trust them, I trust them, and we will do this World Cup 2010 definitely in South Africa...The [FIFA] executive reiterated its trust in the authorities to keep the security situation under control and asserted once again its full confidence in South Africa's organisation of the next World Cup."

(*afrol News*, 2008)

Nevertheless, there was some concern that South Africa was behind in meeting FIFA's critical deadlines in terms of hosting the 2010 tournament, and that a Plan B was being considered. In an interview with *Sky News* in July 2008, Sepp Blatter said: "I have spoken to three possible, not only possible, but three associations and countries that would be able to stage the World Cup in one year's time. They need one year (to prepare)" (FIFA head pursues 'Plan B', 2008). He did not give reasons and did not mention the xenophobic attacks. However, Danny Jordaan responded in the same article that there were no grounds to move the event to another country. "We signed a contract stipulating it can only be taken away if a natural disaster strikes and the chances of that are very small," he said, and continued that "There is no basis for it to be taken away. Even the general secretary himself said that only God can take it away from us. We are even selling our tickets, which means that we are on track."

In his State of the Nation Address on 6 February 2009, President Kgalema Motlanthe referred to the readiness of South Africa to host FIFA 2010:

Virtually all the projects and plans are completed or nearing completion – from stadia, transport infrastructure, security measures, issues of accommodation, to health and immigration plans – confirming the confidence of the global soccer fraternity that ours will be a truly successful tournament. (Motlanthe, 2009: 14)

Once again, in his address there was the rhetorical contention that:

> "The true legacy of this spectacle will be in our ability to showcase South
> African and African hospitality and humanity – to change once and for all
> perceptions of our country and our continent among peoples of the world"
> (Motlanthe, 2009: 15).

A significant omission in President Motlanthe's address was any reference to the
xenophobic attacks of the previous year, or any risks it might present for FIFA
2010. However, the xenophobic attacks continued in 2009, and 25 incidents were
reported. At least 19 migrants lost their lives. Shops operated by migrants were
looted and burnt. About 3 100 migrants were displaced (Crush, Ramachandran
& Pendleton, 2013). In December 2009, Judge Navi Pillay, the UN Commissioner for Human Rights, expressed concern that xenophobia was increasing
"particularly against refugees and migrants.... Attacks against non-nationals in
South Africa... are gravely alarming... These people are frequently excluded
from fully participating in the life of a community, from its economic, political
and social development" (Pillay, 2009: 1). Violent attacks and looting of businesses of foreign nationals continued between January and May 2010. According to the Somali Community Board, 17 migrants were killed during that period
(Crush et al., 2013). Between May and July 2010, there were numerous reports
that foreigners would be attacked immediately after the FIFA 2010 tournament.

4 The mega event and xenophobic threats

As the FIFA 2010 tournament was about to commence, there were threats of
xenophobic attacks after the competition was over. South Africans were warning foreign migrants to leave the country after the soccer games or face violent
attacks (Wilson, 2010). These threats are summarised in Table 6.3. According to
the Consortium for Refugees and Migrants in South Africa (CoRMSA), whose
members include Amnesty International, the South African Red Cross Society
and the Centre for the Study of Violence and Reconciliation, these threats were
very serious and were attributed to various sources such as neighbours, col-
leagues, taxi drivers, passers-by, nurses, social workers and police officers. More
sinisterly, CoRMSA contended that some of the individuals and groups responsible for such threats believed that senior ANC leaders endorsed their actions
(*Nibishaka*, 2010: 1).

At international level, Judge Navi Pillay, the UN High Commissioner for
Human Rights, expressed concern about the contradictions between organising a
successful World Cup and threats against foreigners:

By hosting the World Football Cup, South Africa has shown that it can wel-
come visitors from all over the globe with flair, generosity and warmth. It should
now prove that it is also able to extend such hospitality and tolerance to migrants
seeking a better life and protection.... I am alarmed at recurrent episodes of
attacks against non-nationals in my country. (Pillay, 2009: 14)

Table 6.3 Xenophobic Threats May–June 2010

The threats came from many different people: neighbours, colleagues, taxi drivers, passers-by, nurses, social workers and police officers. Some of those making the threats believed that they had the support of senior political leaders.	Dozens of Zimbabwean women interviewed in Hillbrow, downtown Johannesburg, said they were being intimidated and threatened daily by their landlords and groups of men gathering outside their homes at night.
"They say they will come after the World Cup and they will kill us," said Ethel Musonza, 32, a mother of 4. "These people are serious; they are organised; they know where we live. They say they won't do anything during the World Cup because of the foreign tourists, but afterwards, the police will step aside and some of us will get killed."	In an informal settlement on the East Rand, groups of men who claimed they took part in the "war" of 2008 told foreign migrants and refugees to leave the country before 11 July. "We sat down and talked and said let us leave them until the World Cup is coming to our country," said one, who admitted he broke the law to "protect his country from foreigners" in 2008.
Jilley, who had fled Somalia 22 years before as a teenager to settle in Port Elizabeth, was afraid of what would happen to him when the tournament ended on 11 July: "I feel very scared," he said. "We're getting threatened – told that after the World Cup is over, we're going to attack you, loot your property and chase you away from South Africa."	"The message that's on the street is: 'If you don't have an ID, we are taking you out after the World Cup. We will take you to the police, and if the police don't do something to you, we are going to do it ourselves'", said 22-year-old Asmath Chauke, who lives in Alexandra, a congested neighbourhood of ramshackle houses just a few miles from one of Johannesburg's wealthiest suburbs.

Source: Adapted from Kelly, 2010; Wilson, 2010.

Civil-society organisations played a major role in drawing government and public attention to the threats against foreign nationals. The Nelson Mandela Foundation was worried about rumours that migrants from Africa might be attacked in South Africa. The Foundation hoped optimistically that South African support for African teams would lead to more understanding of and appreciation for the country's connections with the continent, and greater sympathy for the plight of non-nationals. It emphasised that South Africans "are not victims to the influx of foreign people" into the country (Vegter, 2010, p. 1).

The Solidarity Peace Trust (which is supported by churches) called on religious and other community leaders to oppose xenophobic attacks collectively and to ensure that foreigners were protected. Contrary to the assertion of some government officials, the Trust endorsed the view of the South African Council of Churches that the fear of xenophobic violence was not based on unsubstantiated rumours. The threats of violence were real, and the fear among migrants palpable (Makoni, 2010). The South African Institute of Race Relations (SAIRR) reported that casual threats of xenophobic violence were increasing. The SAIRR urged that the government should not deny the incidence of xenophobic threats that continued after May 2008, although not on the same scale (Schulze, 2010).

5 The government response

In "Ministers to assess xenophobia" (2010), the minister of police Nathi Mthethwa acknowledged that there were tensions between local and foreign-owned businesses in the townships and informal settlements where the latter were more dominant. In some areas, criminals exploited those tensions and looted the stores of vulnerable foreigners. He emphasised that attacks on foreigners were unacceptable, and anyone engaged in such violent activities would face the full might of the law. That was reinforced by the minister of defence, Lindiwe Sisulu. She warned that criminals would be arrested and prosecuted. Yet again, the focus was on criminality without acknowledging that xenophobia was a problem in South Africa.

On 2 June 2010, the South African government reestablished the interministerial committee (IMC), set up initially in response to the May 2008 violence, to deal with the renewed threats of harm to foreign nationals. The IMC was chaired by the minister of police, Nathi Mthethwa, and included the ministers of Home Affairs; Social Development; State Security; Basic Education; Cooperative Governance and Traditional Affairs; Arts and Culture; and International Relations and Cooperation. However, the focus was on dealing with crime and criminals without acknowledging xenophobia. The government adopted multipronged strategies to avert violence. That included promoting social dialogue and engaging civil society (churches and NGOs) to flush out criminal elements. The swift policing and justice strategy of FIFA 2010 would continue, with greater regulation of the business operations of foreigners. The lessons learnt from the 2008 xenophobic attacks would be reviewed. Civic education of police and broader society would receive attention, and government communication strategies would be improved (Government outlines plan to deal with xenophobic threats, 2010).

Despite the IMC's strategies, the government's initial response the xenophobic threats appeared to be confusing and contradictory. Some senior government bureaucrats and politicians refuted any prospect of xenophobic attacks. Hence, such threats were viewed as rumours being spread by "prophets of doom" who were disappointed that South Africa had hosted a successful tournament. For example, in a statement issued on 9 July 2010, national executive committee (NEC) member of the ANC Malusi Gigaba scoffed at rumours of xenophobic attacks after FIFA 2010 that made no sense and that he viewed as an envious response to South Africa's successful hosting of the event for the first time on the African continent:

> "The hosting of this very first African World Cup has coincided with endless allegations of its imminent failure.... Suddenly, the pride we felt in being African as we hosted the World Cup soccer tournament dissipates as we face the looming imminence of a savage attack on fellow Africans."
>
> (African National Congress, 2010)

The commissioner of police, General Bheki Cele, alleged that foreign migrants were engaging in criminal activities to embarrass the government and perpetuate perceptions that South Africa was infested with crime during FIFA 2010: "We have observed a trend where foreigners commit crime – taking advantage of the fact that we have an unacceptable crime level – to tarnish our credibility and image" (Masondo, 2010: 1). The deputy minister of police, Minister Fikile Mbalula, maintained that South Africa was not a "banana republic" and that anyone attacking foreigners would be punished:

> "The issue of xenophobic attacks after the World Cup has no foundation except to influence the vulnerable within our society to commit crime. We have confidence in both the police and our people. The ministry of police is unimpressed by the continued engraving of fear in the hearts and minds of our people, including our fellow African brothers and sisters, by the faceless people within our midst." (*Nibishaka*, 2010: 1).

The South African Communist Party (SACP) condemned the threats of attacks on foreigners, which it regarded as not xenophobic but rather criminal acts to undermine poor communities and exploit their vulnerabilities (SACP, 2010). As the threats of violence increased, President Jacob Zuma released a press statement on 15 July 2010 in which he appealed to South Africans and foreign nationals to work together to stop xenophobic attacks and to report any threats to the police. He emphasised that South Africans were peaceful and their support for teams from the African continent demonstrated unity:

> "The 2010 FIFA Soccer World Cup has demonstrated fully that South Africans are warm, peace-loving and hospitable people. The support provided to Ghana and other African soccer teams was impressive and demonstrated African unity in its true sense. This spirit must continue to prevail in our country. Let us isolate all elements who may have sinister agendas, who may want to create havoc and sow pain and destruction in communities, especially foreign nationals residing in our country. We appeal for calm, tolerance and unity amongst all."

> (South African Government, 2010)

By the end of July 2010, the NEC of the ANC concluded that the threats of xenophobia were exaggerated and sensational, but acknowledged that security forces (police and army) had reduced the potential for violent attacks and intimidation (Mantashe, 2010). However, in the June–July 2010 period, there were 31 xenophobic incidents, including looting and pillaging of foreign-owned shops, arson and violent attacks with serious injuries. Five foreign nationals were killed (Crush et al., 2013).

6 Conclusion

This paper analyses the contradictions between organising a successful "African" World Cup and celebrating the continent's humanity, and the xenophobic threats against foreigners from the continent. Violent crime was a known, lingering urban risk for FIFA 2010 in South Africa. However, the organisers, the

South African government and FIFA did not consider xenophobia to be a serious risk to the 2010 tournament. As such, it was downplayed after the May 2008 violence. Nevertheless, the xenophobic attacks and threats of violence posed a major urban risk and contributed to a decline in the number of tourists compared with the initial projections for the 2010 soccer World Cup. The official government response to the threats of xenophobic violence during and after FIFA 2010 was ambiguous and lacked coherence, with senior politicians and officials sometimes contradicting each other. This was attributed to the denialism that characterised the government's response to xenophobia consistently. Current scholarly literature on urban risks presented by mega sports events focuses on crime, safety and security. This chapter links mega sports events to xenophobia, which has been largely ignored.

In bidding for and subsequently marketing FIFA 2010, there was rhetorical reference to Africa in a grand, collective sense. The "African" rhetoric was symbolic to garner the continent's support for the bid, and to influence the outcome from the elite voting block that was morally obligated to award the hosting of FIFA 2010 to an African country. The xenophobic violence, threats and risks exposed the big lie – FIFA 2010 was all about South Africa, its sense of "exceptionalism", and its subliminal disconnection from the continent, which was exacerbated by xenophobia and violent attacks on foreign nationals from the continent. In addition to the well-known threats linked to crime and security, it is evident from this study that other urban risks associated with mega sports events can be connected to the specificities of localities, which requires further research.

Notes

1 South Africa 2010 Bid Book, p. 3.
2 Donaldson, A. Mbeki pledges to make 2010 FIFA World Cup an "African Cup" (http://www.kapweine.15May2004, accessed 10 July 2020).
3 https://www.bizcommunity.com/article/196/147/20019.html
4 UN News Services – South Africa: Football World Cup in country underlines 'African Renaissance' – UN Envoy (http://allafrica.com/stories, accessed 28 June 2010).

References

African National Congress. (2010, July 9). Statement by Malusi Gigaba, African National Congress NEC member, on xenophobia. HTTPS://WWW.POLITY.ORG.ZA/ARTICLE/ANC-STATEMENT-BY-MALUSI-GIGABA-AFRICAN-NATIONAL-CONGRESS-NEC-MEMBER-ON-XENEOPHOBIA-09072010-2010-07-09 (Accessed 10/01/2020).
afrol News (2008). Xenophobic attacks worry FIFA. http://www.afrol.com/articles/29085 (Accessed 12/11/2019).
Alegi, P. (2001). 'Feel the pull in your soul': Local agency and global trends in South Africa's 2006 World Cup bid. *Soccer & Society 2*(3), 1–21.
Alegi, P. (2010*). African Soccerscapes – How a Continent Changed the World's Game*. Athens, OH: Ohio University Press.
Amusan, L. & Mchunu, S. (2017). An assessment of xenophobic/afrophobic attacks in South Africa (2008–2015). *South African Review of Sociology 48*(4), 1–18.

Blumberg, L.H., De Frey, A., Frean, J. & Mendelson, M. (2010). The 2010 FIFA World Cup: communicable disease risks and advice for visitors to South Africa. *Journal of Travel Medicine 17*, 150–152.

British Broadcasting Corporation (BBC) News. (2008, May 23). *Jordaan condemns SA violence.* http://news.bbc.co.uk/sport2/hi/football/africa/7416878.stm (Accessed 15/11/2019).

*Cape Argus, (21/05/*2008) Xenophobia: FIFA voices concern https://www.iol.co.za/ capeargus/sport/xenophobia-fifa-voices-concern-425035. (Accessed 10/01/2020).

Crush, J., Ramachandran, S. and Pendleton, W., (2013). Soft targets: Xenophobia, public violence and changing attitudes to migrants in South Africa after May 2008. https:// www.africaportal.org/publications/soft-targets-xenophobia-public-violence-and-changing-attitudes-to-migrants-in-south-africa-after-may-2008/ (Accessed 11/12/2019).

Desai, A. & Goolam, V. (2010). World Cup 2010: Africa's turn or the turn on Africa? *Soccer & Society 11*, 154–167.

Donaldson, R. & Ferreira, S. (2007). Crime, perceptions and touristic decision making: Some empirical evidence and prospects for the 2010 World Cup. *Politikon 34*, 353–371.

Dube, K. (2020). Tourism and sustainable development goals in the African context. *International Journal of Economics and Finance Studies 12*(1), 88–102.

FIFA head pursues 'Plan B'. (2008, July 10). *Independent Online.* Retrieved from https:// www.iol.co.za/news/south-africa/FIFA-head-pursues-plan-b-407797

Folarin, O. & Adeniyi, O. (2020). Does tourism reduce poverty in sub-Saharan African countries? *Journal of Travel Research 59*(1), 140–155.

George, R. & Swart, K. (2012). International tourists' perceptions of crime risk and their future travel intentions during the 2010 FIFA World Cup™ in South Africa. *Journal of Sport & Tourism 17*, 201–223.

Giulianotti, R. & Klauser, F. (2010). Security governance and sport mega events. *Journal of Sport and Social Issues 34*, 49–61.

Government outlines plan to deal with xenophobic threats. (2010, July 8). https://www. gcis.gov.za/content/newsroom/media-releases/media-releases/government-out-lines-plan-deal-xenophobic-threats (Accessed 12/01/2020).

Gqola, P.D. (2010, May 16). *Whistling a different tune on the World Cup. City Press*, p. 27,

Grant Thornton. (2010). Updated economic impact of the 2010 FIFA World Cup. http:// www.gt.co.za/News/Press-releases/Strategic-solutions/2010/2010eia.asp (Accessed 30 April 2010).

Hansard. (2010, August 17). Debate on successful hosting of the 2010 FIFA World Cup. https://pmg.org.za/hansard/18126/ (Accessed 12/11/2019).

Hoogendoorn, G. & Fitchett, J.M. (2018). Tourism and climate change: A review of threats and adaptation strategies for Africa. *Current Issues in Tourism 21*(7), 742–759.

Human Rights Watch. (2009). *World Report 2009.* https://www.hrw.org/world-report/ 2009/country-chapters/south-africa (Accessed 10 December 2019).

Kelly. A. (2010, May 17). *Warning of xenophobic violence in South Africa after World Cup. The Guardian.* https://www.theguardian.com/world/2010/may/17/south-africa-world-cup-xenophobic-violence (Accessed 12/11/2019).

Ludvigsen, J.A.L. & Millward, P. (2020). A security theatre of dreams: Supporters' responses to "safety" and "security" following the Old Trafford "fake bomb" evacuation. *Journal of Sport and Social Issues 44*, 3–21.

Maharaj, B. (2009). Migrants and urban rights. *L'Espace Politique 8*, 2–15.

Maharaj, B. (2018, May 21). *South Africa's shameful xenophobic decade. Daily Maverick*, https://www.dailymaverick.co.za/opinionista/2018-05-21-south-africas-shameful-xenophobic-decade/ (Accessed 10/01/2020).

Makoni, M. (2010). Churches in drive to help prevent xenophobic attacks. https://www.anglicannews.org/news/2010/07/churches-in-drive-to-help-prevent-xenophobic-attacks.aspx (Accessed 14/11/2019).

Mantashe, G. (2010). Xenophobic threat exaggerated – ANC NEC. https://www.politicsweb.co.za/party/xenophobic-threat-exaggerated--anc-nec (Accessed 15/11/2019).

Masondo, S. (2010, June 14). Foreign crooks, pasop. https://www.timeslive.co.za/news/south-africa/2010-06-13-foreign-crooks-pasop/ (Accessed 10/01/2020).

Mbeki, T. (2008, July 4). *Address of the President of South Africa, Thabo Mbeki, at the National Tribute in Remembrance of the victims of attacks on Foreign Nationals, Tshwane.* https://www.politicsweb.co.za/documents/mbeki-speaks-on-attacks-on-foreign-nationals (Accessed 12/11/2020).

Meth, O. (2008). *South Africa will risk hosting 2010.* Centre for Civil Society, UKZN. http://ccs.ukzn.ac.za/default.asp?10,66,10,3313 (Accessed 15/11/2019).

Ministers to assess xenophobia. (2010, June 7). *news24.* https://www.nes24.com/SouthAfrica/News/Ministers-to-assess-xenophobia-20100712 (Accessed 10/11/2019).

Misago, J.P., Landau, L.B. & Monson, T. (2009). Towards tolerance, law, and dignity: Addressing violence against foreign nationals in South Africa. International Organisation for Migration (IOM). http://www.migration.org.za/wp-content/uploads/2017/08/IOM_Addressing_Violence_Against_Foreign_Nationals.pdf (Accessed 10/01/2020).

Motlanthe, K. (2009, February 6). *State of the Nation Address.* https://www.sahistory.org.za/archive/2009-president-motlanthe-the-state-nation-address-6-february-2009-national-elections (Accessed 15/01/2020).

Musavengane, R., Siakwah, P. & Leonard, L. (2019). "Does the poor matter" in pro-poor driven sub-Saharan African cities? towards progressive and inclusive pro-poor tourism. *International Journal of Tourism Cities*, 5 (3), 392-411, DOI. 10.1108/IJTC-05-2019-0057.

Musavengane, R., Siakwah, P. & Leonard, L. (2020). The nexus between tourism and urban risk. *Journal of Outdoor Recreation and Tourism 29*(100254), 1–13. https://doi.org/10.1016/j.jort.2019.100254.

Mutana, S. & Mukwada, G. (2020). Are policies and guidelines shaping tourism sustainability in South Africa? *Tourism and Hospitality Research 20*(2), 198–209.

Ndebele, S., (2010). *Address at the African Renaissance Conference, Durban*, 25 May. Available from: http://www.polity.org.za [Accessed 8 June 2010].

Ngobese, S. (2015, May 27). Xenophobia and Migration: Adjust our urban policies towards safer cities for all. https://www.saferspaces.org.za/blog/entry/xenophobia-and-migration-adjust-our-urban-policies-towards-safer-cities (Accessed 10 May 2020).

Nibishaka, E. (2010). Threats Of Post-World Cup Xenophobia Another Test For SA`s Government. https://issafrica.org/amp/iss-today/threats-of-post-world-cup-xenophobia-another-test-for-sas-government (Accessed 11/11/2019).

Novelli, M., Burgess, L.G., Jones, A. and Ritchie, B.W., (2018). 'No Ebola… still doomed'–The Ebola-induced tourism crisis. *Annals of Tourism Research, 70*, pp.76-87.

Nyar, A. (2011). *What happened? A narrative of the May 2008 xenophobic violence.* Gauteng City Region Observatory (GCRO)/Atlantic Philanthropies. Synthesis Report.

Panja, T. & Rich, M. (2020, March 30, updated March 31). *Summer Olympics in Tokyo to Start on July 23, 2021.* The New York Times. https://www.nytimes.com/2020/03/30/sports/olympics/tokyo-olympics-date-coronavirus.html (Accessed 10/01/2020).

Pillay, N. (2009, December 10). *Address by the High Commissioner for Human Rights*, Navi Pillay, Freedom Park, Pretoria, South Africa. https://reliefweb.int/report/south-africa/address-high-commissioner-human-rights-navi-pillay-freedom-park-pretoria-south (Accessed 12/11/2019).

Pillay, U., Tomlinson, R. & Bass, O. (Eds). (2009). *Development and dreams: the urban legacy of the 2010 Football World Cup.* Cape Town: HSRC Press.

Polzer, T. & Takabvirwa, K. (2010). Just crime. *South African Crime Quarterly 33*, 3–10.

Rogerson, C.M. (2016). Climate change, tourism and local economic development in South Africa. *Local Economy 31*(1–2), 322–331.

Rogerson, C.M. & Visser, G. (2014). A decade of progress in African urban tourism scholarship. *Urban Forum 25*, 407–417.

SA2010. (2010). Africa's time has come! SA is ready! [Online]. Available from http://www.sa2010.gov.za (Accessed 9/06/2010).

Schulze, C. (2010). Casual xenophobic threats increasing – SAIRR. https://www.politicsweb.co.za/archive/casual-xenophobic-threats-increasing--sairr (Accessed 10/11/2019).

South African Communist Party (SACP). (2010, July 13). *SACP statement on acts of violence directed at foreign nationals.* https://www.politicsweb.co.za/opinion/xenophobia-is-pure-criminality--sacp (Accessed 12/11/2019).

South African Government. (2010, July 15). President Zuma calls for calm and unity around alleged xenophobic attacks. [Press Statement]. https://www.gov.za/president-zuma-calls-calm-and-unity-around-alleged-xenophobic-attacks (Accessed 10/01/2020).

Silke, A. & Filippidou, A. (2019). What drives terrorist innovation? *Security Journal* (Accessed 10/01/2020) https://doi.org/10.1057/s41284-019-00181-x.

Spaaij, R. (2016). Terrorism and security at the Olympics. *The International Journal of the History of Sport 33*, 451–468.

Steinberg, J. (2008). South Africa's Xenophobic Eruption. *ISS Paper 169*, Institute for Security Studies, Pretoria.

Vegter, I. (2010). South Africa's World Cup, xenophobic threats on the rise. https://www.csmonitor.com/World/Africa/2010/0714/After-South-Africa-s-World-Cup-xenophobic-threats-on-the-rise (Accessed 12/11/2019).

Visser, G. (2019). The challenges of tourism and urban economic (re)development in Southern cities. In D. Muller, (ed.). *A Research Agenda for Tourism Geographies*, Edward Elgar Publishing, United Kingdom.

Wilson, G.L. (2010, June 10). *After South Africa World Cup 2010 ends, war on foreigners and poor.* https://www.thedailybeast.com/after-south-africa-world-cup-2010-ends-war-on-foreigners-and-poor (Accessed 20/02/2020).

7 Election risk and urban tourism in sub-Saharan African cities

Exploring peace through tourism in Harare, Zimbabwe

Regis Musavengane

1 Introduction

Tourism is entrenched in social structures, networks and aspects of human behaviour (Farmaki, 2017), hence the tenet that tourism has the ability to foster peace through building strong relations among community members and between the host communities and visitors. This can be attained through the enhancement of human relations and perceptions (Musavengane, 2019) and the cultivation of understanding among people (Musavengane & Simatele, 2016). Tourism has been perceived as pro-peace and thrives in peaceful environments (Kanlayanasukho, 2014; Teye, 1988). This can be attested to by the various forms of tourism that seem to promote 'peace', notably through the pursuance of responsible and sustainable tourism (Wintersteiner & Wohlmuther, 2014). Most of sustainable tourism's constituting elements have peace-building effects and constitute a primary component of sustainable development (see Blewit, 2015). This is exemplified in the World Travel and Tourism Council (WTTC) (2016) report on peace and tourism, which highlights the linkages between tourism and peace. Further, the partnership between the WTTC and the Institute of Economics and Peace (IEP) evidences the importance of enabling peace through tourism. Cities, being hubs of economic, political and social activities, have a high potential to degenerate into chaotic zones or battlefields if good governance is lacking (Siakwah, Musavengane & Leonard, 2020).

Violence, conflict, unrest, protest, xenophobia, coup, police intervention and military intervention are buzzwords in the 21st century in some sub-Saharan African (SSA) cities (Musavengane et al., 2020). Despite apartheid and its colonial past, South Africa was once regarded and labelled as a peaceful part of Africa. Tourists consider visiting the tip of the continent due to its generally peace-loving people, although this cannot be generalized across the whole region, as there are some areas regarded as dangerous zones for tourists. Peace in SSA cities has been threatened by several factors, notably, infrastructure deficits (Dodman et al., 2017), population pressure (Musavengane, Siakwah & Leonard, 2020), high urbanisation (Satterthwaite, 2017), poverty (Muchadenyika, 2020) and crime (Boakye, 2012).

The report on peace and tourism revealed that between 2008 and 2015, none of the SSA countries were in the top ten in terms of tourism openness and sustainability (WTTC, 2016). Instead, they dominated the bottom ten performers: Angola, Rwanda, Togo, Bangladesh, Ethiopia, Benin, Mozambique, Tanzania, Burkina Faso and Nigeria (WTTC, 2016). Further, the report highlighted that internal conflicts in the SAA region have increased instability in the region. Globally, such internal conflicts contribute to an unprecedented forced displacement of almost 70.8 million people; among them are nearly 25.9 million refugees (The United Nations High Commissioner for Refugees [UNHCR], 2019). Most of the displaced persons will find themselves in the major cities of host countries and tend to compete for scarce resources with local people. This situation breeds xenophobic violence against immigrants and causes unrest in countries, and in particular, in South Africa. Most of the internal conflicts in the SSA region are political in nature and power-play driven. Zimbabwe has experienced many internal conflicts that have threatened human rights and caused unrest, and the effects are being felt in the Southern African region. The conflicts date back to the year 1999 when the major opposition party, the Movement for Democratic Change (MDC), was formed. Its formation caused unrest in the quarters of the ruling party, the Zimbabwe African National Union-Patriotic Front (ZANU-PF), and one incident led to another, from land reform in 2000 to the 2017 coup d'état. The episodes of conflict and violence witnessed in the country have a bearing on the brand of place and perception of tourists on the destination. Most often, the political environment in Zimbabwe shapes the progress and planning of urban areas, with the rife contestations between ZANU-PF controlling the national government and the opposition, MDC, controlling the majority of the urban local authorities (Muchadenyika & Williams, 2016). This threatens the governance of cities and tourism, as there will be poor synergetic and coordinated efforts between the local and national authorities (Siakwah et al., 2020). In their definition, the United Nations defines tourism governance as the "process of managing tourist destinations through synergistic and coordinated efforts by governments, at distinct levels and in different capacities; civil society living in the inbound tourism communities; and the business sector connected with the operation of the tourism system" (UNWTO, 2008: 31–32). Thus, continual conflict between political parties, national governments and local governments poses a tremendous threat to tourism development.

The negative impacts of conflict on tourism are seemingly growing and result in a reduction in tourist arrivals, which is either due to negative travel advisories, tourists' perceptions of safety and risk, or to the direct loss of tourist infrastructure and attractions (Lepp, Gibson & Lane, 2011). Nevertheless, tourism is regarded as a resilient industry (Prayag, 2018) that recovers quickly after a conflict, making it an important tool in strategies to reconstruct the destination (Alluri et al. 2014). This chapter is inspired by the United Nations Sustainable Development Goal 16: Promote just, peaceful and inclusive societies. This particular goal makes it clear that sustainability is dependent on peace, justice and sound governance. Tourism is no exception to promoting peace, justice and good governance. Reflecting on the political challenges in urban areas, the chapter traces and identifies possible opportunities and routes to promote peace tourism in Harare.

2 The nexus between peace and tourism

Despite the growing interest in examining the role of tourism in promoting peace, there is sparse debate on the aspect of 'peace tourism' (Van den Dungen, 2014). Peace tourism involves visiting places associated with nonviolence, peaceful conflict resolution, peacemaking, prevention of war, resistance to war, protesting war and reconciliation (Van den Dungen, 2014). These associations can refer to the past, present, national as well as international contexts. The conception of building peace through tourism emerged in the 1920s, leading to the launch of international peace conferences (Wintersteiner & Wohlmuther, 2014). Notably, the 1929 seminal British Travel and Holidays Association's conference was themed 'Travel for Peace'. Further, 1967 was declared the United Nation's 'Tourism: Passport to Peace'. More profoundly, in 1980 the World Tourism Organisation (WTO) declared peace as a force for global tourism in Manila. In 1986, the International Institute for Peace through Tourism was founded by Louis D'Amore with the aim that tourism should become the world's largest peace industry, where every tourist would be an Ambassador for Peace (Salazar, 2006). A series of conferences promoting peace through tourism have been organized to date, including the 2019 Geneva Sixth Annual International Conference on Travel and Sustainable Tourism for Peace and Development, organised by the United Nations. These conferences are enablers to 'world peace'.

Furthermore, realism and liberalism are the two main perspectives in international politics, which are key to understanding tourism politics (Cho, 2007). Realism is more pessimistic and stresses insecurity, force, and survival as the natural relations between states, while liberalism is more optimistic and emphasises economic interdependence between states (Nye, 1993). Therefore, the potential to achieve peace through tourism is a liberal pursuit. Thus, tourism can enable the achievement of peace.

The discourse advocating for tourism as a peacemaking tool anchors on the premise that contact between visitors and hosts induces a positive influence on international politics (Farmaki, 2017). Travel fosters the reduction of cultural and psychological gaps among people and appreciates diversity (Nyaupane, Teye & Paris, 2008). There is a large volume of published studies describing the role of tourism as a change agent, which may unify people from different social classes, nations and cultures (Musavengane & Leonard, 2019; Causevic, 2010; Sarkar & George, 2010). Nevertheless, some scholars critique the validity of the causal relationship between tourism and peace (Salazar, 2006). For instance, some of the critiques argued that tourism does not create peace but is rather a beneficiary of peace (Litvin, 1998). Similarly, Rowen (2014) noted that tourism scholarship overemphasised the role of tourism in peacebuilding without substantive evidence.

Like peace, tourism is delicate – it can easily break (De Villiers, 2014). For example, tourism in a particular destination, country or region can easily be damaged or destroyed by political crises, security threats, financial collapse, natural disasters or military conflicts (Siakwah et al., 2020; Boakye, 2012; Sonmez & Graef, 1998). Furthermore, it is important to note that peace is equally fragile, as it depends on human relations. If the relations are strong, peace will grow, and the opposite threatens the existence of peace. Oftentimes, misconception, prejudice and intolerance are threats to peace and justice. Hence, the reason why tourism is intertwined to peace (De Villiers, 2014). The potential of tourism to break down barriers and divisions between people from diverse cultures, nationalities and beliefs contributes to peacebuilding (Farmaki, 2017). Peace and tourism are interrelated: the absence of peace does not promote tourism in the region, but tourism can contribute to the peace-building process (Van den Dungen, 2014). "Peace is a journey which demands continued effort. It requires that we vigorously protect and advance those rights and values that form the foundation of real peace – rights that can be equated with individual freedom, democracy and the rule of law" (De Villiers, 2014: 81).

Related to peace are justice and governance connotations. It is widely accepted that upholding human rights determines whether a society is just or not. Justice is embedded in the governance system of a nation or organisation. In tourism, governance is defined as a "process of managing tourist destinations through synergistic and coordinated efforts by governments, at distinct levels and in different capacities; civil society living in the inbound tourism communities; and the business sector connected with the operation of the tourism system" (UNWTO, 2008: 31-32). Similarly, Siakwah et al. (2020: 356) conceptualise governance as "a network of interactions, interdependence, and cooperation among varied actors (including locals) in the management of the specific resource, emphasising participation, equitable power relations, trust, justice, fairness, and inclusion". The common feature emerging from these two definitions is the promotion of justice and equity. Justice is a key principle for evaluating the effectiveness of public policy (Fainstein, 2017). Although justice is complex and means different things to people depending on where they are seated in society, it includes rights and duties; income distribution; wealth; principles of fairness, equality, and liberty; power; social well-being; and building a good society (Jamal & Camargo, 2017). Focusing on the promotion of 'peace through tourism' (PPT) facilitates the attainment of the United Nations Sustainable Development Goal 16; Promote just, peaceful and inclusive societies. D'Amore (1988: 9) defines PPT as "peace within ourselves, peace with other people, peace between nations, peace with nature, peace with the universe and peace with our God". It focuses on the forms of tourism that promote peaceful relations. In addition, justice tourism is described by Holden as "a process which promotes a just form of travel between members of different communities. It seeks to achieve mutual understanding, solidarity and equality amongst participants" (cited in Pearce, 1992, p.18).

The above linkage between tourism and peace provides a strong foundation to discuss the relationship between tourism and peace in cities.

3 Methodology

Political events that led to destabilisation or which had the possibility to cause such were sought from various online platforms, including YouTube, hashtag posts and websites of public institutions. The events were identified through a Google search as well as specific online platform searches where single or combinations of terms were used: 'war in Harare', 'coup in Harare', 'destabilization in Harare', 'intervention in Harare', 'police in Harare', 'demonstrations in Harare', 'peace in Harare' and 'opposition in Harare'. The various searches produced a total of 201 of broadly relevant results. Through a process of elimination, the results were narrowed down to 9 different URLs, ensuring that the data obtained addresses the gist of the study. The 9 URLs are:

URL Links:

1. https://www.cwgc.org/find-a-cemetery/cemetery/142302/HARARE%20 MEMORIAL
2. http://apanews.net/en/news/protesters-injured-as-zimbabwe-capital-turns-into-war-zone
3. https://www.youtube.com/watch?v=-a4XTzWAUHQ
4. https://www.youtube.com/watch?v=UWv4o2TjfZM
5. https://www.youtube.com/watch?v=KRoSFq42mA8
6. https://www.youtube.com/watch?v=zKJ23fpkwVc and https://www.youtube.com/watch?v=4NBWPpP5tLI
7. https://www.youtube.com/watch?v=VN68zAVo3j0
8. https://www.youtube.com/watch?v=dzdbO9JIOYo

Five steps were followed to analyse the data. First, the content in the videos was manually transcribed. Then, the textual pages were printed and collated. Thereafter, the data were read twice to make meaning of the content and then coded, highlighting sections that could be used to promote peace through tourism. The next step involved grouping the data into themes, following the identification of patterns. Lastly, the emerging themes were refined and labelled to capture the common essence. Where necessary, quotes were provided to maintain the authenticity of data.

4 Cities, peace and tourism

Worldwide, cities are hubs of economic development, even though they are also the settings of numerous developmental challenges (Fraser et al., 2017). Thus, city or town planners, urban developers and tourism experts identified tourism as a tool that can create positive economic benefits for urban communities (Wei-Ching, 2019; Rogerson, 2002). Therefore, in a globalised world where there are calls for peace, global restructuring and deindustrialisation, tourism offers opportunities for urban renewal (Siakwah et al., 2020; Law, 1996). In Europe, tourism was used to rebuild some cities that were thought to be unrepairable (Owen, 1990). In a couple of past decades, tourism-based regeneration became a major phenomenon, as it has the potential to bring desired development in urban spaces (Steinbrink, 2012).

The most notable city that went through rejuvenation in Asia is Hiroshima in Japan. It was largely destroyed by an atomic bomb during World War II. Today, visitors to Hiroshima are peace-loving tourists rather than war-loving tourists (Van den Dungen, 2014). Some of the visitors to Hiroshima are peace activists, educators, anti-nuclear weapon activists and pilgrims. Hiroshima has long promoted itself as a city of peace, and the world has received and positioned it as such. The city attracts both domestic and international visitors who visit its large peace museum and park with numerous memorials (Kosakai, 2002). Hiroshima and Nagasaki officially opened a peace museum and peace park in 1955 ('Hiroshima Peace Park Guide', 2005). Several renovations, extensions and additions have made both cities veritable destinations of pilgrimage for peace people.

In Europe, Utrecht is celebrated as a peace city. It hosted negotiations that ended a war, and a peace treaty was named after the city. The 'Peace of Utrecht' is a series of peace treaties signed during the war of the Spanish Succession between April 1713 and February 1715. Celebrations are held annually in Utrecht to remember and promote peace today. The events attract people of all age groups as diverse programmes are lined up to attract all tourists (Van den Dungen, 2014). Further, the German cities of Osnabrück and Münster remember the protracted peace negotiations (1643–1648) that took place to end wars, and have been known as peace cities. The legacies of peace-building in both cities led to the end of the Thirty Years' War (1618–1648). During the commemorations, certain customs and traditions are observed (Van den Dungen, 2014).

In America, in the city of Dayton, Ohio, negotiations were held to end the war in Bosnia and Herzegovina in 1995 through the Dayton Peace Accords. A Dayton International Peace Museum was built and opened to allow people to remember the historic events and to promote peace in Bosnia and Herzegovina. The Museum created the Dayton Literacy Peace Prize, which has since become an annual event and it is inscribed in the social and cultural calendar of the city. The museum acts as the main vehicle to promote a culture of peace in the city (https://daytonpeacemuseum.org/).

In Africa, 431 cities in 47 countries and regions are members of the Mayors of Peace (http://www.mayorsforpeace.org/english/membercity/map/africa.html). Mayors of Peace is a grouping of Mayors around the world that have formally expressed support to press for the abolishment of nuclear energy. Most of the Southern African nations are members of the Mayors of Peace, but Zimbabwe is not one of them.

5 Zimbabwe crisis, Harare and peace

Zimbabwe has been in crisis for the past two decades. Since 2000, there have been vigorous debates over the nature of liberation movements in power and the prospects for a new form of politics in southern Africa (Freeman, 2014). However, Moyo and Yeros (2007) noted that the political terrain and *dramatis personae* that existed pre-independence has not changed in Zimbabwe. Concerned African Scholars (2009) highlighted that the ever-ruling party, the ZANU-PF, is finding it difficult to pursue the founding ideologies of liberation, i.e. promoting the will of the people. The 2002 presidential election in the Zimbabwe election marked the beginning of heavy political tension in the country (Pottie, 2003). It was the first deep contest that the late President Robert Gabriel Mugabe faced from the late Morgan Richard Tsvangirai, the then-leader of the main opposition party, Movement for Democratic Change (MDC). Though there were three other candidates for the presidency, namely, Wilson Kumbula, Shakespeare Maya and Paul Siwela, they were relatively unknown and had no significant political support base (Pottie, 2003). The election results in 2002 were allegedly rigged and the MDC challenged them. Violence was visible during the 2002 electoral process.

The script of electoral violence continued in the harmonised presidential and parliamentary elections in 2008, which saw a delay of over a month before the release of the 29 March presidential results. The announced results showed that Tsvangirai had won slightly less than 50% to secure the outright win; a run-off was called for 27 June 2008. This led to the gun-blazing confrontation of alleged MDC officials and supporters. ZANU-PF, with the support of the Zimbabwe Defence Forces (ZDF), launched a clean-up audit on the electorate code-named 'Operation *Mavhoterapapi?*' ('Where did you put your vote?') to unleash opposition party supporters (Rutherford, 2018). "Dozens were killed, 'torture camps' were established, and destruction of property and violence, including rape, were used by activists and state security officials" (Rutherford, 2018: 58). Many escaped the country for safety, including Morgan Tsvangirai, who had to pull out of the run-off presidential election race to calm down the situation and to save lives. The intervention of the international community led to the formation of the coalition government or Government of National Unity (GNU), between the ZANU-PF and two main MDC formations (MDC-T for Tsvangirai and MDC for Arthur Mutambara). Mugabe remained president while Tsvangirai served as the first Prime Minister and Arthur Mutambara the second Prime Minister. ZANU-PF, however, remained in control of the key government ministries, including the security sector, which allowed it to recoup and widen itself in the national political economy (Cheeseman and Tendi, 2010).

The power play continued in Zimbabwe, leading to the forceful removal of President Robert Mugabe in 2017. On the 14 November 2017, the ZDF launched 'Operation Restore Legacy' in a bid to remove President Robert Mugabe from the office and facilitate a transfer of power to his former Vice President, Emmerson Mnangagwa. The whole incident transpired in Harare, the capital of Zimbabwe. The oust of Emmerson Mnangagwa from the Vice Presidency Office by President Mugabe triggered the removal of Mugabe, as he had the support of the ZDF, led by General Constantino Chiwenga (Beardsworth, Cheeseman & Tinhu, 2019). Mnangagwa fled to South Africa for safety, while the ZDF seized control of the Mugabe residence, commonly known as the Blue Roof. Military tanks were deployed in the city of Harare and at key institutions. It is alleged that during the process, Mugabe was held against his will, and those who resisted the actions of the ZDF were detained and questioned, often brutally, with some escaping the country (Beardsworth et al., 2019; Asuelime, 2018). However, not all information about Zimbabwe's political transition is in the public domain because those who stage-managed the process created the impression that it was not a coup, but rather a correction of in-house issues within the ruling party (Beardsworth et al., 2019). This led to the supposed resignation of Mugabe on 21 November 2017 and paved the way for the rule of Mnangagwa. In light of the Merriam-Webster dictionary definition of 'coup d'état', the Zimbabwe 2017 power transition can perfectly be described as a coup d'état. According to Merriam-Webster, a coup d'état is "a sudden decisive exercise of force in politics especially: the violent overthrow or alteration of an existing government by a small group a military coup d'état of the dictator" (Merriam-Webster Dictionary, 2020). The Zimbabwe coup d'état was further sanitised by the citizens who had suffered for a long period and viewed Mugabe as an obstacle to their success. The pain suffered by Zimbabwean citizens is well-captured by linguists, for example:

> …the expressions zvakadhakwa/zvidhekwe lit: 'drunkenness', zvakapenga lit: 'madness', and kuwona moto lit: 'feeling fire' metaphorically refer to the confusing, frustrating, and painfully difficult situation that was occurring in Zimbabwe. These expressions are not isolated because there is a relationship between concrete meanings and new meanings. For example, in the conceptual metaphor 'drunkenness-is-confusing Zimbabwe situation' the SD [Source Domain] is a situation of drunkenness while the TD [Target Domain] is the situation in Zimbabwe. The same thinking applies to the conceptual metaphor, 'difficulties-are-being in fire' in which the TD is the painful Zimbabwe crisis, while the SD is the pain that is inflicted on one who is put in fire. Using the metaphor kuwona moto lit: 'feeling fire' Shona speakers are not just substituting words but the words are defining the Zimbabwean situation in terms of the pain that one goes through after being burnt by fire. This serves to show how the Shona speakers conceptualized the nature of pain that they went through as a result of the crisis that was occurring in their country.
>
> (Kadenge & Mavunga, 2011: 157)

Moving to the 2018 harmonised elections, minimal violence was witnessed across the country. However, it is alleged that the presidential results were marked with serious irregularities (Moyo, 2019). On the first of August 2018, the peaceful Harare turned into chaos when supporters of the main opposition party, the MDC led by Nelson Chamisa (the new leader after the death of Tsvangirai), took to the streets to protest, alleging that the result was being rigged in favour of ZANU-PF. Heavily armed military forces descended on them and seven people were killed in daylight in the streets of Harare. Then, in early 2019, there were protests against an increase in fuel price and general economic hardship; protesters in Harare and Bulawayo were brutally put down by heavily armed security forces, which led to the national shutdown of the internet for national security reasons. In the year 2019, many demonstrations planned by the main MDC were blocked and strong security forces were witnessed in the city. During the Mugabe era, the Zimbabwe Republic Police (ZRP) were always in conflict with motorists that led to 'hit and run' scenarios (rat and cat chase), causing the death of some CBD pedestrians. These episodes tend to scare tourists and threaten the sustainability of urban tourism. Musavengane et al. (2020: 8) noted that "tourists do not inevitably equate security to the existence of uniformed personnel, instead, they conceive (in)security within the triple framework of space, order and professionalism". A key success factor for tourism destinations is the ability to provide a predictable, safe and secure environment for tourists (Speakman and Sharpley, 2012). By nature, tourists are risk-averse and, thus, any actual or perceived threat to their health, safety or security has the potential to influence their decision to visit a particular destination (Lepp and Gibson, 2003). It is in this vein that tourism is highly regarded as susceptible to political, economic, environmental and social influences. Thus, this chapter seeks to interrogate the key tourist areas in Harare that can be established and/or promoted to promote peace through tourism in the city.

6 Moving towards peace tourism in Harare

Four themes emerged during the analysis. These are human rights and the rule of law, a peace museum in Harare, peace music concerts and liberation routes. Data were grouped into these four themes to enable a discussion of possible avenues to invest in peace through tourism in the capital city of Harare.

6.1 Human rights and the rule of law

The videos show that the main source of conflict and violence in Harare is the electoral processes. There is common agreement in the videos that the human rights of locals and the rule of law did not seem to be respected in the city and the country at large. Citizens and tourists love to spend their leisure time at peaceful destinations (Becken and Carmignani, 2016). The speech given by General Constantino Chiwenga during the coup process clearly showed that the ZDF and ZANU-PF were one and seemed to serve the same interests:

> Let us begin by quoting the constitution of this country, particularly the preamble which speaks of "Exalting and extolling the brave men and women who sacrificed their lives during the Chimurenga/Umvukela and national liberation struggles and honouring our forebears and compatriots who toiled for the progress of our country". It is with humility and a heavy heart that we come before you to pronounce the indisputable reality that there is instability in ZANU-PF today and as a result anxiety in the country at large (Daily News Zimbabwe, 2017).

Following a rise in the intervention of the military on civilian issues after the coup, the Zimbabwean Lawyers demonstrated for the restoration of the rule of law in the country. In the interview (see one of the nine URLs above), one of the female lawyers alluded that:

> If you committed a crime, you must be arrested, and due legal process should be followed. There shouldn't be instant justice as we are seeing, and we are saying no state of emergency has been declared so why do we have the army all over the place?

The same sentiments were aired by a male lawyer during the same demonstration, noting that "there were three main demands for this march namely, restoration of the rule of law, compliance with the constitution and respect for human rights". One of the political analysts interviewed highlighted that it was naive to expect a free and fair election after a military coup. Such protests by lawyers signify the need for peace tourism in the city.

6.2 Peace museum in Harare

In all the URLs consulted and used in this study, the element of military intervention dominates over the use of the police. In August 2018, the election protesters met their fate when the Zimbabwe Army used live round bullets against them. The video showed the army using armoured vehicles in the streets of Harare to scare protesters and others. The infantry was mobilized with AK47s, whips and batons. Journalists were told to stop filming, turn off their cameras and some of the cameras were broken during the process (said one of the journalists). The use of army tankers was also done during the 2017 coup where people are seen in a joyous mood and enjoying the event.

In 2019, the opposition party, MDC, organised protests in all cities across the country, including Harare. These led to the nationwide shutting down of the internet for security reasons. In one of the URL links provided, military tankers were also spotted in the streets and soldiers were seen dispersing the crowds and pedestrians. The presence of military causes many to fear for their lives. Another lady is heard saying with a voice full of fear "ndirikutsvaka kombi yekuenda kumba" ("I am looking for a taxi to take me home").

To promote peace tourism in Harare, it will be noble to have a Military Museum in Harare, like the one in Gweru, another city in Zimbabwe. This Military Museum should not only showcase armoury used during the first liberation war, but should also show the recent events that many people born in the post-independence (after 1980) era can relate to. Museum visitors need to relate to incidents they know to promote peace. This will complement the existing Harare Memorial located within the African plot of Harare (Pioneer) Cemetery and the National Heroes Acre. The Harare Memorial commemorates 38 men of the British South Africa Police and 28 of the Rhodesia Native Regiment who fell in the First World War. The National Heroes Acre commemorates war veterans who fought for the independence of Zimbabwe from Rhodesian white superiority. Having a Peace Museum in Zimbabwe will augment these two key historical sites. There seems to be a narrative that the Heroes Acre has lost its value in the sight of the youthful generation or those born after 1980. The generation needs something they can relate to better.

6.3 Peace music concerts

Events promote the growth of tourism globally. Music connects people. Most of the videos in the URLs provided background music, which was played to bring people together for a common goal. It is my opinion that, if music can lead to demonstrations and violence, it can also unify people for peace. In one of the videos showing the demonstration by lawyers, there is a song towards the end of the video that arouses the emotions of people. It was sung in Shona as: "ini handichina nguva yeku bigger masoja vanongotirova zuva ne zuva" ("myself 1 don't have time to respect soldiers anymore, they always beat us every day").

During the coup, a song by Mukudzeyi Mukombe (commonly known as Jah Prayzer) titled "Kutonga kwaro" ("His reign") was used to unseat President Robert Mugabe. Emotions ran high when people heard this song, as they saw hope in the removal of Robert Mugabe by the army. As time went by, and hope began to fade among the Harare urban dwellers and citizens across the country, the song became unpopular among citizens. In another protest against the high cost of living, protesters are seen in a video chanting revolutionary songs near Unity Square in Harare as they energise themselves to protest. It will be honourable to set up a musical theatre dedicated to liberation (albeit of all forms) songs. This will be the only one of its kind in Africa and can attract both domestic and international tourists who love music and peace.

6.4 Liberation routes

In the videos, there is evidence that whenever people arrange for demonstrations and movements, there are specified points of convening and routes to follow. These routes can be labelled, for example, a coup route, where one follows the points where gathering and speeches were given. Having these routes will preserve peace in the city and at the same time promote urban tourism. In other African countries, for example, in Ghana, a route of slavery is traced and marked (see Sibeko & Korokoro, 2019).

7 Conclusions

The chapter aimed to trace and identify possible opportunities and routes to promote peace tourism in Harare. Harare has been the epicentre of violence in Zimbabwe for more than two decades and has degenerated into a 'militarised' sort of zone after the removal of President Robert Mugabe. The chapter revealed that good governance is key to avoid violence. Harare witnessed the death of civilians and protesters at the hands of the military, and this challenges the growth of tourism. Boakye (2012) and Sonmez and Graef (1998) noted that militarisation is not an option to promote tourism but rather repels tourists from a destination. As in other African nations, the increasing conflicts about scarce resources, equality and electoral disputes by the urban populace in Harare, Zimbabwe, have led to continual demonstrations and violence. The chapter adds weight to the existing literature on alternative tourism by discussing a rarely discussed peace tourism approach, which promotes peace and inclusivity. By sharing 'peace elements' essential for destination development, the chapter supports Woyo and Slabbert's (2020) main finding that scenic attractions do not predict repeat visitation, hence the need to reimagine what to sell in African countries. Four main themes emerged during the analysis, namely, human rights and the rule of law, a peace museum, peace music concerts and liberation routes. These were identified as key in promoting peace through tourism in Harare. The findings of this study can be implemented in cities within the same context of Harare. Future studies may consider measuring the impact of these 'new' options for tourism in Harare.

References

Alluri, R. M., Lei Cher, M., Palme, K., Ke Joras, U. (2014). Understanding economic effects of violent conflicts on tourism: Empirical reflections from Croatia, Rwanda and Sri Lanka. In C. Wohlmuther W. Wintersteiner (Eds.), *International Handbook on Tourism and Peace* (pp. 101–119). Klagenfurt: Drava Verlag.

Asuelime, L. (2018). A Coup or not a Coup: That is the Question in Zimbabwe. *Journal of African Foreign Affairs*, 5 (1), 5-24.

Beardsworth, N., Cheeseman, N. Tinhu, S. (2019). Zimbabwe: The coup that never was, and the election that could have been. *African Affairs*, 1–17, DOI:10.1093/afraf/adz009.

Becken, S. & Carmignani, F. (2016). Does tourism lead to peace? *Annals of Tourism Research*, 61, 63–79.

Blewit, J. (2015). *Understanding sustainable development*. 2nd Ed. London: Earthscan.

Boakye, K. A. (2012). Tourists' views on safety and vulnerability. *Tourism Management*, 33, 327–333.

Causevic, S. (2010). Tourism which erases borders: An introspection into Bosnia and Herzegovina. In Moufakkir, O., Kelly, I. Tourism, progress and peace. Oxfordshire, CABI (pp. 48-64).

Causevic, S., & Lynch, P. (2013). Political (in) stability and its influence on tourism development. *Tourism Management*, 34, 145-157.

Cheeseman, N. & Tendi, B. (2010). "Power-Sharing in Comparative Perspective: The Dynamics of 'Unity Government' in Kenya and Zimbabwe." *Journal of Modern African Studies* 48 (02): 203–229.

Cho, M. (2007). A re-examination of tourism and peace: The case of the Mt. Gumgang tourism development on the Korean Peninsula. *Tourism Management*, 28, 556–569

Concerned Africa Scholars. (2009). African Events. Bulletin 82. Online: Accessed 05/01/2020 http://concernedafricascholars.org/bulletin/issue82/.

D'Amore, L. J. (1988). Tourism: The world's peace industry. *Paper presented at tourism: A vital force for peace, 1st global conference*, Montreal, October 23–27).

Daily News Zimbabwe. (2017). Army will step in says Chiwenga (Online: Accessed 22 February 2020 at https://www.youtube.com/watch?v=R7_vcVxD_Bg)

De Villiers, D. (2014). Cornerstones for a Better World: Peace, Tourism and Sustainable Development. In C. Wohlmuther & W. Wintersteiner (Eds.), *International Handbook on Tourism and Peace* (p. 78-84). Klagenfurt: Drava Verlag.

Dodman, D., Leck, H., Rusca, M. & Colenbrander, S. (2017). African Urbanisation and Urbanism: Implications for risk accumulation and reduction. *International Journal of Disaster Risk Reduction* 26, 7–15.

Fainstein, S. S. (2017). Urban planning and social justice. In M. Gunder, A. Madanipour, & V. Watson (Eds.), *The Routledge handbook of planning theory* (pp. 130–142). London: Routledge.

Farmaki, A. (2017). The tourism and peace nexus. *Tourism Management*, 59, 528-540.

Fraser, A., Leck, H., Parnell, S., & Pelling, M. (2017). Africa's urban risk and resilience. *International Journal of Disaster Risk Reduction*, 26, 1–6.

Freeman, L. (2014). A parallel universe – competing interpretations of Zimbabwe's crisis. *Journal of Contemporary African Studies*, 32:3, 349-366, DOI:10.1080/02589001.201 4.956497.

Hiroshima Peace Park Guide. (2005). *Hiroshima: Hiroshima Interpreters for Peace.*

Jamal, T., & Camargo, B. A. (2017). Tourism governance and policy: Whither justice? *Tourism Management Perspectives.* 10.1016/j.tmp.2017.11.009

Kadenge, M. & Mavunga, G. (2011). The Zimbabwe crisis as captured in Shona metaphor. *Journal of African Cultural Studies*, 23:2, 153-164, 10.1080/13696815.2012.637879.

Kanlayanasukho, V. (2014). An analysis of the tourism industry's management responses to political crisis in Thailand. In Ritchie, B.W. and K. Campiranon. *Tourism Crises and Disaster Management in the Asia-Pacific.* Oxfordshire, CABI, 116-131.

Kosakai, Y. 2002. *Hiroshima Peace Reader.* Hiroshima: Hiroshima Peace Culture Foundation.

Law, C. M. (1996). Introduction. In C. M. Law (Ed.). *Tourism in major cities* (pp. 1–22). London: International Thomson Business Press.

Lepp, A., & Gibson, H. (2003). Tourist roles, perceived risk and international tourism. *Annals of Tourism Research*, 30(3), 606–624.

Lepp, A., Gibson, H., & Lane, C. (2011). Image and perceived risk: A study of Uganda and its official tourism website. *Tourism Management*, 32(3), 675–684.

Litvin, S.W. (1998). Tourism: The world's peace industry? *Journal of Travel Research*, 37(1), 63-66.

Merriam-Webster. (2020). "Coup d'état." https://www.merriam webster.com/dictionary/ coup%20d%27%C3%A9tat. Accessed 12 Feb. Merriam-Webster.com Dictionary 2020.

Moyo, J. (2019). *Excelgate: How Zimbabwe's 2018 Presidential Election was Stolen.* Harare, SAPES BOOKS.

Moyo, S. & Yeros, P. (2007). "The Radicalised State: Zimbabwe's Interrupted Revolution." *Review of African Political Economy* 34 (111): 103–121. 10.1080/03056240701340431.

Muchadenyika, D. & Williams, J.J. (2016). Politics and the practice of planning: the case of Zimbabwean cities. *Cities*, 63: 33 – 40.

Muchadenyika, D. (2020). *Seeking Urban Transformation: Alternative Urban Futures in Zimbabwe.* Harare, Weaver Press.

Musavengane, R. (2019). Understanding tourism consciousness through habitus: perspectives of 'poor' black South Africans. *Critical African Studies*, 11 (3), 322-347, 10.1080/21681392.2019.1670702.

Musavengane R, & Leonard, L., (2019) When Race and Social Equity Matters in Nature Conservation in Post-apartheid South Africa. *Conservation & Society*, 17(2), 135-146.

Musavengane, R. & Simatele, D. (2016) Community-based natural resource management: The role of social capital in collaborative environmental management of tribal resources in KwaZulu-Natal. South Africa, *Development Southern Africa*, 33:6, 806-821, 10.1080/0376835X.2016.1231054.

Musavengane, R. Siakwah, P. and Leonard, L. (2020). The nexus between tourism and urban risk: Towards inclusive, safe, resilient and sustainable outdoor tourism in African cities. *Journal of Outdoor Recreation and Tourism*, 29, 100254. 10.1016/j. jort.2019.100254.

Nyaupane, G. P., Teye, V. & Paris, C. (2008). Innocents abroad: Attitude change toward hosts. *Annals of Tourism Research*, 35(3), 650-667.

Nye, J. S., Jr. (1993). *Understanding international conflicts: An introduction to theory and history*. New York: Harper Collins College Publishers.

Owen, C. (1990). Tourism and Urban Regeneration. *Cities: The International journal of Urban Policy and Planning*, 7, 194–201.

Pearce, D. G. (1992). Alternative tourism: Concepts, classifications and questions. In W. R. Eadington & V. L. Smith (Eds.), *Tourism alternatives: Potentials and problems in the development of tourism* (pp. 15–30). Philadelphia, PA: University of Pennsylvania Press.

Pottie, D. (2003). The presidential elections in Zimbabwe, March 2002. *Notes on Recent Elections /Electoral Studies* 22, 516–523.

Prayag, G. (2018). Symbiotic relati onship or not? Understanding resilience and crisis management in tourism. *Tourism Management Perspectives* 25, 133–135.

Rogerson, C. M. (2002). Urban tourism in the developing world: The case of Johannesburg. *Development Southern Africa*, 19(1), 169–190.

Rowen, I. (2014). Tourism as a territorial strategy: The case of China and Taiwan. *Annals of Tourism Research*, 46, 62-74.

Rutherford, B. (2018) Mugabe's shadow: limning the penumbrae of post-coup Zimbabwe. *Canadian Journal of African Studies / Revue canadienne des études africaines*, 52:1, 53-68, 10.1080/00083968.2018.1441037.

Sarkar, S. K., & George, B. P. (2010). Peace through alternative tourism: Case studies from Bengal, India. *The Journal of Tourism and Peace Research*, 1(1), 2010.

Satterthwaite, D. (2017). The impact of urban development on risk in Sub-Saharan Africa's cities with a focus on small and intermediate urban centers. *International Journal of Disaster Risk Reduction*, 26, 16–23.

Salazar, N. B. (2006). *Building a 'Culture of Peace' through tourism: Reflexive and analytical notes and queries*. Universitas humanística, 62, 319–333. Available (25/11/18) <http://www.javeriana.edu.co/Facultades/C_Sociales/universitas/62/salazar.pdf>.

Siakwah, P., Musavengane, R. & Leonard, L. (2020) Tourism Governance and Attainment of the Sustainable Development Goals in Africa. *Tourism Planning & Development*, 17:4, 355-383, DOI: 10.1080/21568316.2019.1600160.

Sibeko, S. & Korokoro, F. 2019. Retracing a slave route in Ghana, 400 years on. (Online:Accessed 05/02/2020 at https://www.reuters.com/article/us-africa-slavery-journey-widerimage/retracing-a-slave-route-in-ghana-400-years-on-idUSKCN1UR4JV.

Speakman, M. & Sharpley, R. 2012. A chaos theory perspective on destination crisis management: Evidence from Mexico. *Journal of Destination Marketing & Management*, 1(1-2), 67-77. 10.1016/j.jdmm.2012.05.003.

Sonmez, S., & Graefe, A. (1998). Influence of terrorism risk on foreign tourism decisions. *Annals of Tourism Research*, 25(1), 112–144.

Steinbrink, M. (2012). 'We did the slum!' – urban poverty tourism in historical perspective. *Tourism Geographies*, 14 (2), 213–234.

Teye, V.B. (1988). Coups d'Etat and African Tourism: A Study of Ghana. *Annals of Tourism Research*, 15: 329-356.

Van den Dungen, P. (2014). Peace Tourism. In C. Wohlmuther & W. Wintersteiner (Eds.), *International Handbook on Tourism and Peace* (pp. 62-77). Klagenfurt: Drava Verlag.

Wei-Ching, W. (2019). The effect of early-life outdoor experiences on residents' attitudes towards sustainable tourism within an urban context. *Journal of Outdoor Recreation and Tourism*, 25, 1–9.

Wintersteiner, W. & Wohlmuther, C. (2014). Peace Sensitive Tourism: How Tourism Can Contribute to Peace. In C. Wohlmuther & W. Wintersteiner (Eds.), *International Handbook on Tourism and Peace* (pp. 31-61). Klagenfurt: Drava Verlag.

World Travel and Tourism Council (2016). *Tourism as a driver of peace.* Available (22/01/2020) https://www.wttc.org/publications/2016/tourism-as-a-driver-of-peace/.

Woyo, E. & Slabbert, E. (2020). Unpacking the motivations, satisfaction and loyalty of tourists travelling to a distressed destination, *Anatolia*, 10.1080/13032917.2020.1794919

UNHCR. (2019). Figures at a glance. Available Online (20/01/2020) https://www.unhcr.org/figures-at-a-glance.html.

United Nations and World Tourism Organization (UNWTO) (2008). *International recommendations for tourism statistics 2008 (IRTS 2008)*. New York. Retrieved from http://unstats.un.org/unsd/tradeserv/tourism/manual.html

8 The role of responsible tourism in peace-building and social inclusion in war-risk cities

Evidence from Goma, Democratic Republic of Congo

Clément Longondjo Etambakonga and Dieudonné Trinto Mugangu

1 Introduction

Urban tourism is an important part of the world economy, particularly in Africa (Musavengane, 2018; World Travel and Tourism Council [WTTC], 2017). There are, however, challenges with urban tourism and its role in peace-building and inclusive benefit-sharing (Alluri, 2009; Duran, 2013; Nunkoo, 2017). The Democratic Republic of Congo (DRC) has been going through warfare and security crises since 1994 (Reyntjens, 2009). The Eastern Congolese city of Goma epitomises such a long-term security crisis since about one and a half million refugees from the Rwandan genocide, in 1994, ran overnight for shelter in the city and its neighbourhoods (Prunier, 2009; Reyntjens, 2009). In the DRC, Goma, the capital city of an eastern province, seemed to be the city most affected by the war, and this has impacted on its tourism industry. Globally, tourism is vulnerable to war while sometimes only benefiting the powerful stakeholders. Goma has always been a transit city for ecotourists who visit some of the world's wonders like the Virunga National Park with its extinct and active volcanoes, water geysers, mountain gorillas and chimpanzees, and thousands of hippopotamuses (Beru, 2009; Brisman, South, & White, 2016; Muhindo, 2010). Additionally, the city serves as one of the last stops to climb the western slopes of Mount Ruwenzori, the third tallest mountain in Africa, splendid with everlasting glaciers on the equatorial line. This area is also endowed with a beautiful tropical forest that is home to lowland gorillas and the rare okapi (Beru, 2009). All of these are very important tourist attraction sites.

Although there is some research in recent years on urban tourism development in sub-Saharan Africa (SSA) (Adu-Ampong, 2018; Musavengane, 2018; Siakwah, 2018), there are rarely studies on responsible tourism (Lorant, 2011) amidst warfare and peace-building. Goma experienced 3 decades of nonconventional warfare with devastating consequences for the ecotourism industry in the area. The conflict that began in August 1998 drastically reduced local economic output, besides illegal exploitation of some of the natural resources by several local, regional and international economic actors (Kolk & Lenfant, 2012). The eastern province of DRC's vast natural resource wealth is viewed as a burden instead of a blessing (Hochschild, 1998). The inverse relations between natural resources and socioeconomic development has been referred to as a 'resource curse' (Auty, 1993). The resource curse explains situations where economies that are rich in natural resources, especially in developing countries, perform poorly economically (Siakwah, 2017). The inverse link between resource abundance and poverty is a paradox because usually, resource endowment should provide wealth for poverty reduction activities. The tourism resources within the Goma region and their impact can be viewed within the frame of the resource curse thesis, where despite the huge tourism potential of the area, it provides minimal benefits to the inhabitants. For instance, the tourism industry in Goma has benefited a few powerful individuals rather than improving lives and reducing poverty among the populace.

Tourism, as one of the world's largest industries, is vulnerable to insecurity and conflicts (Alluri, 2009). It tends to flourish during peacetime, not during conflicts. However, Goma as an urban safe haven has witnessed a thriving urban tourism industry despite insecurity in the area over the past 30 years. Tourism development has been driven by the construction of houses and hotel businesses. However, it is only responsible tourism that will benefit most of the stakeholders, including the marginalised groups that can contribute to security, peace-building and economic development (Alluri, 2009; Booyens & Rogerson, 2016). Through pro-poor policies, training and social empowerment, voiceless people can be employed in the tourism industry and thus prevent them from being recruited into recurrent armed groups in the area.

By exploring the role of responsible tourism in peace-building and social inclusion, this chapter contributes to the complexity of responsible and inclusive urban tourism amidst conflict and insecurity. This chapter sheds light on inclusive urban tourism building from a fragile economy made of mineral trafficking, peacekeeping and humanitarian presence. Additionally, the existing ecotourism has fostered a putative urban tourism built around a growing economy of peacekeeping and artisanal mineral mining. It contributes to a broader discussion on how a responsible urban tourism industry can develop and become resilient with a peace-building presence, despite ongoing security risks (Alluri, 2009; Boas, 2013). In the next sections, we will pay attention to literature on responsible tourism, peace-building and social inclusion to generate a framework for analysis. We will discuss methodology and understanding of responsible and inclusive tourism in Goma.

2 The nexus between responsible tourism, peace-building and social inclusion

In the last 2 decades, we have seen a change in the way the tourism industry has operated. According to Frey (2008), the mid-1990s witnessed a change in the way tourists, local individuals and companies saw tourism and its impacts on the environment; specifically, its contribution to climate change, increasing solid waste generation and air/water pollution, as well as diminution of fauna and flora. The concept of responsible tourism has been entrenched in discussions about sustainable tourism by receiving some scholarly attention in the past (Eraqi, 2014; Lorant, 2011; Saarinen, 2014; Spenceley, 2008). Responsible tourism is, however, differently defined by authors. Goodwin and Font (2007), for instance, define the concept as a movement aimed to increase economic, social and environmental benefits, and to minimise costs for destinations. Further, Saarinen (2014) suggests that it denotes changes in principles and practices of tourism that are intended on improving the places where people live and visit. In this study, responsible tourism is used to denote tourism activities that operate in the social and economic interests of all stakeholders, including having a contribution to peace-building in the context of conflicts and insecurity. Blackstock et al. (2008) are of the view that responsible tourism may have similarities to sustainable tourism, even though they differ, with responsible tourism advocating for proactive examination and reasoning by visitors and the industry. We use responsible tourism and sustainable tourism interchangeably to refer to tourism that improves living conditions of most people within a safe operating space. The commonality of the two concepts resides in their importance in reducing adverse effects of tourism on the environment and local communities by encouraging conservation practices and economic sustainability and increasing social benefits-sharing (Booyens & Rogerson, 2016; Goodwin et al., 2002). Saarinen (2014) is of the view that responsible tourism should be extended beyond economic indicators to integrate social benefits and environmental protection constraints.

Tourism is sometimes recognised as a source of creating affluence in disadvantaged regions, while some focus on its potential of encouraging local social and economic development (Dieke, 2003). Unlike short-term epidemics, conflicts and insecurity can affect the image of a destination for years (Alluri, 2009). For many conflict-affected regions, tourism can be a route to integration into an inclusive economy (Ashley et al., 2000). It could play a positive role in a post-conflict peace-building, given its capacity to offer responsible and equitable growth (Hall & Brown, 2011; Novelli & Hellwig, 2011). Alluri (2009) notes that peace-building is important in supporting socioeconomic, political, security and reconciliation processes whilst helping to reduce the risk of conflict recurrence. Similarly, Cho (2007) argues that peace-building through tourism highlights the proposition that tourism can be mobilised as a tool for avoiding war or securing peace. In the *Agenda for Peace*, Boutros-Ghali (1992) defines post-conflict peace-building as an action to identify and support structures that will strengthen and solidify peace to avoid conflict relapse. Smith (2004: 10) categorises peacebuilding activities into 4 goals: to provide security; establish the socioeconomic foundations; establish the political framework of long-term peace; and to generate reconciliation, a healing of the wounds of war and justice. Usually considered the responsibility of state and UN peacekeepers, peace-building is today taken up by a range of actors, including corporate entities (Kolk & Lenfant, 2012). The private sector can reinforce peace promotion through tourism. As Goma emerges from shattering civil unrest and chronic insecurity, tourism is important in peace promotion and social inclusion.

Globally, inclusion is one of the key principles for the achievement of Sustainable Development Goals (SDGs). Yet, as observed by United Nations

Development Program (UNDP 2015), many marginalised groups are excluded from the development process. Development can be inclusive when all groups contribute to creating opportunities, share benefits and participate in decision-making. Inclusive tourism comprises a concern with broadening the participation of voiceless groups in tourism, on terms that are sympathetic to them with a wider transformative effect (Jamal & Camargo, 2014; Scheyvens & Biddulph, 2018). Thus, inclusive tourism needs to include previously marginalised people in decision-making about tourism and safeguarding the wider benefits of tourism (Scheyvens & Biddulph, 2018). Scheyvens and Biddulph (2018) note that inclusive tourism needs to enable low-income people to acquire better employment or entrepreneurship opportunities, and to engage in ethical production or consumption of tourism and the sharing of its benefits. In the context of Goma, it seems most people have been excluded from tourism development efforts in the past. There is the need to find ways to overcome marginalising people in benefits-sharing from tourism, and reduce insecurity and contribute to peace-building. Responsible tourism and social inclusion are the appropriate ways to achieve such efforts in Goma.

3 Methodology

The city of Goma is the Congolese's capital of tourism (Muhindo, 2010). Goma's economy partly thrives through hosting and catering for ecotourists. Goma had become, by 1998, a safe haven with thousands of UN peacekeeping forces, humanitarian NGOs (nongovernmental organisations) and a resilient economy revolving around mineral trafficking and the construction of thousands of houses and dozens of hotels (Boas, 2013; Büscher & Vlassenroot, 2010). As one of the main tourism cities in the country, visitor centres are important and thrive in the area. Even after the refugee crisis, Goma has again been transformed into an urban tourist attraction. The main urban tourism attractions in Goma are Mount Goma, the Tschukudu singular wooden bicycle invented to help carry loads of merchandises and a thriving canoe and boat construction industry on the methane gas-laden Lake Kivu, endowed with spectacular islands and landscapes. These natural features are becoming hubs of tourism attraction.

This study employs a qualitative case study methodology by intensively investigating a case and focusing on details within a context (Neuman, 2011). Yin (2014) denotes that the case study research method is used to contribute knowledge to our understanding of individual group, organisational, social, political and related phenomena. Data for this study are drawn from existing policy and strategy documents and research papers related to tourism, governance and nature conservation of North Kivu Province. Even though interviews can allow participants to tell their stories on tourism and peace-building, secondary data are more readily available, given time and resources. The document analysis was supplemented by 12 semi-structured interviews conducted in Goma as part of data triangulation. Interviews were administered via email and telephone. The interviewees included: representatives from the tourism sector in Goma, local government officials (4), the tourism private business actors (4), the UN peacekeepers and conflict and peace experts (2) and National Government officials (2). The interviews increase the credibility of the data and findings.

During the sampling, we first contacted the local ministry of justice, human rights, tourism, arts and culture of North Kivu Province, who gave us a list of 20 key actors in the tourism space in the province. However, after screening, only 7 met the criteria (e.g. those with touristic activities in Goma, located in Goma and been established in the last 10 years) and were included. As tourism actors are sometimes hard to find in the city, we employed a nonprobability snowballing sampling process, which entails a chain referral sampling used in social sciences in hard-to-reach populations (Biernacki & Waldorf, 1981). The unit of analysis was an actor's testimony on the role of responsible tourism in peace-building and social inclusion. To analyse that data, we used the individuals' discourse to create aggregate narratives of group constructions of the role of responsible tourism (Currie & Brown, 2003). These were constructed by the researcher based on individuals' discourses and further transformed into aggregate narratives. The data were further triangulated with archival data to increase the credibility of the findings.

4 Understanding urban tourism in Goma

4.1 The potential of urban tourism in Goma

In 1990, the city of Goma was inhabited by around 200 000 people. By 2010, the city of Goma had tripled in population to 800 000 dwellers. In 2020, the city of Goma is at around 1 200 000 dwellers, 6 times more than it had 30 years before. There were only a few major sources of income and employment. These included the ecotourism industry, a small airport, Lake Kivu Port connecting to Bukavu towards South Kivu Province, local agropastoral industry coupled with a retail commerce for imported manufactured goods, cattle farming, coffee plantations and manufacturing industry, and retail services. There was an asphalted road of 200 km to Virunga's Rwindi tourist bungalows that continued by a bumpy road to Butembo, Beni, Bunia and Kisangani. The Rwindi had an asphalted road to Sake, passing by the southern sector of Virunga National Park and Hotel Karibu (150 rooms). That road continued as a dirt road to Masisi (farming lands) and Walikale (an artisanal mineral centre), and it led to Kisangani through Lubutu and Maiko National Park. These circumstances highlight the precarious nature of the transportation network in the area and how it can negatively affect tourism. But, there were also dozens of locally owned hostels in the city. Virunga National Park had a striving tourist visitor centre within the city of Goma. Only a few hotels were present, including Grand Lac Hotel (80 rooms), Rif(t) Hotel (30 rooms) and Hotel Karibu (150 rooms). It is worth it to note that amidst its challenges, Goma has a lot of touristic opportunities.

Based on the data, the potential of urban tourism was very low in Goma in 1990 due to a low capacity of tourist lodging, mostly oriented towards elite eco-tourism in the Virunga National Park, with its mountain gorillas, volcanoes visitation, large game viewing in the plains and Mount Ruwenzori climbing. Things, however, changed in 1994 with the moving in of refugees and subsequent developments. First, millions of refugees from Rwanda lived in tent camps that looked like city centres, which were organised by Humanitarians and were seemingly larger than Goma itself. The refugees, the humanitarian agencies and the military were thought to visit and loot the parkland, especially poaching for wildlife and making charcoal out of the protected areas trees as a striving business to feed those refugee camps. But by 2000, they were joined by a large peace-keeping mission. These do not only have excess cash from UN salaries, but also, they are outfitted with so many vehicles that they use to roam the town. High rentals in Goma by those peace-keeping forces and humanitarian agencies prompted the city dwellers and refugees from neighbouring countries to start building houses and hotels. Additionally, many of the Rwandan refugees progressively invaded the artisanal mining industries in Walikale, Masisi and Lweshe, and soon, the warlords started to transit in Goma to trade their looted mineral ores (coltan, wolfram, molybdenum, etc.) with worldwide traffickers crossing out of Rwanda and Uganda. Many homes and hotels were constructed, and by 2000, a government made of Rwandan and local rebellers elected Goma as their capital city for the whole Eastern Congo region. The city population more than doubled by around 600 000 people, including local people displaced out of the insecure villages taken away by armed foreign invaders and refugees.

Summaries of archival data indicate that ever since then, peacekeepers and humanitarian organisations look for weekend opportunities for tourism. As prostitution became rampant, more hotels were built in the area. Meanwhile, DRC protected areas entered into ecotourism revenue-sharing schemes with Rwanda's protected areas, especially the Volcanoes National Park contiguous with Virunga National Park in Jomba and Bukima. In these places, two large bungalow facilities were built by local businessmen and protected by the UN peacekeepers. Goma became the third-largest urban tourist centre, based on visitors and hotel occupancy, in DRC after Kinshasa (DRC's capital city) and Lubumbashi.

The Tchukudu monument and several boat buildings spots were built along the shores of the lake under the spectacular Mount Goma. Land reclamation in the Lake Kivu area, augmented with spectacular villas and hotels along the lake shoreline, all point to the tourism potential of the area. More vehicles and tarmac roads were made after Nyiragongo volcano erupted and spilled over its lava in the city. The airport runway was cut into two parts, but with the help of UN peacekeepers, the lava was removed. The government of DRC enlarged the runway above the homes in the city centre. These developments promoted tourism in the area. It can be observed that these caused the economy to thrive with both urban and ecotourism.

4.2 The challenges of responsible tourism in Goma

There are many challenges and impediments for a responsible urban tourism in Goma. First, there is no freshwater system in hotels in Goma, as water out of the faucet is pumped from Lake Kivu. This is, at the same time, a cesspool for city wastes with high methane levels in the salty water. The people we interviewed suggested that bringing water from the freshwater springs or rivers upland from the Katale plantations or elsewhere would be helpful in improving the clean freshwater supply. The little freshwater found in Goma faucets comes from Gisenyi in Rwanda. Water issues are common in many SSA cities, but access to clean water will attract tourists and promote the tourism industry. Secondly, there are no pathways for pedestrian hiking or bicycling in the city. The roads in the city are narrow. These discourage people from visiting the surroundings. Third, the Goma airport runway is difficult for aircraft landing and take-off. Mount Nyiragongo, an active volcano, stands tall just north of the runway. The only way in and out of this airport is to fly south to Lake Kivu, but the airport runway is overhanging the city houses. During 2019, several aircrafts ended up above homes and killed innocent people in their homes. These poor airport infrastructure conditions impede tourism promotion. Good infrastructure, including roads and airports, is crucial for any business, including the tourism industry. Fourth, there is no organised transportation dedicated to tourists, such as lake canoes, boats or catamarans; buses; horse carts; or scenic-viewing aircrafts. Also, to the less fit are able to climb Mount Nyiragongo and Mount Goma. These mountains would also boost urban tourism if flying and/or gliding kites were available. These inadequacies in infrastructure limit tourism development.

Fifth, another impediment for tourism during dry seasons is volcanic ash and dust particles in the air. Sixth, the city of Goma lacks professional guides and tour operators, especially speaking both local and foreign languages. Seventh, there is limited organised and publicised tourist circuitry in Goma. Eighth, DRC and Goma are known for administrative corruptions and red tape that discourages tourists. It is frequently reported that tourists are being asked to pay money to secure entrance visas at the border or for any acquisition of paperwork, and these services are actually free. Ninth, to reach Goma as a tourist, one needs to go through neighbouring cities and across borders, which are more competitive in terms of tourist facilities and existing tour operators. Tenth, cultural settings and economic exclusion around Goma discourage local people from engaging in local tourism, as they lack time and money to spend on leisure, and as they dedicate their savings to livelihood and survival. Eleventh, no investment banks exist to support tourism infrastructure and investment. Twelfth, almost no evacuation system exists, nor first aid care for tourist accidents or injury. Finally, in Goma and DRC in general, life, health or evacuation insurances for incoming tourists are abnormally high. To engage in a responsible tourism, the sector needs serious reengineering. Good governance is important to promote the tourism industry. However, the current tourism industry in Goma is not nearly sustainable enough to operate in a responsible and inclusive manner.

4.3 Resilience of urban tourism in an economy of crises

For urban tourism to become resilient, removal of impediments to sustainability is vital. In some cases, an economic crisis can provide opportunities for people to rethink issues of sustainability and resilience. Economic crises do not necessarily mean doom; they can help people to innovate and find technological solutions to challenges. The wooden wheelbarrow, called 'Tchukudu', was invented in Goma during a time of economic crisis when the people needed to transport heavy loads. This helped the community to move loads easily downhill or uphill. Resilient urban tourism can promote innovative practices to enhance the sustainability of its operations, such as cooperation with other businesses and collaboration with all tourism actors, acknowledgement of customer relations and market, and competent management.

5 Moving towards responsible urban tourism in Goma

5.1 A responsible tourism for peace-building and social inclusion

Goma, as one of the leading tourist destinations in the DRC, has seen that potential resource as sometimes a burden rather than a way of improving the lives of its inhabitants. Instead of improving the lives of many, the tourism industry in Goma benefits only a few powerful individuals, and poverty seems widespread.

The tourism industry in Goma needs to ensure that the sector is socially and economically sustainable to profit the poor, local communities that were formerly excluded. By empowering local communities and creating job opportunities for poor people in Goma, tourism will discourage the local youth communities from joining armed groups, which fuel conflict as a livelihood strategy. It can supplement state and UN peacekeepers' peace-building efforts. As one of the biggest industries in the city, tourism can be mobilised as a means to promote reconciliation, social inclusion and securing peace. The industry can create opportunities for the people, including sharing its benefits with marginalised groups in the city. Below are two overriding factors that have contributed to thriving tourism in Goma during nonconventional warfare, conflict and security crises.

5.2 Safe haven due to peacekeeping and humanitarian presence

Urban tourism has recently surfaced in Goma. This happened during the warfare in its hinterlands, while the city served as a safe haven for United Nations peacekeeping forces, humanitarian personnel and internally displaced people and refugees from neighbouring countries. Indeed, such a diversified mixture of stakeholders brought up a booming economy, despite long-lasting conflicts and security crises.

To keep such an incipient urban tourism growing, and to become sustainable amidst warfare and security crises, there is the need to find replacements for current driving forces of urban tourism, i.e. peacekeeping and humanitarian agencies. Peacekeeping forces and humanitarian operations brought a steady cash flow into the economy of Goma, which in turn prompted the construction of newer housing for rental by peacekeepers, and hotel construction for visitors. Such a growing economy needs to be sustained for urban tourism to thrive and flourish. Based on data from interviews with the key actors in tourism in Goma, it was revealed that there are emerging opportunities to sustain the economy after the warfare and insecurity crises. These include: (a) introduction of an added-value mineral industry for export; (b) support of an agropastoral and dairy industry with bio-produce or cash crops, such as coffee or cacao; (c) fostering a diversified tourism industry coupled with trained professionals to run it; (d) creation of investment banking as well as affordable life and health insurance for local stakeholders and visitors; (e) diminishing and eradicating red tape; and (f) training tourism professionals and qualified hotel managers and chefs. These conditions are supposed to help in the promotion of urban tourism in Goma.

5.3 Replacement of a mineral-trafficking economy with a legal, diversified economy

To sustain the nascent urban tourism in Goma, especially when peacekeeping efforts end, the generic solution is to diversify and strengthen the economy. Policy and strategic documents from both national and local ministries of tourism, suggest some pragmatic steps for responsible and sustainable tourism in the city. First, this will require the introduction of an added-value mineral industry that processes these products before export. Goma is a transaction centre for trading raw minerals, especially in the underground or informal economy during warfare. Second, it is advisable to bring in new investments, introduce organic agriculture and support farming and dairy industries, as well as processing and transforming cash crops such as coffee or cacao for export. Third, we recommend to foster a diversified tourism industry, offering more organised circuitries, including cable vehicles, city-touring buses, aircraft touring, waterskiing, kite-flying or soaring from mountaintops, etc. Fourth, let's create investment banks, along with insurance companies offering affordable life and health insurances for local stakeholders and visitors. This will encourage investment in the tourism sector. Fifth, it is important to lessen and eradicate red tape and introduce legal economy taxes, and slowly move away from the widespread underground economy. Finally, it is critical to train tourism professionals, hotel managers and chefs, as well as to promote a boat-building industry to efficiently run the urban tourist industry. Tourism curricula are already offered in Goma at the secondary and college levels. Tourism professionals and culinary experts, as well as a better education of the people in Eastern DRC, would altogether add up to sustaining the urban tourism.

All these emerging opportunities create new jobs and a middle class of blue-collar employees that would need and could afford urban tourism for their recreation during their spare time and weekends. Industry proceedings, legal taxes and salaries of the middle-class workers would sustain a cash flow into the economy to contribute to the tourism industry.

5.4 Recommendations for Africa

African governments should develop an enabling environment to stop a small group of rich people from having control over most of the tourism industry. This would be done by including community representatives in the management of the tourism resources. Sub-Saharan African cities need inclusive pro-poor tourism approaches that are resiliency-centred to encourage urban tourism (Musavengane, Siakwah & Leonard, 2020). Governance systems need to strengthen tourism regulatory and policy procedures, and remove administrative obstacles. As Musavengane et al. (2019) noted, in developing tourism governance, including collaboration among all actors, the inclusion of particularly marginalised groups is paramount. This collaboration becomes even more crucial in promoting governance based on justice, trust, inclusion and equitable power relations by extending to the international actors, private sector and government institutions (Siakwah et al., 2020).

Privatisation and regulation of new businesses of the tourism sector by African governments could help develop competition and efficiency. Building an image of Africa as a safe and attractive destination while recognising the outstanding challenges of peace-building is also critical. Promotion strategies should not only focus on tourism that generates income, but also attempts to promote social inclusion and peace-building activities. Efforts should be directed at tourism to contribute to social inclusion and support peace-building actions. A planning of pertinent actors, potential destinations and adverse effects of tourism should be recognised. Tourism actors should develop activities that cater to the needs and capacities of the vulnerable groups, such as orphans, women, children and soldiers who are extremely affected by the conflicts.

Develop employment and training processes that allow local communities, particularly voiceless people, the opportunity to have employment. We have to aim at organising local training programmes that provide service training together with conflict-compassion practices. This is mostly crucial for the African countries that are facing conflict and insecurity, if they want to improve their local tourism market. In addition to creating employment, community development and tourism entrepreneurship cultures should be promoted in Africa. A shift away from benevolent aid is a crucial step towards the development of a workforce that is motivated and independent. Given the state's decreasing capacity in many SSA countries, an increasing cooperation with non-state actors, such as private businesses and civil-society organisations, would contribute to alleviating poverty and in achieving Sustainable Development Goals (SDG) – ending poverty in all its manifestations by 2030.

6 Conclusion

While tourism is not the only sector in Goma that can contribute to the peace-building efforts and alleviating poverty, responsible tourism has a huge potential in contributing to building socioeconomic institutions, reconciliation and promoting justice, trust, inclusion and equitable power relations. Responsible tourism promotes peace-building and social inclusion by working together with other stakeholders such as government institutions, the United Nations peacekeepers, multinational enterprises, civil-society organisations and marginalised groups. By adopting pro-poor policy and strategy approaches, responsible tourism in Goma can take into account the concerns of voiceless people in addressing the real causes of conflicts and promote social inclusion.

This chapter contributes to the role of responsible tourism towards peace promotion and social inclusion by documenting how tourism was promoted even amidst conflicts, war and peace-building in Goma. It is a unique study, as not much has been written about war-risk countries pertaining to responsible tourism. It enriches discussions on how a nascent urban tourism industry is developed out of (a) a long-standing ecotourism that has been stressed for long periods of time during warfare; and (b) it has become resilient during a peace-building presence despite ongoing security risks, as long as a wide range of existing and new stakeholders were involved. Stakeholders participate in urban tourism management and visitation when a consensual system of responsibilities and revenue-sharing is adopted among them.

We have seen in this chapter how crises and challenges can bring about new opportunities for people to think about alternative solutions and innovations. For example, we discussed, among other things, how the warfare and insecurity crises have prompted warlords in Goma to tap into artisanal mining to fuel an underground economy that supported and sustained an unconventional warfare for 3 decades. In response to the warfare, the international community introduced a peacekeeping and a humanitarian presence, which brought about, in the existing system of ecotourism, new stakeholders, having access to cash and who needed recreation during their spare time. This fuelled the construction business for hotels and rental homes, resulting in urban tourism. Finally, existing ecotourism, characterised by insecurity and risks, has catalysed an urban tourism in Goma as a safe haven city amidst warfare. Urban tourism, thus, became a surrogate substitute to existing ecotourism. The research outcomes reveal that tourism development needs policies to be more oriented towards responsible tourism in order to enhance peace-building efforts and equitable benefits-sharing to improve the quality-of-living standards of the marginalised locals in Goma.

References

Adu-Ampong, E. A. (2018). Tourism and national economic development planning in Ghana, 1964–2014. *International Development Planning Review.* doi:10.3828/idpr.2018.2.

Alluri, R. M. (2009). The role of tourism in post-conflict peacebuilding in Rwanda. Available at: http://edoc.vifapol.de/opus/volltexte/2011/2447/pdf/2_2009.pdf, accessed January 2020.

Ashley, C., Boyd, C., & Goodwin, H. (2000). *Putting poverty at the heart of the tourism agenda. Natural resource perspectives. Briefing paper 51.* London: ODI June 2000.

Auty, R. (1993). *Sustaining development in mineral economies: the resource curse thesis.* London, Routledge.

Beru, M. (2009). *Les sites touristiques dans la ville de Goma et sa périphérie: état de lieu et perspective d'avenir. Unpublished master's thesis submitted to the Tourism National Institute of (ISTou)*, Goma, Democratic Republic of Congo.

Biernacki, P., & Waldorf, D. (1981). Snowball Sampling: Problems and Techniques of Chain Referral Sampling. *Sociological Methods & Research, 10(2)*, 141–163.

Blackstock, K. L., White, V., McCrum, G., Scott, A., & Hunter, C. (2008). Measuring responsibility: An appraisal of a Scottish National Park's sustainable tourism indicators. *Journal of Sustainable Tourism, 16(3)*, 276–297.

Boas, M. (2013). A Tale of Two Cities: The Peacekeeping Economy of Goma and Monrovia. In: *5th European Conference on African Studies*, Lisbon, Portugal, 26–29.

Booyens, I., & Rogerson, C. M. (2016). Responsible tourism in the Western Cape, South Africa: an innovation perspective. *Turizam: međunarodni znanstveno-stručni časopis, 64(4)*, 385–396.

Boutros-Ghali, B. (1992). An agenda for peace: Preventive diplomacy, peacemaking and peacekeeping. *International Relations, 11(3)*, 201–218.

Brisman, A., South, N., & White, R. (2016). Gorillas and Guerrillas: Environment and Conflict in the Democratic Republic of Congo. In: *Environmental Crime and Social Conflict* (pp. 73–89). Routledge.

Büscher, K., & Vlassenroot, K. (2010). Humanitarian presence and urban development: new opportunities and contrasts in Goma, DRC. *Disasters, 34*, S256–S273.

Cho, M. (2007). A re-examination of tourism and peace: The case of the Mt. Gumgang tourism development on the Korean Peninsula. *Tourism Management, 28(2)*, 556–569. 10.1016/j.tourman.2006.04.019.

Currie, G., & Brown, A. D. (2003). A narratological approach to understanding processes of organizing in a UK hospital. *Human Relations, 56(5)*, 563–586.

Dieke, U. C. (2003). Tourism in Africa's economic development: Policy implications, management decisions. *The Emirates Academy of Hospitality Management, 41(3)*, 287–295.

Duran, C. (2013). Governance for the tourism sector and its measurement, UNWTO statistics and TSA issue paper series STSA/IP/2013/01. Retrieved from http://statistics. unwto.org/en/content/papers.

Eraqi, M. I. (2014). Responsible tourism management as an integrated approach for enhancing standards of living of local people in Egypt. *International Journal of Services and Operations Management, 17(1)*, 1–35.

Frey, N. (2008). *Responsible Tourism Management: The Missing Link between Attitude and Behaviour in an Emerging Market*. Cape Town: University of Cape Town.

Goodwin, H., & Font, X. (2007). Advances in responsible tourism. Retrieved from Leeds:

Goodwin, H., Spenceley, A., & Maynard, B. (2002). *Development of responsible tourism guidelines for South Africa*.

Hall, D., & Brown, F. (2011). Tourism and welfare: Ethics, responsibility a wellbeing. In: S. Cole & N. Morgan (Eds.), *(2010) Tourism and inequality: problems and prospects* (pp. 143–163). Oxford, Cabi.

Hochschild, A. (1998). *King Leopold's ghost*. London, MacMillan.

Jamal, T., & Camargo, B. A. (2014). Sustainable tourism, justice and an ethic of care: Toward the just destination. *Journal of Sustainable Tourism, 22(1)*, 11–30.

Kolk, A., & Lenfant, F. (2012). "Business-NGO collaboration in a conflict setting: partnership activities in the Democratic Republic of Congo". *Business and Society, 51(3)*, 478–511.

Lorant, D. (2011). Tourism ecology: towards a responsible, sustainable tourism future. *Worldwide Hospitality and Tourism Themes, 3(3)*, 210–216.

Muhindo, S. R. (2010). *La redynamisation du secteur touristique et son impact sur le développement de la vie socioéconomique de la population de Goma*, Unpublished master's thesis submitted to the Tourism National Institute of (ISTou), Goma, DR Congo.

Musavengane, R. (2018). Toward pro-poor local economic development in Zimbabwe: The role of pro-poor tourism. *African Journal of Hospitality, Tourism and Leisure, 7(1)*, 1–14.

Musavengane, R., Siakwah, P., & Leonard, L. (2019). "Does the poor matter" in pro-poor driven Sub-Saharan African cities? towards progressive and inclusive pro-poor tourism. *International Journal of Tourism Cities*, ISSN: 2056-5607.

Neuman, W. L. (2011). *Social research methods: qualitative and quantitative approaches* (7th ed.). Needham Heights, MA, Allyen and Bacon.

Novelli, M., & Hellwig, A. (2011). The UN MDGs, tourism and development: A tour operators' perspective. *Current Issues in Tourism, 14(3),* 1–17.

Nunkoo, R. (2017). Governance and sustainable tourism: What is the role of trust, power and social capital? *Journal of Destination Marketing & Management, 6,* 277–285.

Prunier, G. (2009). *Africa's World War: Congo, the Rwandan genocide and the making of a continental catastrophe.* Oxford, Oxford University Press.

Reyntjens, F. (2009). *The great African war: Congo and regional geopolitics, 1996-2006.* Cambridge, Cambridge University Press.

Saarinen, J. (2014). Critical sustainability: Setting the limits to growth and responsibility in tourism. *Sustainability, 6(11),* 1–17.

Sala-i-Martin, X., & Subramanian, A. (2013). Addressing the natural resource curse: An illustration from Nigeria. *Journal of African Economies, 22*(4), 570-615.

Scheyvens, R., & Biddulph, R. (2018). Inclusive tourism development. *Tourism Geographies, 20(4),* 589–609.

Siakwah, P. (2018). Tourism geographies and spatial distribution of tourist sites in Ghana. *African Journal of Hospitality, Tourism and Leisure, 7(1),* 1–19.

Siakwah, P. (2017). Political economy of the resource curse in Africa revisited: the curse as a product and a function of globalised hydrocarbon assemblage. *Development and Society, 46(1),* 83–112.

Siakwah, P., Musavengane, R. & Leonard, L. (2020) Tourism Governance and Attainment of the Sustainable Development Goals in Africa. *Tourism Planning & Development*, 17: 4, 355-383, 10.1080/21568316.2019.1600160.

Smith, D. (2004). Towards a strategic framework for peacebuilding: Getting their act together. Royal Norwegian Ministry of Foreign Affairs: Evaluation Report 1/2004.

Spenceley, A. (ed) (2008). *Responsible tourism: critical issues for conservation and development.* London, Earthscan.

United Nations Development Programme (UNDP). (2015). *Sustainable development goals (SDGs).* Nairobi: Author.

World Travel & Tourism Council (WTTC). (2017). *Travel and tourism economic impact 2017 world.* London: Author.

Yin, R. (2014). *Case study research: design and methods* (5th ed.). Thousand Oaks, CA, Sage.

Tourism, climate change and flood risks

9 Factors influencing tourism accommodations' lack of preparedness for flooding in Lagos, Nigeria

Eromose E. Ebhuoma and Llewellyn Leonard

1 Introduction

Tourism is one of the most economically viable sectors globally, as it accounted for 10.3% of the world's gross domestic product (GDP) in 2019 (World Travel and Tourism Council, 2020). African countries like South Africa (Fitchett, Robinson & Hoogendoorn, 2017), Kenya (Balala, 2018), Mauritius (Mahadew & Appadoo, 2019) and Tanzania (Kilungu et al., 2017) have benefited immensely from tourism. Unfortunately, the same cannot be said of Nigeria, the largest economy on the continent. Nigeria's unenviable reputation for violent crime and corruption acts as major deterrent to potential international tourists (Bankole, 2002; Sanni & Chile, 2018). Consequently, Nigeria loses out on tourism revenues to competing African countries perceived to be safer, such as Kenya, Ghana and The Gambia (Sanni & Chile, 2018). Domestic tourism has, nonetheless, increased slightly from 2010 to 2018 (Nwanne, 2018; Rosa, 2018), partly because of stringent visa restrictions in clienteles' preferred destination choices, such as the United States of America, Europe and South Africa (United Nations Conference on Trade and Development [UNCTD], 2017; Rosa, 2018). Also, the plunging of the Nigerian economy into recession in 2016, which reduced disposable income significantly and more than doubled the exchange rate from 160 to 360 naira (NGN) to US$1 (Rosa, 2018), inadvertently fuelled the growth of local tourism. Nigeria's tourism industry realised NGN757.3bn (US$2.1bn) in 2013 (Metilelu, 2016). By 2024, the tourism industry is expected to directly contribute 1.6%, the equivalent of NGN1 366bn (US$3.8bn), to Nigeria's GDP (Metilelu, 2016). This projected growth, however, could be severely compromised by climatic risks such as flooding (Intergovernmental Panel on Climate Change [IPCC], 2014).

According to Hoogendoorn and Fitchett (2016), the nature and frequency of climate change will largely determine the extent to which tourism accommodations will remain operational and sustainable globally. In Nigeria, for example, increased flooding occurrences are anticipated to become the new normal by 2030 (Shepherd et al., 2013). Under the current state of affairs, this will have severe consequences for urban tourism in Nigeria and will, most likely, result in the closure of some small and medium-sized tourism accommodation establishments

(SMTEs) and job losses. In this chapter, a small-sized accommodation is defined as one with up to 50 rooms, while a medium-sized accommodation has 51–100 rooms (Ingram et al., 2000).

The closure of SMTEs with subsequent job losses will be catastrophic for Nigeria, especially at a time when the government is seeking avenues to diversify its economy from depending solely on crude oil (Ebhuoma & Simatele, 2019). The President Obasanjo-led administration, 1999 to 2007, considered tourism as one of the 6 priority sectors for economic and social development (Metilelu, 2016). Thus, the need to protect SMTEs in Nigeria is crucial for a nation whose unemployment rate continues to skyrocket. This is partly due to the inability of the Nigerian government and industries to provide jobs that correspond with the rate at which new graduates enter the job market annually. Tourism provides 1.2 million direct jobs in Nigeria (Nwanne, 2018). Therefore, the need for SMTEs to prepare adequately for flooding cannot be underestimated, especially since contingency planning, as well as the creation and implementation of containment mechanisms, can be challenging during a disaster (Hystad & Keller, 2006).

Against this background, this chapter analyses the factors undermining Nigeria's SMTE's preparedness for flooding in Nigeria and the implications for tourism development. Nigeria makes for an exciting case study because of scant literature on the topic and the sluggishly growing local tourism industry, which comprises predominantly SMTEs (Sanni & Chile, 2018). Spending is projected to increase in the coming years, especially among the Nigerian middle class with a desire for leisure holidays (Rosa, 2018). This study focuses specifically on Lagos State, one of the most visited destinations by both domestic and international tourists (Bada, 2013). It is hoped that this chapter will trigger healthy debate on possible ways SMTEs in Lagos State can remain viable and operational in the face of increased flooding occurrences. This chapter proceeds in 4 parts. The first considers the impacts and preparedness of tourist accommodations to flooding. The second presents a snapshot of the study area and the methodology applied – a review of relevant literature. The third part highlights the factors undermining SMTEs from preparing for flooding. We demonstrate how historical narratives, lack of financial and human capital, failure to utilise nonstructural measures and lack of cohesion among tourism accommodation operators contribute to a lack of flood preparedness. The last part draws decisive conclusions and makes relevant recommendations.

2 Flooding in tourist accommodations: Impacts and preparedness

The 2007 Davos Declaration includes a compelling remark that, globally, climate change is the greatest singular threat to sustainable tourism in the 21st century (United Nations World Tourism Organisation [UNWTO], 2007). Chief among climate change threats is flooding. Accommodation enterprises under threat are usually classified as vulnerable to floods (Southon & Van der Merwe, 2018). As the United Nations Office for Disaster Risk Reduction (UNISDR) (2015) notes, the high exposure of accommodations to flooding and other disasters reflects tourists' preference to be close to aesthetically appealing natural environments such as rivers and coastlines. Thus, demystifying ways to manage flooding and risks associated with sea-level rise to reduce the negative impacts on accommodation establishment is crucial. As Shaw et al. (2012) note, accommodation establishments are unaware of the magnitude of their vulnerability to floods, yet the impact of floods on accommodations is enormous.

Flooding results in damage to properties and infrastructure (Bernard & Cook, 2015), and severely compromises the aesthetic appeal of tourist accommodation in various countries (Becken, 2013; Wyss, Abegg & Luthe, 2014). This, in turn, results in reduced tourist reservations and shorter vacation periods, which adversely affect profits and competitiveness (Changnon, 1998; Mondlane, 2010; Atta-ur-Rahman & Khan, 2011; Hamzah et al., 2012). There have also been instances where flooding has resulted in employees being laid off (Changnon, 1998; Mondlane, 2010). These impacts are especially catastrophic for SMTEs that often find it extremely challenging to implement disaster-related repairs because of limited financial resources and lacking insurance, a reality that will, arguably, compromise rebranding and advertising to regain tourists' confidence. Thus, the need to adopt more proactive and strategic planning instead of waiting for floods to occur before embarking on reactive responses and recovery efforts is overwhelmingly essential (Ritchie, 2008).

Yet, globally, very few accommodation enterprises have adopted readiness strategies in some form to minimise the negative impacts of floods (Ritchie, 2008; UNISDR, 2015). Negative attitudes towards disaster planning, a lack of responsibility for dealing with crises, limited finances, a lack of knowledge and downplaying the magnitude of disasters are regarded as some of the reasons for this (Wang & Ritchie, 2012). Hystad and Keller (2006), for example, documented that barriers to proactive disaster planning by tourism businesses in Canada included: a lack of finances (68%); a lack of knowledge about disaster management planning (47%); inability to make changes due to small business size (23%); and a perceived dearth of solidarity in the industry (14%). Despite Hystad and Keller's (2006) study, tourist accommodation enterprises' level of preparedness for disasters remains under-researched, yet such research is necessary to help inject strategies to inspire preparation and appropriate responses among businesses in vulnerable regions like sub-Saharan Africa (SSA) that are anticipated to suffer the adverse effects of future climate change (IPCC, 2014).

3 Study areas and methodology

3.1 Snapshot of Lagos State

Lagos is located between latitude 6.5244°N and longitude 3.3792°E of the equator (Figure 9.1). It is the second-largest megacity in Africa after Cairo. "The status of Lagos as Nigeria's economic capital is evident in the fact that the city contributes about 30% ($52bn) to the nation's gross domestic product (GDP) and is the leading contributor (62%) to the nation's non-oil sector GDP" (LMEPB, 2013, cited in Adelekan, 2016: 256). Lagos has witnessed years of rapid urbanisation.

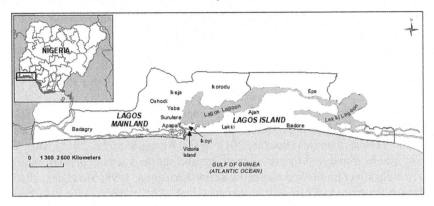

Figure 9.1 Map of Lagos State.
Source: Authors, 2020.

From a population of about 3.3 million in 1975 (United Nations Department of Economic and Social Affairs [UNDESA], 2012, cited in Adelekan, 2016), Lagos now has approximately 14 million people (World Population Review, 2020). The population concentration is largely due to the concentration of economic activities in the city. The population density of 20 000 persons/km² (Lagos State Government [LASG], 2012) far exceeds the global average population density of 112 persons/km² for coastal zones (International Human Dimension Programme [IHDP], 2012).

Lagos' climate is tropical and humid all year round with an average temperature of 27°C. It has two seasons: the rainy (or wet) and dry seasons. Normally, the rainy season begins in April and ends in October, with a short dry spell in August. The dry season begins in November and ends in May (Ajibade & McBean, 2014). The mean monthly rainfall between May and July is about 300 mm, while it decreases to 75 mm in August and September. In January, it is as low as 35 mm (Okoye & Ojeh, 2015). Increased variations in rainfall intensity and spatiality, storm surges and changes in land use combined with an increased urban population, a shortage and blockages of drainage systems and ineffective urban planning have increased flood risks in Lagos (Asiyanbi, 2015; Adelekan, 2016; Adelekan & Asiyanbi, 2016). This is amplified by the city's low-lying topography (see for example Nkwunonwo, Whitworth & Baily, 2015). For over 2 decades, flooding, especially from July to October, has become an annual occurrence with increasing frequency and severity.

A case-in-point is the development of Eko Atlantic. Concern for the safety of its citizens due to rising sea-levels was cited as the reason why the Lagos State government sacrificed Lagos' Bar Beach, once a vibrant and famous tourist hotspot for Lagosians as well as other domestic and international tourists, for Eko Atlantic, officially Nigeria's International Commerce City (Orient News, 2010). Prior to its closure, Bar Beach often experienced the lowest visitor figures during the brief, intermittent dry spells during the rainy season referred to as 'August break'. That was due to fears of the beach overflowing its banks (The Weather

Channel, 2018). Visitors' fears were justified by the number of lives lost (approximately 45) between 2000 and 2004 as a result of unprecedented tidal waves. A further example of the impact of climate change is the incident that took place at another popular relaxation spot in Lagos in August 2012. There was no rainfall on the day, yet a surge from the Atlantic Ocean hit Kuramo Beach, and at least 16 lives were lost (This Day, 2012). These events have cascaded into reduced tourist visits, with severe implications for SMTEs.

3.2 Methodology

This study is based on secondary data. It is worthwhile to mention that documented evidence on climate change impacts on tourism establishments in Lagos is limited. Thus, this paper draws on literature documenting the impacts of climate change on urban households, as it provides valuable insights on how climate change impacts will likely affect tourism establishments. It is also important to state that news from online tabloids was included in the analysis. Examples of some keywords inserted in search engines like Google Scholar, PubMed and Web of Science are: 'climate change and tourism in Nigeria', 'tourism establishments in Lagos', 'flood risk perception in Lagos', 'impacts of flooding on Nigeria's tourism', 'vulnerability to climate change in Lagos', 'adaptation to climate change in Lagos', 'disaster management in Lagos' and 'disaster preparedness and tourism in Lagos'. To begin with, titles and abstracts were scrutinised to determine their relevance. Next, the full texts were downloaded to ascertain whether they addressed issues of climate change and adaptation in Lagos State directly and indirectly. Finally, the reference list of each relevant article was assessed to identify other relevant article(s). The search strategy, screening and selection processes are illustrated in Figure 9.2.

Themes were generated by drawing on the findings of Hystad and Keller (2006), Pennington-Gray et al. (2011) and Orchiston (2013) on barriers to proactive disaster planning by tourism businesses, the only empirical studies that highlighted such limitations. The barriers identified in these studies include a lack of finances, a lack of knowledge about disaster management planning, an inability to make changes due to small business size and a perceived absence of cohesion in the industry. These themes formed the basis for the searches, resulting in the selection of 28 pieces of literature relevant to Lagos, and guided the analysis of flooding risks and tourism development in Lagos.

4 Results

4.1 Tourism and urban development in Lagos

Due to its well-preserved traditions and cultures, Nigeria is endowed with several unique structures and festivals that could make any tourist visit a worthwhile investment. With over 250 ethnic groups, the nation has ample opportunities for cultural tourism in terms of historical sites, annual traditional festivals and folk art, such as crafts, carvings and sculpture. It is, therefore, not surprising that the

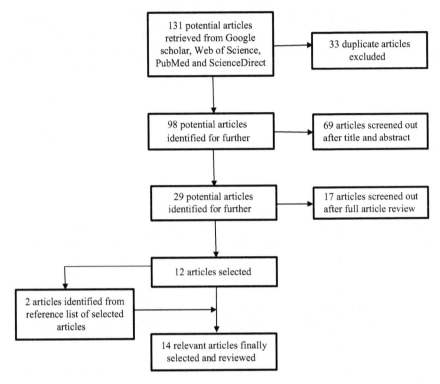

Figure 9.2 Flow chart of article screening and selection.
Source: Authors, 2020.

Nigerian embassy stated that, due to the nation's tropical weather, well-preserved culture, astonishing waterfalls and historical relics, it has the potential of becoming a tourist paradise (Bankole, 2002). Despite all the breathtaking and enchanting attractions Nigeria has to offer, the tourism sector performed abysmally in previous decades (Bankole, 2002). From 2010 to 2018, however, domestic tourism witnessed a slight growth, partly because of the burgeoning Nigerian middle class. According to Rosa (2018), travel has become a status symbol for Nigerians. One of the states that attracts a massive influx of domestic tourists is Lagos.

As such, tourism is steadily becoming a key contributor to the GDP of Lagos State. In 2017, for example, activities within the tourism sector contributed about NGN800bn (just over US$2.2bn) to the State's GDP. In the last quarter of 2018, Lagos State government captured total spending in excess of NGN50bn (over US$138m) in cash transactions, especially in the weeks preceding and following the Yuletide season (The Guardian, 2019). According to a report published in the British Daily Mail in April 2018, Lagos along with Nairobi in Kenya were listed as some of the top non-European destinations for the summer holiday planning of British travellers (The Guardian, 2019).

A notable tourism event in Lagos is the *Eyo* festival (Emmanuel, 2014). *Eyo* is the name given to the costumed dancers popularly referred to as masquerades that come out during the festival. In the past, the function of the festival was to accompany the 'spirit of a dead Lagos king or high chief and to usher in the new king or chief' (Olawale, 2018: 1). While Lagos has lost a significant number of its traditional Yoruba followers to Christianity and Islam, the festival still is celebrated as a tourist attraction (Olawale, 2018), especially because some Lagos indigenes regard *Eyo* as their ancestral and illustrious father (Emmanuel, 2014). The *Eyo* festival, which currently takes place on Lagos Island in Lagos State, attracts tourists from various parts of Nigeria and the world (Olawale, 2018).

In January 2019, the Lagos State government rolled out its art, culture and entertainment events calendar for the year to inform local and foreign tourists about the rich cultural events on offer. These included over 80 events either sponsored or endorsed by the State. These events were concentrated in April and the last quarter of the year up to December, when the weather in Lagos is usually most favourable for outdoor events. The idea behind creating such a calendar, which commenced in 2018, was because the 'State enjoyed a considerable increase in the consumption of its tourism products by improving access to tourism information' (Nigeria Travel Digest, 2019: 1). Such organised events have an impact on tourism businesses, including tourist accommodations (Olawale, 2018).

A study by Eruotor (2014) found that accommodations and restaurants had increased significantly in Lagos, especially close to the coastline, which is a hotspot for domestic and international tourists. The study also found that due to the booming tourism, the Lagos State government employed cleaners called highway managers to keep the coastline tidy so as to not compromise its aesthetic appeal. Also, there is evidence of the government benefiting from the bourgeoning tourism industry via tax revenues (Eruotor, 2014; Okonkwo, 2014).

Due to the huge potential of tourism to scale up GDP contributions in Nigeria, which some believe has not yet been maximised (Ovat, 2003; Taxaide, 2019), the Nigerian Tourism Development Cooperation (NTDC) has publicised the unique and diverse cultures and attractions of Lagos and other states to the outside world (Festus, 2014). While crucial, failure to contextualise how flooding will impact on Lagos' tourism and SMTEs will set the sector on a trajectory to failure. Lagos is exposed to frequent and intense rainfall, storm surges and coastal flooding (Pelling et al., 2018). According to Maplecroft's (2012) Climate Change Vulnerability Index (CCVI), Lagos is among the top 10 cities in the world facing 'high risk' from climate change. Thus, failure to take cognisance of, as well as finding innovative and sustainable ways of adapting to, climate variability and change will prove catastrophic for tourism in Lagos and for SMTEs.

5   Factors undermining tourism establishments from preparing for flooding

5.1   Historical narratives

A major constraint that undermines some tourism establishments' flood preparedness in Lagos is downplaying the severity of floods concerning tourism development (see, for example, Asiyanbi, 2015; Ojomo et al., 2015; Adelekan

& Asiyanbi, 2016). The underestimation of flooding is partly underpinned by historical narratives, especially from those who have not been impacted severely. Historical narratives play a pivotal role in the way climatic risks are construed. For example, "the *availability heuristic* states that events are judged to be more probable if imagining or recalling similar instances from memory is easier" (Eiser et al., 2012: 8). Thus, some tourism operators and managers whose establishments in Lagos have, thus far, not been affected adversely by floods may assume that they are in a "buffer zone" where future flooding impacts will not be severe. Consequently, the need to implement readiness measures to minimise future flooding events is not taken seriously.

In view of the above, climate education is necessary for operators and managers of SMTEs to trigger behavioural changes aimed at implementing proactive measures to reduce the negative impacts of floods (Anderson, 2012; Monroe et al., 2017). That will enlighten those less knowledgeable about the science of future flooding projections and those downplaying the potential risks of flooding to their establishments. Climate education can equip tourism operators and managers with the prerequisite skills to facilitate flooding preparedness to mitigate the adverse effects of floods. Since "climate change education interventions are most successful when they focus on local, tangible and actionable aspects, especially those that can be addressed by individual behaviour" (Anderson, 2012: 197), the need to prioritise the replacement and retrofitting of old materials with flood-resistant building materials is essential. As the International Federation of Red Cross and Red Crescent Societies (IFRC) (2013) notes, a dollar spent on disaster preparedness saves four dollars spent on response and recovery measures.

5.2 Lack of human and financial capital

Following the identification of tourism as a key priority area for development in Nigeria by the Obasanjo administration, a presidential committee was set up with a mandate to development a master plan to make Nigeria become a preferred choice for international tourists. Among key issues raised that needed to be tackled decisively was the level of human capital development that lags far behind in the delivery of quality services to clienteles (Metilelu, 2016). This also inhibits SMTEs in Lagos from embarking on flood preparation. Similar sentiments have been shared concerning South Africa (Faling, Tempelhoff & Van Niekerk, 2012) and the coastal regions of developing countries where most tourism attractions are often located (Agrawala et al., 2004; Oladipo, 2010). Nonetheless, it is argued that limited financial capital also prevents SMTEs from preparing adequately for floods (Bankole, 2002; Oladipo, 2010).

Arguably, the profitability mindset coupled with the likelihood of going extinct usually deters long-term planning, which is often expensive (Idahosa & Ebhuoma, 2020). The question now, as Hoogendoorn and Fitchett (2016) put forward, is how best these SMTEs can adapt to remain sustainable and operational with minimal capital investments. Perhaps the NTDC should adopt incentives such as tax reductions or holidays for SMTEs that implement preparedness measures against floods. Also, regulatory measures from the NTDC could be enforced on insurance companies, mandating them to charge higher premiums from SMTEs that have no preparedness measures in place. While such proposed measures may seem stringent, it is necessary if the projected 4.3% (NGN3.61bn or approximately US$10m annually) that tourism will contribute to Nigeria's GDP by 2028 wants to be achieved (Nwanne 2018).

5.3 *Failure to utilise nonstructural measures*

Lagos State government has invested in structural and nonstructural measures to tackle flood risks. These include a flood awareness campaign, the establishment of an emergency control centre by the Lagos State Emergency Management Agency (SEMA), drainage construction and the provision of weather warnings by the Nigerian Meteorological Agency (NIMET), among other things (Figure 12.3) (Adelekan, 2016). Yet, no literature indicated that SMTEs worked closely with any of these agencies or used early weather warnings to scale up flood preparedness. The common disaster management planning practices put in place to minimise the adverse effects of floods include drain construction in front of accommodations, the clearing of drainage systems, the use of sandbags and the building of high walls to prevent floodwater from entering accommodation establishments, among other things (Adelekan, 2010, 2016). While such preparations are necessary, plugging into nonstructural measures like early weather warnings is essential to protect, and minimise damages to, fixed assets, infrastructures and human lives.

SMTEs stand to benefit from the utilisation of early weather warnings. Firstly, confidence would be boosted if risk messages were inserted on the websites of accommodation enterprises explaining what prospective tourists could expect in the event of heavy rainfall that could result in flash flooding, and what measures are in place to ensure the safety of guests. Implementing this strategy is crucial at a time when guests use hashtags in online ratings to express their experiences at accommodation establishments. Secondly, the rainy season may be the time for SMTEs to reduce costs on online advertising or to re-strategise their advertising based on the seasonal weather outlook for Lagos. Scott, Lemieux and Malone (2011), for example, document that a tourism brochure for Brittany in France informs tourists that prejudice and misconceptions have depicted Brittany as a region notorious for rain when just breathing its unique, rich iodine sea air is, in fact, an opportunity to enjoy nature's free health properties.

It is noteworthy to mention that no literature documented the presence of a laid-down protocol that provides tourists with stepwise actions to be taken in the event of a flood or any other disaster. A laid-down protocol is necessary, as tourists from different geographical regions may under- or overestimate the risks associated with floods (Law, 2006). Also, a study conducted in the Asia-Pacific region suggests that retreat organisers, tour operators and travel agents from Europe request "risk management information and audit hotel risk management" (UNISDR, 2015: 1). This suggests that any SMTE that develops standardised protocols that meet the needs of tourists is likely to have a competitive advantage over its contemporaries. A plausible reason why no SMTEs have laid-down

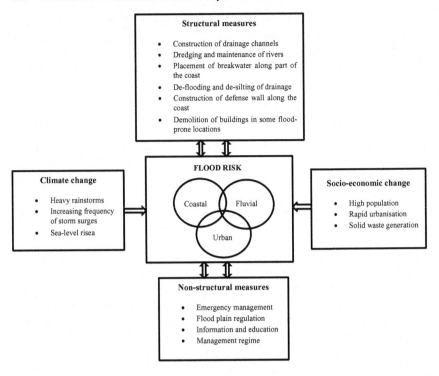

Figure 9.3 Flood risk management by public agents in Lagos.
Source: Adelekan, 2016.

protocol in place is the absence of a certification scheme for tourism establish-ments in Nigeria that shows compliance with the laid-down standards for extreme weather preparedness.

5.4 Lack of cohesion among tourist accommodation operators

Another limitation is the lack of a structure (regional monthly meetings) or plat-form (online) that brings SMTEs together. With a structure that brings SMTEs together, it will be much easier for agencies like the Specialty Equipment Mar-ket Association (SEMA) and the Nigerian Meteorological Agency (NIMET) to disseminate vital information that will facilitate flood preparedness. The lack of communication, as Hystada and Keller (2006) argue, was one of the rea-sons why some small tourist businesses in Kelowna, British Columbia, Canada, were affected adversely by a forest fire disaster, despite the well-planned and well-practiced emergency response plan put in place by the provincial gov-ernment. To concretise the need for a structure or platform that brings SMTEs together, key industry leaders in the Asia-Pacific region suggest that hotels working with other hotels in a region is crucial for building adaptive capacity and promoting early adoption of laid-down procedures (UNISDR, 2015). Thus, mediums that bring SMTEs in Lagos together can be used, among other issues relating to tourism, to share experiences and concerns, including tips on adapting to flooding, especially from those with an accommodation that has been affected in the past. As Southon and Van der Merwe (2018) argue, learning from previous flood events is useful to enhance the knowledge of tourist accommodation managers, which is necessary to build resilience to future flood events.

6 Conclusion and recommendations

Tourism is expected to directly contribute 1.6%, the equivalent of NGN1 366bn (US$3.8bn), to Nigeria's GDP by 2024 (Metilelu, 2016). For a nation striving relentlessly to diversify its economy from crude oil, the need for the tourist accommodation sector, which has been identified as a key priority area for economic growth and development (Metilelu, 2016), to prepare adequately for extreme weather like flooding cannot be taken for granted. According to Shepherd et al. (2013), increased occurrences of extreme weather will become the norm in Nigeria by 2030. By unpacking relevant literature, this chapter analysed the factors that undermine flood preparedness among SMTEs in Lagos, Nigeria, one of the most-visited destinations by local and international tourists.

Factors that hamper flood preparedness include downplaying the severity of flood disasters, especially by operators and managers whose establishments have never been affected adversely by floods. The tendency towards flood denial among some accommodation operators and managers is not implausible because they assume that their establishments are situated in a 'buffer zone' where the severe effect of flooding will not be felt. A lack of financial and human capital, a lack of cohesion among tourist accommodation establishments and failure to utilise early weather warnings are some additional factors that undermine flood preparedness. In proffering possible solutions to facilitate flood preparedness, incentives such as tax reductions or holidays for SMTEs that implement preparedness measures, such as retrofitting old materials with flood-resistant building materials, are essential. Also, a platform that brings SMTEs together to ease emergency information dissemination by SEMA and NIMET is crucial to ensure adequate flood preparedness.

References

Adelekan I. O. (2010). Vulnerability of poor urban coastal communities to flooding in Lagos, Nigeria. *Environment and Urbanisation*, 22, 443–450.

Adelekan, I. O. (2016). Flood risk management in the coastal city of Lagos, Nigeria. *Journal of Flood Risk Management*, 9, 255–264.

Adelekan, I. O. & Asiyanbi, A. P. (2016). Flood risk perception in flood-affected communities in Lagos, Nigeria. *Natural Hazards*, 80, 445–469.

Agrawala, S., Moehner, A., El Raey, M., Conway, D., Van Aalst, M., Hagenstad, M., & Smith, J. (2004). *Development and climate change in Egypt: Focus on coastal resources and the Nile*. Paris: Organisation for Economic Co-operation and Development.

Ajibade, I. & McBean, G. (2014). Climate extremes and housing rights: A political ecology of impacts, early warning and adaptation constraints in Lagos slum communities. *Geoforum*, 55, 76–86.

Anderson, A. (2012). Climate change education for mitigation and adaptation. *Journal of Education for Sustainable Development, 6*(2), 191–206.

Asiyanbi, A. P. (2015). 'I don't get this climate stuff!' Making sense of climate change among the corporate middle class in Lagos. *Public Understanding of Science, 24*(8), 1007–1024.

Atta-ur-Rahman & Khan, A. N. (2011). Analysis of flood causes and associated socioeconomic damages in the Hindukush region. *Natural Hazards, 59*(3), 1239–1260.

Bada O. (2013). *The emerging role of fashion tourism and the need for a development strategy in Lagos, Nigeria. Case study: Lagos fashion and design week, thesis.* Centria University of Applied Sciences, Kokkola-Pietarsaar Unit, Finland.

Balala, N. (2018, February 2). Tourism sector performance report–2018. Retrieved from http://ktb.go.ke/wp-content/uploads/2019/01/Tourism-Performance-2018-Presentation-Final2.pdf.

Bankole, A. (2002). The Nigerian tourism sector: Economic contribution, constraints and opportunities. *Journal of Hospitality Financial Management, 10*, 71–89.

Becken, S. (2013). Developing a framework for assessing resilience of tourism subsystems to climatic factors. *Annals of Tourism Research, 43*, 506–528.

Bernard, K. & Cook, S. (2015). Luxury tourism investment and flood risk: Case study on unsustainable development in Denarau island resort in Fiji. *International Journal of Disaster Risk Reduction, 14*, 302–311.

Changnon, S. A. (1998). The historical struggle with floods on the Mississippi river basin –impacts of recent floods and lessons for future flood management and policy. *Water International, 23*(4), 263.

Ebhuoma, E. & Simatele, D. (2019). "We know our terrain": Indigenous knowledge preferred to scientific systems of weather forecasting in the Delta State of Nigeria. *Climate and Development, 11*(2), 112–123.

Emmanuel, O. K. (2014). Religious tourism and sustainable development: A study of eyo festival in Lagos, Nigeria. *International Journal of Social Science and Education, 4*(2), 524–535.

Eruotor, V. (2014, June 6). *The economic importance of tourism in developing countries: Case study of Lagos, Nigeria.* Unpublished thesis, Central University of Applied Sciences, Kokkola-Pietarsaari Unit, Finland. Retrieved from https://core.ac.uk/download/pdf/38104881.pdf.

Faling. W., Tempelhoff, J. W. N. & Van Niekerk, D. (2012). Rhetoric or action: Are South African municipalities planning for climate change? *Development Southern Africa, 29*(2), 241–257.

Festus, A. A. (2014). An assessment of the impact of culture and tourism on international public relations practice: A study of Nigerian Tourism Development Corporation (NTDC). *Journal of Culture, Society and Development, 4*, 11–18.

Fitchett, J. M., Robinson, D. & Hoogendoorn, G. (2017). Climate suitability for tourism in South Africa. *Journal of Sustainable Tourism, 25*(6), 851–867.

Hamzah, J., Habibah, A., Buang, A., Jusoff, K., Toriman, M. E., Mohd Fuad, M.J., Er, A. C. & Azima, A. M. (2012). Flood disaster, impacts and the tourism providers' responses: The Kota Tinggi experience. *Advances in Natural and Applied Sciences, 6*(1), 26–32.

Hoogendoorn, G. & Fitchett, J. M. (2016). Tourism and climate change: A review of threats and adaptation strategies for Africa. *Current Issues in Tourism, 21*(7), 742–759.

Hystada, P. & Keller, P. (2006). Disaster management: Kelowna tourism industry's preparedness, impact and response to a 2003 major forest fire. *Journal of Tourism and Hospitality Management, 13*, 44–58.

Idahosa, L. & Ebhuoma, E. (2020). Limitations to Sustainable Resource Management in the Global South: Evidence from the Accommodation Industry in the Cape. *Tourism and Hospitality Management, 26* (2), 337– 358.

Ingram, A., Jamieson, R., Lynch, P. & Bent, R. (2000). Questioning the impact of the 'graduatization' of the managerial labour force upon the management of human resources in the Scottish hotel industry. *Journal Consumer Studies and Home Economics, 24*(4), 212–222.

Intergovernmental Panel on Climate Change (IPCC). (2014, October 19). *Africa. Intergovernmental Panel on Climate Change.* Retrieved from https://www.ipcc.ch/pdf/ assessment-report/ar5/wg2/WGIIAR5-Chap22_FINAL.pdf

International Federation of Red Cross and Red Crescent Societies (IFRC). (2013, April 20). *Disaster preparedness saves lives and saves money.* Retrieved from https://www.ifrc.org/fr/nouvelles/nouvelles/common/disasters-preparedness-saves-lives-and-saves-money-61204/.

International Human Dimension Programme (IHDP) on Global Environmental Change. (2012, February 4). *Background on coastal zones.* Retrieved from http://www.ihdp.unu. edu/article/coasts.

Kilungu, H., Leemans, R., Munishi, P. K. T. & Amelung, B. (2017). Climate change threatens major tourist attractions and tourism in Serengeti National Park, Tanzania. *Climate Change Adaptation in Africa, 375–392.*

Lagos State Government. (2012, February 4). *Lagos state government official website on population.* Retrieved from http://www.lagosstate.gov.ng/index.php?page= subpage&spid=12&mnu=null.

Law, R. (2006). The perceived impact of risks on travel decisions. *International Journal of Tourism Research, 8*(4), 289–300.

Mahadew, R. & Appadoo, K. (2019). Tourism and climate change in Mauritius: Assessing the adaptation and mitigation plans and prospects. *Tourism Review, 74*(2), 204–215.

Maplecroft. (2012, January 30). World's fastest growing populations increasingly vulnerable to the impacts of climate change – 4th global atlas reports. Retrieved from http:// maplecroft.com/about/news/ccvi_2012.html.

Metilelu, O. O. (2016). Human capital development trends in the hospitality and tourism industry: A case of southwest Nigeria. *African Journal of Hospitality, Tourism and Leisure, 5*(4), 1–16.

Mondlane, A. I. (2010). *GIS-based flood risk management – the case of Limpopo river basin in Mozambique.* 10th International Multidisciplinary Scientific Geoconference and EXPO – Modern Management of Mine Producing, Geology and Environmental Protection, SGEM 2010, *1,* 1019–1026.

Monroe, M., Plate, R., Oxarart, A., Bowers, A. & Chaves, W. (2017). Identifying effective climate change education strategies: A systematic review of the research. *Environmental Education Research,* 1–22.

Nkwunonwo, U. C., Whitworth, M. & Baily, B. (2015). A review and critical analysis of the efforts towards urban flood reduction in the Lagos region of Nigeria. *Natural Hazards and Earth Systems Sciences, 3,* 3897–3923.

Nwanne, C. (2018, April 7). *Report predicts growth for Nigeria's domestic tourism.* Retrieved from https://guardian.ng/saturday-magazine/report-predicts-growth-for-nigerias-domestic-tourism/.

Ojomo, E., Elliott, M., Amjad, U. & Bartram, J. (2015). Climate change preparedness: A knowledge and attitudes study in Southern Nigeria. *Environments, 2,* 435–448.

Okonkwo, C. H. (2014, April 18). *The socio-economic contribution of tourism in Nigeria and North Cyprus: A comparative approach.* Published Maters in Business

Administration Thesis frp, Cyprus International University. Retrieved from https://www.grin.com/document/276394.

Okoye, C. B. & Ojeh, V. N. (2015). Mapping of flood prone areas in surulere, Lagos, Nigeria: A GIS approach. *Journal of Geographic Information System, 7*, 158–176.

Oladipo, E. (2010, February 3). *Towards enhancing the adaptive capacity of Nigeria: A review of the country's state of preparedness for climate change adaptation.* Report submitted to Heinrich Boll Foundation. Retrieved from https://s3.amazonaws.com/academia.edu.documents/31030940/Nigeria_Prof_Oladipo_final_CGA_study.pdf?response-content-disposition=inline%3B%20filename%3DTOWARDS_ENHANCING_THE_ADAPTIVE_CAPACITY.pdf&X-Amz-Algorithm=AWS4-HMAC-SHA256&X-Amz-Credential=AKIAIWOWYYGZ2Y53UL3A%2F20200203%2Fus-east-1%2Fs3%2Faws4_request&X-Amz-Date=20200203T091029Z&X-Amz-Expires=3600&X-Amz-SignedHeaders=host&X-Amz-Signature=7638d87214a1e0c5c884e9c150d50403c9da3c2e8494870177ae68bdb57c17eb.

Olawale, J. (2014, April 18). *Yoruba festivals and holidays in Nigeria.* Retrieved from https://www.legit.ng/1143388-yoruba-festivals-holidays-nigeria.html.

Orchiston, C. (2013). Tourism business preparedness, resilience and disaster planning in a region of high seismic risk: The case of the Southern Alps, New Zealand. *Current Issues in Tourism, 16*(5), 477–494.

Orient News. (2010, February 1). *Eko Atlantic: Live and work.* Retrieved from https://www.ekoatlantic.com/latestnews/press-clipping/lagos-bar-beach-moves-from-ocean-violence-to-eko-atlantic-city/.

Ovat, O. O. (2003). Tourism and economic development in Nigeria: an empirical investigation. *Global Journal of Social Sciences, 2*(1), 33–44.

Pelling, M., Leck, H., Pasquini, L., Ajibade, I., Osuteye, E., Parnell, S., et al. (2018). Africa's urban adaptation transition under a 1.5° climate. *Current Opinion in Environmental Sustainability, 31*, 10–15.

Pennington-Gray, L., Thapa, B., Kaplanidou, K., Cahyanto, I. & McLaughlin, E. (2011). Crisis planning and preparedness in the United States tourism industry. *Cornell Hospitality Quarterly, 52*(3), 312–320.

Eiser, R. J., Bostrom, A., Burton, I., Johnston, D. M., McClure, J., Paton, D., Van der Pligt, J. & White, M. P. (2012). Risk interpretation and action: A conceptual framework for responses to natural hazards. *International Journal of Disaster Risk Reduction, 1*, 5–16.

Ritchie, B. W. (2008). Tourism disaster planning and management: From response and recovery to reduction and readiness. *Current Issues in Tourism, 11*(4), 315–348.

Rogerson, C. M. (2016). Climate change, tourism and local economic development in South Africa. *Local Economy, 31*(1–2), 322–331.

Rosa, N. (2018, January 13). #Africa Month: *The rise of Nigeria - why we should be paying attention to this travel market.* Retrieved from https://www.bizcommunity.com/Article/196/373/176753.html.

Rosselló, J. & Waqas, A. (2015). The use of tourism demand models in the estimation of the impact of climate change on tourism. *Revista Turismo em An_alise, 26*(1), 4.

Sanni, S. & Chile, N. (2018, January 13). *Nigerian millennials fuel domestic tourism.* Retrieved from https://www.reuters.com/article/us-nigeria-tourism/nigerian-millennials-fuel-domestic-tourism-idUSKCN1NL1MI.

Scott, D. (2011). Why sustainable tourism must address climate change. *Journal of Sustainable Tourism, 19*(1), 17–34.

Scott D., Lemieux C. & Malone, L. (2011). Climate services to support sustainable tourism and adaptation to climate change. *Climate Research, 47*, 111–122.

Scott, D., Gössling, S. & Hall, C. M. (2012). International tourism and climate change. *WIREs Climate Change, 3,* 213–232.

Shaw, G., Saayman, M. & Saayman, A. (2012). Identifying risks facing the South African tourism industry. *South African Journal of Economic Management Systems, 15*(2), 190–206.

Shepherd, A., Mitchell, T., Lewis, K., Lenhardt, A., Jones, L. & Muir-Wood, R. (2013, November 24). *The geography of poverty, disasters and climate extremes in 2030.* Retrieved from http://www.odi.org/sites/odi.org.uk/files/odi-assets/publications-opinion-files/8633.pdf.

Southon, M. P. & Van der Merwe, C. D. (2018). Flooded with risks of opportunities: Exploring flooding impacts on tourist accommodation. *African Journal of Hospitality, Tourism and Leisure, 7*(1), 1–16.

Taxaide. (2019, April 19). *Unlocking Nigeria's tourism potentials.* Retrieved from https://taxaide.com.ng/2019/04/18/unlocking-nigerias-tourism-potentials/.

The Guardian. (2019, February 4). *Nigeria: Lagos and the tourism goldmine.* Retrieved from https://allafrica.com/stories/201901310737.html.

The Weather Channel. (2018, February 2). *Exodus: the climate migration crisis.* Retrieved from https://features.weather.com/exodus/chapter/page/2/.

This Day. (2012, February 4). *Nigeria: Lagos ocean surge levels kuramo beach.* Retrieved from https://allafrica.com/stories/201208190103.html.

United Nations Conference on Trade and Development (UNCTAD). (2017, January 13). *Economic development in Africa: Tourism for transformative and inclusive growth.* Retrieved from https://unctad.org/en/PublicationsLibrary/aldcafrica2017_en.pdf.

United Nations Office for Disaster Risk Reduction (UNISDR). (2015, April 17). *Developing strategies to strengthen the resilience of hotels to disasters. A scoping study to guide the development of the Hotel Resilient Initiative.* Retrieved from https://reliefweb.int/sites/reliefweb.int/files/resources/ScopingStudy_HotelResilientInitiative_0.pdf.

United Nations World Tourism Organization (UNWTO). (2007). *Davos Declaration: Climate change and tourism–responding to global challenges.* Davos, Switzerland, 3 October.

Wang, J., & Ritchie, B. W. (2012). Understanding accommodation managers' crisis planning intention: An application of the theory of planned behaviour. *Tourism Management, 33*(5), 1057–67.

World Bank. (2011, February 1). *Transformation through tourism: harnessing tourism for growth and improved livelihoods.* Washington, DC: The World Bank. Retrieved from http://documents.worldbank.org/curated/en/115431468204252582/pdf/700990ESW0P1170ing0the0Economic0Pow.pdf.

World Travel and Tourism Council. (2020, June 3). *Economic impact report.* Retrieved from https://wttc.org/Research/Economic-Impact.

World Population Review. (2020, April 24). *Lagos population 2020.* Retrieved from https://worldpopulationreview.com/world-cities/lagos-population/.

Wyss, R., Abegg, B. & Luthe, T. (2014). Perceptions of climate change in a tourism governance context. *Tourism Management Perspectives, 11,* 69–76.

10 Climate change impacts and adaptation strategies for tourism hotspots Mombasa and Cape Town

Francini van Staden

10.1 Introduction

For the African continent, the tourism sector is showing steady to fast growth, and this trend is mirrored for sub-Saharan Africa. Africa's international tourist arrivals increased by 7% in 2018, amounting to 67 million international tourists and earnings of US$38 billion (United Nations Tourism Organization [UNWTO], 2019). For sub-Saharan Africa, tourism is the fastest-growing economic sector (Messerli, 2011) and 33.8 million tourist arrivals were recorded in 2012, a significant increase from only 6.7 million in 1990 (Christie et al., 2014). Africa has been identified as highly vulnerable to the impacts of climate change (Intergovernmental Panel on Climate Change [IPCC], 2014a; Niang et al., 2014), exacerbated by an increasingly faster pace of climate change (Adger et al., 2003; Bauer & Scholz 2010). There are notable variances in the expected climate change and sectoral impacts for sub-Saharan Africa – the strongest degree of reduced rainfall and drought risk is for South Africa, with East Africa, including Kenya, at a higher risk of flooding (Serdeczny et al., 2017). Although low- and high-emission scenarios lead to different climate change projections, even the low-emission scenario anticipates a substantial increase in extreme heat occurrences across sub-Saharan Africa (Serdeczny et al., 2017). Considering the region's reliance on tourism as a mechanism for economic development (Binns & Nel, 2002), sustainable urban tourism comes into focus when relating climate change adaptation and sustainable development. Sustainable urban tourism also prominently links to the 2030 Agenda for Sustainable Development and several of the Sustainable Development Goals (SDGs), as was unanimously adopted in 2015 by United Nations members.

10.2 Interconnections between climate and tourism

The IPCC defined climate change as a global phenomenon of climate variability, attributed to anthropogenic influence and or natural processes that are internal to the global climate system (2014a); the United Nations Framework Convention on Climate Change (UNFCCC) emphasises direct and indirect human activity altering the composition of the global atmosphere (1992). Climate risk is defined as the potential for adverse consequences on lives; livelihoods; health; infrastructure; ecosystems and species; economic, social and cultural assets and services; and such consequences in the context of uncertain outcomes (IPCC, 2014a). Three conceptual components of climate risk are hazard, exposure and vulnerability (Cardona et al., 2012; IPCC, 2014b; Oppenheimer et al., 2015). The urban areas of developing countries are described as regions of increased risk (Hallegatte et al., 2016; Revi et al., 2014; Romero-Lankao & Dodman, 2011) and have been linked to declining international investment for local economic development, negative impacts on environmental and cultural assets, disruptions to operations and transport – all of which are likely to affect tourist demand patterns (Scott et al., 2016). Based on impacts and risks, adaptation is needed and involves the adjustment of systems to moderate or cope with climate change impacts (Adger et al., 2003).

Climate is both a tourism attraction and a tourism driver, influencing when and where tourists travel and how tourism interactions are experienced (Hoogendoorn & Fitchett, 2018; Scott et al., 2012). Since the 1960s, literature described this relationship alongside the rise of climate and weather-related research, with weather generally linked to favourable tourism experiences (Becken, 2013; Falk, 2014; Martín, 2005). As a global concern, the link between climate change and tourism extends to how tourism contributes to climate change. Tourism substantially contributes to global greenhouse gas (GHG) emissions – the emission of substances that fuel climate change by their radiatively active nature (IPCC, 2012). Estimates reveal that the global tourism sector may contribute anywhere between 5% and 14% of all global anthropogenic emissions (Hall et al., 2015; UNWTO 2008). In the current scenario, approximately 75% of emissions come from transport-related tourist activities, with air transport being the key contributor. Further estimates have also suggested that the remaining 21% of tourism-driven emissions can be attributed to the industry's accommodation sector (UNWTO, 2008). A growing body of literature has noted the degree to which climate change is already impacting tourism (Köberl et al., 2016; Scott et al., 2012; Smith, 1990), with more recent discussions highlighting the knowledge gaps that persist despite increasing levels of climate change research (Becken, 2013; Gasper et al., 2011; Kaján & Saarinen, 2013) and a lack of investigations surrounding the implementation of adaptation strategies (Pandy, 2017). Climate change impacts are not uniform, and not all destinations will be impacted equally or negatively. The dynamics of climate change risks therefore remain diverse (Jurgilevich et al., 2017), and understanding these dynamics are crucial for effective adaptive strategies and their implementation (Bhave et al., 2016; Dilling et al., 2015). The interconnection between climate change and tourism thus revolves around climate being a positive driver of tourism; however, climate change places tourism in specific regions at risk by impacting tourism's overall sustainability and long-term viability (Hoogendoorn & Fitchett, 2018). An important shift is taking place in literature that links this interconnection to that of sustainable tourism and sustainability principles (Ashworth & Page, 2011; Edwards et al., 2008; Timur & Getz, 2009). This is expanding understandings on the potential of urban tourism to respond to sustainable development challenges (Aall & Koens, 2019; Paskaleva-Shapira, 2007).

This chapter considered tourism destination hotspots of Mombasa in Kenya and the city of Cape Town in South Africa within the framework of the risks and the impacts associated with climate change. Both cities are recognised as highly vulnerable to the direct and indirect impacts of climate change, including similarities of rainfall variability, drought and water stress, flooding, sea-level rise, storm surges and loss of biodiversity. The chapter provides an overview of the interplay between climate change and tourism with references from secondary published literature. This discussion was expanded through case-specific information for Mombasa, Kenya, and Cape Town, South Africa. The chapter described each case separately, reviewing climate change and tourism policies and strategies from both national and local level governments as key documents. This information was applied comparatively towards an analysis of policy integration and mainstreaming that would support sustainable urban tourism in Mombasa and Cape Town, with findings and recommendations made.

10.3 Tourism and climate trends: Mombasa, Kenya

Mombasa is Kenya's second-largest city after Nairobi and had an estimated population of 925 137 in 2009 (National Council for Population Dynamics [NCPD], 2013), with the Mombasa coastal region known for high levels of urban poverty. It continues to develop as a major urban centre and is East Africa's largest seaport city. It is a low-lying coastal city at 45 m above sea level and with a coastal plain up to 6 km wide and a high concentration of tourism facilities and infrastructure. The city's tourism appeal includes its combination of marine and coral environment, mangroves, warm water for a variety of coastal activities and a rich local culture and history. Fort Jesus on Mombasa Island is the city's most visited tourist attraction and is one of two local UNESCO World Heritage Sites, together with the sacred Kaya forests, the home to the Mijikenda tribes. Business tourism is becoming a priority niche for Mombasa, alongside its long-established coastal tourism (Kenya Ministry of Tourism and Wildlife, 2017). Mombasa's coastal tourism is, however, a cause of strain on the coastal environment, impacting coral reefs and mangroves (Visser & Njuguna, 1992).

At a national level, tourism represents Kenya's fastest-growing economic sector (Njoya & Seetaram, 2018). Annual tourism earnings increased by 31.2% between 2017 and 2018, and the reported increase in international tourist arrivals was attributed to growth and market union in the aviation and transport sector, as well as shared economy growth (Kenya Ministry of Tourism and Wildlife, 2018). Although estimates are that Kenya's tourism sector contributed approximately 10% to the national GDP, greater impact is evident from how tourism is embedded in the Kenyan economic fabric, including the high percentage of the tourism purchases originating from domestic sources and suppliers, making the sector highly integrated economically with strong backward multipliers (World Bank, 2017). Mombasa's international tourist arrivals increased by 46% in 2018 (Kondo, 2018), and this can, in part, be attributed to improved travel connectivity, including daily nonstop flights between Kenya and New York, the new Standard

Gauge Railway, offering express rail between Mombasa and Nairobi, and the upgrading of Mombasa's Moi International Airport.

Kenya has an arid to semi-arid climate with a high susceptibility to drought and low rainfall, but also a wide range of annual precipitation variability (Uhe et al., 2018). In recent years, Kenya has experienced several extreme weather patterns including more than a decade of drought since 2000. Extreme patterns have been linked to the El Niño–Southern Oscillation and La Niña as negative phase; strong correlations exist between the phenomena El Niño–Southern Oscillation and the Indian Ocean Dipole (Uhe et al., 2018). Extreme events are also known to be triggered in cases where these phenomena are independent of each other (Ashok et al., 2003). The Indian Ocean Dipole phenomenon has been associated with destructive flooding and, in 2019, displaced thousands of Mombasa's citizens and caused significant infrastructure damages. Although Mombasa has a history of extreme climate events and severe flooding is a regular occurrence (Awuor et al., 2008), the frequency and intensity of flooding are increasing due to climate change. Flood impacts are far-reaching and include cumulative human health impacts – waterborne diseases of which cholera outbreaks are a main concern, and other indirect impacts, including the spread of vector-borne diseases, such as malaria. Urban design can worsen the impact and, in the case of Mombasa, its infrastructure and hardened surface designs are recorded as worsening flood impacts (Kithiia & Dowling, 2010). The context of Mombasa's tourism impacts arises from climate change projections for its low-lying coastal environment and its island nature within the Indian Ocean. The IPCC (2013) projected an upper boundary of 0.82 m for global mean sea-level rise by 2100, while it is projected that sea-level rise of only 0.3 m – well below the global mean – will inundate up to 17% of Mombasa (Awuor et al., 2008). As Mombasa's tourism facilities are mostly within the city's coastal zone, these climate change projections will impact the local tourism sector through loss of coastline and environmental resources, loss or severe damaging of historic and cultural tourist attractions, such as Fort Jesus, and a change in shape and potential access to beaches, islands and other coastal attractions. Infrastructure and populations in low-lying coastal zones are at risk and will create pressure on the city's capacity for a growing tourism market, especially if water supply, human health, infrastructure, transport and the natural environment suffer sudden changes because of climate change.

10.3.1 Policy context

Kenya's National Climate Change Action Plan (2013) linked adaptation and development as complementary goals and proposes achieving this through the mainstreaming of climate change action across aspects of development planning. The Kenya Vision 2030 taps into the socioeconomic significance of the country's fast-growing tourism sector and promotes this as a key driver of national economic growth (Kenya Ministry of Wildlife and Tourism, 2017). Adaptation and climate actions are prioritised for the tourism sector at a national level through the National Adaptation Plan (2016). The National Adaptation Plan included tourism sector recommendations for short-, medium- and long-term adaptation within the overarching sector goal of enhancing tourism value chain resilience. It also indicates awareness for known adaptation challenges by calling for the integration of ecosystem and community-based approaches towards long-term feasibility and community support. It specified criteria for determining adaptation priority, namely short-term urgency and ease of implementation. This developed further to include priority adaptation actions in the National Climate Change Action Plan (2018), such as developing and implementing resilience actions plans for vulnerable tourism areas, expanding local sustainable tourism projects, guideline development on resource efficiency for tourism operation, governance strengthening and capacity-building programmes for sector climate resilience. For Mombasa, at a local level, climate change adaptation remains largely within this national governance context. One local-level document with reference to this context is the Mombasa District Development Plan (2002), which included projections for sea-level rise and resulting local impacts for Mombasa and its citizens, highlighting the urban poor and the lack of urban adaptation.

10.4 Tourism and climate trends: Cape Town, South Africa

Located in the southern peninsula of South Africa's Western Cape Province, Cape Town, with its population of 4.2 million people (Western Cape Government, 2017), is the country's second-largest city with an extensive coastline stretching over 240 km. Cape Town remains favoured for international tourism and destination visits (Rogerson & Rogerson, 2014). As one of South Africa's higher tourist-demand regions, it benefits from expanding air connectivity, such as a direct flight option between New York and Cape Town that was introduced in 2019. Two UNESCO World Heritage Sites are found in the city: the Cape Floral Region and Robben Island. Cape Town's city centre is highly popular with tourists, and most tourists spend time engaging with urban tourism, including heritage, cultural and retail tourism activities, as well as expanding niches, such as township tourism that uncovers ethnic and cultural identities in a post-apartheid South African urban context (Goudie et al., 1999). Tourism contributed 9% to South Africa's national GDP in 2018; a notable increase from the 4.6% contribution in 1993 prior to South Africa's democracy (Tourism, 2019). Tourism for 2018 was, however, reported as a second consecutive low-growth year with a 2.2% growth rate, which is lower than the global average growth rate of 6% for 2018 (Tourism, 2018, 2019). International arrivals declined by more than 1%, which contributed to the overall slower growth rate for 2018; the 2016-2018 multi-year Cape Town drought situation is thought to be one contributing factor amongst other factors leading to a decline in international arrivals during this time (Department of Tourism, 2019; Parliamentary Monitoring Group, 2018). Corresponding to the decline in arrivals, a 1.7% decline in GDP contribution was reported, in contrast to global trends of increased GDP contributions (Department of Tourism, 2018). Some recovery is noted, and for 2019, Cape Town reported a 2% increase in the year-on-year arrivals after the severity of the drought subsided. Yet South Africa's national forecasts made by the National Department of Tourism follow the recent 'below average global trends' – including a GDP contribution growth projection of 9.6% by 2029, which is lower than the expected 14% of global contributions (Department of Tourism, 2018).

South Africa's climate change projections within the current emissions context indicate temperature increases above the average 20th-century intensity and rate, and national projections include a general warming of 2.7°C and an annual rainfall reduction of between 30% and 50% (Schewe et al., 2014). By 2050, it is expected that the country's coastal regions will experience a temperature increase of 1.5°C, and the interior regions up to 3°C (DEA & DP, 2016). Cape Town is characterised by a warm and dry Mediterranean summer climate and a moderately wet winter season. This immediately places tourism in a context of concern – Mediterranean climate regions are considered climate 'hot spots' because of their warming and drying trends (Paeth et al., 2017). Climate change projections for the city include changed seasonality of rainfall and a likely overall decrease in annual average rainfall, higher maximum temperatures, increase in frequency and intensity of heat waves, an increase in wind strength (CSAG, 2016) and an increase in both frequency and intensity of storm occurrences (Brundrit, 2009). Sea-level rise projections vary between different climate change scenarios, with projections between 2.5 and 6.5 m of rise with variance based on locality and inundation of up to 4% (Brundrit, 2009). Coupled with extensive coastal development of an already dynamic coastline, storm surges and sea-level rises are exposing the city to a range of contemporary risks (Colenbrander et al., 2015). Arising from these climate change projections, Cape Town faces impacts such as loss or damaging of environmental resources, shifts in agricultural production regions with changes in food security, coastal erosion, human settlement and infrastructure damages, and increasing risk of vector-borne diseases. These impacts are not manifesting equally. The city remains challenged by the legacy of apartheid spatial planning and impacts are exposing this through settlement and infrastructure damages (Colenbrander et al., 2015). For Cape Town's tourism, climate change projections indicate sector risks and losses – including overall destination attractiveness, with weather attractiveness as an influencing factor, the sector's economic feasibility, water security and a shift in tourism activities as a result of cumulative impacts, such as potential changes faced by the wine industry or weather-dependent accessibility to Table Mountain as one of Cape Town's top tourist attractions.

10.4.1 Policy context

South Africa's National Climate Change Response Strategy (2004) recognised that the country at large is vulnerable to negative climate impacts. The strategy emphasised the need for adaptation and mitigation through responses and interventions that simultaneously serve as sustainable development drivers. Sustainability challenges are responded to by promoting actions that meet key policy criteria – responses and interventions that are sustainable, culturally compatible, community supported and socially acceptable. In a key contribution to climate change adaptation mainstreaming, the National Tourism and Climate Change Action Plan (Department of Tourism, 2011) combined the priorities of South African tourism and climate change adaptation with several proposed dynamic actions. This corresponds to the need for purposeful and integrated adaptive action and to avoid the isolation of adaptation actions (Pandy, 2017; Smit & Wandel, 2006). The National Climate Change Response Policy followed in 2011, and developing from this, the National Tourism and Climate Change Response Programme and Action Plan (Department of Tourism, 2012). Five specific actions were identified in this action plan, bearing responsibility for both the tourism sector and governance: improve understanding of tourism's vulnerability to climate change, reduce the GHG emissions from tourism activities, accurate and effective information-sharing from government to industry, development of a national implementation protocol and the maintaining of a positive climate change position in key markets.

The Draft National Climate Change Adaptation Strategy (2019) is the country's first national adaptation strategy offering a collective national vision for climate resilience by 2050. Flagship priorities have been identified for several sectors, including mining, energy and agriculture amongst others, but no implementation priorities have been identified for the tourism sector. The strategy, however, emphasised that climate change will exacerbate pressure on the natural environment with negative implications for the tourism industry. At local level, Cape Town is one of the country's leading cities in terms of mainstreaming adaptation and mitigation, including integration with urban planning (Mukheibir & Ziervogel, 2007; Pasquini et al., 2015). The City of Cape Town Responsible Tourism Policy was adopted in 2009 with a clear commitment to climate change adaptation. Similarly, the City of Cape Town Tourism Development Framework (2013-2017), identified climate change as a risk factor that impacts the tourism sector. Aligning to the national climate resilience vision, the City of Cape Town Climate Change Policy (2017) responded to the highly localised and contextual nature of climate change by identifying where and how resilience should be developed against climate change risks. It adopted several strategic areas for adaptation which equally enables adaptation through participatory approaches, including the protection of environmental resources and the sustaining and expanding of the ecotourism sector.

10.5 Analysing policy integration and mainstreaming

There are risk similarities between Mombasa and Cape Town relating to the coastal-city localities favoured by tourism, such as climate change projections of drought, sea-level rise and flood occurrences and the resulting tourism impacts of environmental resource loss, settlement and infrastructure damages, impaired basic services provision, water security and health risks. In comparing national-level policies of Kenya and South Africa, it is recognised that similar visions have been adopted to the extent that climate change adaptation is to be guided by biophysical and socioeconomic vulnerabilities and the need for resilience. The approaches taken towards these shared visions are, however, contrasting: Kenya adopted a 'low regrets' adaptation approach; South Africa adopted a 'no regrets' adaptation approach. Possibly explaining these different approaches is:

the availability of climate change data and projections; how well local context adaptation is understood from a risk-based approach, including the costs and benefits of adaptation; the availability of technologies; and track records or evidence of best practice. In analysing adaptation policies and strategies, it is important to emphasise that adaptation strategies may demonstrate effectiveness in reducing short-term risk probability, but they do not exclude the possibility of increased long-term vulnerability or risk exposure (Cardona et al., 2012). It further applies that adaptive actions are not necessarily sustainable, particularly if they are not based on local context; therefore, successful adaptation can be highly contextual (Kaján & Saarinen, 2013). The contrasting city-level adaptation policy contexts of Mombasa and Cape Town are thus indicative of the several key determinants in developing and adopting a 'low regrets' or 'no regrets' adaptation approach.

At the city level, Cape Town has a narration of climate change adaptation strategies and policies that are distinct from the national-level strategies and policies. This responds to a requirement for effective adaptation planning – recognising that risk is highly localised and uniquely shaped by local contexts (Ziervogel et al., 2017). Although climate change knowledge globally presents as incomplete with on-going uncertainties (Beland Lindahl et al., 2016), Cape Town policymaking is utilising multiple years of data and projection records that are available, some of which have been commissioned by the city itself. This has guided detailed, risk-based understandings of the city's infrastructure and settlements under various climate change scenarios and informed the Framework for Adaptation to Climate Change in the City of Cape Town (2006) and the Cape Town Climate Change Policy (2017).

In contrast, Mombasa is not benefitting from detailed climate change data and projections to inform its climate change adaptation. The city is largely reliant on national-level climate adaptation strategies and plans that provide a support framework but without a localised data and modeling context. This limitation aligns to what is described for the global South – adaptation strategies and their implementation are weakened by climate change uncertainty and gaps in projected impacts (Dessai et al., 2007; Refsgaard et al., 2013). Mombasa's limited city-level climate change data is evident in policy and planning, with the national-policy context only offering general adaptation guidance and lacking specific adaptation for the local tourism sector. Although climate change risks for Mombasa are widely acknowledged, adaptation is not yet strengthened by policy integration and mainstreaming into local government strategies. The case of Mombasa is likely affected by competing challenges within the global South context – urgencies of basic service provision, infrastructure, healthcare and education are superseding the priority of climate change adaptation and the financial, planning and policy intervention it requires (Hoogendoorn & Fitchett, 2018). Comparatively considering the respective policies highlighted another challenge; namely, that the messaging from the Kenya's National Tourism Blueprint 2030 and the Kenya National Adaptation Plan 2015–2030 are not fully aligned. The Tourism Blueprint promotes Mombasa beach node developments and the enhancing of coastal tourism development without reference to or guidance on the urgency for the tourism sector's climate change adaptation, whilst the

National Adaptation Plan identified Mombasa as particularly exposed to climate change impacts and calls for adaptation actions that will enhance the resilience of the tourism sector. This indicates the need for more proactive mainstreaming in the policy space, which could improve alignment at the local level for climate change adaptation and sustainable urban tourism development.

10.6 Conclusion

The impacts of climate change on the tourism sectors of Mombasa and Cape Town, alongside projections for more frequent and severe impacts, are elevating the prominence of climate change risk and resilience across climate change and tourism policies. Adaptation challenges are, however, evident, and more so as the tourism sectors of these respective cities are confronted by the challenge of adapting to climate change risks, which may have a slow onset according to the process of climate change, yet must be resilient to impacts that can occur more suddenly. The associated adaptation, development and governance challenges do not exist in isolation from opportunities, such as the combining of development deficits with adaptation deficits. Climate change adaptation for both cities are guided by national-level policies and action plans, with Cape Town presenting policy integration and mainstreaming at local level, which is strengthening its capacity to implement climate change adaptation and indicating early shifts towards climate change adaptation. Such integration and mainstreaming, however does not manifest across Mombasa's policymaking, which weakens its progress in climate change adaptation and isolates its tourism sector from climate change adaptation policies. At a broader level, this indicates that the United Nations' 2030 SDGs, – specifically SDG target 8.9: "development and implementation of sustainable tourism policies", SDG target 12.b: "monitoring of sustainable development impacts for sustainable tourism", Goal 11: "make cities and human settlements inclusive, safe, resilient and sustainable", and Goal 13: "take urgent action to combat climate change and its impacts" are coinciding priorities and that alignment through policy integration and mainstreaming can contribute to the progress of sustainable urban tourism. From the policy analysis, it was found that both cities face policy gaps that influence the effectiveness of their climate change adaptation, including the prominence of market-led adaptation rather than community-based adaptation. Policy gaps did not enable sustainable tourism urban development. In outcome, The following key recommendations are proposed:

- There must be support for climate change adaptation and tourism development in Mombasa through climate change research that advances risk-based understanding of the city's infrastructure, settlements and tourism facilities under various climate change scenarios.
- Expanding and strengthening There is a need to expand and strengthen Mombasa and Cape Town's climate change adaptation by involving the local sustainable urban tourism sectors through community-based approaches in the development and implementation of climate change adaptation.

References

Aall, C., & Koens, K. (2019). The Discourse on Sustainable Urban Tourism: The Need for Discussing More Than Overtourism. *Sustainability,* 11(15), 4228. doi:10.3390/su11154228

Adger, W. N., Huq, S., Brown, K., Conway, D., & Hulme, M. (2003). Adaptation to climate change in the developing world. *Progress in Development Studies*, 3(3), 179–195.

Ashok K., Guan Z., & Yamagata T. (2003). A look at the relationship between the ENSO and the Indian Ocean dipole. *Journal of the Meteorological Society of Japan,* 81(1), 41–56.

Ashworth, G. J., & Page, S. J. (2011). Urban tourism research: Recent progress and current paradoxes. *Tourism Management,* 32(1), 1–15.

Awuor, C. B., Orindi, V. A., & Ochieng Adwera, A. (2008). Climate change and coastal cities: the case of Mombasa, Kenya. *Environment and Urbanization, 20*(1), 231–242.

Bauer, S., & Scholz, I. (2010). Adaptation to climate change in Southern Africa: New boundaries for sustainable development?. *Climate and Development,* 2, 83–93. doi:10.3763/cdev.2010.0040

Becken, S. (2013). A review of tourism and climate change as an evolving knowledge domain. *Tourism Management Perspectives,* 6, 53–62.

Beland Lindahl, K., Baker, S., Rist, L., & Zachrisson, A. (2016). Theorising pathways to sustainability. *International Journal of Sustainable Development and World Ecology,* 23(5), 399–411.

Bhave, A. G., Conway, D., Dessai, S., & Stainforth, D. A. (2016). Barriers and opportunities for robust decision making approaches to support climate change adaptation in the developing world. *Climate Risk Management,* 14, 1–10.

Binns, T., & Nel, E. (2002). Tourism as a local development strategy in South Africa. *Geographical Journal*, 168(3), 235–247.

Brundrit, G. (2009). Global climate change and adaptation: City of Cape Town sea-level rise risk assessment. *Cape Town.* Retrieved from https://resource.capetown.gov.za/documentcentre/Documents/City%20research%20reports%20and%20review/Phase%205%20-%20SLRRA%20Full%20assessment+vulnerability%20Section_1_2_combined.pdf

Cardona, O. D., Van Aalst, M. K., Birkmann, J., Fordham, M., Mc Gregor, G., Rosa, P., ... Keim, M. (2012). Determinants of risk: exposure and vulnerability. In *Managing the Risks of Extreme Events and Disasters to Advance Climate Change Adaptation: Special Report of the Intergovernmental Panel on Climate Change* (pp. 65–108). New York: Cambridge University Press.

Christie, I., Fernandes, E., Messerli, H., & Twining-Ward, L. (2014). *Tourism in Africa: Harnessing tourism for growth and improved livelihoods.* Africa Development Form. Washington, DC: World Bank. doi: 10.1596/978-1-4648-0190-7

City of Cape Town (2006). *Framework for Adaptation to Climate Change in the City of Cape Town.* Retrieved from http://resource.capetown.gov.za/documentcentre/Documents/City%20strategies,%20plans%20and%20frameworks/Framework_for_Adaptation_to_Climate_Change_(FAC4T)_08_2006_38200713832_465.pdf

City of Cape Town (2009). *City of Cape Town Responsible Tourism Policy.* Retrieved from http://resource.capetown.gov.za/documentcentre/Documents/Bylaws%20and%20policies/Responsible%20Tourism%20Policy%20for%20the%20City%20of%20Cape%20Town%20-%20approved%20on%2026%20November%202009.pdf

City of Cape Town (2013). *Tourism Development Framework: 2013 to 2017.* Retrieved from https://resource.capetown.gov.za/documentcentre/Documents/City%20strategies,%20

plans%20and%20frameworks/Tourism%20Development%20Framework%20for%20 the%20City%20of%20Cape%20Town.pdf

City of Cape Town (2017). *Climate Change Policy, 2017.* (Policy Number 46824). Retrieved from http://resource.capetown.gov.za/documentcentre/Documents/City%20 strategies,%20plans%20and%20frameworks/Climate%20Change%20Policy_ 2019-20.pdf

City of Cape Town (2018). *State of Cape Town 2018.* Retrieved from http://resource. capetown.gov.za/documentcentre/Documents/City%20research%20reports%20 and%20review/State%20of%20Cape%20Town%202018.pdf

Climate Systems Analysis Group (CSAG) (2016). *Climate change projections for the City of Cape Town: An update based on most recent science.* University of Cape Town. Retrieved from http://www.csag.uct.ac.za/~cjack/CSAG_CCT%20report.pdf

Colenbrander, D., Cartwright, A., & Taylor, A. (2015). Drawing a line in the sand: managing coastal risks in the City of Cape Town. *South African Geographical Journal*, 97(1), 1–17.

Department of Environmental Affairs (2019). *Draft National Climate Change Adaptation Strategy. South African National Government.* Retrieved https://www.environment.gov.za/ sites/default/files/gazetted_notices/draftnational_climatechange_adaptationstrategy_ g42446gon644.pdf

Department of Environmental Affairs & Development Planning (DEA&DP) (2016). *Western Cape Climate Change Response Strategy Biennial Monitoring & Evaluation Report 2015/16.* Western Cape Government. Retrieved from https://www.westerncape. gov.za/eadp/files/atoms/files/Climate%20Change%20Response%20Strategy_ M%26E%20Report_2015-16.pdf

Department of Environmental Affairs & Tourism (2004). *A National Climate Change Response Strategy for South Africa. South African National Government.* Retrieved from https://www.environment.gov.za/sites/default/files/legislations/national_ climatechange_response_whitepaper.pdf

Department of Tourism (2011). Final Draft National Tourism and Climate Change Action Plan (2011). South African Government. Retrieved from https://www. tourism.gov.za/CurrentProjects/ResponsibleTourism/Responsible%20Tourism/ TourismClimateChangePlan-January2011_1.pdf

Department of Tourism (2012). *First National Tourism and Climate Change Response Programme and Action Plan. South African National Government.* Retrieved from https://tkp.tourism.gov.za/Documents/National%20Tourism%20and%20Climate%20 Change%20Response%20Programme%20and%20Action%20Plan.pdf

Department of Tourism (2018). *State of Tourism Report 2017/18.* South African National Government. Retrieved from https://www.tourism.gov.za/AboutNDT/Publications/ State%20of%20Tourism%20Report%20(STR)%202017-18.pdf

Department of Tourism (2019). *Bojanala.* Edition 3. South African National Government. Retrieved from https://www.tourism.gov.za/AboutNDT/Publications/Bojanala%20 Edition%20-%20January%202019.pdf

Dessai, S., O'Brien, K., & Hulme, M., (2007). Editorial: On uncertainty and climate change. *Global Environmental Change,* 17 (1), 1–3.

Dilling, L., Daly, M. E., Travis, W. R., Wilhelmi, O. V., & Klein, R. A. (2015). The dynamics of vulnerability: why adapting to climate variability will not always prepare us for climate change. *Wiley Interdisciplinary Reviews: Climate Change*, 6(4), 413–425.

Edwards, D., Griffin, T., & Hayllar, B. (2008). Urban tourism research: developing an agenda. *Annals of Tourism Research,* 35(4), 1032–1052.

Falk, M. (2014). Impact of weather conditions on tourism demand in the peak summer season over the last 50 years. *Tourism Management Perspectives, 9,* 24–35.

Gasper, R., Blohm, A., & Ruth, M. (2011). Social and economic impacts of climate change on the urban environment. *Current Opinion in Environmental Sustainability*, 3(3), 150–157.

Goudie, S. C., Khan, F., & Kilian, D. (1999). Transforming tourism: black empowerment, heritage and identity beyond apartheid. *South African Geographical Journal*, 81(1), 22–31.

Government of Kenya (2002). *Mombasa District Development Plan 2002–2008.* Nairobi: The Government Printer.

Government of Kenya (2016). *Kenya National Adaptation Plan: 2015–2030.* Retrieved from https://www4.unfccc.int/sites/NAPC/Documents%20NAP/Kenya_NAP_Final.pdf

Government of Kenya (2018). *National Climate Change Action Plan (Kenya): 2018–2022. Nairobi ministry of Environment and Forestry.* Retrieved from http://www.lse.ac.uk/GranthamInstitute/wp-content/uploads/2018/10/8737.pdf

Hall, C. M., Amelung, B., Cohen, S., Eijgelaar, E., Gössling, S., Higham, J., ... Aall, C. (2015). No time for smokescreen scepticism: A rejoinder to Shani and Arad. *Tourism Management*, 47, 341–347.

Hallegatte, S., Bangalore, M., Bonzanigo, L., Fay, M., Kane, T., Narloch, U., Rozenberg, J., Treguer, D., & Vogt-Schilb, A. (2016). *Shock Waves: Managing the Impacts of Climate Change on Poverty.* Climate Change and Development Series. Washington, DC: World Bank. doi:10.1596/978-1-4648-0673-5

Hoogendoorn, G., & Fitchett, J. M. (2018). Tourism and climate change: A review of threats and adaptation strategies for Africa. *Current Issues in Tourism*, 21(7), 742–759.

Intergovernmental Panel on Climate Change. (2012). *Managing the risks of extreme events and disasters to advance climate change adaptation: special report of the intergovernmental panel on climate change.* Field, C. B., Barros, V., Stocker, T. F., & Dahe, Q. (Eds.). Cambridge: Cambridge University Press.

Intergovernmental Panel on Climate Change. (2013). *Climate change 2013: The physical science basis. In Working Group I Contribution to the Fifth Assessment Report of the Intergovernmental Panel on Climate Change. Summary for Policymakers.* New York: Author.

Intergovernmental Panel on Climate Change (2014a). *Climate Change 2014: Synthesis Report. Contribution of Working Groups I, II and III to the Fifth Assessment Report of the Intergovernmental Panel on Climate Change.* R. K. Pachauri & L. A. Meyer (Eds.). Geneva: Author.

Intergovernmental Panel on Climate Change (2014b). *Climate Change 2014: Impacts, Adaptation, and Vulnerability. Part A: Global and Sectoral Aspects Contribution of Working Group II to the Fifth Assessment Report of the Intergovernmental Panel on Climate Change.* C. B. Field, V. Barros, D. Dokken, K. Mach, M. Mastrandrea, T. Bilir, ... L. White, (Eds.). Cambridge: Cambridge University Press.

Jurgilevich, A., Räsänen, A., Groundstroem, F., & Juhola, S. (2017). A systematic review of dynamics in climate risk and vulnerability assessments. *Environmental Research Letters*, 12(1), 013002.

Kaján, E., & Saarinen, J. (2013). Tourism, climate change and adaptation: a review. *Current Issues in Tourism,* 16(2), 37–41.

Kenya Ministry of Environment and Mineral Resources (2013). National Climate Change Action Plan. Retrieved from https://cdkn.org/wp-content/uploads/2013/03/Kenya-National-Climate-Change-Action-Plan.pdf

Kenya Ministry of Tourism and Wildlife (2017). *National Tourism Blueprint 2030.* September 2017. Retrieved from http://www.tourism.go.ke/wp-content/uploads/2018/06/NTB2030-Web-Version-1.0-1.pdf

Kenya Ministry of Tourism and Wildlife (2018). *Tourism Sector Performance Report 2018.* Retrieved from http://ktb.go.ke/wp-content/uploads/2019/01/Tourism-Performance-2018-Presentation-Final2.pdf

Kithiia, J., & Dowling, R. (2010). An integrated city-level planning process to address the impacts of climate change in Kenya: The case of Mombasa. *Cities*, 27(6), 466–475.

Köberl, J., Prettenthaler, F., & Bird, D. N. (2016). Modelling climate change impacts on tourism demand: A comparative study from Sardinia (Italy) and Cap Bon (Tunisia). *Science of the Total Environment*, 543, 1039–1053.

Kondo, V. (2018, October 28). *Tourist arrivals at Moi International Airport grows by 46pc Standard.* Retrieved from https://www.standardmedia.co.ke/article/2001300668/tourism-grows-in-the-kenyan-coast

Martín, M. B. G. (2005). Weather, climate and tourism a geographical perspective. *Annals of Tourism Research*, 32(3), 571–591.

Messerli, H. (2011). Transformation through tourism: Harnessing tourism as a development tool for improved livelihoods. *Tourism Planning and Development,* 8(3): 335–337.

Mukheibir, P., & Ziervogel, G. (2007). Developing a Municipal Adaptation Plan (MAP) for climate change: the city of Cape Town. *Environment and Urbanization,* 19(1), 143–158.

National Council for Population Dynamics (NCPD) (2013). *Kenya Population Situation Analysis.* Government of Kenya. Retrieved from https://www.unfpa.org/sites/default/files/admin-resource/FINALPSAREPORT_0.pdf

Niang, I., Ruppel, O. C., Abdrabo, M. A., Essel, A., Lennard, C., Padgham, J., & Urquhart, P. (2014). Africa. In: *Climate change 2014: impacts, adaptation and vulnerability. Contribution of Working Group II to the Fifth Assessment Report of the Intergovernmental Panel on Climate Change.* Cambridge: Cambridge University Press.

Njoya, E. T., & Seetaram, N. (2018). Tourism contribution to poverty alleviation in Kenya: A dynamic computable general equilibrium analysis. *Journal of Travel Research,* 57(4), 513–524.

Oppenheimer, M., Campos, M., Warren, R., Birkmann, J., Luber, G., O'Neill, B., ... Hsiang, S. (2015). Emergent risks and key vulnerabilities. In *Climate Change 2014 Impacts, Adaptation and Vulnerability: Part A: Global and Sectoral Aspects* (pp. 1039–1100). Cambridge: Cambridge University Press.

Paeth, H., Vogt, G., Paxian, A., Hertig, E., Seubert, S., & Jacobeit, J. (2017). Quantifying the evidence of climate change in the light of uncertainty exemplified by the Mediterranean hot spot region. *Global and Planetary Change* 151, 144–151.

Pandy, W. R. (2017). Tourism enterprises and climate change: Some research imperatives. *African Journal of Hospitality, Tourism and Leisure*, 6(4), 1–18.

Parliamentary Monitoring Group (2018). *Budgetary Review and Recommendation Report of the Portfolio Committee on Tourism.* Retrieved from https://pmg.org.za/page/PCTourBRRR

Paskaleva-Shapira, K. A. (2007). New paradigms in city tourism management: Redefining destination promotion. *Journal of Travel Research*, 46(1), 108–114.

Pasquini, L., Ziervogel, G., Cowling, R. M., & Shearing, C. (2015). What enables local governments to mainstream climate change adaptation? Lessons learned from two municipal case studies in the Western Cape, South Africa. *Climate and Development,* 7(1), 60–70.

Refsgaard, J. C., Arnbjerg-Nielsen, K., Drews, M., Halsnæs, K., Jeppesen, E., Madsen, H., Christensen, J. H., (2013). The role of uncertainty in climate change adaptation strategies—a Danish water management example. *Mitigation and Adaptation Strategies for Global Change,* 18(3), 337–359.

Revi, A., Satterthwaite, D. E., Aragón-Durand, F., Corfee-Morlot, J., Kiunsi, R. B. R., Pelling, M., ... Solecki, W. (2014). Urban areas. In *Climate Change 2014: Impacts, Adaptation, and Vulnerability. Part A: Global and Sectoral Aspects. Contribution of Working Group II to the Fifth Assessment Report of the Intergovernmental Panel on Climate Change.* Field, C.B., Barros, V., Dokken, V. R., Mach, K. J., Mastrandrea, M. D., Bilir, T. E., ... White, L. L. (Eds). Cambridge: Cambridge University Press.

Rogerson, C. M., & Rogerson, J. M. (2014). Urban tourism destinations in South Africa: Divergent trajectories 2001–2012. *Urbani ization*, 25, S189-S203.

Romero-Lankao, P. and Dodman, D., (2011). Cities in transition: transforming urban centers from hotbeds of GHG emissions and vulnerability to seedbeds of sustainability and resilience. *Current Opinion in Environmental Sustainability*, 3(3), 113–120.

Schewe, J., Heinke, J., Gerten, D., Haddeland, I., Arnell, N. W., Clark, D. B., ... Gosling, S. N. (2014). Multimodel assessment of water scarcity under climate change. *Proceedings of the National Academy of Sciences*, 111(9), 3245–3250.

Scott, D., Gössling, S., & Hall, C. M. (2012). International tourism and climate change. *Wiley Interdisciplinary Reviews: Climate Change*, 3(3), 213–232.

Scott, D., Hall, C. M., & Gössling, S. (2016). A review of the IPCC Fifth Assessment and implications for tourism sector climate resilience and decarbonization. *Journal of Sustainable Tourism*, 24(1), 8–30.

Serdeczny, O., Adams, S., Baarsch, F., Coumou, D., Robinson, A., Hare, W., ... Reinhardt, J. (2017). Climate change impacts in Sub-Saharan Africa: from physical changes to their social repercussions. *Regional Environmental Change*, 17(6), 1585–1600.

Smit, B., & Wandel, J. (2006). Adaptation, adaptive capacity and vulnerability. *Global Environmental Change*, 16(3), 282–292.

Smith, K. (1990). Tourism and climate change. *Land use Policy*, 7(2), 176–180.

Timur, S., & Getz, D. (2009). Sustainable tourism development: How do destination stakeholders perceive sustainable urban tourism?. *Sustainable Development*, 17(4), 220–232.

Uhe, P., Philip, S., Kew, S., Shah, K., Kimutai, J., Mwangi, E., ... Cullen, H. (2018). Attributing drivers of the 2016 Kenyan drought. *International Journal of Climatology*, 38, e554-e568.

United Nations. (2015). *Transforming our world: The 2030 agenda for sustainable development. United Nations Seventieth General Assembly 25,* New York.

United Nations Framework Convention on Climate Change. Secretariat. (1992). *United Nations framework convention on climate change.* UNFCCC: New York.

United Nations Tourism Organization (UNWTO) (2019). *International Tourism Highlights, 2019 Edition,* UNWTO, Madrid, pp. 2–3, doi: 10.18111/9789284421152

United Nations World Tourism Organization (UNWTO) (2008). *Climate Change and Tourism - Responding to Global Challenges*; UNWTO and UNEP, Madrid, pp. 13, 21 and 37.

Visser, N., & Njuguna, S. (1992). Environmental impacts of tourism on the Kenya coast. *Industry and Environment*, 15(3/4), 42–52.

Western Cape Government (2017). *Socio-Economic Profile: City of Cape Town.* Retrieved from https://www.westerncape.gov.za/assets/departments/treasury/Documents/Socio-economic-profiles/2017/city_of_cape_town_2017_socio-economic_profile_sep-lg_-_26_january_2018.pdf

World Bank (2017). *Standing Out from the Herd: An Economic Assessment of Tourism in Kenya.* World Bank, Nairobi © World Bank. Retrieved from https://openknowledge.worldbank.org/handle/10986/28577 License: CC BY 3.0 IGO.

Ziervogel, G., Pelling, M., Cartwright, A., Chu, E., Deshpande, T., Harris, L., ... Pasquini, L. (2017). Inserting rights and justice into urban resilience: a focus on everyday risk. *Environment and Urbanization*, 29(1), 123–138.

11 Risk of floods impacting tourism in the coastal cities of West Africa

A case study of Accra, Ghana

Raphael Ane Atanga and Tembi Tichaawa

11.1 Introduction

Although tourism may induce negative impacts on destination communities, it contributes positively to the socioeconomic development of nations (World Travel and Tourism Council [WTTC] 2020). According to the WTTC (2020), the industry accounted for 10.4% of the world's gross domestic product (GDP) in 2018, which amounts to about US$8.8 trillion. This contribution was 1.7 times higher than the mining sector (WTTC, 2020). Similarly, the tourism industry contributed to a total of about 319 million jobs across the world in 2018, yielding about 10% of all jobs. WTTC (2019) further confirmed that the travel and tourism sector was the fastest-growing sector in the world in 2018 compared to other sectors of the global economy. Thus far, tourism contributes positively to the economic, social and environmental development of developing nations (Rogerson, 2012). It is an important contributor towards achievement of the Sustainable Development Goals (SDGs). Consequently, Agenda 2063 of the Africa Union sees tourism as an engine for the socioeconomic development of Africa (Gowreesunkar, 2019).

However, the impact of extreme weather and climate events including floods, droughts, storms and high temperatures poses significant threats to the tourism industry (Hernandez & Ryan, 2011; Merz et al., 2010; Southon & Van der Merwe, 2018). Research shows that extreme weather and climate events negatively affect infrastructure and the environment, impacting the tourism industry in affected countries. From local to global scales, Douglas (2017) demonstrated the causes, teleconnections, vulnerability and impacts of floods on African cities, which directly affect infrastructure, environment and business with a likelihood to affect the tourism industry. The literature suggested that the poorly planned and managed nature of the cities, coupled with squatter settlements, explain the frequent flood occurrences in West African cities and their counterparts on the continent.

Literature further argues that coastal cities in West Africa are vulnerable to extreme flood events with the potential to affect development, including tourism (Twum & Abubakari, 2019). In line with this argument, Adjibade et al. (2016) applied the concept of sustainability to risk management and adaptation issues in Lagos. The authors illustrate that Lagos is exposed to frequent intense rainfall, coastal flooding and storm surges that negatively affect physical, social and economic development infrastructure in the city. Furthermore, Engel and Fink (2017) used specific flood events in Dakar as a coastal city and Ouagadougou as an inland city to support the argument that West African cities are predisposed to extreme precipitation and flood disasters. Other studies focused on flood risk in the cities of Lome and Cotonou to explain the urgency of the problem and its impacts on socioeconomic development (Adelekan, 2010; Ouikotan et al., 2017). In addition, studies about the vulnerability of Accra to frequent flood events with damaging impacts on urban life, infrastructure and socioeconomic development cannot be overlooked (Atanga, 2019; Jha et al., 2012; Karley, 2009; Rain et al., 2011). The problem of flooding in cities of West Africa is therefore evident in existing literature without specific emphasis on its impact on urban tourism.

The flood events in the cities also affect urban tourism (Rain et al., 2011; Twum & Abubakari, 2019). The impact of floods can be devastating, to the extent of physically destroying tourist attractions, urban infrastructure, businesses and social events (Yankson et al., 2017). Floods can result in fatalities, cancellation of tourist itineraries and halting of social activities with direct and indirect losses to tourism businesses and economies (Rajendra, 2020). However, there is evidence of extensive research on extreme weather and climate events in coastal cities in West Africa (Yankson et al., 2017) without specific emphasis on the impact of floods on urban tourism in the affected cities. Additionally, research on tourism in West Africa focuses more on rural than urban tourism studies (Siakwah, 2018). Particularly, current studies about urban tourism in Accra (Musavengane et al., 2020; Yankholmes, 2013) have not yet addressed this topic. There is thus a knowledge gap that needs to be filled. Accordingly, this chapter is a review of the impact of floods resulting from extreme weather and climate events on coastal cities in West Africa, using flood disaster events in Accra from the 1990s to 2015 as an example. This period is relevant because it has recorded chronic flood events in Accra, similar to other cities in West Africa (Asumadu-Sarkodie et al., 2015; Diagne, 2007; Douglas, 2017; Rain et al., 2011). The case of Accra is used as a classic example as floods occur almost annually, leading to a potential direct and indirect impact on tourism (Karley, 2009; Yankson et al., 2017).

Moreover, the specific analysis of floods and how they shape and impact tourism in the urban space is an emerging area that needs urgent research. The research is crucial, as management of floods further affects the urban poor who may be benefitting from urban tourism (Musavengane et al., 2020; Siakwah et al., 2020). Management of floods through the eviction of squatter settlers is not only to reduce flood risk but is also embedded in city authorities' plans to beautify cities in order to attract investors and develop tourism. The aim of this research is to contribute to the literature and provide direction for future research on the impact of flood risk on urban tourism in coastal cities in West Africa. The research will contribute to flood risk management policy and practice, and policies in the tourism sector.

Besides the section 11.1, which focuses on background and research problem, this chapter is structured into the following sections. Section 11.2 theoretically describes the concepts of flood impacts and urban tourism. Section 11.3 describes the study site, while section 11.4 describes the research methods. Section 11.5 is a presentation and discussion of results. This section is subdivided into 4 subsections.

Subsection 11.5.1 discusses results of flood disaster events in Accra, while subsection 11.5.2 focuses on urban tourism resources at risk of flood disaster in Accra. Subsection 11.5.3 discusses the direct and indirect impact of floods on tourism. In subsection 11.5.4, the management of flood risk regarding urban tourism and the challenges faced are discussed. Section 11.6 addresses the implications of flood risk for urban tourism in the future, and section 11.7 concludes and provides recommendations for future research.

11.2 Impact of floods and urban tourism

Extreme weather and climate events have a direct and indirect impact on the tourism industry. Flooding occurs when there is inundation the of land by water, affecting vulnerable elements (Douglas, 2017). Inundation can lead to the destruction of the vulnerable elements. Inundation of coastal cities can result from pluvial floods, fluvial floods, tsunamis, storm surges and sea rises (Hamzah et al., 2012; Scott & Lemieux, 2010; Yankson et al., 2017).

Floods directly and indirectly affect natural and built tourist attractions such as ecosites, beaches, resorts and outdoor activities. The direct impacts emanate from the physical disruption of floods. For instance, Hamzah et al. (2012) confirmed that floods directly affected historical and nature-based urban tourism in Malaysia, with a further explanation that the flood event inundated tourism sites, causing a drop of about 90% in tourism. Schuckert et al. (2015) explained that the drop in tourism is obvious because itineraries to tourism destinations either get cancelled or postponed in the wake of a flood event. Flood events can destroy tourism accommodations, retail, services, travel and infrastructure (Hamzah et al., 2012). Moreover, insurance of tourism businesses may also experience an increase in premiums due to flood impacts (Hamzah et al., 2012; Southon & Van der Merwe, 2018). Besides the direct costs of cleaning and rebuilding flood-affected infrastructure, there is loss of business during the period of a flood event. This is because outdoor businesses cease operating during a flood event.

On the other hand, the indirect impact of floods on tourism is difficult to assess (Schuckert et al., 2015; Southon & Van der Merwe, 2018). Indirect impacts of floods are related to socioeconomic and public activities that can benefit from the operations of hotels, travel services, resorts and restaurant experiences. Losses to the tourism industry as a result of floods have a spiral impact on other sectors of the economy. The concept of indirect impact further explains the negative image that people may attribute to cities after the impact of flood events (Hamzah et al., 2012; Vila et al., 2019). Flood can exacerbate poverty, which in turn can cause tourism activities to dwindle since tourism usually depends on the savings of individuals (Schuckert et al., 2015). Thus, floods are likely to reduce tourist influx to a region. Therefore, there is a need for flood risk management measures that consider the impact of floods on the industry (Southon & Van der Merwe, 2018).

Managing flood risks could be done through strategic policy or technical interventions, which can include preparedness, prevention, mitigation and adaptation
measures (Steyn, 2012). Individual as well as corporate and state interventions
can be useful for flood management. Literature suggests that state authorities
resort to early warning, emergency response and evacuation during a flood event.
After a flood event, clean-ups, rebuilding of infrastructure and subsidies to rees-
tablish businesses are required (Hamzah et al., 2012; Merz et al., 2010). Individual and corporate responses to the impact of floods on tourism include the
closure of tourism businesses and the evacuation of people and animals from
property during a flood event (Hamzah et al., 2012; Merz et al., 2010). Other
flood measures in the industry include cancellation of reservations, clean-ups and
flood insurance (Vila et al., 2019).

Indeed, the impact of floods on urban tourism may require specific policy-related and technical measures to reduce the consequences on sustainable development. However, evidence shows that policy-related and technical measures with
regard to flood hazards and vulnerabilities end up rendering the people living
in squatter settlements homeless as a result of relocation and eviction (Hamzah
et al., 2012; Musavengane et al., 2020). This impact, in addition to a potential
increase in cost of living due to urban tourism, could make living in such communities difficult.

11.3 Description of study site

This section describes the study site in order to provide readers with an insight
into the case-study area. Figure 11.1 shows Accra, the capital city of Ghana. With
similar geographical features to other coastal cities of West Africa, Accra has
tropical climate conditions with dry and wet seasons. February and March have
warm and dry conditions with an average temperature of 27°C. The average temperature for July and August is above 18°C with an average annual rainfall of
800 mm. Accra experiences 2 seasons of rainfall: from March to June and from
August to October (Agyirifo & Otwe, 2011). The topography of Accra indicates
−4 to 350 m contours. The built-up area of Accra consisted of less than 10 km² in
1877. Accra has since expanded uncontrollably to cover almost the entire Great
Accra Region. The 2010 population census of Ghana revealed that the Greater
Accra Region is about 3 245 km² with a population of over 4 million, constituting
about 16% of the national population. Accra's population stands at 1 695 136
million people, according to the 2010 national population census held in Ghana.
With an annual population growth rate of more than 3%, over 90% of Accra
is urban, with many more people living in slums than ever before in the city's
history. The colonial administration of Ghana did not plan Accra with a capacity
for the rapid expansion it has experienced over recent years (Grant & Yankson,
2003). The postcolonial governments expanded the city but have not been able to
address its planning problems. The residential areas have more organised infrastructure than the slum communities, some of which were colonially segregated
settlements with poor infrastructure, social amenities and overcrowding (Grant
& Yankson, 2003).

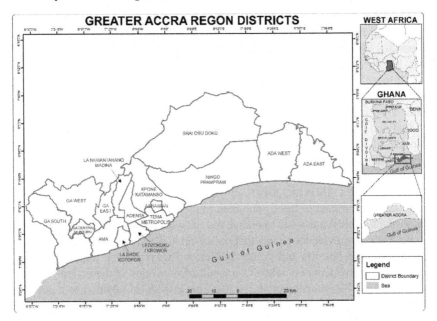

Figure 11.1 Map of study area.
Source: Authors, 2020.

Thus, the urban planning history of Accra is fragmented with the uncontrolled development of settlements. Moreover, land-use management in Accra is poorly coordinated and encroachment on waterways is a big problem, leading to an increase in the development of properties in flood-risk zones. Localised flooding usually occurs in Accra in the main rainy season and sometimes in the minor rainfall season.

The occurrence of localised floods is usually associated with rainfall, although the average rainfall has not increased since the 1960s (Okyere et al., 2013). Reports indicate that much of the Greater Accra Metropolitan Area (GAMA) drainage problem is unsolved. Most serious flood events occurred in the years of 1986, 1994, 1995, 1997, 2001, 2002, 2004, 2007, 2009, 2010, 2011 and 2015 (Karley, 2009; Okyere et al., 2013; Yankson et al., 2017). Accra links Ghana to overseas countries, and it is essential for the travel and tourism industry in the country.

11.4 Research methods

This research applied the thematic method of data analysis. Thematic data analysis is a useful qualitative research method for obtaining insights from existing documents (Braun & Clarke, 2013). This method generally allows researchers to see and make sense of relevant textual materials for qualitative analysis. It is a suitable method that enables researchers to identify and analyse patterns of a phenomenon from documents (Braun & Clarke, 2006). The method is a reflexive process for the intuitive engagement of analysis with the aim to develop a story from the textual data (Neuendorf, 2019). Accordingly, data from existing documents about flood events and urban tourism of coastal cities that focused on Accra were thematically analysed, interpreted and presented following the main themes of this research. Themes about the direct and indirect impact of flood events in coastal cities, especially Accra, were employed for a meaningful analysis of the impact of floods on the tourism industry. Table 11.1 is a summary of the direct and indirect impact of floods drawn from literature.

The risk analysis of the impact of floods on tourism in the study draws insights from Table 11.1. Other useful documents include the Ghana National Tourism Development plan (2013-2027), the Ghana Tourism Authority, the World Travel and Tourism Council (WTTC) and literature providing additional insights for interpretation.

11.5 Results and discussion

11.5.1 Overview of flood disaster events in Accra

This section presents and discusses the history of floods in Accra to offer readers some background on flood events at the study site. Historical records about flood disasters in Accra seem to be inconsistent and uncoordinated before the establishment of the National Disaster Management Organisation (NADMO) in Ghana. However, newspapers, literature and other records have captured flood events that occurred in the colonial and postcolonial days. The establishment of NADMO to coordinate disaster management could be one reason for the more consistent and coordinated flood data. Table 11.2 shows the main flood disasters in Accra from 1995 to 2015, and their impact on Accra. This period is chosen as it has consistent records of flood events that occurred in Accra.

The information in Table 11.2 suggests that most of the floods occurred in the summer. This is also a period in which tourism activities are high in the city. Thus, one can assume that besides the physical damage of floods to tourist attractions and infrastructure, flood disasters have a likelihood of directly and indirectly affecting travel and tourism businesses in the city.

11.5.2 Urban tourism resources at risk of flood disasters in Accra

This section presents and discusses results concerning urban tourist attractions that can be affected by flood disasters in Accra. Urban tourism includes activities of international and domestic tourists in urban communities, such as cities and towns (Cave & Jolliffe, 2012).

A review of documents revealed the following findings. Accra, like other major coastal cities in West Africa, has tourist attractions including travel, tours, hotels and entertainment services that make the city a special hub for tourists. The Legon Botanical Gardens of about 50 ha was established in 1950 and has about 110 km of canopy walkways (Siakwah, 2018). Beaches and resorts in Accra such as Labadi Beach Resort and Bojo Beach attract domestic and international tourists. Siakwah (2018) confirms that 16th- to 18th-century castles and forts are

Table 11.1 Schematic Analysis of the Direct and Indirect Impact of Flood Events

Authors	Year	Direct and indirect impact of floods		Methodology
		Direct impact	*Indirect impact*	
Asumadu-Sarkodie et al.	2015	Coastal communities have a 20% inundation. A 10-year flood has a 10% probability of occurring and could cause US$98.5 million in urban damage and affected GDP of US$50.3 million, with an affected population of 34 000 in Accra.	Psychological impact affected people, cancellation of social events, travel and tour events.	Secondary hydrometeorological data of Accra, Meteonorm 7 software was used to generate meteorological dataset from 1981-2010
Okyere et al.	2013	Deaths of about 1 133 people from 1980 to 2010. Huge economic costs, halt businesses, physical damage to houses, transportation, communication and other infrastructure.	Eviction of Old Fadama community, outbreak of cholera, long-term economic impact and trauma on individuals.	Literature review and secondary data.
Aboagye	2012	At Alajo, Accra, floods in 1995, 2001 and 2007 had an impact of 58%, 72% and 77%, respectively. With the homeless, 80% of households in Alajo lost belongings in 1995, 86% in 2001 and 77% in 2007. Employment losses in 1995 were 83%, 2001 were 86% and 2007 were 89%. Seventy-five percent of the population at Alajo has not recovered from the 2007 flood, and none of the homeless has recovered.	After flood impact, diseases and cancellation or delay in social events can reduce expenses in the economy.	Surveys and interviews.

Rain et al.	2011	Estimated 172 000 residents at risk of 10-year 24-hour 167.6 mm rainfall total.	Slum communities along Korle Lagoon.	Flood modelling using Geographic Information Systems (GIS) system.
Ouikotan et al.	2017	Inundation of settlements and properties and the destruction of assets. For instance, the 3 June 2015 floods in Accra killed about 200 people and caused damage to property with huge economic cost.	Diseases and epidemics such as cholera, malaria, dysentery and diarrhoea. In Dakar, floods occurred in 2005 and 2006, and cholera affected 25% of the population.	Case studies of Dakar in Senegal, Accra in Ghana, Cotonou in Benin and Lagos in Nigeria. Secondary data.
Douglas	2017	Loss of lives and property, diseases, displacement of people and homelessness, damage to road surfaces and inundation of farms.	Increase in food prices, reduction in economic activities and increase in poverty.	Case studies of cities in sub-Sahara.
Karley	2009	Loss of lives, halting of businesses and social activities, and breakdown of infrastructure. Financial costs associated with flooding was more than US$2 million in 2008.	Cases of diarrhoea, dysentery and cholera increased.	Case study of a city and involved a visit to the city to interview local experts.
Hamzah et al.	2012	Ninety percent drop in tourist arrivals and hotel occupancy due to cancellation of hotel reservations and closure of resorts, tourist attractions, tourism services and other urban activities.	Psychological impacts due to loss and decline of businesses, and bad image of region created.	Case study with mixed methods.

Table 11.2 Flood Disasters and Their Characteristics in Accra.

Date of flood event	Affected areas and impact
5 July 1995	The affected areas included low-lying neighbourhoods of the Accra metropolis. Flooding of the Achimota VRA substation resulted in power failure and a lack of lights. The flood disrupted businesses and commuter activities.
13 June 1997	Two days of rainfall caused floods that affected various parts of Accra including the Odaw and Onyasia areas. The flood affected properties and displaced people from homes.
28 June 2001	Madina, Achimota, Dzorwulu, Avenor, Santa Maria and Adabraka Official Town were affected. The floods displaced people and damaged properties.
5 May 2010	Central Accra, Ofankor and Begoro were affected, resulting in property damage and disruption of businesses.
24 February 2011	Adabraka, Kisseman, Alajo Junction, Santa Maria and the Tema Timber Market were flooded. The floods destroyed property and businesses.
1 November 2011	Many parts of Accra were flooded. About 43 087 people were affected, with 14 people dying.
31 May 2013	Kwame Nkrumah Circle, Darkuman Kokompe, Obetsebi Lamptey Circle, Santa Maria and the Dansoman Roundabout were affected, having a direct and indirect impact.
6 June 2014	Adabraka, Kwame Nkrumah Circle, Mallam, North Kaneshie and Dansoman were affected. There were direct and indirect impacts on life and property.
4 July 2014	Taifa, Dansoman, Kaneshie, Adabraka, Awoshie, Kwame Nkrumah Circle, Mallam and Odorko were flooded.
3 June 2015	The flood in parts of Accra affected about 52 622 people and led to a fire explosion at a filling station, which caused the death of 150 people.

Sources: Disaster reports from the National Disaster Management of Ghana, 1995 to 2015.

mostly located along the coast of Ghana, which attract tourists to Accra. The Osu Castle, James Fort, Christianborg Castle, Ussher Fort and Fort Augustaborg are relics of the Europeans dotted along the coast of Accra, which attract tourists. The modern architecture of the city as administrative capital further attracts tourists. With a relatively better transportation network and tourism facilities than other urban areas in Ghana, the city has modern accommodation, travel, touring and entertainment facilities to offer tourists. The Ghana National Tourism Plan (2012–2027) confirms the commissioning of a tourism information centre in Accra. The Marine Drive project is a long-term development project to improve coastal tourism in Ghana. The findings further indicate that over 240 acres of land have been issued to the Ministry of Tourism, Culture and Creative Arts in Ghana for this project. Natural environments including the coastline, beaches, parks and gardens, as well as the Accra Zoo, lure tourists to the city. Cultural tourist attractions include museums, arts and cultural events. The Pan-African Historical

Theatre Festival, also known as PANAFEST, takes place in Accra and it is known as a popular event that attracts tourists from around the world worldwide who have historical roots in Africa. Findings from the reviews suggest that the threat of floods in the study site are increasing. There is a possibility that tourist attractions in Accra will be inundated.

11.5.3 Direct and indirect impact of floods on tourism

The potential impact of floods on urban tourism can be deduced from the impact of flood disasters on lives, fixed assets, businesses, infrastructure and the social and economic activities in cities in the past (Merz et al., 2010). This section analyses the potential direct and indirect impact of floods on tourism in Accra with reference to Table 11.1. The results in Table 11.1 show the impact of floods in Accra. The city experiences regular 10-year flood events that cause loss of life. The most recent example was the flood event of 3 June 2015 that triggered the explosion of a filling station in Accra. This is the most recent deadly flood event, which claimed 150 lives (Ouikotan et al., 2017). Records further show that the floods of 26 November 2011 affected 43 087 people and caused the death of 14 people.

Although specific records of tourist fatalities in Accra have not been cited, tourists also stand a chance of being affected by flood hazards in the city. Research further finds that the coastline of Accra is vulnerable to inundation with about 20% of the communities being at risk of flooding annually (Asumadu-Sarkodie et al., 2015). The results suggest that fixed tourism assets, infrastructure and businesses are also at risk of being destroyed by floods in Accra. Tourism facilities including beaches, hotels, restaurants and retail shops are also at risk of being destroyed by flood disasters in Accra (Aboagye, 2012). Due to this destruction, tourism businesses would require financial input for reconstruction, which could delay tourism businesses. Another direct impact of floods on tourism is loss of jobs. Resort owners, hoteliers and other tourism business owners could lose jobs when their businesses are directly destroyed by floods. During a flood event, tourism activities, similar to other socioeconomic ventures, would come to a halt. Tourism businesses that operate daily will lose profits and may eventually risk collapsing due to floods in the city. Flood events also cause cancellation of travel and tourism activities, which affects the tourism sector directly. As a result of the potential threat of death and physical damage, tourists cancel travel plans and hotel reservations during flood events. This eventually decreases the profits of businesses in the travel, tour and hotel industry. These direct consequences could further affect other socioeconomic activities that are linked to the tourism industry.

Although difficult to identify, the indirect impact of floods on tourism can also be seen in Tables 11.1 and 11.2 (Merz et al., 2010; Ouikotan et al., 2017). The indirect impact can be described as the consequences that are indirectly linked to the impact of a flood event. With reference to Tables 11.1 and 11.2, one can argue that environmental hygiene and public health problems exist after a flood event, which could result in the spread of diseases in Accra. Accra floods have been linked to causes of cholera, dysentery and diarrhoea over the years (Asumadu-Sarkodie et al., 2015; Okyere et al., 2013). After the 26 November 2011 flood in Accra, for example, cholera cases increased as a result of the flood impact. These conditions are unpleasant and could possibly cause negative impressions for tourists, leading to a low interest in future visits to the city. Negative experiences and low interest in future revisits could potentially affect businesses, jobs and livelihood activities. For example, craft and restaurant businesses can be induced by a growth in the tourism industry. Thus, a decline in tourism and outdoor activities during flood events would indirectly affect the informal retail sector in Accra. The 3 June 2015 floods in Accra, which took several days to be cleaned up and recovered from, halted and delayed outdoor activities and business operations in the affected neighbourhoods. This could eventually cause the delay and breakdown of businesses that relied on tourism to operate. Clubs, restaurants and businesses were affected for days by the 2015 floods in Accra. Furthermore, the overall flood impact on tourism leads to spiral effects on local and national economies.

11.5.4 Management of urban tourism flood risk and challenges

Essentially, flood risk management employs structural and non-structural measures in response to the impact of floods in cities. However, the impact of floods on urban tourism is sector-specific and would benefit from management measures in the sector. The discussion in this section focuses on flood management measures for the impact of floods on tourism in Accra. The structural measures have to do with engineering approaches to flood risk reduction. These are physical constructions that are aimed at preventing and controlling flood hazards and vulnerabilities. The Accra city authorities use channels and drainage structures to regulate flood water. These structures, especially the Odaw drains, are dredged and expanded seasonally to ease the flow of stormwater. The objective of such public projects is to protect lives, property and businesses. Property, businesses and stakeholders in the tourism sector are also protected. Individuals in the tourism sector apply physical flood measures to reduce the impact of flood hazards on their property.

In Accra, tourism accommodation and business owners use flood-proof designed foundations, platforms and walls to reduce the impact of flood waters. Hotel owners also use sandbags and drains around the buildings as flood impact measures in the city. These technical measures could minimise the direct physical impact of floods on buildings to reduce potential damage. Other flood management projects in Accra, which include the Korle Lagoon Restoration Project (KLERP) and the Accra Sanitary and Storm Drainage Alleviation Project 2013 (the Conti Project) are also aimed at reducing floods and making the city attractive to investors and tourists (Atanga, 2019; Farouk & Owusu, 2012). Government policies further include planning and land-use regulations that focus on preventing building in waterways. Tourism business owners are required to follow these land-use regulations for the development of their properties in the city.

Nonstructural measures are the social interventions that focus on saving lives and property through emergency response, recovery and mitigation measures for the reduction of flood risk. In the context of tourism, the flood response in Accra includes early warning systems that give information to tourists, resorts and travel and hotel operators. The Ghana Meteorological Agency and NADMO support the distribution of flood warning information to tourists and tourism business owners to be used for accommodation bookings and travel arrangements. For recovery purposes, clean-up exercises after floods allow hotel and tourism businesses to return to normal operations. Government sometimes compensates registered businesses that are affected by floods, from which tourism business operators can also benefit. Evacuation and public education on safety measures can further help to minimise the impact of floods on tourism in the city. The relocation programmes in Accra, which started in 2003, intend to remove physical structures on waterways as part of flood risk management (Farouk & Owusu, 2012). Tourism businesses are to follow building regulations to avoid developments in waterways.

There are challenges that make public and individual responses to the impact of floods on the tourism sector in Accra few and ineffective. The main problems facing flood risk management in the sector are inadequate resources and capacity to deal with flood hazards and reduce vulnerability to the impact of floods. Weather forecasting is poorly developed and does not provide reliable forecasts. The problem in Accra and other cities of developing nations is lack of reliable weather information for public use. The weather forecast is usually inaccurate and comes too late, with daily predictions that do not allow for advance preparation. Tourism business owners also resort to flood insurance in response to the potential impact of floods, but this measure is not advanced.

11.6 Implications of flood risks for future urban tourism

This section discusses the implications of floods for urban tourism in Accra. The reviews confirmed that flooding in Accra and other West African coastal cities seems to be an annual problem. The increase in flood occurrences seems to suggest that the impact of flood events in the cities would also affect tourism. The implications for future tourism seem severe due to an increase in extreme weather events and urbanisation, and the importance of the study for urban tourism development in West Africa cannot be overemphasised. However, literature also indicates that tourism and climate change affect each other. Thus, management needs to look at both causes and solutions to the problem. Flood management and climate risk policies need to include tourism stakeholders in disaster risk management in the future. Redeveloping the flood-prone communities in Accra by improving infrastructure will reduce flood risks and attract tourists, increase tourism and decrease poverty. Current trends of an increased urban population suggest that urban tourism is likely to increase, and it is thus crucial to have a corresponding improvement of flood management. However, trying to increase urban tourism through an inner-city development approach has the tendency to dispossess squatter settlers of homes and their source of livelihood in Accra. The approach results in a forced displacement of settlers who are less privileged in society.

11.7 Conclusions and recommendations

This chapter reviewed the risk of floods in coastal cities in West Africa, using Accra as the case study. Data were obtained from secondary sources. The review revealed that Accra experiences a risk of coastal submergence and the occurrence of 10-year flood events. These events could result in direct and indirect impacts on tourism. Floods could directly destroy tourist attractions, accommodations, beaches and resorts with the likelihood of reducing tourism resources and tourist activities. The indirect impact of flood events on tourism were also considered, because a reduction in the tourism sector could affect other sectors of socioeconomic development in the city. Flood disasters could give the city a bad image, which will discourage future tourists from visiting. Besides, attempts at dealing with flood risk usually result in a dislocation of the urban poor from their places of abode, which increases levels of poverty and inequality. Strategic flood risk management measures and programmes need to consider specific measures for decreasing the impact of floods on urban tourism in the city and similar coastal cities in West Africa. Moreover, there is a need for reliable weather information for tourists and residents alike to reduce the direct and indirect impacts of floods on the sector at the study site. One major limitation of this study is that it obtained data from secondary sources and literature. It would be useful for future research to consider more empirical work involving qualitative and quantitative research approaches. In conclusion, research about the impact of floods on urban tourism at the study site is new and needs further research to provide more practical solutions to the problem.

References

Aboagye, D. (2012). The political ecology of environmental hazards in Accra, Ghana. *Journal of Environment and Earth Science*, 2(10), 157–172.

Adelekan, I. O. (2010). Vulnerability of poor urban coastal communities to flooding in Lagos, Nigeria. *Environment and Urbanisation*, 22 (2), 433–450.

Adjibade, I., Pelling, M., Agboola, J., & Garschagen, M. (2016). Sustainability transitions: exploring risk management and the future of adaptation in the Megacity of Lagos. *Journal of Extreme Events*, 3(3), 1–25.

Agyirifo, D. S., & Otwe, E. P. (2011). *Profile of temperature and rainfall patterns in Ghana from 1940–2010*. Conference: Proceedings of the University of Ilorin, Nigeria, and University of Cape Coast, Ghana, 2nd Joint International Conference on Climate Change and Sustainable Development, 11 May 2011, at Ilorin, Nigeria., Volume: 1.

Asumadu-Sarkodie, S., Owusu, P. A., & Rufangura, P. (2015). Impact analysis of flood in Accra, Ghana. *Advances in Applied Science Research*, 6(9), 53–78.

Atanga, R. A. (2019). The role of local community leaders in flood disaster risk management strategy making in Accra. *International Journal of Disaster Risk Reduction*, 43, 101358. DOI:10.1016/j.ijdrr.2019.101358

Braun, V., & Clarke, V. (2006). Using thematic analysis in psychology. *Qualitative Research in Psychology*, 3, 77–101.

Braun, V., & Clarke, V. (2013). *Successful qualitative research: A practical guide for beginners*. London, UK: Sage.

Cave, J., & Jolliffe, L. (2012). Urban tourism. In P. Robinson (Ed.). *Tourism: The key concepts*. (pp. 268–270) London, UK: Routledge.

Diagne, K. (2007). Governance and natural disasters: Addressing flooding in Saint Louis, Senegal, *Environment and Urbanisation*, 19(2), 552–562.

Douglas, I. (2017). Flooding in African cities, scales of causes, teleconnections, risks, vulnerability and impacts. *International Journal of Disaster Risk Reduction*, 26, 34–42.

Engel, T., Fink, A. H., Knippertz, and Pante, G. (2017). Extreme precipitation in the West African cities of Dakar and Ouagadougou: Atmospheric dynamics and implications for flood risk assessments. *Journal of Hydrometeorology*, 18, 2937–2957.

Farouk, B. R., & Owusu, M. (2012). 'If in doubt, count': The role of community-driven enumerations in blocking eviction in Old Fadama, Accra. *Environmental Urbanisation*, 24(1), 47–57.

Government of the Republic of Ghana (2013). *Ghana national tourism development plan (GNTDP) 2013–2027*, Ministry of Tourism, Accra, The Republic of Ghana.

Gowreesunkar, V. (2019). African Union (AU) Agenda 2063 and tourism development in Africa: contribution, contradiction and implications. *International Journal of Tourism Cities*, 5(2), 288–300. doi:10.1108/IJTC-02-2019-0029.

Grant, R., & Yankson, P. (2003). Accra. *Cities*, 20(1), 65–74.

Hamzah, J., Habibah, A., Buang, A., Jusoff, K., Toriman, M. E., Er, J. A. C., & Azima, A. M. (2012). Flood disaster impacts and the tourism providers' responses: The Kota Tinggi experience. *Advances in Natural and Applied Science*, 6(1), 26–32.

Hernandez, A. B., & Ryan, G. (2011). Coping with climate change in the tourism industry. *Tourism and Hospitality Management*, 17(1), 79–90.

Jha, A. K. R., Bloch, R., & Lamond, J. (2012). *Cities and flooding: A guide to integrated urban flood risk MANAGEMENT for the 21st century*. New York, USA: The World Bank.

Karley, N. K. (2009). Flooding and physical planning in urban areas in West Africa: Situational analysis of Accra, Ghana. *Theoretical Empirical Resources Urban Management*, 4, 25–41.

Merz, B., Kreibich, H., Schwarze, R., & Thieken, A. (2010). Review article "Assessment of economic flood damage". *Natural Hazards Earth Systems Science*, 10, 1697–1724.

Musavengane, R., Siakwah, P., & Llewellyn, L. (2020). The nexus between tourism and urban risk: Towards inclusive, safe, resilient and sustainable outdoor tourism in African cities. *Journal of Outdoor Recreation and Tourism*, 29 (2020), 100,254.

Neuendorf, K. A. (2019). Content analysis and thematic analysis. In P. Brough (Ed.), *Research methods for applied psychologists: Design, analysis and reporting* (pp. 211–223). New York: Routledge.

Okyere, C. Y., Yacouba, Y., & Gilgenbach, D. (2013). The problem of annual occurrences of floods in Accra: An integration of hydrological, economic and political perspectives. *Theoretical and Empirical Researches in Urban Management*, 8(29), 45–79.

Ouikotan, B. R., Van der Kwast, J., Mynett, A., & Afouda, A. (2017). *Gaps and challenges of flood risk management in West African coastal cities. 16th World Water Congress, International Water Resources Association*, Cacum, Quintana, Mexico, 29 May–3 June 2017.

Rain, D., Engstrom, R., Ludlow C., & Antos, S. (2011). Accra Ghana: A city vulnerable to flooding and drought-induced migration for Chapter 4: Human Settlements Background Study UN Publications. *Global report on human settlements 2011*. UN-HABITAT, Nairobi, Kenya.

Rajendra, R. (2020). Climate change impacts on the coastal tourist. *IOP Conference Series: Earth and Environmental Science*, 423, 012044.

Rogerson, C. M. (2012). The tourism development nexus in sub-Saharan Africa – progress and prospects. *African Insight*, 42(2), 28–45.

Schuckert, M., Liu, X. & Law, R. (2015). Hospitality and tourism online reviews: Recent trends and future directions. *Journal of Travel & Tourism Marketing*, 32(5), 608–621.

Scott, D., & Lemieux, C. (2010). Weather and climate information for tourism. *Procedia Environmental Sciences*, 1(1), 146–183.

Siakwah, P. (2018). Tourism geographies and spatial distribution of tourist sites in Ghana. *African Journal of Hospitality, Tourism and Leisure*, 7(1)–(2018) ISSN: 2223-814X.

Siakwah, P., Musavengane, R. & Leonard, L. (2020) Tourism governance and attainment of the sustainable development goals in Africa. *Tourism Planning & Development*, 17:4, 355–383, DOI: 10.1080/21568316.2019.1600160.

Southon, M. P., & Van der Merwe, C. D. (2018). Flooded with risks or opportunities: Exploring impacts on tourism accommodation. *African Journal of Hospitality, Tourism and Leisure*, 7(1), 1 –27.

Steyn, J. N. (2012). Managing climate change impacts on tourism: Mitigating and adaptive strategies with special reference to the Western Cape Province of South Africa. *African Journal for Physical, Health Education, Recreation and Dance,* 18(3), 552–564.

Twum, K. O., & Abubakari, M. (2019). 'Cities and floods: A pragmatic insight into the determinants of households' coping strategies to floods in informal Accra, Ghana'. *Jàmbá: Journal of Disaster Risk Studies* 11(1), a608. https://doi.org/10.4102/jamba.v11i1.608

Vila, N. A. R., Toubes, D. R., & Brea, J. A. F. (2019). Tourism industry's vulnerability upon risk of flooding: The aquis querquennis complex. *Environments*, 6, 122.

World Travel & Tourism Council (WTTC) (2019). *Ghana 2019 annual research report: Key highlights*. World Travel & Tourism Council, London, UK. file:///C:/Users/rapta/Downloads/Ghana2020_.pdf

World Travel & Tourism Council (WTTC) (2020). *Travel and tourism economic impact 2019 – Ghana.* (http://www.wttc.org/site_media/uploads/downloads/ghana2013.pdf. 20.2.2020).

Yankholmes, A. K. B. (2013). Residents' stated preference for scale of tourism development in Danish-Osu, Ghana. *Cities*, 31, 267–275.

Yankson, P. W. K., Owusu, A. B., Owusu, G., Boakye-Danquah, J., & Tetteh, J. D. (2017). Assessment of coastal communities' vulnerability to floods using an indicator-based approach: A case study of Greater Accra Metropolitan area, Ghana. *Natural Hazards,* 89, 661689.

12 The nexus of climate change and urban tourism in South Africa

Triaging challenges and optimising opportunities

Felix Kwabena Donkor and Kevin Mearns

12.1 Introduction

12.1.1 Tourism, environment and human society

The climatic conditions of an area are a core factor in its appeal as a tourist destination and a critical part of its tourism appeal (Gossling et al., 2012). Yearly fluctuations in climatic conditions affect tourism seasonality, whilst daily conditions generally determine the satisfaction levels of leisure destinations (Rossello & Waqas, 2015). Thus, climate impacts are already evident in the tourism industry and are informing policymaking in the sector (Hoogendoorn & Fitchett, 2016). These are inclusive of impacts on biodiversity, scenic beauty, wildlife presence, coastal resources, ecosystem integrity and overall local tourism infrastructure (Hoogendoorn & Fitchett, 2016). Ultimately, climate change could affect the comparative allure and competitivity of tourism destinations (Rossello & Waqas, 2015). This is because climate projections indicate an increase in the severity of natural hazards and extreme events, including an increased impact on key tourism destinations and sectors (Fitchett et al., 2016; Rogerson, 2016). This makes it imperative to understand the interaction between climate change and the tourism industry in order to apply adaptive measures that effectively mitigate the harmful impacts (Becken & Wilson, 2013; Hambira & Saarinen, 2015). Moreover, such an understanding is crucial to the sustainability of the tourism industry in different locales, including the urban milieu.

Tourism depends on and substantially affects the natural ecosystem where it takes place (Winter & Brom, 2018). Although it is acknowledged that several areas across the globe are being preserved by way of parks and protected areas, the growth in tourism results in serious negative impacts (Boateng et al., 2017). Moreover, some of the notable environmental challenges associated with tourism are the degradation of critical natural resources (such as water sources and forest areas), ecological pollution (such as the polluting of the air, noise pollution, sewage, garbage and littering) and physical effects (such as construction projects, marine projects and the destruction of biodiversity) (United Nations Environment Programme, 2003). The ecological effects of tourism can go beyond local areas to have an impact on the global ecosystem. Spiralling air travel is a typical instance and identified as one of the main factors in climate change. It is argued that the connection between climate change and tourism is complicated; however, tourists do react to the vagaries of the weather in their immediate environs, comprising elements such as inclement conditions, precipitation and sunlight duration. This scenario is intensified for areas that are endowed with a comparatively high number of outdoor attractions, such as nature-based tourism, adventure tourism and beach tourism sites (Agnew & Viner, 2001). Overall, whether advantageous or disadvantageous, tourism is a key agent of socioeconomic transformation globally, whilst the sector continues to change at an impressive rate. The complex interaction between climate change and the tourism sector makes it imperative to involve key stakeholders in a holistic approach to effectively address the challenges posed (Figure 12.1). Ultimately, the tourism industry is climate-sensitive, which exacerbates the associated risks in different environments ranging from rural to urban milieu. Not addressing risks such as drought compromises the goal of sustainable tourism and ultimately the attainment of the Sustainable Development Goals (Figure 12.1).

This interconnection makes it necessary to address some of the core socioeconomic factors that can help mitigate the risks associated with climate change in the sector to safeguard the industry (Figure 12.1). This includes reinforcing policy and related institutions whilst local actors such as the tourists and service providers become more proactive in their conduct (Mearns & Lukhele, 2015). The core sectors that underpin tourism are often linked to environmental resources and can be subject to vagaries of the weather. This scenario exacerbates the risks

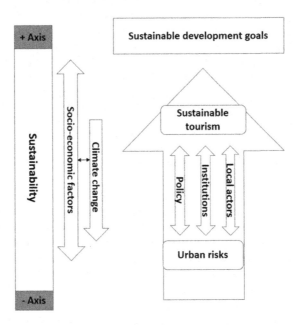

Figure 12.1 The nexus of tourism and urban risks.

associated with the tourism sector. Thus, despite the importance of the tourism industry in recent times, discourses about the industry have become progressively linked by the issues of climate change. Although Africa is recognised as a climate hot spot and argued to bear the brunt of climate change impacts globally, there is a dearth of research on its local tourism industry and climate fluctuations (Hoogendoorn & Fitchett, 2016). Furthermore, several Intergovernmental Panel for Climate Change (IPCC) reports have highlighted the vulnerability and significant diversity in tourism, pointing to the need for further research on climate adaptation in the sector (Donkor et al., 2019). This article contributes to the debate about the connections between climate change and urban tourism, with a focus on adaptive measures that actors in the urban sector, such as Cape Town, can employ to safeguard their niche in the industry. Furthermore, the United Nations Sustainable Development Goals (SDGs) provide a global blueprint for the peace and prosperity of humankind and the planet. The thematic areas addressed have implications for the SDGs, particularly Goal 8 ("decent work and economic growth") and Goal 11 ("sustainable cities and communities"), as tourism and urban risk lie at the intersection of these specific goals.

12.1.2 Profile of South Africa's tourism sector

South Africa is a tourism hub in Africa and a suitable case study for the dynamics of climate-induced impacts on the tourism industry. It is endowed with myriad outdoor tourism destinations, ranging from coastal locations and beachfronts to the Kruger National Park, with ancillary national parks, waterfalls, rivers and mountain-based adventures (Rogerson & Visser, 2006). South Africa's diverse weather embraces summer and winter precipitation locales in subtropical to mid-latitude areas, coupled with both moist and dry conditions (Nicholson, 2000). Furthermore, South Africa is categorised as a climate hot spot subject to dire consequences owing to its limited adaptive capacity and pressing developmental needs (Reid & Vogel, 2006). The industry's capacity to thrive is mediated by climate dynamics and depends on the adaptive capacity of both the tourism industry and the entire nation (Rogerson, 2016). Tourism in South Africa has been on an upward trend in the post-apartheid era, with figures rising from 1 million visits in 1990 to 14.3 million by 2013 (Stats SA, 2016). The industry represents 3% of the country's gross domestic product (GDP), with tourists' expenditures recording R218.9 billion (US$21.1 billion) in 2013 (Stats SA, 2016). Given the high unemployment figures, the tourism sector supplies livelihoods for about 655 609 people and is touted as a pathway out of poverty (Briedenhann & Wickens, 2004; Leonard, 2016; Mearns & Lukhele, 2015). The prevalence of outdoor destinations, coupled with the comparatively limited adaptive resources available, makes the industry highly susceptible to climate impacts with dire consequences for the most vulnerable in the sector (Rogerson, 2016). The mitigation of climate-induced risks to the tourism industry is in consonance with the United Nations SDGs, as they translate into poverty alleviation coupled with addressing social inequality and climate consequences for burgeoning climate-sensitive enterprises (Musavengane & Leonard, 2019; Siakwah et al., 2019).

12.1.3 Study setting

South Africa (Figure 12.2) is defined by the geographical coordinates 22°S-35°S and 17°E-33°E stretching from the subtropics to the midlatitudes (Karmalkar et al., 2012). The country records wintery precipitation climes in the southwest together with midsummer precipitation stretching from its centre to the north (Nicholson, 2000). The country's temperature variation includes heightened temperatures above 32°C in summertime to under 0°C at altitudes along the interior plateaux, with its conducive climate a major allure for tourists (Jawtusch, 2014). The City of Cape Town (Figure 12.2) in South Africa has a population of 3 740 026 and is governed by a 231-member city council, with the executive mayor being voted in by the council and exercising executive authority for the city (City of Cape Town, 2017). The City of Cape Town is an extensive urban expanse and highly populous, with a dense traffic of people, goods and services, widespread development and numerous business districts and industrial areas. It embodies hubs of economic activity with intricate and varied economies, distinct features of which are integrated development planning and robust, interdependent socioeconomic connections between its integral units (City of Cape Town, 2017). South Africa is essentially an arid area. However, Cape Town's most conspicuous land mass, Table Mountain, catches onshore

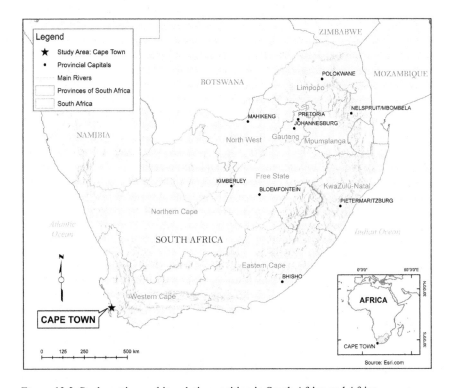

Figure 12.2 Study setting and its relative position in South Africa and Africa.

breezes emanating from warm ocean waters, producing localised precipitation that fills rivers and underground aquifers. In short, Cape Town is an idyllic oasis with a Mediterranean climate (SA-Venues.com, 2019). Such natural splendour has fostered population escalation and enhanced wealth and prosperity. The city is endowed with natural pools and water parks aside wineries and lush gardens. Nevertheless, as the city has industrialised, a significant section has continued to be characterised by stark poverty and impoverished settlements, with unemployment that tops 25%. Cape Town thrives on its tourism sector, which affords an estimated 300 000 jobs (Horn, 2018). Furthermore, climate change is triggering far-reaching changes in weather, with more severe storms and harsher extreme events.

The next section details the approaches adopted in pursuing the study objectives.

12.2 Methodology

12.2.1 Research design

This study was conducted using the case study approach. Literature and theoretical studies are important qualitative methods of gaining understanding of the related thematic areas under investigation (Creswell, 2013).

12.2.2 Case study

The case study approach to qualitative research was employed in this study. Case studies are utilised when empirical assessments of contemporary phenomena within real-life settings are needed; when the difference between phenomenon and context is vague; and when diverse sources of proof are involved (McCombes, 2020). The case study approach was utilised in this instance because it enables profound insights to be gained on the nexus of tourism and urban risk, which is under consideration, and because it permits the making of valid generalisations.

12.2.3 Literature review as a methodological approach

In addition, a literature review permits a critical analysis of the current state of scholarship on a theme of interest within a particular timeframe (Ralph et al., 2014). Some key documents were studied to understand the status quo on the diverse thematic areas of this study. Thus, scientific articles and journals were perused as the core information sources in the literature review process. Systematic searches on scientific databases such as Science Direct were utilised to collect data on diverse themes. The searches were organised around specific keywords such as "*climate change*" and "*urban risk*", which were paired with Boolean operators such as *AND* and *OR*. Examples of such searches included phrases such as "*tourism and climate change*" and "*urban risk and resilience*".

12.2.4 Data interpretation

Through a thematic content analysis (Bernard & Ryan, 2010), the core themes emanating from the literature were strung into similar paragraphs by way of *meaning condensation*. Meaning condensation involves a summary of repetitive themes into terse formulations (Creswell, 2013). The meaning condensation approach to analysis comprises 5 main steps: the entirety of a selected text is first evaluated to afford a comprehensive overview; the *meaning units* are recognised by the researcher; the key thematic areas as per the meaning units are paraphrased succinctly; the meaning units are then cross-evaluated; and ultimately, the critical themes of the overall text are merged to compose a descriptive statement (Torraco, 2016).

12.3 Results and discussion

The tourism industry is one of the fastest-growing service industries globally and represents a critical component in the development of the South African economy (Smith, 2020). Unlike countries in the northern hemisphere, the opportunities for tourism in the southern hemisphere and the constraints on urban tourism posed by climate fluctuations are mediated by the competing interests of economic development on the one hand and social upliftment on the other (Krige, 2019). This compromises and often limits adaptation and mitigation measures (Long & Ziergovel, 2020; Rogerson, 2016). The nexus of climate change and urban tourism is an intricate interrelation that is largely site-specific but has received a dearth of research. This article helps bridge this gap by addressing the subject to enhance knowledge and adaptation strategies, with a focus on the role of urban industry players in South Africa.

12.4 Threats and adaptation strategies

12.4.1 Rising temperatures and beach tourism

Ultimately, climate change affects the vulnerability of coastal attractions and hence their sustainability. The susceptibility of a destination to climate change is reflected in its loss of attractiveness due to such change, coupled with the negative implications of adaptation and mitigation strategies. Urban tourism operators in Cape Town and across Africa have the opportunity to develop a low-carbon industry by co-developing technology and processes with minimal environmental impact. Eco-efficiency, according to the World Business Council for Sustainable Development, characterises products that limit the usage of resources and minimise environmental impacts (Grimm et al., 2018). Industry operators who have carved a niche in beach tourism are confronted with the risk of scorching temperatures, increased rainfall, fluctuations in wave dynamics and a rising sea level (Fashae & Onafeso, 2011; Fitchett et al., 2016). Cape Town's pristine beaches are set against the impressive landscapes of the Cape Fold Mountain range and are amongst the core attractions of tourists annually. With the Atlantic Ocean bordering the coastal city, Cape Town offers large stretches of white sandy beach nearby and attractive spots for surfing, including kite surfing. Outdoor beach games in a relaxed atmosphere include volleyball, soccer and touch rugby, and games with beach bats. The warm weather, scenic beaches and cool water are the perfect ingredients for a day of soaking up the sun whilst also offering long strolls on the beach (Love Cape Town, 2020). The location of the city's beaches so close to the central business district (CBD), with its many shops and eateries, make them popular after-work hangouts amongst the locals whilst relishing in the incomparable sunsets and, in summer, enjoying longer sunshine hours (SA-Venues.com, 2019). Paddling is relatively safe owing to the level expanses of beach, but swimming can pose hazards, so there is an abundance of lifeguards. Safety measures are an additional cost to the industry but are considered important to protect the reputation of the area for beach tourism. There is something for animal lovers too, as animal sightings are a huge tourist attraction, from colonies of penguins to schools of whales.

Moreover, aside from the scenic attributes of destinations and the effects of climate change, public policies are a core determinant of the viability or vulnerability of destinations (Scott & Lemieux, 2010). Poor policies are also the cause of poor integration between tourism and climate change guidelines, and the absence of coordination amongst core stakeholders in the sector (Santos-Lacueva et al., 2017; Stern, 2006). This is because weak policy frameworks are a hurdle to effectively dealing with climate change. Thus, there is a direct connection between public policies and the vulnerability of destinations (Donkor et al., 2019). This explains why 2 tourist destinations with similar scenic attributes and subject to the same climate impacts can vary in vulnerability (Santos-Lacueva et al., 2017). Climate change exacerbates flooding and worsens erosive processes (e.g. beach erosion) whilst coastal urban tourism infrastructure is destroyed. Beach tourism is a vital market that demands comparatively high temperatures. Studies from other urban tourism hot spots in Africa indicate that there is an urgent need for a long-term adaptation management framework to mitigate climate risks to the tourism industry. Boateng et al. (2017) argue that such a framework is necessary to stem the tide of coastal erosion and flooding in tourism operations along Ghana's coastline. Fashae and Onafeso (2011), with reference to Lagos, Nigeria, point to the need to enhance sea-defence policies to minimise loss of lives and property by introducing robust flood warning systems and implementing requisite building codes. Similar observations have been made for Cairo (Shaltout et al., 2015) and Dar es Salaam (Kebede & Nicholls, 2011).

12.4.2 *Drought in Cape Town*

Coastal cities are susceptible to the synergistic impacts of climate change and anthropogenic turbulence owing to their responsive ecologies, escalating populace and exposure to rising sea levels and climate change. Drought in the Western Cape is a major worry for industry players (Steyn, 2012; Simpson et al., 2020b). It is estimated that fears about the impact of the drought crisis in the Western Cape threatened its projected increase of 20% in tourist visits (Brophy,

2018). This translates into an income loss of about R90 million owing to concerns about "Day Zero", when water supplies to the city would be cut off. Owing to the unique experience of Cape Town, its operators in the urban tourism sector are arguably well-positioned to champion adaptation measures in tackling water stress and thereby helping to create a hub that is resilient in the face of climate change and that rival destinations worldwide can learn from (Simpson et al., 2020a). As the region's water resources come under increasing pressure, it is prudent to encourage visitors to partner with locals in the judicious use of water (Simpson et al., 2020a, 2020b). Accordingly, industry players have encouraged visitors to experience fantastic holidays whilst consuming less water and thus to safeguard Cape Town as a breathtaking destination for future generations through conserving its resources. Industry players have used several platforms to educate their clients on water resource conservation and displayed brief tips on using water as a local, including limited toilet flushing, reusage of towels and bedding, and reduced showering times (Brophy, 2018). Tourism operators have introduced measures such as reduced-flow taps and showers, hand sanitizers in bathrooms, buckets in showers to trap grey water for flushing the toilet, bottled water and using water from boreholes and rainwater tanks for gardens and pools. In the hot summers, tourism operators are known to have covered swimming pools and blocked the showers in gyms (Brophy, 2018). Some urban tourism operators have built their own desalination plants whilst others have sourced boreholes and well points to extract ground water. All these measures were initially introduced to improve tourists' awareness and cooperation in grappling with water scarcity, enabling them to become water-wise and environmentally conscious without compromising their positive experience of the city and its environs (Pace, 2018). Some tourism operators have placed advisory notifications in hotel rooms in the quest to conserve water. The stringent limit of 87 litres of water per person daily was introduced to stave off Day Zero, together with punitive measures, against the backdrop of a public awareness campaign.

12.4.3 *Sanitation and health*

Climate-induced water scarcity comes with health risks (Chitonge et al., 2020; Rother et al., 2020). Urban hospitality operators have had to confront not only the huge waste that comes with hosting visitors, but also the necessity of implementing measures to safeguard their health whilst also conserving water. Examples are the use of specialised bio-enzymatic formulae that can be sprayed into toilets or urinals to eliminate harmful bacteria whilst eradicating malodour (Rother et al., 2020). Not only industry players but the entire city, nation and world have been alerted to ways of conserving water and energy.

Climate change impacts the distribution and availability of wildlife as it comes into closer contact with humans and surfaces in new places (Carlson et al., 2020; Gudoshava et al., 2020). It is also noteworthy that the outbreak of pandemics such as COVID-19 have thrown the spotlight on human and wildlife interactions in a bid to stem the transfer of viruses from wildlife to humans (Colyn et al.,

2020; Rother et al., 2020). Given that industry players are on a drive to increase tourist arrivals, including from areas of the world with a poor record of regulating wildlife trade and consumption, it is imperative to improve such regulations in this country. Additionally, the fluctuating climate and land-use fuel alterations in the geographic range of wildlife, result in the novel grouping of species and opportunities for viral distribution between hitherto isolated species. This exacerbates the potential spillover into humans – a likely connection between climate change and emerging zoonotic disease. Changing mammalian species are forecast to converge in areas with high elevation, in biodiversity hot spots and in places with dense human populations in Asia and Africa, sharing novel viruses between 3 000 and 13 000 times.

Higher standards of safety, cleanliness, amenities and environmental health at beaches in South Africa are promoted and recognised by the award of Blue Flag status to beaches that meet the benchmarks. The Mother City has a reputation as hosting some of the best such beaches across the globe (The Guardian, 2016). Ten beaches in Cape Town were awarded the Blue Flag for the December 2019 to January 2020 season. The blending of two oceans around Cape Point, namely the Atlantic and Indian Oceans (separated until this point by a 1 000 m high peninsula), translates into two differing styles of beach, making Cape Town an unrivalled holiday destination.

12.4.4 Powering urban tourism with alternative energy

The Western Cape represents approximately 13% of South Africa's GDP (Odendaal, 2018). Tourism operators are dealing with intermittent power cuts as the state utility provider has introduced electricity rationing. The need to weather the city's energy crisis is particularly urgent, as it comes on the heels of a drought crisis there, putting the urban tourism industry into steady crisis mode (Sanderson, 2019). The load-shedding scenario, unlike the drought, gives ample opportunity to plan, as one knows when the power is scheduled to be cut. With measures being rolled out to increase tourist arrivals, challenges related to energy may become pronounced. However, renewable energy sources can be introduced in forms that address sustainability imperatives (Fitchett et al., 2017). To effectively address the challenge of climate change, urban tourist operators need to embrace energy-saving measures and the increased use of renewable energy sources. This is especially necessary as the tourism industry also relies on transportation and is based on energy resources in many respects (Jiricka et al., 2010). Urban tourist operators have a unique opportunity to transform energy consumption into a climate-friendly process underpinned by sustainability principles. The tourism experience can be conducted in a sustainable way such as via *solar camps* employing solar mobility together with energy for camping, accommodation and related activities. This comes with impacts on long-term sustainability, as it can influence others to embrace renewable energy technologies in their lives (Jiricka et al., 2010). Synergy between thermal and hydroelectric plants is another option that can be explored in collaboration with local government authorities to optimise renewable energy technologies (Jiricka et al., 2010; Michalena, 2008). For this to be successful, a high level of acceptance is necessary amongst operators (Scott et al., 2004; Shaaban & Ramzy, 2010). Renewable energy offers a wide range of opportunities, from solar systems usage in luxury tourism to the use of wind parks or biomass combustion in ecotourism and geothermal greenhouse applications in agrotourism (Jiricka et al., 2010; Michalena, 2008).

12.4.5 Storms and fires

Tourism operators have often cited strong winds and wildfires as being amongst their biggest challenges, with lightning causing more issues. The threat of storms and wildfires for South Africa's urban operators is exacerbated by climate change, with strong winds often driving flames that leave parched terrain and devastated landscapes (Western Cape Government, 2017). This is exemplified by the recurrent outbreak of wildfires in Knysna, attributed to severe weather conditions, which have damaged urban tourism infrastructure. Several tourism establishments were destroyed, including large tracts of indigenous forest, 1 059 homes and approximately 500 beds lost. The effects of fire and storms often lead to claims in excess of R22 million for fire and R1 million for storms, respectively (Western Cape Government, 2017). Destruction attributed to storms is often relatively superficial – involving damage to roofs, doors and tiles, and the collapse of smaller buildings – with fire causing more widespread damage. The Southern Africa Tourism Services Association (SATSA) collaborates closely with emergency services. Popular destinations like the Garden Route have been affected by severe fires and fall within a disaster zone. Supplementary resources can be marshalled to combat fires in the area, including fire trucks from the City of Cape Town and the Overberg district (Western Cape Government, 2017). The collaboration amongst tourism operators to assist stranded tourists and afford help for health emergencies, search and rescue, coupled with trauma counselling services, underscores the need for operators to be proactive. Operators cannot afford to be reactive only, given the devastation and health implications. Copious amounts of smoke and ash, amongst others factors, may cause potential visitors to seek alternative destinations (Simpson et al., 2020a; Tesfaye & Berhanu, 2015). It has become necessary to provide useful, comprehensive and practical information for potential tourists and make it available on tourist sites. The rising threat of fires highlights the need to integrate wildfire planning into tourism planning (Scott et al., 2004; Shaaban & Ramzy, 2010). Wildfires are also considered social disasters because of the complexity of gaining fire insurance, with implications for both operators and their employees. Fires are also a problem for tourism marketers, as negative images often go viral, tending to tarnish the branding process, complicating perception issues and becoming an existential threat to tourism; indeed, some popular destinations are cited as being in fire-prone areas (Boustras & Boukas, 2013). Such multifaceted challenges necessitate that the bar be raised in terms of service delivery and more creative marketing strategies in order to overcome the competitive challenge from rival destinations.

12.4.6 Opportunities

Tourism opportunities presented by climate change include the following:

- By virtue of their location in Africa, which is a climate hot spot, tourism operators are strategically located to take the lead in developing new tourism niches. Thus, the urban tourism industry can make gains in terms of creating an eco-efficiency outlook through introducing measures that are deemed more sustainable.
- Operators can become proactive in formulating and influencing relevant policies (Figure 12.1) to secure the sector and fulfil their corporate social responsibilities.
- Urban operators can benefit from addressing climate-induced effects such as a rising sea levels and water scarcity, and can integrate environmental quality concerns into their offerings whilst diversifying their products. In addition, short- and medium-distance beach tourists can gain from seasonal climate forecasting.
- Cape Town's urban tourist operators are uniquely placed to serve as global ambassadors in terms of industry-wide best practices and service delivery, impacting both clients and operators.
- The diversification of water sources can be promoted, and long-term strategies can be embraced, instead of only reactive piecemeal gestures.
- Urban tourism operators have a unique opportunity to support viral surveillance and discovery initiatives with biodiversity surveys tracing range shifts. This is particularly relevant as pandemics such as COVID-19 have affected urban tourism operators immensely and call for their proactivity.
- Growing global concerns about fighting climate change and improving energy efficiency provide avenues for exploring novel tourism niches, such as energy tourism. Merging sustainability sensitisation with novel experiences can serve as a marketing tool and simultaneously enhance opinions on climate change adaptation measures.
- Energy tourism can be combined with other tourism products in the area to make the Cape Town area an eco-energy region. The prospects for renewable energies are good, and geothermal energy sources and those from wind and waves can be explored and harnessed.
- Urban tourism operators can be engaged in awareness creation and adaptation-planning processes. This includes involvement in disaster planning processes related to fire, which is considered a threat that affects them immensely.

12.5 Conclusion

South Africa is replete with idyllic landscapes and attractions set in a rich, multicultural and historical context. This accounts for its popularity as a tourist destination for international tourists, amongst others, in the aftermath of apartheid, when the country was welcomed into the comity of nations. It is not surprising that the industry has become a critical segment of the burgeoning economy and sustains the social and economic livelihoods of a great number of locals annually. Thus, issues that affect the success of the sector are of keen interest, given their potential to impact the value chain. Climate change is affecting the local tourism industry and related actors, as evidenced by the rising incidence of drought, storms and wildfires. Nevertheless, urban tourist operators in Cape Town are well-placed to be leaders in novel niches in the tourism sector, introducing features that can cause clients to become environmentally conscious whilst co-developing interventions and shaping related policy. This includes combining energy tourism with other tourism products to create an eco-energy region; becoming active in formulating and influencing relevant policies, including disaster planning; diversifying water and energy sources; promoting environmental conservation and sensitisation; and ultimately serving as ambassadors of sustainability. This will also substantially amplify their contributions to the SDGs and cement their position as key stakeholders.

References

Agnew, M.D., & Viner, D. (2001). Potential impacts of climate change on international tourism. *Tourism and Hospitality Research,* 3(1), 37–60.

Becken, S., & Wilson, J. (2013). The impacts of weather on tourist travel. *Tourism Geographies,* 15(4), 620–639.

Bernard, H.R., & Ryan, G.W. (2010). *Analyzing qualitative data: systematic approaches.* Los Angeles, CA: Sage.

Boateng, I., Wiafe, G., & Jayson-Quashigah, P. (2017). Mapping vulnerability and risk of Ghana's coastline to sea level rise. *Marine Geodesy,* 40(1), 23–39. https://doi.org/10.1080/01490419.2016.1261745.

Boustras, G., & Boukas, N. (2013). Forest fires' impact on tourism development: a comparative study of Greece and Cyprus. *Management of Environmental Quality,* 24(4), 498–511. https://doi.org/10.1108/MEQ-09-2012-0058.

Briedenhann, J., & Wickens, E. (2004). Tourism routes as a tool for the economic development of rural areas – vibrant hope or impossible dream? *Tourism Management,* 25(1), 71–79.

Brophy, S. (2018). *Hanekom: Tourism vulnerable to real SA challenges.* https://www.traveller24.com/News/hanekom-tourism-vulnerable-to-real-sa-challenges-20180321.

Carlson, C.J., Albery, G.F., Merow, C., Trisos, C.H., Zipfel, C.M., Eskew, E.J., Olival, K.J., Ross, N. & Bansal, S.. (2020). Climate change will drive novel cross-species viral transmission. *bioRxiv.* https://doi.org/10.1101/2020.01.24.918755.

Chitonge H., Mokoena A., & Kongo M. (2020). Water and sanitation inequality in Africa: challenges for SDG 6. In: Ramutsindela M., & Mickler D. (Eds), *Africa and the sustainable development goals,* 207–218. Cham: Springer.

City of Cape Town. (2017). *Meet the city.* https://www.capetown.gov.za/.

Colyn, R.B., Henderson, C.L., Altwegg, R., & Smit-Robinson, H.A. (2020). Habitat transformation and climate change: implications for the distribution, population status, and colony extinction of Southern Bald Ibis (*Geronticus calvus*) in southern Africa. *The Condor*, 122(1), 1–17 duz064.

Creswell, J.W. (2013). *Research design: qualitative, quantitative, and mixed method approaches.* (4th ed.). Thousand Oaks, CA: SAGE.

Donkor, F.K., Howarth, C., Ebhuoma, E., Daly, M., Vaughan, C., Pretorius, L., Mambo, J., MacLeod, D., Kythreotis, A., Jones, L., Grainger, S., Golding, N., & Anderson, A.A.

(2019). Climate services and communication for development: the role of early career researchers in advancing the debate. *Environmental Communication*, 13(5), 561–566. https://doi.org/10.1080/17524032.2019.1596145.

Fashae, O.A., & Onafeso, O.D. (2011). Impact of climate change on sea level rise in Lagos, Nigeria. *International Journal of Remote Sensing*, 32(24), 9811–9819. https://doi.org/10.1080/01431161.2011.581709.

Fitchett, J.M., Hoogendoorn, G., & Swemmer, T. (2016). Economic costs of the 2012 floods on tourism in the Mopani District Municipality, South Africa. *Transactions of the Royal Society of South Africa*, 71(2), 187–194.

Fitchett, J. M., Robinson, D., & Hoogendoorn, G. (2017). Climate suitability for tourism in South Africa. *Journal of Sustainable Tourism*, 25(6), 851–867. https://doi.org/10.1080/09669582.2016.1251933.

Gossling, S., Scott, D., Hall, C.M., Ceron, J.P., & Dubois, G. (2012). Consumer behaviour and demand response of tourists to climate change. *Annals of Tourism Research*, 39(1), 36–58.

Grimm, I.J., Alcântara, L.C.S., & Sampaio, C.A.C. (2018). Tourism under climate change scenarios: impacts, possibilities, and challenges. *Revista Brasileira de Pesquisa em Turismo*, 12(3), 1–13. https://doi.org/10.7784/rbtur.v12i3.1354.

Gudoshava, M., Misiani, H.O., Segele, Z.T., Jain, S., Ouma, J.O., Otieno, G., Anyah, R., Indasi, V.S., Endris, H.S., Osima, S., & Lennard, C. (2020). Projected effects of 1.5° C and 2° C global warming levels on the intra-seasonal rainfall characteristics over the Greater Horn of Africa. *Environmental Research Letters*, 15(3), 034037.

Hambira, W.L., & Saarinen, J. (2015). Policy-maker's perceptions of the tourism-climate change nexus: Policy needs and constraints in Botswana. *Development Southern Africa*, 32, 350–362.

Hoogendoorn, G. & Fitchett, J.M. (2016). Tourism and climate change: a review of threats and adaptation strategies for Africa. *Current Issues in Tourism*, 21(7), 742–759.

Horn, G. (2018). *The impact of tourism on the drought*. https://www.countrylife.co.za/news/38380.

Jawtusch, J. (2014). *Climate change and disaster risk guide: which climate and disaster risks affect South African and how do they affect South Africa?* http://www.brotfueralle.ch/fileadmin/deutsch/2_Entwicklungpolitik_allgemein/.

Jiricka, A., Salak, B., Eder, R., Arnberger, A., & Pröbstl, U. (2010). Energetic tourism: exploring the experience quality of renewable energies as a new sustainable tourism market. *Transactions on Ecology and the Environment*, 139, 1–14.

Karmalkar, A., McSweeney, C., New, A., & Lizcano, G. (2012). *UNDP climate change country profiles: South Africa*. http://www.geog.ox.ac.uk/research/climate/projects/undp-cp/?countryDSouth_Africa&d1DReports.

Kebede, A.S., & Nicholls, R.J. (2011). Population and assets exposure to coastal flooding in Dar es Salaam (Tanzania): vulnerability to climate extremes. *Regional Environmental Change*, 12, 81–94.

Krige, N. (2019). *Statistics show that the South African tourism sector is in decline*. https://www.thesouthafrican.com/travel/tourism-in-south-africa-on-the-decline-2019/.

Leonard, L. (2016). Mining and/or tourism development for job creation and sustainability in Dullstroom, Mpumalanga. *Local Economy*, 31(1–3), 249–263. https://doi.org/10.1177/0269094215621875.

Long D., & Ziervogel G. (2020). Vulnerability and adaptation to climate change in urban South Africa. In: Massey R., & Gunter A. (Eds), *Urban geography in South Africa*, 139–153. Cham: Springer.

Love Cape Town. ©2020. *A guide to beaches in Cape Town.* https://www.capetown.travel/a-guide-to-beaches-in-cape-town/.

McCombes, S. (2020). *How to write a literature review.* https://www.scribbr.com/dissertation/literature-review/.

Mearns, K.F., & Lukhele, S.E. (2015). Addressing the operational challenges of community-based tourism in Swaziland. *African Journal of Hospitality Tourism and Leisure,* 4(1), 1–12.

Michalena, E. (2008). *Using renewable energy as a tool to achieve tourism sustainability in Mediterranean islands.* https://doi.org/10.4000/etudescaribeennes.3487

Musavengane, R., & Leonard, L. (2019). When race and social equity matters in nature conservation in post-apartheid South Africa. *Conservation and Society,* 17(2), 135–146.

Nicholson, S.E. (2000). The nature of rainfall variability over Africa on time scales of decades to millennia. *Global and Planetary Change,* 26(1), 137–158.

Odendaal, N. (2018). *Cape Town drought hits tourism, threatens province's credit ratings.* https://www.engineeringnews.co.za/article/cape-town-drought-hits-tourism-threatens-provinces-credit-ratings-2018-02-07/rep_id:4136.

Pace, A. (2018). *Drought affects tourism industry.* https://www.capetownetc.com/travel/drought-affects-tourism-industry/.

Ralph, N., Birks, M., & Chapman, Y. (2014). Contextual positioning: using documents as extant data in grounded theory research". *SAGE Open,* 4(3),1-7 215824401455242. https://doi.org/10.1177/2158244014552425.

Reid, P., & Vogel, C. (2006). Living and responding to multiple stressors in South Africa – glimpses from KwaZulu-Natal. *Global Environmental Change,* 16(2), 195–206.

Rogerson, C.M. (2016). Climate change, tourism and local economic development in South Africa. *Local Economy,* 31(1–2), 322–331.

Rogerson, C.M., & Visser, G. (2006). International tourist flows and urban tourism in South Africa. *Urban Forum,* 17(2), 199–213.

Rossello, J., & Waqas, A. (2015). The use of tourism demand models in the estimation of the impact of climate change on tourism. *Revista Turismo em Análise,* 26(1), 4–20.

Rother H.A., Sabel C.E., & Vardoulakis, S. (2020). A collaborative framework highlighting climate-sensitive non-communicable diseases in urban sub-Saharan Africa. In: Ramutsindela, M., & Mickler, D. (Eds), *Africa and the sustainable development goals,* 267–278. Cham: Springer.

Sanderson, A. (2019). *One year after the water crisis, Cape Town recovers from tourism drought.* https://www.dw.com/en/one-year-after-the-water-crisis-cape-town-recovers-from-tourism-drought/a-47966335.

Santos-Lacueva, R., Clavé, S.A., & Saladié, Ò. (2017). The vulnerability of coastal tourism destinations to climate change: the usefulness of policy analysis. *Sustainability,* 9, 2062. https://doi.org/doi:10.3390/su9112062.

SA-Venues.com. (2019). *Cape Town beaches.* https://www.sa-venues.com/attractionswc/beaches.htm.

Scott, D., & Lemieux, C. (2010). Weather and climate information for tourism. *Procedia Environmental Sciences,* 1, 146–183.

Scott, D., McBoyle, G., & Schwartzentruber, M. (2004). Climate change and distribution of climatic resources for tourism in North America. *Climate Research,* 27(2), 105–117.

Shaaban, I., & Ramzy, Y. (2010). The impact of climate change on tourism in Egypt as perceived by both policymakers and tourism managers. *WIT Transactions on Ecology and the Environment, 139,* 241– 251.

Shaltout, M., Tonbol, K., & Omstedt, A. (2015). Sea-level change and projected future flooding along the Egyptian Mediterranean coast. *Oceanologia*, 57(4), 293–307. https://doi.org/10.1016/j.oceano.2015.06.004.

Siakwah, P., Musavengane, R., & Leonard, L. (2019). Tourism governance and attainment of the Sustainable Development Goals in Africa. *Tourism Planning & Development.* https://doi.org/10.1080/21568316.2019.1600160.

Simpson, N.P., Shearing, C.D., & Dupont, B. (2020a). When Anthropocene shocks contest conventional mentalities: a case study from Cape Town. *Climate and Development*, 12(2), 163–169.

Simpson, N.P., Shearing, C.D., & Dupont, B. (2020b). Gated adaptation during the Cape Town drought: mentalities, transitions and pathways to partial nodes of water security. *Society & Natural Resources*. https://doi.org/10.1080/08941920.2020.1712756.

Smith, S. (2020). *SA tourism industry needs special attention, Mr. President.* https://www.fin24.com/Economy/South-Africa/sa-tourism-industry-needs-special-attention-mr-president-20200212.

Stats SA. (2016). *An economic look at the tourism industry.* http://www.statssa.gov.za/?pD4362.

Stern, N. (2006). *Stern review: the economics of climate change.* https://webarchive.nationalarchives.gov.uk/20100407172811/http://www.hm-treasury.gov.uk/stern_review_report.htm

Steyn, J.N. (2012). Managing climate change impacts on tourism: mitigating and adaptive strategies with special reference to the Western Cape province of South Africa. *African Journal for Physical, Health Education, Recreation and Dance (AJPHERD)*, 18(3), 552–564.

Tesfaye, S., & Berhanu, K. (2015). Improving students' participation in active learning methods: group discussions, presentations and demonstrations: a case of Madda Walabu University second year tourism management students of 2014. *Journal of Education and Practice,* 6(22), 1–5.

The Guardian. (2016). *The world's best hidden beaches: Cape Town.* November 23. https://www.theguardian.com/travel/2016/nov/23/worlds-best-hidden-beaches-cape-town.

Torraco, R.J. (2016). Writing integrative literature reviews: using the past and present to explore the future. *Human Resource Development Review.* 15(4), 404–428. https://doi.org/10.1177/1534484316671606.

United Nations Environment Programme. (2003). *Negative socio-cultural impacts from tourism.* http://www.unep.org/resourceefficiency/Business/Sectoral Activities/Tourism/FactsandFiguresaboutTourism/ImpactsofTourism/Socio-CulturalImpacts/NegativeSocio-CulturalImpactsFromTourism/tabid/78781/Default.aspx

Western Cape Government. (2017). *Latest on impact of fires on Knysna tourism.* https://www.westerncape.gov.za/news/latest-impact-fires-knysna-tourism-0.

Winter, K., & Brom, P. (2018). *How cities can work with nature when droughts take their toll.* https://theconversation.com/how-cities-can-work-with-nature-when-droughts-take-their-toll-100396.

Theme 4

Inclusive urban tourism and enclaves

13 Human settlements and tourism development in Kenya

Prospects for tackling urban risks in informal settlements

Prudence Khumalo

13.1 Introduction

Urbanisation in Africa has brought about opportunities to cities, but at the same time, it poses threats to the well-being of many people, especially in the big cities (Croese et al., 2016; Khumalo, 2019; Musavengane et al., 2020). Human settlements inadequacy plagues many of the continent's urban areas, and informal settlements are common features across Africa. If the United Nations' 2030 Sustainable Development Goal (SDG) 11 on sustainable cities is to be achieved, urban risks caused by informal settlements need to be revisited. Any risk that affects tourism indirectly impacts on the fight against poverty, especially in countries such as Kenya where the tourism industry is a significant forex earner. Conversely, if mechanisms meant to promote urban tourism are implemented without supportive, participatory and inclusive development consciousness, these may increase urban risks such as impoverishment and exclusion of certain sections of urban dwellers. As can be drawn from Siakwah et al. (2020), tourism in its various forms and expressions seems to have linkages to the SDGs. Besides being a forex earner, tourism, particularly pro-poor tourism, has the potential to contribute to the attainment of SDG 1: ending poverty (Siakwah et al., 2020). While sub-Saharan Africa (SSA) is expected to grow its urban tourism, most cities are set to confront a number of urban risks associated with future developments (Musavengane et al., 2020).

This chapter examines informal settlements,[1] urban risks and tourism development in Nairobi, Kenya. Kenya is a good case for the study owing to its demography; as of 2016, 26.11% of its populace has lived in urban areas, and of this percentage, 46.5% has lived in informal settlements (Knoema, 2020). Informal settlements, by their nature, connote a space akin to crime, inadequacy, indignity and general lack of access to basic services (Chege & Mwisukha 2013, Khumalo, 2019). It is on grounds of these squalid conditions that informal settlements are viewed as havens of social ills. As in most parts of SSA, the common term used to refer to an informal settlement in Kenya is a 'slum'. According to the Republic of Kenya's (2016) National Slum Upgrading and Prevention Policy, a slum is a contiguous settlement where inhabitants are characterised as having inadequate housing and basic services. Furthermore, the basic characteristics of a slum as contained in the policy include inter alia high population density, dilapidated housing structures, overcrowding and inaccessible and inadequate basic physical and social services such as storm water drainage, electricity, safe water, sanitation and solid waste disposal. The term 'slum' and 'informal settlement' are used interchangeably in this chapter. Informal settlements are areas where groups of dwelling units are constructed on lands that the occupants have no legal claim to, and dwelling units are not in compliance with planning and building regulations. In other words, informal settlements or slums are areas or settlements where development and occupancy do not comply with the legal urban land-use standards set by the governing authority (Castro et al., 2015).

This chapter employs participatory development lenses to unpack the risks inherent in informal settlements and how these impact on tourism and developmental aspirations. The informal settlements and tourism nexus becomes important, especially considering that tourism is one of the key contributors to Kenya's GDP. The country's vision for 2030 spells out 6 (agriculture, wholesale and retail, manufacturing, business process outsourcing, tourism and financial services) priority areas to increase its GDP growth rate per annum by 10%, and tourism is identified as a leading sector amongst them (Kieti & Magio, 2013). The importance of tourism to the Kenyan economy is such that urban risks can have far-reaching negative impacts and effects. This is critical, especially noting that while for several years, Kenya's tourism relied on its traditional forms, such as wildlife, beach and culture, we are recently witnessing new forms of tourism, like slum tourism (Kieti & Magio, 2013). In addition to this introduction, the work is organised into 5 sections. Section 2 presents the theoretical base for the study and unpacks the concept of slum-tourism and its links with urban risks. In section 3, the methodological framework employed is presented, exposing the qualitative nature of the study and how empirical and secondary data were collected and analysed for the discussion. Section 4 presents the findings, giving policy and practical recommendations. Finally, we conclude the chapter by summarising the urban risks for tourism development in Kenya and policy recommendations for future research in section 5.

13.2 Informal settlements, urban risk and tourism

In order to unpack the question of urban risks and tourism, it is important to briefly highlight pertinent issues surrounding informality, urban risk and tourism development. In fact, the question of informal settlements has been viewed from various perspectives – human rights, human dignity, economic impact and poverty. The state of many informal settlements exemplifies what Datta (2012) calls the "violence of urban development". Within this frame, urban development is viewed as a violent process that relegates many into zones of illegality, lack of access and extreme poverty. It must be noted that terms used for informal settlements in different countries denote squalid conditions (Khumalo, 2019). Articulating the causal factors of urban informality, the UN-HABIT (2007) describes Kenyan informal settlements or slums as a combination of demographic, economic and political realities, particularly rapid physical urbanisation and growth that is beyond the ability of the local authorities to guide. This translates into an inability of the urban authorities to provide essential services for urban dwellers, especially in the rapidly built informal settlements.

The discourse on the causal factors of informal settlements is not new (Khumalo, 2019; Croese, Cirolia & Graham, 2016; Fox, 2014; Penglase, 2014; Datta, 2012; Perlman, 2010). The rapid growth and manifestation of slums in Nairobi is a result of the combined effects of rural–urban migration, increasing urban poverty and inequality, marginalisation of poor neighbourhoods, high cost of living, the inability of the urban poor to access land for housing, insufficient investment in new low-income housing and poor maintenance of existing housing. These challenges have effects on living conditions. Satterthwaite (2017) points out that in the absence of risk-reducing infrastructure, overcrowding and other ills such as use of unclean energy heightens the risks of premature death, serious illness and injury in urban areas. As observed by Musavengane et al. (2020), these socioeconomic ills, which are linked to poor governance, tend to lead to unsustainable tourism development as they create, among others ills, nepotism, patronage, clientelism, corruption and institutionalised crime, which threaten physical urban spaces with the whole likelihood of repelling tourists. These urban risks could partly be traced to the neoliberal economic system, where market forces tend to push out the poor from urban areas to create space for tourism expansion and other economic activities.

The development complexities surrounding informal settlements should be understood beyond the streets and shelter. Hernandez-Garcia (2013) intimates that informal settlements are more than the streets and houses; they have social, economic and cultural characteristics, politics and governance. Fox (2014: 200) also argues that the political economy of the informal settlements shows that these settlements provide opportunities for the cultivation of politically useful patron-client networks and rent-seeking opportunities, which create strong incentives to uphold the status quo. However, informal settlements also have a role to play in the promotion of tourism, especially when proper governance and a concerted effort involving all key players is harnessed to undo the ills that bedevil informal settlements. The nexus between informal settlements and tourism is complex because of the negatives and positives that underpin it. Hernandez-Garcia (2013) observes that despite its elusive nature, the subject of informal settlements has gained traction in city branding. It is critical at this point to highlight how urban tourism relates to informal settlements and the whole idea of city branding. City branding denotes the means through which the city achieves a competitive advantage in order to increase inward investment and tourism, as well as community development, local identity and identification of citizens with their city. This also entails activation of social forces to avoid social exclusion and unrest.

The question that emanates from this discussion is how Kenyan urban centres leverage on the informal settlements to promote tourism. The Latin-American case alluded to by Hernandez-Garcia (2013), however, spells out 3 ways by which informal settlements can enrich urban tourism. Firstly, there is the realisation that informal settlements are a constitutive and consistent part of urban areas, exhibiting distinctive physical and social features. In a sense, they are a differentiated space with 'strong identity associations'. The second aspect relates to some of the cultural expressions obtained in these areas, which can be of interest beyond their own boundaries. Informal settlements are known for creativity and cultural richness, which can positively contribute to branding. The argument here is that the cultural heritage of slums, such as their stories of resilience and the traditional dishes served therein, can be utilised as a resource to remake their images in the face of deeply rooted prejudices against slum residents. The third aspect points to the distinctive architecture of these areas, which arguably can contribute to the idea of place branding. A case-in-point is that of the New Kibera Soweto East flats. These 3 aspects are more acceptable than the idea of 'gazing at the poverty of others', as intimated by some scholars such as Steinbrink (2012). 'Slum tourism' is still a new phenomenon, especially in the Global South (Steinbrink, 2012), concept has attracted debates from some sectors of the society who view such tourism as violating the rights of the poor, thus questioning the appropriateness of the practice (Kieti & Magio, 2013). One of the criticisms of slums borders is about the morality or appropriateness of making other people's underprivileged position a feature of attraction. It can be very insensitive to use the condition of the poor as a gaze for attraction. Despite the ongoing contestations about slum tourism, a number of cities in the Global South such as Rio de Janeiro, Johannesburg, and Cape Town have slum tours as part of their urban tourism programme (Steinbrink, 2012). In the case of South Africa, Booyens and Rogerson (2019) observe that the phenomenon has increased in recent years, with places such as Soweto Township in Johannesburg and Khayelitsha in Cape Town becoming some of the target attractions for tourists. The residents of these townships have embraced this as an opportunity for business. Slum tourism gives an opportunity for local residents to tell their stories to an interested audience, particularly in places like Soweto, where locals seize the tourist opportunity to recount their apartheid history (Booyens & Rogerson, 2019).

The nexus between tourism and informal settlements could also be understood through the negative impact that slums have on urban tourism. As aforementioned, most informal settlements are potential crime zones, and this has adverse effects on the attractiveness of urban areas for tourism. Slum tourism exposes the risks associated with modern city tourism, where the socioeconomic context relegates a section of the city to what some scholars such as Steinbrink (2012) has termed the 'culturalisation of poverty'. This seems to be quite a typical feature of slum tourism. However, slum tourism should not always be seen as all about a gaze at poverty, since some historical and socio-cultural factors can provide a broader appreciation of informal settlements. The rise of what came to be known as 'township tourism' in South Africa, particularly in Johannesburg, is linked to the struggle against apartheid, where resistance against the oppressive regime can be traced back to areas where key figures like Nelson Mandela lived (Booyens & Rogerson, 2019). Their former houses have become heritage sites, which attract many tourists. These examples, in a sense, broaden slum tourism to more than an activity where the better-off gaze at the squalid conditions of the less privileged. Slum tourism is a way of reconnecting with history. This is important for local economic development, as it increases financial circulation within the locality. Previous studies on Kibera, Nairobi, argue that a visit by tourists has an impact on local businesses as the tourists boost the local business, especially those involved in art and craft (Fox, 2014). Kibera became one of the key political battle sites for the presidential race following the disputed presidential election of 2007, which finally culminated in a power-sharing agreement between Mwai Kibaki and Raila Odinga (Fox, 2014).

The processes involved in bringing about an upgrade of organic informal settlements to formalised structures, as in the case of the Kibera informal settlements, presents a huge opportunity for other areas who are still stuck in the makeshift dwellings to emulate. Upgrading informal settlements stands to improve tourist visits, as tourists seek to learn the culture, taste local foods, hear local life stories and, importantly, inject money into the locality. More creative forms of tourism can be developed in a space where myriad repulsive elements are minimised. In this context, informal settlements become spaces of opportunity in the tourism development discourse.

13.3 Methodology

In order to unravel the factors and urban risks impacting informal settlements and tourism development, this chapter adopts a qualitative approach to bring out the lived experiences of officials and people who have been involved with informal settlements in urban spaces. The study looks at the informal settlements in Nairobi, Kenya, with Kibera Soweto East Project specifically as a case study. This case is unique due to its situation within a vast space covered by slums and a portion of high-rise newly upgraded houses. Kibera is the most visited slum in Kenya, with tours organised by some private companies (Chege & Waweru, 2014). The data collection approach is twofold, consisting of both secondary and primary data sources. First, the primary step was to engage with relevant literature on the subject and explore official and other documents on informal settlements in Kenya, critically interrogating the policies, strategies and programmes put in place to deal with informal settlements' challenges. The relevance of the literature used was determined and selected on the basis of two main criteria. Firstly, articles addressing urban risks, tourism and informal settlements in general, and those related to Kenya, were reviewed. Besides the scholarly literature, government policy documents such as the National Slum Upgrading and Prevention Policy were analysed. These were critical in understanding the background and policy intentions of government and the socioeconomic factors at play.

Second, the secondary sources are augmented by an empirical study that involved site visitation and in-depth interviews with 9 key informants. These key informants included persons from the Directorate of the Kenya Slum Upgrading Programme (KENSUP). The director and the deputy director were interviewed to obtain the vision, strategies and methods of slum upgrading. Additionally, the project manager for Kibera Soweto East Project was interviewed as well. First-hand experience in managing processes and stakeholder engagements was very important in unpacking informal settlements risks and developing better human settlements for the slum dwellers. Respondents who lived in the Kibera slum before and after the upgrade were critical to the study. The views of the chairperson of the community housing executive committee, who also happens to be a clergyman, were also sought. Five other dwellers of the slum were interviewed, including the youth. The interviews with the slum dwellers focused on firsthand information and lived experiences in the slum. The data from the interviews were recorded, transcribed, coded, thematised and compared with literature and information obtained from official reports. Themes were developed based on the main research question and those emanating from the data concerning the challenges of informal settlements and urban tourism development in Kenya.

13.4 Kenya's policy and strategy on informal settlements

Statistics have shown that there are more than 46% of people dwelling in informal settlements in urban areas in Kenya (Knoema, 2020). This population often lives in conditions that are virtually not conducive for habitation – mostly, slums. These slums are characterised by lack of access to water and sanitation, adequate housing and secure tenure, with many facing security and health problems. Residents have to rely on informal networks for survival in hostile urban spaces. These challenges are indicative of the complexities that the government of Kenya and other actors or players are faced with in addressing the informal settlements difficulties. Instead of viewing informal urban settlements as problem-makers, there is need for a shift in perspective to see them as areas for improvement and possible solutions to urban challenges. It is in light of this background that the Kenyan government's policies and strategies relating to informal settlements are brought under scrutiny. As shown by the Latin-American case (see Hernandez-Garcia, 2013), informal settlement spaces can bring positive as well as negative outcomes depending on how they are handled. The exclusion and abandonment of informal settlements cannot be sustained, hence the need to address the question of informal settlements' development and risks to tourism development.

The Kenyan Government, through the Ministry of Land, Housing and Urban Development, has come up with ways of improving housing and human settlements for its populace. In relation to informal settlements/slums, one of the key policies guiding development is the National Slum Upgrading and Prevention Policy (Republic of Kenya, 2016). The policy arose from the realisation that while the urban areas have grown to be attractive as places of better living, attracting 6-7% growth annually, a number of the people drawn to these areas are the unemployed and low-income earners. This means that in the absence of social housing, as the case is in Kenya, these poor urban dwellers cannot afford the high price of housing on the open markets. As a result, there has been a continuous growth in the number of informal settlement dwellers. Given this state of affairs, the objective of the policy is to recognise and integrate the slums into the urban fabric, guaranteeing access to adequate housing while taking into account the local livelihoods. It also seeks to provide a regulatory and institutional framework to guide coordinated and accountable implementation of Slum Upgrading and Prevention at the national and subnational level in Kenya. The policy also seeks to promote and protect dignified livelihoods of the underprivileged working and living in slums by integrating them into the social, political and economic framework in line with the Constitution of the Republic of Kenya (2016). The policy is quite explicit on government intentions to improve the lives of people living in slums, detailing interventions such as community mobilisation and organisation, urban development strategies to guide urban development, social and physical infrastructure and income generation activities. The policy also entails strategies to upgrade shelter and environmental and waste management. The intended outcomes stand to benefit tourism in the area by reducing factors that repel tourists, such as poor hygiene, while providing the infrastructure that can enable and support tourism. In the succeeding sections, the implementation of some aspects of the policy are presented to highlight urban risks and tourism in informal settlements.

13.5 Informal settlements, urban risks and tourism in Kenya

The data highlight the significance of informal and slum settlements to Kenya's urban landscape. By virtue of their urban share, informal settlements cannot be ignored in the promotion and preservation of tourism, especially urban tourism. While there are a number of perspectives to explain the relationship between informal settlements and tourism, it is clear from literature that their cultural, historical and social connections explain the tourists' attraction to slums. The empirical data collected from key informants indicate that while the government has been making efforts to improve the state of informal settlements, urban informal settlements remain high-risk threats to the socioeconomic development of the inhabitants. The respondents[2] from the directorate of the Kenya Slum Upgrading Programme identified poor infrastructure such as drainage, roads and other communication infrastructure, and sewage systems as some of the areas of concern in the informal settlements. In underscoring the vulnerability of these areas, the respondent from the Kibera Slum Upgrading Project[3] pointed to the adverse effects of a small river separating the upgraded section of the informal settlements and the rest of the area still informally settled. This small river overflows its banks during times of heavy rains and sweeps away some of the slum structures, including the possessions of those who dwell therein. This is one of the risks that the informal settlement dwellers are confronted with from time to time. These areas are also prone to the devastating impact of fires. Poor or inadequate sanitation poses one of the biggest health risks such as cholera. Some of the respondents[4] narrated the unfortunate cases of what is known as 'flying toilets', where some dwellers of the informal settlements would dispose of their human waste by throwing it out into the open at night. This unfortunate and despicable state of affairs has been responded to by government and other development partners by putting in resources to improve sanitation in these settlements, although some challenges still persist. The absence of proper waste management means that waste, especially plastic waste, is disposed of anyhow, and it collects in streams and rivers, which sometimes in the end affect plants and animals. These make the informal settlements vulnerable to waterborne diseases and thus unattractive to tourists.

The key informants from the directorate explained the challenge of criminality within the informal settlements. Some cartels control structures in the settlements and dwellers pay rentals to them. It came to light that only 8% of the slum dwellers own the structures in the settlement. One of the key informants explained how these slum lords who happen to live lavishly outside the slum area were behind the resistance to efforts by the government to improve the slum areas.[5] There was further indication that informal settlements have become lucrative sites for some political entities who solicit votes by giving handouts and promising networks of patronage. Due to poverty levels, most people fall for these handouts, and in some cases, sabotage lasting solutions that improve their socioeconomic status. The key informants from the directorate expressed disappointment at the manner in which the 8% absentee owners were manipulating the majority who rent from them to stand in the way of the participatory approach government was embarking on to improve the area. One might easily dismiss the directorate's responses as a top-down approach to the informal settlement development; however, visiting the site of these developments and interacting with residents of the informal structures and those who have benefitted from the collective action by government and the communities to upgrade the settlements gives a different picture. The Kenya Slum Upgrading Programme that saw 822 households (about 5 000 people) accommodated in new high-rising flats in informal settlements on a rent-to-buy basis presents an interesting case. The landlords of the informal structures worked to frustrate the pace of upgrading the settlement for selfish reasons, slowing a development process that could unlock more room for tourism. The perpetuation of the status quo means the necessary infrastructure to support tourism development is stifled.

An interview with the chairperson of the community settlements committee indicates that there was active participation of the community and the first group to benefit was transparently selected and the allocation was fairly done. Those who were on the waiting list expressed hope of also getting the opportunity in the future to upgrade to similar structures. The community had even nicknamed the new upgraded structure 'Canaan' after the biblical Promised Land to express improvement of life for those who benefitted.[6] The important part of this development is that it overcame the risks of disrupting social networks and support systems as it is in situ. It is important to note that the chairperson of the settlements committee is a clergyman, which brings about the importance of allowing the community to select their own structures. His social standing within the settlement made it easy for him to rally the inhabitants to embrace the idea of improving their housing and sacrifice the necessary resources to attain this.

One of the risks emanating from the empirical study, which is also evident from the literature, is the lack of access to educational facilities, which may result in high illiteracy and the possibility of children being trapped in the cycle of poverty. An interesting interview with one former dweller[7] of the informal settlement at the site of the new development was quite enlightening on what scholarship can do to transform the livelihoods of the informal settlement dwellers.

The respondent narrated how he worked hard to get himself to school and caught the interest of one sponsor who granted him a scholarship, and he managed to go to good schools until he got his law qualifications. He came back to his former home to mobilise youths to pursue their education and helped them identify scholarships to pursue their dreams and to be active in the improvement of their area. The expectation is that once residents are empowered through education, they will be able to explore the tourism potential dormant in the slum.

It was evident from the directorate respondents that while there are success stories in terms of curbing the risks associated with developing informal settlements, the rate of development was very slow due mainly to lack of funding. The government with other players such as the World Bank sponsored most of the work. The findings point to the fact that the main attraction to tourists in Kibera is the gaze at poverty, and this poses a risk of perpetual poverty, as the potential of this type of tourism does not help much in improving the economic status of the residents. This is because most of the tourists are interested in sightseeing, and those benefitting from this aspect of tourism are non-residents of the slum. This validates Booyens and Rogerson (2019)'s argument for more creative tourism that goes beyond the historical heritage and gaze at the poor for tourism development and socioeconomic empowerment of the residents of the slums.

13.6 Conclusion

The chapter brings to the fore the nexus between informal settlements and urban tourism risk. The social context, cultural uniqueness and historical features or heritage of informal settlements make them attractive places for tourists. Conversely, factors such as crime, poor hygiene and lack of supportive infrastructure stifle the growth and development of tourism in these areas. It is drawn from the literature and the empirical study on informal settlements in Nairobi, Kenya, that, by their nature, informal settlements pose a number of risks to urban tourism. The study highlights that there has been a growing interest in what some scholars term 'poverty tourism' or 'negative sightseeing', which entails tourists who visit informal areas to gaze at the poverty of others. This aspect of tourism has faced serious criticism from a number of writers and understandably so, as it borders on unethical practices that break some moral codes. However, this study argues that there is more to informal settlement tourism than a gaze at poverty. The study unravelled the risks associated with informal settlements. These include the high rate of crime that scares tourists from visiting these places, the poor or inadequate sanitation and drainage, and vulnerability to adverse weather conditions and disasters such as fires. The absence of proper waste management and removal from these settlements poses a health hazard to flora and fauna. The study argues that informal settlement improvement programmes, especially in situ, such as the Kenya Informal Settlements Improvement Programme, should not be viewed as disrupting the social fabric and support systems, as they actually improve the socioeconomic status of dwellers.

Notes

1 This work is part of a bigger study examining Prospects of Human Settlements in an integrated Africa, which is funded by UNISA & the African Union Commission.
2 Two members of KENSUP Directorate, March 2019.
3 Official from Kenya Upgrading Programme, Kibera Project, March 2019.
4 Two current dwellers of Kibera Slum who have not yet benefited from the upgrading programme, March 2019.
5 Official from Kenya Slum Upgrading Programme, Kibera Project, March 2019.
6 Two respondents who are beneficiaries of the Slum Upgrading Programme, March 2019.
7 Law professional who previously lived in the Kibera slum, March 2019.

References

Booyens, I., & Rogerson, C. M. (2019). Re-creating slum tourism: Perspectives from South Africa. *Urbani Izziv*, 30, 52–63.

Castro, C. P., Ibarra, I., Lukas, M., Ortiz, J., & Sarmiento, J. P. (2015). Disaster risk construction in the progressive consolidation of informal settlements: Iquique and Puerto Montt (Chile) case studies. *International Journal of Disaster Risk Reduction*, 13, 109–127.

Chege, P. W., & Mwisukha, A. (2013). Benefits of slum tourism in slum in Nairobi, Kenya. *International Journal of Arts and Commerce*, 2(4), 94–102.

Chege, P. W., & Waweru, F. K. (2014). Assessment of status, challenges and viability of Slum Tourism: Case Study of Kibera Slum in Nairobi, Kenya. *Assessment*, 4(6).

Croese, S., Cirolia, L. R., & Graham, N. (2016). Towards Habitat III: Confronting the disjuncture between global policy and local practice on Africa's 'challenge of slums'. *Habitat International*, 53, 237–242.

Datta, A. (2012). *The illegal City: Space, law and gender in a Delhi squatter settlement.* Burlington, USA, Ashgate.

Fox, S. (2014). The political economy of slums: Theory and evidence from Sub-Saharan Africa. *World Development*, 54, 191–203.

Hernandez-Garcia, J., (2013). Slum tourism, city branding and social urbanism: the case of Medellin, Colombia. *Journal of Place Management and Development*, 6(1), pp.43–51.

Kieti, D. M., & Magio, K. O. (2013). The ethical and local resident perspectives of slum tourism in Kenya.

Khumalo, P. (2019). Rethinking informal settlements in the Global South: Imagining a new approach of tackling informal Settlements in Africa in Albert IO & Lawanson T (Editors).*2019. Urban crisis and crisis management in Africa. A festschrift for Prof. Akin Mabogunje.* Austin TX, Pan African University Press.

Knoema (2020). https://knoema.com/atlas/Kenya/Urban-population Accessed 18/04/2020.

Musavengane, R., Siakwah, P., & Leonard, L. (2020). The nexus between tourism and urban risk: Towards inclusive, safe, resilient and sustainable outdoor tourism in African cities. *Journal of Outdoor Recreation and Tourism*, 29, 100254.

Penglase, R. B. (2014). *Living with insecurity in a Brazilian favela: Urban violence and daily life.* Rutgers University Press.

Perlman, J. (2010). *Favela: Four decades of living on the edge in Rio de Janeiro.* Oxford University Press.

Republic of Kenya, 2016: *National slum upgrading and prevention policy.* Ministry of Land, Housing and Urban development, Nairobi.

Satterthwaite, D. (2017). The impact of urban development on risk in sub-Saharan Africa's cities with a focus on small and intermediate urban centres. *International journal of disaster risk reduction*, 26, 16–23.

Siakwah, P., Musavengane, R. & Leonard, L. (2020) Tourism governance and attainment of the sustainable development goals in Africa. *Tourism Planning & Development*, 17:4, 355–383, DOI: 10.1080/21568316.2019.1600160.

Steinbrink, M. (2012). 'We did the Slum!'–urban poverty tourism in historical perspective. *Tourism Geographies*, 14(2), 213–234.

UN-Habitat. 2007. *UN-HABITAT and the Kenya Slum Upgrading*. UNHABITAT, Nairobi, Kenya.

14 Conservation tourism challenges and opportunities on the Cape Flats, South Africa

Michael Dyssel

14.1 Introduction

Conservation tourism is dependent on a destination's conservation estate – that is, its conservation-worthy biodiversity, geodiversity and cultural history attributes – as well as how that destination is managed within the broader geographical context of its specific location. Depending on the location, this geographical context can either enable or impede conservation and tourism. The purpose of this study is to identify and analyse the factors that govern conservation tourism on the Cape Flats, the immediate hinterland of Cape Town, as a way of engaging with the city's efforts to reduce urban risks and enhance bioresilience. Specifically, it looks at how 4 nature reserves in this part of the city are impacted by the difficult socioeconomic conditions in the surrounding communities. Furthermore, it examines how impediments to successful and sustainable conservation tourism, such as safety concerns and conservation apathy, can be transformed into conservation tourism enablers.

The case-study approach and qualitative data collection methods used are rooted in political ecology as an overarching theoretical lens and in the Sustainable Development Goals (SDGs) as an overarching ethical framework. The results reveal the extent of the threats to protected areas on the Cape Flats and point to the necessity of inclusive co-management strategies (involving both authorities and communities) in responding to these threats. Ultimately, the study's contribution is rooted in the idea that a nuanced appreciation of a city's conservation estate, including its neglected or forgotten aspects, can assist in thinking through and addressing urban risk and resilience concerns.

14.2 Background

14.2.1 Conservation through a political ecology lens

Human–nature relationships are complex, fraught and continually evolving. On both a theoretical and an ethical level, there is a need to carefully and constantly interrogate the links between conservation on the one hand and vested interests, resource needs and tourism practices on the other hand (Adams & Hutton, 2007).

The destructive and exclusionary role that many protected conservation areas have played, and are still playing, is particularly contentious. Globally, there has been a wide variation in the 'officialisation' and use of protected areas. More often than not, though, these protected areas leave an imprint of leisure, hunting, tourism, economic agendas and large-scale environmental destruction on the natural landscape (Adams, 2004; Adams & Hutton, 2007; Kelleher, 1999) – all while physically and economically displacing dependent communities (Brockington, 2008).

Certainly, the establishment and spatial expansion of conservation areas are not always a function of bona fide conservation concerns alone. Scholars have identified other key catalysts of these moves (such as political-strategic concerns, power relations and capitalist accumulation) in order to illustrate that conservation, as a philosophy and practice, is not necessarily benign (Adams & Hutton, 2007; Brockington & Igoe, 2006; Carruthers, 1989; Ramutsindela, 2007, 2012; Wolmer, 2003). In their critique of conservation, Büscher and Dressler (2007, 2012) frame it in terms of the commodification of nature, as defined and fuelled by capitalist and neoliberal interests. In general, the murky ethics surrounding conservation mean that conservation efforts aimed at sustainable resource use and benefit-sharing are often out of sync with real community needs (Brockington & Wilkie, 2015). The literature suggests that uncontrolled corporate-style or business-focused conservation leads to the 'undermining of social goals' (Fletcher, 2010: 3) – and, by implication, of socially responsible conservation.

Political ecology is a useful theoretical approach for navigating the thorny dynamics surrounding conservation. Conservation is understood, first and foremost, as a socially embedded practice. In particular, political ecology is aimed at critically analysing and questioning the power relations that emanate from the (mostly) genuine ecological concerns of individuals, land-owners and conservation entities (Dyssel, 2019). Robbins (2004) classifies these power relations according to 4 main 'theses', 2 of which are particularly relevant to the South African conservation context:

- The first one deals with conservation and control. It asserts that conservation's failures are often divorced from the political and economic contexts within which they are, in fact, deeply embedded.
- The second one deals with environmental identities and social movements. It links livelihood challenges with conservation agendas at different spatial levels.

South Africa's lingering apartheid spatial patterns mean that conservation in the country tends to be especially divided along political and economic lines, with markedly damaging effects on lives and livelihoods. In the following section, this point is illustrated through a discussion of conservation practices in what is arguably South Africa's most segregated city: Cape Town (Western, 2002; Wainwright, 2014).

14.2.2 Conservation tourism in Cape Town:
Urban resilience and risk

Scholars have repeatedly shown the historical linkages between conservation and colonialism, imperialism and the subjugation of indigenous peoples (Brockington & Igoe, 2006; Büscher, 2017; Nustad, 2015; Ramutsindela, 2007). These linkages are particularly apparent in South Africa, whose long history of racial segregation has run parallel to its conservation history (Büscher & Dressler, 2012; Nustad, 2015; Paterson, 2011; Ramutsindela, 2007). As Licht, Kenner and Roddy (2014: 5) observe, "[h]istorically, parks and reserves in [the] country were established and managed primarily for the pleasure and benefit of the wealthy and privileged white minority". Even today, popular conservation areas such as the Kruger National Park exist as enclaves of wealth in a sea of surrounding poverty. In political ecology terms, vested interests continue to override social concerns when it comes to conservation.

In Cape Town, the legacy of the past manifests most strikingly at the intersection of conservation and tourism. The spatial and socioeconomic divisions established through apartheid-era city planning and forced removals have given way to a situation where tourist sites are visited and consumed differently according to geography, with conservation management running along similarly unequal lines.

The 'iconified' Cape Town of the city centre (see 'Cape Town CBD' in Figure 14.1) is nestled against the majestic Table Mountain, recently declared one of the seven new 'Wonders of Nature' (Table Mountain, 2012), and flanked by the azure waters of the Atlantic Seaboard and the False Bay coast. This side of Cape Town is characterised by rare scenic beauty, as well as by various sites of cultural historical importance related to the city's colonial and slave histories and to the anti-apartheid liberation struggle (Brodie, 2015; Richmond et al., 2018). These and other appealing features have earned the city widespread acclaim and various top tourism awards and accolades (Forbes, 2018; Travel and Leisure, 2019; IOL, 2020; UK Post Office, 2018).

The 'uniconified' Cape Town, however, is mostly invisible to tourists and encompasses the city's immediate hinterland – the Cape Flats (spanning part of the areas marked 'South' and 'East' in Figure 14.1). The Cape Flats is home to more than a million people, of whom the vast majority reside in poverty-stricken and crime-ridden suburbs, townships and informal settlements. This part of Cape Town is the most enduring remnant of the violent and extensive forced removals that took place in the wake of the 1950 Group Areas Act, at the height of apartheid. As Williams (2014) puts it, "people from widely divergent backgrounds and experiences were uprooted from their communities and thrown together in the wasteland that has become known as the Cape Flats". The result has been widespread poverty, unemployment, gangsterism and substance addiction. With 6 out of South Africa's 10 murder capitals located on the Cape Flats (Etheridge, 2019), it is hardly surprising that tourism barely penetrates the area. Although interest in township tourism is slowly growing among certain international visitors who wish to embrace the different cultures of South African cities (Booyens & Rogerson, 2019; Mengich, 2011; Rolfes, Steinbrink & Uhl, 2009; Turan, 2017), ongoing safety concerns cement the view of the Cape Flats as a risky 'no-go' area and

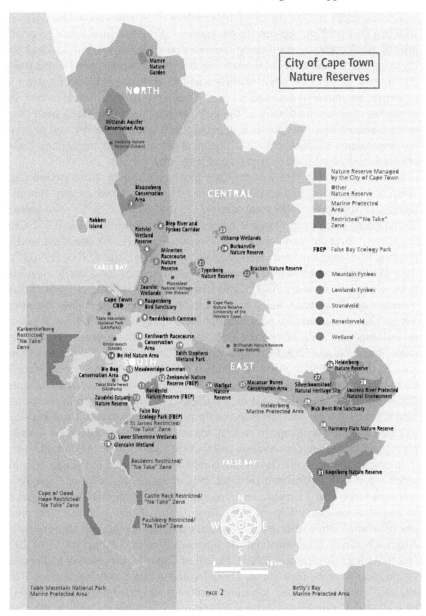

Figure 14.1 Locations of protected and conservation areas in the metropolitan area of Cape Town.
Source: City of Cape Town, 2010.

make it difficult for the area to sustainably attract local and international visitors. This view is not helped by the segregated marketing strategy of the City of Cape Town, which markets the city centre and the Cape Flats as distinct tourist zones (City of Cape Town, 2020).

The accolades and successes of the iconified Cape Town should no doubt be seen in a positive light. Against the background of South Africa's poor economic growth, weak currency, debilitating socioeconomic challenges, political and policy uncertainties and series of devastating droughts in recent years (World Bank, 2018), they speak to the city's resilience and its ability to maintain its status as a premier international destination despite these severe obstacles. However, the exclusion of uniconified parts of the city (such as the Cape Flats) from these tourism-related successes points to unequal access and opportunity, and suggests the perpetuation and reenactment of historical divisions along racial lines. It also affects the way conservation is practiced in the city.

In terms of ecology, the Western Cape province of South Africa (where Cape Town sits) has unrivalled biodiversity compared to the rest of the country. It hosts 6 biomes, 19 veld types, 9 489 plant species, 153 mammal species, 305 bird species, 39 amphibian species and 52 reptile species (Republic of South Africa, 2005). Cape Town itself lies at the centre of the Cape Floristic Region (CFR), one of the world's foremost floral kingdoms and a UNESCO World Heritage site as of 2004 (UNESCO, n.d.). The CFR includes some 6 200 endemic fynbos species that occur nowhere else in the world (Frazee et al., 2003). Table Mountain alone is home to 1 470 of these species (Cape Point, n.d.), which is part of its abiding appeal as a tourist attraction. Yet the Cape Flats area also possesses rich biodiversity and geodiversity. It houses several important endemic species, including the critically endangered Cape Flats Dune Strandveld and Cape Flats Sand Fynbos (Trimple, 2020). The 4 conservation areas on the Cape Flats used as case studies in this chapter – Edith Stephens Wetland Park, Wolfgat Nature Reserve, Macassar Dunes Conservation Area and Driftsands Nature Reserve – are all located on the Cape Flats, and they contain spectacular natural scenery on par with that found on the popular tourist circuit. These key sites, and the Cape Flats landscape in general, require sustainable conservation management practices if their conservation and tourism value is to be maximised.

In practice, though, the Cape Flats is relatively neglected in the conservation space – just as it is sidelined from the tourism space. The City of Cape Town manages more than 31 nature reserves and other conservation areas as part of its conservation estate (City of Cape Town, 2010). These local reserves, much like provincial nature reserves and national parks, are managed in terms of South Africa's National Environmental Management Protected Areas Act 57 of 2003 (South African Government, 2003). Not all of Cape Town's reserves and conservation areas have the same status. Those located in historically white areas of the city can – by virtue of their locations, resources and management advantages – be considered 'privileged', especially compared to those located on the Cape Flats (including the 4 sites mentioned above). Unsurprisingly, the low status of these sites gives rise to high levels of community apathy with regard to conservation (Eksteen, 2012). This further degrades the sites and reduces their appeal to visitors, who are already deterred from visiting the Cape Flats on account of safety concerns. It goes without saying that ineffective resource management and site degradation also have ecological consequences: they reduce the biophysical resilience of the city and are therefore risks in their own right, beyond any socioeconomic risks that may follow from them.

The ecological repercussions of neglecting significant tracts of Cape Town's protected natural landscape cannot be afforded. The Western Cape in general, and Cape Town in particular, are already in a risky place ecologically. The Western Cape's protected area network does not adequately protect the ecosystems and biodiversity of the province (Turner, 2012), and the same is true of Cape Town. Of the 1.1 million ha that make up the CFR biome, for example, a mere 9% are protected through the different nature reserves and conservation areas in the City of Cape Town's network (Cape Nature, n.d.). Expanding this network and carefully and fairly managing existing reserves – regardless of their geographical location and other impediments – is therefore of critical importance in terms of bioresilience, given the low rate of overall protection.

The situation is further jeopardised by the concentration of the Western Cape's biodiversity (and specifically plant-species diversity) in and around metropolitan Cape Town, which is rapidly expanding and developing in response to its ever-increasing population. This expansion poses a serious threat to the integrity and management of conservation in the city. Graham and Ernston (2012: 2) capture the challenges of urban biodiversity conservation in Cape Town:

> [N]atural resource management, and biodiversity conservation in particular, are faced with novel sets of complexities in the rapidly suburbanising areas of Cape Town, South Africa, and in the nexus between apartheid past, informal settlements, remnant biodiversity patches, and urban poverty.

In order to mitigate these various urban risks and dynamics, it is necessary to highlight the plight of Cape Town's 'stepchild' nature reserves located on the Cape Flats. The perpetuation, in whatever form, of preferential conservation tourism in Cape Town hampers these nature reserves' ability to shake off their 'no-go' status, and this in turn hampers the environmental/ecological, sociocultural and economic resilience of the city as an integrated space. These neglected conservation zones play a vital role in supporting the already-fragile ecosystem of the city and should be viewed in this light.

Using the 4 aforementioned sites on the Cape Flats – Edith Stephens Wetland Park, Wolfgat Nature Reserve, Macassar Dunes Conservation Area and Driftsands Nature Reserve – as case studies, this study is aimed at identifying their unique advantages and disadvantages, and critically engaging with their real and perceived importance within Cape Town's conservation estate. It asks the following crucial question: if safety concerns and conservation apathy are the major impediments to the flourishing of conservation tourism on the Cape Flats, to what extent can these impediments be transformed into conservation tourism enablers? It also asks the following secondary question: to what extent can communities, in the face of adversity and socioeconomic struggle, along with authorities, co-create and co-manage spaces in which conservation and tourism can flourish?

To this extent, the study not only uses a political ecology lens, but also follows in the tradition of urban risk assessment. Dickson et al. (2012) consider such assessment an important prerequisite for sustainable risk alleviation and prevention. Since this study deals with the interplay between conservation and tourism, the focus is primarily on the premise of hazard impact assessment, which focuses on and measures the impact of natural and environment-related hazards on an urban area (Dickson et al., 2012). However, the other two pillars of urban risk assessment – institutional factors and economic factors – should not be ignored, given the historical and ongoing impact of their structural footprint on the landscape. They might represent an avenue for further research. The ultimate goal of urban risk assessment is to obtain a nuanced appreciation and awareness of the complexity and hybridity that underpins human–nature relations in particular urban environments, and to use that awareness as the basis for constructive action. This localised approach represents an alternative to the uncritical advocacy of best practices as they pertain to other realities.

14.2.3 Recent conservation legislation and SDGs

Before turning to the case studies, it is important to touch on the legislative and policy framework in which this study is grounded. The use of political ecology and urban risk assessment as theoretical ways of looking at urban risk and resilience is only as effective as its ability to explain conditions prevailing in reality. The situation described in the previous section mandates that any legislative or policy moves be grounded in socioeconomic redress, benefit-sharing and the upliftment of marginalised groups. In this regard, the City of Cape Town and the Western Cape Provincial Government recently took some steps in the right direction.

In particular, a new bylaw was introduced and aimed at both preserving all the nature reserves within the city's municipal boundaries and increasing the safety of visitors to these areas. The city's Mayoral Committee Member for Spatial Planning and Environment Marian Nieuwoudt was quoted as saying:

> Thousands of people visit our nature reserves every month. They want a safe space and an environment that contributes to the pleasure and enjoyment of being in nature. We have a responsibility to these visitors (Tourism Update, 2020).

The relevance of the new bylaw to the city's overall ecological well-being was highlighted by one commentator: "these protected areas provide important ecosystems and contribute to Cape Town's future sustainability and resilience to climate change" (Tourism Update, 2020). Indeed, the city's prioritisation of biodiversity conservation by way of the nature reserves in its care is encouraging.

In 2019, the Western Cape Provincial Government also recognised the importance of its biodiversity endowments through the Draft Western Cape Biodiversity Bill. The Provincial Gazette Extraordinary, in which the draft bill was published, emphasises

> the unique biodiversity in the Western Cape, the Republic's international obligations, the Province's dependence on ecosystem services, the need for access and benefit sharing and the need to ensure long-term ecological resilience (Province of the Western Cape, 2019).

The direct reference to "access and benefit sharing" and to "long-term ecological resilience" suggests an awareness on the part of the provincial government of the urgency of these issues. Since the bill – like the bylaw – is a recent measure, the success thereof will be determined by the level of eventual buy-in and the implementation of the measures it outlines.

The bill mentions South Africa's "international obligations", which presumably refers to the country's responsibilities in relation to the global ecological crisis. These responsibilities are articulated nowhere more cogently than in the United Nations' SDGs, particularly SDG 11 and SDG 15, which are concerned with the intersection of natural landscapes and urban populations. The stated purpose of SDG 11, Sustainable Cities and Communities, is to "[m]ake cities inclusive, safe, resilient and sustainable" (United Nations, 2016a). The stated purpose of SDG 15, Life on Land, is to "[s]ustainably manage forests, combat desertification, halt and reverse land degradation, halt biodiversity loss" (United Nations, 2016b). Given the obvious relevance of these 2 SDGs to the various urban risks surrounding Cape Town, and the Cape Flats in particular, it is worth briefly establishing the conceptual role of the SDGs within the concerns of this study.

SDGs, like their predecessors the Millennium Development Goals, serve as general guidelines and protocols for how the world's different developmental and environmental challenges can be addressed. In introducing the SDGs in 2015, the United Nations effectively mandated the global community to consider planet, people and prosperity as fundamental and fundamentally linked (Jamali, 2018; Langford, 2016). The universality of the SDGs is generally acceptable; however, the complexities of place and time specificities are not fully captured by the policy framework (Jamali, 2018).

Real complexities are therefore often used as the basis for critiques against the SDGs (Moyer & Hedden, 2020; Swain, 2017). These critiques range from postcolonial feminist perspectives on sustainable development (Struckmann, 2017) to revisiting the politics underpinning the overall transformation agenda of the SDGs (Langford, 2016). Swain (2017: 1) believes that on a more practical level, SDGs can be criticised "for being inconsistent, [and] difficult to quantify, implement and monitor". Moyer and Hedden (2020), Sultana (2018) and Swain (2017) argue that the attempt to lend weight to the SDGs and their targets led to a strong emphasis on economic growth. Consumption became entrenched in the SDG project, which in turn led to imbalances among the project's environmental, economic and social goals (Moyer & Hedden, 2020; Sultana, 2018; Swain, 2017).

One need not accept these more granular arguments, but the general point about the need to weigh the SDGs against the real complexities of place and time does hold. This study is committed in principle to the ethos of SDG 11 (with its focus on building sustainable cities and communities) and of SDG 15 (with its focus on building sustainable ecosystems), but it is also aimed at better understanding the unique challenges involved in realising these goals in the Cape Town context. In mapping the space–time complexities and challenges that prevail at the 4 study sites on the Cape Flats, this study hopes to inform the role that conservation tourism – guided by the SDGs – can play in balancing urban risk with urban resilience.

14.2.4 The Cape Flats: Four case studies

This section provides some contextual details on each of the 4 study sites investigated and discussed in the remainder of the chapter: Driftsands Nature Reserve, Macassar Dunes Conservation Area, Wolfgat Nature Reserve and Edith Stephens Wetland Park. These 4 sites were chosen based on their unique biophysical characteristics as well as their shared context of surrounding communities that are generally less conservation-orientated, experience harsh socioeconomic conditions and use the land in particular ways. In short, the risks and opportunities associated with conservation tourism on the Cape Flats are best exemplified by this sample of (relatively neglected) nature reserves. The 4 sites are clearly demarcated and numbered in Figure 14.1 (see the 'South' and 'East' parts of the map).

14.2.4.1 Driftsands Nature Reserve

This reserve is located inland of the False Bay coast. It is surrounded by the largely poverty-stricken communities of Emfuleni to the east, Khayelitsha to the south and Delft to the west. The Kuils River drains the eastern part of the reserve and the central part comprises seasonal wetlands surrounded by some vegetated dunes on which patches of undisturbed Cape Flats Dune Strandveld and Cape Flats Sand Fynbos flourish. Some dunes are overgrown with invasive vegetation such as rooikrans and black wattle. Although the reserve is located in a dense and highly urbanised setting, it is managed by Cape Nature (the Western Cape's provincial conservation authority) as an urban park in conjunction with local government structures, nongovernmental organisations and other stakeholders. The broad, long-term vision for the reserve is as follows: "a nature reserve with ecosystem integrity, which reinforces a resilient landscape in a changing urban environment" (Saul et al., 2015).

14.2.4.2 Macassar Dunes Conservation Area

This reserve is also located along the False Bay coast, east of Melkbaai Beach in the town of Strand, one of the most popular tourist destinations on this stretch of the coast. It is host to some of the highest dunes in the Cape region. These dunes are made up of "Strandveld (dune thicket), dune fynbos on calcareous sand and dwarf fynbos on calcrete" and are home to more than 179 indigenous plant species (Davey, 2001: 6). The challenges associated with the site include sand mining; off-road driving, walking, fishing and other recreational activities; the harvesting of flora by nearby communities; cattle grazing; the presence of 2 sewage plants; and the pressures of possible future urban use (Davey, 2001).

14.2.4.3 Wolfgat Nature Reserve

This reserve is located between the beaches of Monwabisi to the east and Mnandi to the west. It is bordered by Tafelsig, a residential area of Mitchell's Plain, to the north and the False Bay coastline to the south. Its primary conservation foci are marine fauna, Strandveld and dwarf coastal fynbos, and it is the only terrestrial breeding location of the black-backed seagull. Wolfgat's rugged limestone cliffs (the Swartklip Cliffs) offer dramatic vistas of the False Bay coastline, which can and should be a bigger tourist drawcard. Due to safety concerns, however, potential visitors avoid them.

14.2.4.4 Edith Stephens Wetland Park

This wetland park is located inland of the False Bay coast between 2 important motorways on the Cape Flats: Govan Mbeki Road and Jakes Gerwel Drive. It is surrounded by the impoverished communities of Nyanga, Gugulethu, Philippi, Hanover Park and Mannenberg. The wetland park contains significant biodiversity elements despite its small size. Facilities and services at the site include a primary-school science programme and an environmental education section. The reserve is boundary-fenced, and access control is conducted by security personnel. Picnic and recreational facilities are available in the park.

14.3 Methodology

The case-study design of this study was supported by an overarching survey method that included both primary and secondary data collection. The primary data were collected in and around Macassar Dunes Conservation Area, Wolfgat Nature Reserve, Edith Stephens Wetland Park and Driftsands Nature Reserve. Convenience sampling was used, with the participants selected based on their willingness and availability.

For the Driftsands and Wolfgat sites, the data were collected through unstructured interviews with reserve managers, domestic and international visitors, and local reserve consumers, as well as through focused observation over the period of September 2019 to October 2019. For the Macassar and Edith Stephens sites, the primary data were collected through extensive focused observation over a longer period. The secondary data sources included the reserve management plans for the different sites (City of Cape Town, 2011a, 2011b, 2012; Cape Nature 2014) as well as academic literature.

- The conversations with the official reserve representatives focused largely on conservation management challenges, safety issues, perimeter-fencing concerns and relationships with surrounding communities.
- The conversations with the reserve visitors included categories such as their reasons for visiting, the frequency of their visits, the resources and amenities they used, their transport and access to the sites, the highlights of their visits and any concerns regarding the sites.
- The conversations with the local consumers or harvesters of the reserves' resources (for example, fuelwood, wood for construction, sand for construction, grazing land for livestock and harvesting of flora to sell to passersby) touched on their reasons for illegal harvesting, their level of access to the reserve and their relationship with law enforcement and the reserve authorities.

The focused observations explored these same issues through site visits. Relevant observations were recorded in field notes. Document analysis was used to make sense of the reserve management plans, field notes and other key texts.

14.4 Findings

14.4.1 Risk factors and resilience factors

Table 14.1 summarises the findings that emerged from the interviews, the observations and the document analysis. In keeping with the format of a hazard impact assessment, the tabulated findings on the 4 study sites are presented in terms of resilience factors (cultural heritage endowment and ecological endowment) and risk factors (urban and environmental threats and challenges).

Resilience and risk factors are differentiated in the table, but it is important to note that the distinction between these factors is not always clear-cut. The biodiversity, geodiversity and cultural heritages attributes of the sites can largely be considered as bases for their resilience per se, yet they can also contribute to the risk factors listed, on account of the endowments themselves – for example, poor people in proximity to the reserves plundering the biodiversity (wood, sand, flora and fauna) for livelihood purposes.

14.4.2 Key spatial variables

In addition to the identification of the key risks and opportunities present at each site, the data were organised thematically according to 4 main spatial variables that emerged during the analysis. These spatial variables are:

- Tourism value
- Location
- Accessibility
- Association

These spatial variables provide a way to reflect on the risk levels associated with the 4 study areas as a whole and to think differently about the impediments and complexities surrounding conservation tourism on the Cape Flats. They also provide a potential framework for linking SDG 11 and SDG 15 to the real-world complexities of sustainable development and conservation management in this part of Cape Town. These thematic findings are described in the remainder of this section.

14.4.2.1 Tourism value

The research reveals that the inherent value of the conservation attributes associated with an area's biodiversity, geodiversity and cultural diversity are often influenced by externalities such as management efficiency, resource availability and educational initiatives to promote such attributes. In other words, the attributes

Table 14.1 Key resilience and risk factors at the four study sites

	Conservation area			
	Driftsands Nature Reserve	**Macassar Dunes Conservation Area**	**Wolfgat Nature Reserve**	**Edith Stephens Wetland Park**
Size	433 ha	1116 ha	248 ha	39 ha
		Resilience factors		
Cultural heritage endowment	Political instability and factional feuds in the 1980s gave rise to informal settlements in Driftsands, which became a refuge for people who fled townships such as Cross Roads.	The area is linked to the Khoikhoi, its first inhabitants. It became the birthplace of the first Muslim community in South Africa. The Kramat of Sheikh Yusuf in Macassar bears testimony to that history.	The reserve is named after the brown hyena, or *strandwolf*, that used to roam this part of the False Bay coastline.	The environmental commitments of Edith Stephens, a former botanist, saw her buying the land on which the wetland sits and securing it for conservation and education purposes.
Ecological endowment (biodiversity and geodiversity)	Characterised by endemic, endangered and poorly protected Cape Flats Dune Strandveld. Sensitive seasonal and floodplain wetland system.	178 plant species. Endemic, endangered Cape Flats Dune Strandveld. Endangered white milkwood trees. Variety of bird species. Animals include mongoose, porcupine, tortoise and buck hares. Boasts some of the highest dunes in the Cape Town metropolitan area.	150 plant species. Endemic, endangered Cape Flats Dune Strandveld. Vegetation includes evergreen shrubs, succulents, arum lilies and daisy varieties. Birds include kelp gulls and black oyster catchers. Boasts spectacular limestone cliffs.	Large seasonal wetland. Endemic, endangered Cape Flats Dune Strandveld and Cape Flats Sand Fynbos. Several red data plant species. Approximately 100 species of birds, reptiles and mammals. Endangered frog (Western Leopard Toad). Endemic, highly endangered Cape Quillwort (*Isoetes capensis*).
		Risk factors		
Urban and environmental threats and challenges	Illegal resource uses, such as sand and fuelwood harvesting, livestock grazing and dumping. Invasive vegetation. Safety.	Uncontrolled sand mining, cattle grazing, off-road vehicle use, angling and medicinal plant and fuelwood harvesting. Safety.	Invasive alien rooikrans (*Acacia cyclops*). Impact of neighbouring communities. Safety.	Safety (located in the heart of Cape Town's gangland).

can either be cultivated and capitalised on, or they can remain deactivated and neglected. The lingering legacies of spatial apartheid in Cape Town have had – and continue to have – consequences for the city's conservation landscapes, as this study confirms. Based on the analysis conducted, it is evident that the risk factors impacting conservation and tourism in the study areas (see Table 14.1) are multilayered.

14.4.2.2 Location

The very geographical places, or the so-called 'absolute locations', of the reserves are givens (that is, they are determined by their ecological attributes). The presence of patches of endangered Cape Flats Dune Strandveld, Cape Flats Sand Fynbos and renosterveld in some of the conservation areas, as well as other biodiversity, geodiversity and cultural historical attributes, are place-based realities that have to be dealt with by the conservation authorities. But so are the socioeconomic challenges of the communities surrounding these areas. The tension between the locations of conservation areas and the locations of severe socioeconomic suffering and poverty in Cape Town is best exemplified in the protected areas studied.

In other words, the absolute locations of the reserves also make them risky spaces. The concept of 'place' becomes more an operational space, shaped by all the relevant socioeconomic variables. Traversing these risky spaces in order to get to the core conservation 'place' can be, and generally is, risky for visitors and tourists. This points to the need for stronger and more sustainable relationships with the people living in these spaces and the enhancement of opportunities through partnerships and capacity-building (discussed in more detail in the next section).

14.4.2.3 Accessibility

The absolute and relative accessibility of specific locations, areas and services has always been contentious in the highly divided South African context. Except for Edith Stephens Wetland Park, access to the other 3 reserves is unrestricted. They have almost no access control due to the absence of physical boundaries – or, in the case of Driftsands Nature Reserve, damaged boundaries. For outsiders, the accessibility of the reserves in question is also relative and may be influenced by other factors. Motorways in proximity to these areas are often the stages for the service delivery protests that have become commonplace throughout the city. Such protests naturally pose safety risks to locals in the area and visitors alike, which impacts accessibility. On account of these safety concerns, roads are often closed to traffic. Baden Powell Drive (which runs through Wolfgat Nature Reserve), the Old Faure Road and Hindle Road (close to Driftsands Nature Reserve), and Govan Mbeki Drive (close to Edith Stephens Wetland Park) are notorious locations for service delivery protests.

Therefore, perceptions of accessibility and safety are oftentimes shaped by conditions beyond the control of the management of the reserves. The frequency and persistence of destabilising activities influence the relative level of access to Cape Flats reserves and can negatively affect planned visits to some reserves—a point alluded to by management representatives of the Driftsands and Wolfgat nature reserves.

14.4.2.4 Association

The close association of the 4 study sites with the socioeconomic and safety challenges plaguing the communities in proximity to them can be considered a disabling factor for the promotion of conservation tourism on the Cape Flats. The open or porous boundaries of Driftsands Nature Reserve, Macassar Dunes Conservation Area and Wolfgat Nature Reserve are of particular concern, as the open vegetation in these areas often facilitates criminal activities and contributes to the risk surrounding these sites.

Interviews with reserve managers as part of this study, as well as informal conversations with recreational fishers and beachgoers in the author's personal capacity, revealed that safety is indeed a major stumbling block for efforts to improve pro-conservation and pro-tourism attitudes and activities at these sites. It was reported that each incident of mugging or assault involving people visiting the reserves stifles attempts to build sustainable co-management initiatives between the City of Cape Town (as conservation authority) and the nearby communities of Khayelitsha, Makhaza and Mitchell's Plain.

Visitors to Driftsands Nature Reserve are, for example, strongly advised not to go into the reserve without being accompanied by Cape Nature officials. The situation at Wolfgat Nature Reserve is even more dire in terms of porousness and protection, as the site is spatially bisected by Baden Powell Drive, which connects Stellenbosch with the Muizenberg area. According to management personnel at Wolfgat, the proposed realignment of Baden Powell Drive as part of the city's Urban Renewable Programme intends to consolidate and enhance the reserve's spatial and ecological integrity, environmental education programme and tourism value. However, concerns around implementation remain.

14.5 Discussion: Turning risk into resilience

This study explored two main questions: are safety concerns and conservation apathy the major impediments to conservation tourism flourishing on the Cape Flats, and to what extent can these impediments be transformed into conservation tourism enablers? To what extent can communities, in the face of adversity and socioeconomic struggle, along with authorities, co-create and co-manage spaces in which conservation and tourism can flourish?

The findings confirm the centrality of safety concerns and conservation apathy as impediments to the sustainable management of nature reserves on the Cape Flats, with apathy arising directly from the desperate socioeconomic conditions of the surrounding communities, and inappropriate land-use occurring almost entirely for livelihood and survival purposes. As the background section highlighted, these socioeconomic and livelihood challenges are a direct legacy of apartheid-era urban planning and spatial segregation, which remain almost entirely intact in Cape Town.

The background section also highlighted the preferential conservation tourism practices that see certain nature reserves relegated to 'stepchild' status on account of their location in uniconified Cape Town, which contributes to their relative neglect compared to more privileged or iconified reserves. The findings confirm the strong need for intervention at the study sites on the Cape Flats, in order (i) to turn the existing risk factors into resilience opportunities and (ii) to safeguard the existing bioresilience factors against the encroaching risks (see Table 14.1). However, the findings also suggest the equally strong need for community involvement in any potential intervention. This is because the risk factors are almost entirely located in the troubled relationship between the nature reserves and the socioeconomic contexts in which they exist.

There are different ways to approach this challenge and bring the Cape Flats closer to the vision articulated in SDG 11 and SDG 15. Identifying the space–time complexities and challenges that prevail at the 4 study sites on the Cape Flats, as this study has done, should pave the way for more *inclusive* co-management or 'convivial' conservation (Büscher, 2017) rather than more *exclusive* perimeter-fence or 'fortress' conservation (Doolittle, 2007). Fortress conservation practices normally lead to enclaves that further alienate disenfranchised people, as has largely been the case in South Africa's conservation history to date. It is therefore imperative that the safety and apathy narratives be continually (re) contextualised to reflect the plight of the disenfranchised so that these communities are not blamed or further marginalised in relation to conservation.

The recent biodiversity bill and conservation bylaw discussed in the background section are encouraging, given their progressive and inclusive wording, although rollout and implementation will need to be carefully monitored. In terms of tourism, the City of Cape Town's latest Tourism Development Framework is also encouraging. It emphasises the important role of the conservation of the city's natural and cultural environments in its tourism offerings, and commits itself to "community involvement, benefits and support" (Tourism Update, 2019). It is evident that enhancing the potential benefits that can be accrued from the city's conservation–tourism nexus would be for the good of society and the environment at large. Generating tangible advantages for people on the Cape Flats in particular through conservation tourism could also lead to the emergence of less-risky tourism spaces in this part of Cape Town.

What would such upliftment look like, exactly? In a comparative study of different African cities' inclusiveness, safety, resilience and sustainability, Musavengane, Siakwah and Leonard (2020) make the case that the promotion of sustainable tourism is dependent on broad-based urban renewal initiatives. Such initiatives, they argue, should be inclusive of poor and disenfranchised people in unfavourable urban locations (Musavengane et al., 2020). Unfortunately, area-based urban renewable programmes in South Africa have to date shown limited success in terms of addressing the issues of more inclusivity and less division.

Donaldson et al. (2013) studied these programmes in detail. As they explain, South Africa's democratic government has initiated different plans since 1992 to address the interwoven spatial, economic and social legacies of apartheid: most notably, the Special Integrated Presidential Projects, the National Urban Renewal

Programme and the Neighbourhood Development Programme. The National Urban Renewal Programme is strongly area-based and focuses on upgrading and changing earmarked places in cities and towns to enhance living conditions and address urban socioeconomic ills. Urban rejuvenation projects in former areas of decay, such as Woodstock and Salt River in Cape Town, are prime examples of the National Urban Renewal Programme. Renewal programmes like these can have unintended consequences if the renewal approach is not holistic and sensitive to urban complexities, or where initiatives are demand- and profit-driven (Donaldson et al., 2013). In Woodstock, for instance, property prices became unaffordable for most of the people who used to live there after the area was 'renewed'.

It can therefore be argued that area-based National Urban Renewal Programme initiatives in predominantly poverty-stricken and crime-ridden areas such as Mitchell's Plain and Khayelitsha on the Cape Flats will always be questionable if they are not in sync with other pressing societal needs. When these initiatives occur in conservation areas, fostering and maintaining healthy partnerships between conservation authorities and communities are vital for the protection and integrity of the landscape. Donaldson et al. (2013) believe that sector-specific initiatives through public–private partnerships can go a long way in supporting area-based programmes, and this may indeed be something to consider in conservation areas on the Cape Flats.

Another useful guiding framework for inclusive, convivial conservation might be strategic adaptive management (SAD). SAD in the context of conservation allows for strategic forward-thinking in terms of the physical planning and protection of conservation attributes. It promotes an adaptive approach to achieving desired outcomes: in other words, learning and refining as the project unfolds. Most crucially, it advocates for the incorporation of as many stakeholders, and interested and affected parties, as possible into the management of nature reserves as a means of creating a representative and capacitated critical mass that can assist reserve officials. Eksteen (2012: 1) believes that "[b]alancing social needs with conservation needs is a struggle for conservators, but many successes came in cases where this balance was realised". Because conservation tourism is one possible weapon in the armoury for fighting poverty and uplifting disenfranchised communities, conditions should be created for conservation tourism to be fully operationalised. Partnerships and adaptive co-management arrangements are arguably the most sustainable ways of establishing synergies between conservation and tourism needs on the one hand and social needs on the other hand.

14.6 Conclusion

From the many challenges facing the protected areas investigated, it is clear that these pockets of conservation value cannot be separated from the communities surrounding them through the establishment of hard boundaries and perimeter-fencing or other exclusionary measures. It is also clear that the conservation risks for neglected nature reserves on the Cape Flats have a negative effect on the further development of tourism in the area, and vice versa. Concerted efforts by the Western Cape Provincial Government and the City of Cape Town to enhance the resilience of the city through legislation are promising. Such legislation, guided by the framing ethos of the SDGs, that is appropriately implemented could effectively protect Cape Town's conservation assets while allowing for benefit-sharing and supporting the sustainable socioeconomic upliftment of communities. As such, it could contribute to the betterment of conservation on the Cape Flats and to the gradual cultivation of the area's tourism potential.

References

Adams, W. M. (2004). *Against extinction: The story of conservation.* London: Earthscan.

Adams, W. M., & Hutton, J. (2007). People, parks and poverty: Political ecology and biodiversity conservation. *Conservation and Society,* 5(2), 147–183.

Booyens, I., & Rogerson, C. (2019). Re-creating slum tourism: Perspectives from South Africa. *Urbani Izziv, 30,* 52–63.

Brockington, D. (2008). Powerful environmentalisms: Conservation, celebrity, and capitalism. *Media, Culture and Society,* 30(4), 551–568.

Brockington, D., & Igoe, J. (2006). Evictions for conservation: A global overview. *Conservation and Society,* 4(3), 424–470.

Brockington, D., & Wilkie, D. (2015). Protected areas and poverty. *Philosophical Transactions of the Royal Society B,* 370(1681). DOI: 10.1098/rstb.2014.0271.

Brodie, N. (2015). *The Cape Town book: A guide to the city's history, people and places.* Cape Town: Struik Travel and Heritage.

Büscher, B. (2017). *Towards 'convivial conservation': Radical ideas for saving nature in the Anthropocene. Seminar presented at the Programme for Land and Agrarian Studies (PLAAS), University of the Western Cape,* 23 May 2017.

Büscher, B., & Dressler, W. (2007). Linking neo-protectionism and environmental governance: On the rapidly increasing tension between actors in the environment–development nexus. *Conservation and Society,* 5(4), 586–611.

Büscher, B., & Dressler, W. (2012). Commodity conservation: The restructuring of community conservation in South Africa and the Philippines. *Geoforum,* 43, 367–376.

Carruthers, J. (1989). Creating a national park: 1910 to 1926. *Journal of Southern African Studies,* 15(2), 188–216.

Cape Nature (n.d.). *Cape for nature: Cape Floristic region.* Retrieved from https://www.capenature.co.za/care-for-nature/biodiversity/cape-floristic-region/..

Cape Nature (2014). *Driftsands nature reserve: Protected area management plan 2015–2020.* Retrieved from https://www.capenature.co.za/wp-content/uploads/2014/05/DRFS-PAMPS_merged-1.pdf.

Cape Point (n.d.). *Plants of the park: Part 1.* Retrieved from https://capepoint.co.za/plants-of-the-park-part-1/.

City of Cape Town (2010). *City of Cape Town nature reserves: A network of amazing biodiversity.* Second edition. Retrieved from http://resource.capetown.gov.za/documentcentre/Documents/Graphics%20and%20educational%20material/CCT_Nature_Reserves_book_2010-02.pdf.

City of Cape Town (2011a). *Integrated management plan for the Edith Stephens Nature Reserve 2011.* Retrieved from http://resource.capetown.gov.za/.

City of Cape Town (2011b). *Integrated Reserve Management Plan: Wolfgat Nature Reserve.* Retrieved from https://nanopdf.com/download/integrated-reserve-management-plan-wolfgat-nature-reserve_pdf.

City of Cape Town (2012). *Conservation implementation plan for Strandveld in the Metropole.* Retrieved from https://studylib.net/doc/10392873/conservation-implementation-plan-for-strandveld-in-the-metropole....

City of Cape Town (2020). *Peninsula map.* Retrieved from https://www.capetown.travel/wp-content/uploads/2019/02/CTT-Cape-Town-Peninsula-map.pdf.

Davey, S. (2001). *Environmental governance of sand mining in an urban setting: Macassar Dunes, Cape Town, South Africa.* Master's thesis, University of Cape Town. Retrieved from https://open.uct.ac.za/bitstream/item/4725/thesis_sci_2001_davey_s.pdf?sequence=1.

Dickson, E., Baker, J. L., Hoornweg, D., & Tiwari, A. (2012). *Urban risk assessments: Understanding disaster and climate risk in cities.* Washington, D.C.: World Bank.

Donaldson, R., du Plessis, D., Spocter, M., & Massey, R. (2013). The South African area-based urban renewal programme: Experiences from Cape Town. *Journal of Housing and the Built Environment,* 28, 629–638. DOI: 10.1007/s10901-013-9348-3.

Doolittle, A. (2007). Fortress conservation. In P. Robbins (ed.), *Encyclopedia of environment and society* (pp. 705–705). Thousand Oaks, CA: SAGE Publications.

Dyssel, M. (2019). *The political ecology of private nature reserve tourism on the West Coast of South Africa. The Political Economy of Tourism International Seminar, Department of Geography,* University of São Paulo, 26–31 October 2019.

Eksteen, L. (2012). *Relationships between conservators, community partners and urban conservation areas: A case study of nature reserves on the Cape Flats.* Master's thesis, University of the Western Cape.

Etheridge, J. (2019, September 12). Murder stats: 6 out of 10 worst murder areas in Cape Town—and Nyanga remains murder capital. *News24.* Retrieved from: https://www.news24.com/SouthAfrica/News/murder-stats-6-out-of-10-worst-murder-areas-in-cape-town-and-nyanga-remains-murder-capital-20190912.

Fletcher, R. (2010). Neoliberal environmentality: Towards a poststructuralist political ecology of the conservation debate. *Conservation and Society,* 8(3), 171–181.

Forbes (2018, June 22). *The 12 coolest neighborhoods around the world.* Retrieved from https://www.forbes.com/sites/annabel/2018/06/22/the-12-coolest-neighborhoods-around-the-world/#40f9db706eb1.

Frazee, S. R., Cowling, R. M., Pressey, R. L., Turpie, J. K., & Lindenberg, N. (2003). Estimating the costs of conserving a biodiversity hotspot: A case-study of the Cape Floristic Region, South Africa. *Biological Conservation,* 112, 275–290.

Graham, M. & Ernston, H. (2012). Co-management at the fringes: Examining stakeholder perspectives at Macassar Dunes, Cape Town, South Africa, at the intersection of high biodiversity, urban poverty, and inequality. *Ecology and Society,* 17(3), 34.

IOL (2020, May 14). *Cape Town ranked as best destination to have an international meeting in Africa.* Retrieved from https://www.iol.co.za/travel/south-africa/western-cape/cape-town-ranked-as-best-destination-to-have-an-international-meeting-in-africa-47919346.

Jamali, H. (2018). *Critical perspectives on the Sustainable Development Goals: Are universal indicators meaningful?* Retrieved from https://flows.hypotheses.org/1460.

Kelleher, V. (1999). *Slow burn.* London: Penguin.

Langford, M. (2016). Lost in transformation? The politics of the Sustainable Development Goals. *Ethics & International Affairs,* 30(2), 167–176.

Licht, D. S., Kenner, B. C., & Roddy, D. E. (2014). A comparison of the South African and United States models of natural areas management. *ISRN Biodiversity.* Retrieved from http://dx.doi.org/10.1155/2014/737832/.

Mengich, O. (2011). *Township tourism: Understanding tourist motivation.* Unpublished thesis, University of Pretoria.

Moyer, J. D., & Hedden, S. (2020). Are we on the right path to achieve the sustainable development goals? *World Development*, 127(C), 1–13.

Musavengane, R. Siakwah, P. and Leonard, L. (2020). The nexus between tourism and urban risk: Towards inclusive, safe, resilient and sustainable outdoor tourism in African cities. *Journal of Outdoor Recreation and Tourism*, 29, 100254. Doi.10.1016/j.jort.2019.100254.

Nustad, K. G. (2015). *Creating Africas: Struggles of nature, conservation and land*. New York: Oxford University Press.

Paterson, A. R. (2011). *Legal Framework for protected areas: South Africa. IUCN environmental policy and law paper (IUCN-EPLP No. 81)*. Retrieved from http://cmsdata.iucn.org/downloads/south_africa.pdf/.

Province of the Western Cape (2019). *Provincial Gazette Extraordinary 8094.* 7 May 2019. Retrieved from https://cer.org.za/wp-content/uploads/1975/02/Draft-WC-Biodiversity-Bill-2019.pdf.

Ramutsindela, M. (2007). *Transfrontier conservation in Africa: At the confluence of capital, politics and nature*. Wallingford: CABI.

Ramutsindela, M. (2012). *The 'Gang of Nine' and the trajectory of cross-border conservation in Africa. Paper presented at the 9th Biennial Conference of the Society of South African Geography*, University of Cape Town, 6–8 May.

Republic of South Africa (2005) *South African yearbook 2005–2006*. Pretoria: Government Communication and Information System.

Richmond, S., Bainbridge, J., Carillet, B., & Corne, L. (2018). *Cape Town and the garden Route travel guide*. Franklin, TN: Lonely Planet.

Robbins, P. (2004). *Political ecology*. Hoboken, NJ: Blackwell Publishing.

Rolfes, M., Steinbrink, M., & Uhl, C. (2009). *Townships as attraction: An empirical study of township tourism in Cape Town*. Potsdam: University of Potsdam. Retrieved from http://info.ub.uni-potsdam.de/verlag.htm/.

Saul, L., Hayward, N., Cleaver-Christie, G., & Maliehe, T. (2015). *Protected area management plan: 2015–2020*. Retrieved from https://www.capenature.co.za/wp-content/uploads/2014/05/DRFS-PAMPS_merged-1.pdf.

South African Government (2003). *National Environmental Management Protected Areas Act 57 of 2003*. Retrieved from https://www.gov.za/documents/national-environmental-management-protected-areas-act.

Struckmann, C. (2017). *A postcolonial feminist critique of the 2030 Agenda for Sustainable Development: A South African application*. Master's thesis, University of Stellenbosch, Cape Town, South Africa.

Sultana, F. (2018). An(other) geographical critique of development and SDGs. *Dialogues in Human Geography,* 8(2), 186–190.

Swain, R. B. (2017). A critical analysis of the sustainable development goals. In W. Leal Filho et al. (eds.), *Handbook of sustainability science and research*. New York: Springer.

Table Mountain (2012). *It's official: Table Mountain is a new 7 wonder of nature*. Retrieved from https://www.tablemountain.net/blog/entry/its_official_-_table_mountain_is_a_new7wonder_of_nature.

Tourism Update (2019, April 30). *Cape Town's draft tourism development framework a game-changer*. Retrieved from http://www.tourismupdate.co.za/article/190430/Cape-Town-s-draft-tourism-development-framework-a-game-changer/10.

Tourism Update (2020, February 27). *Cape Town proposes new bylaw to protect nature reserves*. Retrieved from http://www.tourismupdate.co.za/article/198390/Cape-Town-proposes-new-by-law-to-protect-nature-reserves.

Travel and Leisure (2019, July 10). *Cape Town named best city in Africa and Middle East*. Retrieved from https://www.travelandleisure.com/worlds-best/cities-in-africa-middle-east.

Trimple, M. (2020, March 6). *Cape Town's critically endangered Cape Flats Sand Fynbos.* Retrieved from https://storymaps.arcgis.com/stories/c8591e4bd6f04e229d8293c07e675fb4.

Turan, A. (2017). The role of tour guides in opening the eyes of tourists during a slum experience. *Paper presented at the 5th International research forum on guided tours,* Anadolu University, Eskişehir, Turkey. Retrieved from https://www.researchgate. net/publication/321443741_The_Role_of_Tour_Guides_in_Opening_the_Eyes_of_ Tourists_During_a_Slum_Experience/.

Turner, A. A. (ed.) (2012). *Western Cape Province state of biodiversity 2012.* Stellenbosch: Cape Nature Scientific Services.

UK Post Office (2018, January 13). *Worldwide barometer reveals price falls in holiday hotspots.* Retrieved from http://www.mynewsdesk.com/uk/post-office/pressreleases/ worldwide-barometer-reveals-price-falls-in-holiday-hotspots-2372899.

UNESCO (n.d.). *Cape Floral region protected areas.* Retrieved from http://whc.unesco. org/en/list/1007.

United Nations (2016a). *Goal 11: Make cities inclusive, safe, resilient and sustainable.* Sustainable Development Goals. Retrieved from https://www.un.org/sustainabledevelopment/ cities/.

United Nations (2016b). *Goal 15: Sustainably manage forests, combat desertification, halt and reverse land degradation, halt biodiversity loss.* Sustainable Development Goals. Retrieved from https://www.un.org/sustainabledevelopment/biodiversity/.

Wainwright, O. (2014, April 30). Apartheid ended 20 years ago, so why is Cape Town still 'a paradise for the few'? *The Guardian.* Retrieved from https://www.theguardian.com/ cities/2014/apr/30/cape-town-apartheid-ended-still-paradise-few-south-africa.

Western, J. (2002). A divided city: Cape Town. *Political Geography, 21,* 711–716. DOI: 10.1016/S0962-6298(02)00016-1.

Williams, V. (2014). *Overview of the Cape Flats.* Retrieved from http://capeflats.org.za/ modules/home/overview.php/.

Wolmer, W. (2003). Transboundary protected Area governance: Tensions and paradoxes. *Paper prepared for the workshop on transboundary protected areas in the governance stream of the 5th World Parks Congress,* Durban, South Africa.

World Bank (2018). *An incomplete transition: Overcoming the legacy of exclusion in South Africa.* Republic of South Africa systemic country diagnostic. Retrieved from https://openknowledge.worldbank.org/bitstream/handle/10986/29793/WBG-South-Africa-Systematic-Country-Diagnostic-FINAL-for-board-SECPO-Edit-05032018. pdf?sequence=1&isAllowed=y.

15 Resilience, inclusiveness and challenges of cosmopolitan cities' heritage tourism

The case of the balancing rocks in Epworth, Harare

Zibanai Zhou

Introduction

Southern African cities face several challenges such as the management of rapid urbanisation, unsustainably burgeoning populations, expanding informal settlements and a host of governance challenges (Fraser et al., 2017; Muchadenyika & William, 2017). These challenges pose an unprecedented threat to leisure spaces, tourist sites and tourism resources in cities. It is against this backdrop that a need has been identified for a paradigm shift at policymaking level that includes the adoption of new approaches to managing urban tourism spaces as a way of addressing the complexities that arise when multiple socio-economic actors lay claim to such urban tourism resources. This chapter addresses the resilience, inclusivity and multifaceted challenges of urban heritage tourism at the Chiremba balancing rocks (CBRs) in Harare. The analysis of this chapter findings is based on an adaptive management perspective. The chapter seeks to respond to Ashworth and Page's (2011) call for more theoretically informed research on urban tourism, including urban heritage tourism that "situates urban tourism in a more explicitly theoretical context, and thus remedies a persistent weakness in many forms of tourism research that remain case study driven and implicitly descriptive in manner" (p. 2). Although urban tourism has attracted the attention of scholars in the last decade and has emerged as a worldwide form of tourism, existing literature shows that it is still underexplored as a line of research study in the global south (Hoogendoorn et al., 2019; Law, 1993; Page & Hall, 2003). In support of this, Ashworth and Page (2011) noted that urban tourism receives a disproportionately small amount of attention from scholars.

Ismael and Baum (2006: 214) acknowledged a steady, burgeoning body of literature on urban tourism in mega cities. However, it remains skewed in favour of advanced economic jurisdictions. Recently, Hoogendoorn et al. (2019) stated that urban heritage tourism has received intensive attention mainly in the global north. However, while such research is expanding to other global cities in southern countries such as Egypt and South Africa, the topic remains under-researched and lacks theoretical and empirical depth. Moving to a country level, a case-in-point is Zimbabwe. Despite Zimbabwe laying claim to iconic, world-class heritage sites, information on urban heritage tourism in that country remains limited in current tourism discourse. With urban heritage tourism is growing as a topic of investigation internationally, the aim of this chapter is to argue for inclusivity and to unpack the challenges confronting this form of tourism in the Zimbabwean context and in other precarious urban spaces mainly in the global south. Therefore, the chapter seeks to: analyse the resilience of heritage tourism at the CBRs; establish the inclusiveness of urban heritage tourism at the CBRs in Epworth, Harare; identify and document the multifaceted challenges the CBRs' heritage tourism site is grappling with; and suggest policy recommendations.

The rationale for this chapter is that there still seems to be limited scholarship on urban tourism despite its increased popularity. Very few studies, such as Spirou (2010) and Ashworth and Page (2011), have analysed this line of enquiry comprehensively. In addition, there still appears to be a glaring disconnect between tourism and cosmopolitan cities in most previous studies. Ashworth's observation (Ashworth, 2003: 143) that "those studying tourism neglected cities while those studying cities neglected tourism" is still relevant in contemporary times. Clearly, most previous researchers seem to have focused on large cities, while research on urban heritage tourism sites surrounded by slums is limited (Maitland, 2006). Naumov (2014: 72) stressed that "the relationship between urban heritage and tourism needs further research". Looking at the southern African region in general and Zimbabwe in particular, there is scant information on urban heritage tourism.

This chapter feeds into the wider natural-resource-resilience and community-inclusiveness debate meant to enhance the "seeping through" of tourism benefits to immediate communities. At the same time, it aims to unravel the capacity of the CBRs to survive in Zimbabwe's tourism landscape, which is characterised by political, socioeconomic, image and ecological challenges (Zhou, 2014). The chapter also contributes to the evolving debate on strengthening the resilience of tourist sites in the light of dynamic urban ecosystems. It is mindful of and reinforces the United Nations World Tourism Organization's (UNWTO's) declaration on sustainable and inclusive tourism in socioeconomically disadvantaged communities. As such, the chapter echoes and adds weight to the inclusive tourism conversation in the context of southern Africa, amplifying the need for policymakers to ensure that the socioeconomic spin-offs of urban heritage resources filter through to marginalised local communities and social actors as the primary beneficiaries.

In the context of Zimbabwe, previous work of Vumbunu and Manyanhaire (2010), and Mukoroverwa and Chiutsi (2018) related to heritage tourism, explored tourist visitation levels at Chiremba and examined the potential for urban township tourism in Harare's Mbare Musika, respectively. However, conspicuously absent in previous research is an analysis of the interplay of resilience, inclusivity and the challenges of urban heritage tourism within the framework of an adaptive management approach. This constitutes the theoretical contribution of this chapter to the broad area of urban heritage tourism.

The chapter is structured as follows: firstly, an introduction with chapter objectives is given. This is followed by a literature review section that provides an overview of heritage tourism and the adaptive management theory. The third section covers the geo study site and methods. An analysis and discussion of chapter results follow in the fourth section. A conclusion and recommendations are offered in the last section.

Overview of urban heritage tourism

Worldwide, the numbers of urban tourist arrivals have been increasing steadily on the back of globalisation and an increasing demand for authentic cultural products (Vumbunu & Manyanhaire, 2010). Rogerson and Rogerson (2014) suggested that urban tourism is now recognised globally as a critical sector offering the potential for economic and job growth. In this regard, attention is drawn to the spin-offs of urban heritage tourism, in respect to which the critical rights of communities residing in and around tourist heritage sites are sometimes neglected (Nisbett, 2017).

Urban tourism emerged as a field of study in the past few decades on the back of urban renewal, globalisation and mass tourism. It subsequently gained the interest of tourism industry professionals, policy makers and academia (Ashworth & Page, 2011; Law, 1993; Page, 1995). Broadly speaking, heritage tourism grew as a segment of tourism largely due to the desire to experience cultural heritage places and activities that represent the stories and people of the present and past authentically. Given its ability to stimulate economic activity, tourism has been embraced as an agent of economic development and social transformation in urban areas. Worldwide, heritage tourism has thus become a source of national pride. Timothy (2011) theorised that heritage tourism has the potential to enhance urban economies through reviving and sustaining local traditions and local craft industries.

Mbaiwa et al. (2007) highlighted that urban tourism has recently been recognised as a field of academic study. Urban tourism is a complex concept and its definition has been the subject of intense debate. Law (1993) and Page (1995) explained urban tourism as travelling to urban cities, neighbourhoods, towns and areas with the main motivation being the enjoyment of attractions, facilities and services. Given that the concept of urban tourism is relatively new, previous studies, such as Kidane-Marian (2015), noted many opportunities and challenges.

Heritage tourism represents the authentic and genuine cultural and historical attributes of a given area. Heritage sites are visited by different people with various social and intellectual backgrounds. Consequently, heritage can be regarded as a socially and contextually constructed phenomenon. Chang et al. (1996) argued that the consumption of heritage tourism is influenced by the interpretation of historical and cultural aspects, and that heritage tourism provides opportunities for economic and urban regeneration at no extra cost, since it uses available resources.

The convergence of heritage and tourism causes problems associated with conflicts of interest among various stakeholders such as urban planners and conservationists (Orbasli, 2000). This raises pertinent questions about the sustainability of tourism in urban centres. Sustainability is therefore a function of the harmonisation of preservation, conservation and planning (Park, 2014). Sustainable heritage tourism appears problematic, since it is somewhat difficult to provide a clear-cut role for heritage tourism resources like CBRs as tourist attractions in urban centres. On the one hand, they are resources that need protection and preservation; on the other, they become the main profit in the economic channel. This represents a dichotomy within the concept of sustainability (Saarien, 2014).

Urban heritage tourism and an adaptive management approach

Selby (2004: 191) argued that, in urban contexts, both residents and "tourists are dynamic social actors, interpreting and embodying experience, whilst creating meaning and new realities through their actions". There is also a potential for tension between the multiple uses of urban heritage environments, for example, on a renovated historic street between tourists and local residents, because these environments are seldom solely produced for or consumed by just one user group such as tourists (Ashworth & Page, 2011). Tensions can also occur between tourists and city residents when tourist numbers grow markedly in a city (Novy & Colomb, 2017), and conflict is set to occur when space is reserved exclusively for tourists, as is the case at the CBRs, hence the underpinning of the analysis with the adaptive management approach.

An adaptive management approach is a process of robust decision-making in the face of uncertainty. Its aim is to reduce uncertainty over time via system monitoring. The concept emerged in literature in the 1970s. It has since been adapted increasingly and is used in natural resource management (Mackenzie & Keith, 2009). As its underlying ideology, the approach stresses participation by those outside the management institution to manage conflict and increase the pool of contributions to potential management solutions. The CBRs are a natural heritage resource, hence an adaptive management approach is best suited to analyse its potential for heritage tourism. Plummer and Fennell (2009) stated that a broad objective of the adaptive management approach is to enhance and sustain natural resources and improve the social-ecological resilience of environmental systems. Resilience entails the capacity of an enterprise to survive, adapt and grow in the face of turbulent change. Adaptive management is a process linking a set of networked adaptive capacities to a positive trajectory of functioning and adaptation in constituent populations after a disturbance (Dahles & Susilowati, 2015). It is predicated on the participation of diverse stakeholder groups, including local communities, in decision-making processes. This approach, therefore, seems appropriate in contexts characterised by uncertainty or complexity and in situations where local communities are disempowered, such as the Epworth community.

Adaptive management is an effective and well-established framework that supports the management of natural resources, as it increases knowledge and reduces uncertainty (Rist et al., 2012; Walters, 1986). The perspective provides a role for wider stakeholder participation, reversing the traditional approach to management based on centralised planning, top-down decision-making and control. In the context of this study, instead of the National Museums and Monuments of Zimbabwe (NMMZ) wielding so much power over the affairs of the CBRs, it is about time to devolve power and authority to the Epworth Local Board (ELB) and community to run the heritage site. In essence, adaptive management is a dynamic approach to governance whereby institutional arrangements and ecological knowledge are continuously revised through a process of learning by doing. It has been used extensively in the governance of natural resources contexts for its efficacy, and is founded on the active participation and collaboration of diverse stakeholder groups (Armitage et al., 2009; Bramwell, 2011; Jamal & Stronza, 2009; Larson & Poudyal, 2012). The CBRs tourist heritage site fits this context.

Geo study site – Chiremba balancing rocks (CBRs)

The CBRs are located 13 km southeast of Harare in the Epworth settlement (Manjengwa et al., 2016). The balancing rocks are a national heritage site run by the NMMZ (Vumbunu & Manyanhaire, 2010). The rocks are a geomorphological feature comprised of igneous rocks and came into being through natural processes. The CBRs site is funded by the government of Zimbabwe, with additional financial resources generated through entrance fees to the site and donor funds. The rocks are the anchor heritage tourism attraction at Chiremba. The choice of the CBRs for this study was informed by their lofty national significance as an epitome of the country's heritage and rich culture with potential to be a rich source of data. The revered national heritage site attracts leisure, adventure and business tourists. The Reserve Bank of Zimbabwe (RBZ) has also used the rocks as a picture on Zimbabwean banknotes as a symbol of peace and the stability of the nation's economy. However, the site is increasingly coming under threat from creeping urbanisation. The CBRs are surrounded by the informal and highly populated settlement of Epworth run by the ELB. It is an area characterised by haphazard planning, housing of poor structural quality and inadequate infrastructure. There is no refuse collection, only limited access to electricity and inadequate access to sanitation and safe water, which results in rampant use of unprotected shallow wells because residents rely mostly on one borehole that is shared by the entire settlement. Other features are extreme overcrowding, brought about mostly

Figure 15.1 Chiremba Balancing Rocks image.
Source: Zimfieldguide.com.

To Harare

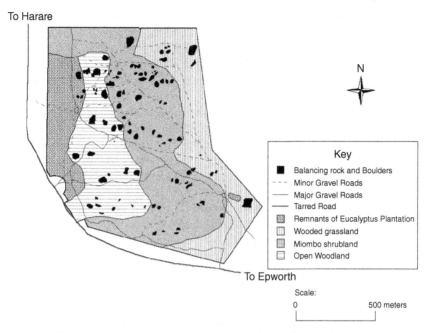

Key

■   Balancing rock and Boulders
--- Minor Gravel Roads
—   Major Gravel Roads
—   Tarred Road
▨   Remnants of Eucalyptus Plantation
▥   Wooded grassland
▨   Miombo shrubland
▤   Open Woodland

N

To Epworth

Scale:
0   500 meters

Figure 15.2 Chiremba Balancing Rocks map.
Source: Maroyi, 2011.

by people displaced during the infamous Murambatsvina purge of 2005, and insecure residential status (Muchadenyika, 2015; Tawodzera, 2012). Epworth has very high levels of income poverty, with large families of seven and more people with low education levels and no income from permanent employment living together in cramped shanty cabins (Manjengwa et al., 2016). Residents live under adverse socioeconomic and materially deprived conditions. Their survival revolves around selling goods by the roadside and international remittances. The unemployment level stands at 80% and the crime rate is very high, with crimes ranging from prostitution to illicit drug dealing, housebreaking, illegal urban cultivation, illegal stone crushing and vending. The population of the settlement was 167 462 in 2012 (ZEC, 2013; Zimstats, 2013; GOZ, 2010).

Methods

A combination of archival data, document analysis, site observation and questionnaires were employed for data collection. Documents studied include CBRs' annual reports, historical visitor statistics, the greater Harare master plan, the national tourism sector master plan of the Zimbabwe Tourism Authority (ZTA), Zimbabwe Electoral Commission (ZEC) delimitation reports and the 2012 national census report of the Zimbabwe National Statistics Agency (ZIMSTAT). Objectives, target respondents, theory and the information to be collected informed the questionnaire design. Data were recorded in a notebook, coded and sorted according to emerging themes and content. Thematic content analysis was then used to ana-lyse data. The method involved identifying, analysing and reporting themes within data. Data were collected over a two-week period in November 2019 through a self-administered questionnaire handed to the following 60 purposefully selected CBRs key stakeholders: the ZTA; the Harare City Council (HCC); the NMMZ; the Tourism Business Council of Zimbabwe (TBCZ); the Combined Harare Residents Association (CHRA); the ELB; the Environmental Management Agency (EMA); Epworth residents; visitors; the Ministry of Home Affairs and Cultural Herit-age (MoHACH); the Ministry of Environment Tourism and Hospitality Industry (MoETHI); and workers at the CBRs. Questions were non directive and open-ended to allow respondents to frame and express opinions in their own way. The questionnaire survey yielded 51 usable returns; that is, 85% broken down as fol-lows: ZTA, 5 returns; HCC, 5 returns; NMMZ, 3 returns; ZBCT, 5 returns; CHRA, 4 returns; ELB, 4 returns; EMA, 2 returns; Epworth residents, 6 returns; visitors, 5 returns; MoETHI, 4 returns; MoHACH, 4 returns; and workers at CBRs, 4 returns.

For the purpose of triangulation, tourists' reviews were also examined for their experiences. The early stages of data analysis sought to gain a hermeneutic appre-ciation of the concerns and views associated with urban heritage tourism. Sub-sequently, data from multiple sources were synthesised into specific themes and patterns based on the resilience and challenges of urban heritage tourism at the CBRs following Miles and Huberman's (1994: 10) guidelines on qualitative data analysis. Four themes were identified: the resilience of urban heritage tourism; the inclusivity of urban communities; multifaceted challenges; and future pros-pects and intervening restorative mechanisms. Each theme is discussed below.

Results and discussion

Resilience of urban heritage tourism amid socioeconomic and political headwinds

It was established that despite the uncertainty and socioeconomic challenges fac-ing the city of Harare in general and the CBRs heritage tourism site in particular, tourism activity at the CBRs has been resilient, albeit in a subdued form.

According to respondents' narratives, the rebounding local tourism market segment, comprising especially schools, churches and social events like wed-dings, kept heritage tourism 'alive' at the CBRs. From observations, the site has not been maintained properly, but it still records modest business during school terms, over weekends and during public holidays. A CBRs official, informant D, who has been working at the heritage site for the past 40 years, had this to say:

Although business is very low especially from foreign visitors we have remained operational. We have not been very fortunate as we went through a challenging operational history; political instability of the 1980s; ESAP [the Economic Structural Adjustment Programme]; land reform; Muram-batsvina; invasion of open urban recreational spaces; political and eco-nomic crisis of the 1990s; international isolation; 2008 cholera epidemic;

negative publicity; hyperinflationary era; fuel and currency crisis; but we survived and still operational (self-administered questionnaire, 10 November 2019).

One would have thought that, given the threat of creeping urbanisation in the late 1990s, the CBRs would be invaded by menacing rock-mining syndicates that crush stones to make quarry stones, which are in high demand in settlements around Harare. However, this has not been the case. Rather, the setbacks the informant referred to almost brought Zimbabwe's tourism industry to its knees.

The adaptive management approach dictates that, in the face of upheavals, one has to institute survival mechanisms such as turning to the local tourism market segment and increasing awareness in schools to stimulate demand for the heritage site. According to national regulatory authority official, informant B, who is responsible for meetings, incentives, conventions and exhibitions (MICE) tourism development, the heritage site's resilience has resulted from a combination of factors (self-administered questionnaire, 12 November 2019). These include the following: the CBRs heritage tourism site attracts a variety of tourists because of the mystery surrounding the balancing rocks. Its location in close proximity to the capital city resonates with tourists and shoppers alike, who combine their shopping excursions with a visit to the CBRs. The heritage site is within easy reach of the Robert Gabriel Mugabe (RGM) International Airport and very close to the National Heroes Acre. Business executives attending corporate meetings and parliamentarians on legislative business form another cohort of regular visitors to the site. The balancing rocks are located near major prestigious hotels such as the Meikles, the Rainbow Towers, the Crowne Plaza and the Holiday Inn, and are in close proximity of major sporting facilities like the giant national sports and Rufaro stadia. Furthermore, Harare is the seat of government, the judiciary and the legislature. Together, these factors have sustained heritage tourism at the CBRs, making it resilient through spill over business.

Inclusion of urban communities in urban heritage tourism

Findings showed that urban communities are not included in tourism development activities at the CBRs. A local government heritage tourism development official, informant A (self-administered questionnaire, 10 November 2019), stated that local communities were left out completely in terms of job inclusiveness, entrepreneurial opportunities, involvement and a trickling down of benefits to women, the elderly and youth. The majority of informants supported this. Their narratives revealed that not even a single community member worked at the heritage site, that no one from the local communities was allowed to operate micro-entrepreneurial ventures at the site and that the local communities were not involved in any decision- making about the heritage site.

Regulatory authority informants A, C and D all stated that it would be judicious for the communities to take charge of and benefit from resources in line with devolution as spelt out in the Zimbabwean constitution (self-administered questionnaire, 9 November 2019). Given the heritage site's location near Epworth, a high-density settlement accommodating many unemployed youth, one would expect that job opportunities would be made available to Epworth residents in line with the guarantees stipulated in the constitution that communities should benefit from the resources in their localities.

A youth from the Epworth settlement, informant F, echoed similar sentiments:

> As youth, we have not been given an opportunity to contribute to CBR. There are many of us here in Epworth without formal employment. My proposal to open an eatery facility was turned down as it was felt to be conflicting with the city's bylaws and NMMZ's imperial regulations.

However, NMMZ and HCC officials, informants A and E, who are responsible for community liaison, differed (self-administered questionnaire, 5 November 2019). They insisted that operating a business had to comply with city bylaws and indicated that local residents were given first preference, provided they had the requisite qualifications.

The very high unemployment rate among communities living in the informal settlement around the CBRs saw the youth engaging in all manner of illicit drug trafficking and abuse, and house-breaking. Giving the communities a chance to engage in some entrepreneurial activities adjacent to the heritage site would go a long way towards helping the hopeless situation. This is the tragedy that heritage tourism is facing at the CBRs. In some other jurisdictions, urban heritage tourism is celebrated as a panacea to the scourge of youth and community unemployment. Cases-in-point are the Egyptian pyramids at Giza and youth employment opportunities availed in Addis Ababa in Ethiopia (Kidane-Marian, 2015). The lack of inclusivity at the CBRs is in sharp contrast to claims made by Timothy (2011) that urban heritage tourism opens vast entrepreneurial opportunities for the youth. Since global trends gravitate more towards the involvement of local people in the conservation, management and exploitation of business opportunities arising from local resources, embracing the adaptive management approach at the CBRs could be the answer. Holding back communities from benefiting meaningfully from tourism activities at the CBRs is retrogressive and defies the UNWTO's much-vaunted inclusive tourism and 2030 sustainable development goals (SDGs) (UNWTO, 2018). It is an affront to calls to harness tourism as a vector for poverty reduction within communities and contradicts the UNWTO's advocacy for local communities to be the primary beneficiaries of tourism resources.

Multifaceted challenges confronting the CBRs as an urban heritage tourism site

The numerous challenges facing the CBRs are as follows:

i)   *Breakdown of a social service delivery system*

ELB informant C, who is responsible for community services in Epworth, stated that the city of Harare is in the throes of a critical clean water supply shortage, experiences electricity downtime of up to 18 hours and poor waste disposal due to a depleted refuse collection fleet (self-administered questionnaire, 8 November 2019). This has exerted a heavy toll on the CBRs. EMA officials confirmed this. Such basic services should not be interrupted at any tourist-designated facility. This finding is in line with what The Guardian (2016) established in the city of Mecca in Saudi Arabia, where pilgrimages resulted in population growth that outstripped the ability to service demand and culminated in severe stresses on the city's physical and social capacities. In addition, MoETHI official informant B, who is responsible for visitor exit surveys, stated that the city of Harare had not fully recovered from the 2008 cholera epidemic, which had a devastating effect on the city's overstretched health delivery system (self-administered questionnaire, 8 November 2019). The respondent lamented that recurrent disease outbreaks repel tourists in a manner reminiscent of West Africa's Ebola, China's coronavirus and the UK's mad cow disease that saw a massive decline in tourist traffic.

ii) *Traffic congestion*

Informant A, a visitor to the heritage site, stated that the Harare city council has, of late, not been able to cope with increased traffic loads, likening the city's driveways to a jungle that poses touting, mugging and sporadic robbery risks to tourists (self-administered questionnaire, 9 November 2019). It has become too dangerous to drive through robots from the city centre to the CBRs heritage site because of the possibility of being robbed at robots and in traffic lanes due to congestion. Not only does this spoil a tourist's experience, but it also jeopardises tourism development in such a crime-rife environment.

iii) *Littering, site graffiti and vandalisation of the perimeter fence at the CBRs.*

A respondent from the EMA stated that littering has become a menace in the city centre, with open spaces having the worst of it. Littering causes visual pollution at the CBRs, thus impairing the aesthetic appearance of an overall ambience at the heritage site through the defacing of the rock paintings. Inadequate security provision at the site makes it possible for people to break down the poorly maintained and unmanned perimeter fence to access the heritage site. This finding conforms to what Kidane-Marian (2015) established in Addis Ababa, where similar challenges of poor sanitation, neglect and lack of strict control and regulation of tourist-related infrastructures and services are faced. An escalation in the vandalisation of the CBRs perimeter fence could also be acts of sabotage by certain sections of the urban community who feel excluded. This is ample evidence of lack of shared goals among CBRs stakeholders in general.

iv) *Covert conflict in the use of urban spaces and resources.*

According to NMMZ, EMA and ELB officials, informants C, D and A, there were subtle conflicts between the NMMZ and local residents over the land surrounding the CBRs relating to tourism and housing (self-administered questionnaire,

9 November 2019). Demand for accommodation space has grown enormously, with open spaces being invaded by housing cooperatives with the full backing of the corrupt political elite. This finding is in tandem with Orbasli's (2000) observation that it is not uncommon for urban tourism to cause problems associated with a conflict of interest among stakeholders. To this end, urban housing settlements are rapidly encroaching on the perimeter fence of the CBRs with huge implications for the attractiveness of the heritage site.

v)   *Lack of tourism amenities.*

Informants A, C, F and B from the ZTA, the ELB, the CHRA and the NMMZ, respectively, concurred that there was an acute underinvestment in proper hospitality-related amenities, which was a cause of concern at the CBRs (self-administered questionnaire, 10 November 2019). The unavailability of proper, world-class hospitality facilities and failure to attract meaningful investment over the years on this front are worrisome and featured most in customer reviews. There are no eateries, no ablution facilities and no information desks, which are basic requirements at any functional tourist facility. The decline in tourist arrivals meant a corresponding decrease in gate-takings that could help salvage the funding deficit. Excerpts from customer online reviews of their experiences at the heritage site confirm the sad state of affairs at the CBRs:

> … no toilets, too expensive, not well-kept, roads filled with weeds, very poor maintenance … involve the surrounding community to work and maintain it, it has potential.
>
> Facility run down … dying state of an awesome heritage site … poor management of the heritage … area is run down, no guides available to direct and interact with visitors.

In Zimbabwe, the NMMZ is the statutory juristic body in charge of all heritage sites; private companies and individuals are shut out. Different actors, social groups and institutions have differential powers concerning the governance and coordination of urban heritage tourism. This fits in well with Khirfan (2014), who found that in the Middle East, national agencies control the development and marketing of heritage sites in cities, which minimises residents' input in heritage tourism planning.

Applying the adaptive management approach in the face of shrinking donor funds and squeezed fiscal space, CBRs authorities need to open up to accommodate private-public partnerships (PPPs), which have resulted in success stories within the region and on the international stage. Furthermore, given the inability of the government to finance investment in proper facilities at heritage sites, built-operate-transfer (BOT) partnerships with investors are another option. The case of the Vilakazi precinct in Soweto is worth mentioning. Booyens and Rogerson (2018) posit that the precinct has expanded considerably as a result of public and private investment. It now boasts an array of shops, stalls and restaurants. This can be replicated easily at the CBRs.

Future prospects and intervening restorative mechanisms

Results indicated that the CBRs heritage site is not yet a write-off. What needs to be done is some rehabilitative work followed by a sustained marketing strategy biased towards growing the local market. Going forward, the focus should be on scaling up multi- and intersectoral linkages and collaboration with tourism-sector-specific players to spruce up the facility. A funding mechanism other than the government grant should be explored through interministerial collaboration. This would apply to the Ministry of Transport and Infrastructural Development to prioritise sprucing up the access roads at the site; the MoHACH, under the jurisdiction of which the NMMZ falls; the MoETHI, under the auspices of which the ZTA falls; and the Ministry of Local Government and Urban Development, under the auspices of which the city of Harare falls. These ministries need to work together to restore the allure of the CBRs.

Conclusion and recommendations

In conclusion, urban heritage tourism at Harare's CBRs, though resilient, is laden with enormous challenges that are surmountable through the adoption of an adaptive management perspective. The non-inclusive nature of heritage tourism at the CBRs frustrates poverty-reduction efforts within communities. It remains an uphill task for the NMMZ to satisfy the expectations of different socioeconomic actors laying claim to the CBRs. Though not a panacea, the adoption of an adaptive management perspective can help the NMMZ navigate the complexity and challenges confronting the CBRs.

This requires an understanding of the functioning of urban ecosystems and interaction among diverse social actors in the built and natural environment, which falls within the realm of an adaptive management perspective. An adaptive management perspective can thus be an innovative way of nudging multistakeholder engagement and, as such, constitutes a useful approach to increase resilience and community inclusiveness at the CBRs heritage tourism site. Tourism planners need to respond creatively and develop systematic and sustainable solutions that will enhance tourism enterprises' resilience and community inclusiveness. An argument has thus been advanced from the perspective that cities are connected, complex and vulnerable entities that can be regarded as urban ecosystems. Hence, silo approaches offer limited results in addressing multifaceted societal challenges and complexities involving multiple social actors. The multifaceted and interconnected nature of several challenges that transverse the CBRs' ecological-socio-economic divide can best be improved by an adaptive management approach.

The following recommendations are submitted:

- Make heritage tourism more inclusive through devolution to ensure that local communities are at the front end of tourism processes.
- Direct more marketing efforts at the local market.
- Spruce up the infrastructural facilities and tourism amenities through smart PPPs, BOT and lease and collaborative arrangements.

- The city of Harare must enforce bylaws, particularly for land zoning, to protect the CBRs heritage site.
- Prosecute politicians and land barons who dole out recreational land unlawfully.
- Increase NMMZ funding to enable rehabilitative programmes, for example, the Great Zimbabwe National Monument, where a funding partnership with international development agencies has paid off.
- Introduce a tourism police service in the CBDs to tame traffic congestion and related challenges.

References

Armitage, D.R., Plummer, R., Berkes, F., Arther, R.I., Charles, A.T., Davidson-Hunt, I. J., (2009). Adaptive co-management for social ecological complexity. *Frontiers in Ecology and the Environment 7*(2), 95–102.

Ashworth, G.J. (2003). Urban Tourism: Still an imbalance in attention? In Cooper, C. (Ed.), *Classic reviews in tourism* (pp. 143–163). Clevedon: Channel View.

Ashworth, G.T., & Page, S.J. (2011). Urban tourism research: Recent progress and current paradoxes. *Tourism Management 32*(1), 1–15.

Booyens, J., & Rogerson, C.M. (2018). Creative tourism: South African township explorations. *Tourism Review 74*(2), 256–267.

Bramwell, B. (2011). Governance, the state and sustainability of tourism: A political economy approach. *Journal of Sustainable Tourism 19*(4–5), 459–477.

Chang, T.C., Milne, S., Fallon, D., & Pohlmann, C. (1996). Urban heritage tourism: The global–local nexus. *Annals of Tourism Research 23*(2), 284–305.

Dahles, H., & Susilowati, T.P. (2015). Business resilience in times of growth and crisis. *Annals of Tourism Research 51*, 34–50.

Fraser, A., Parnell, S., Leck, H., & Pelling, J. (2017). Africa's urban risk and resilience. *International Journal of Disaster Risk Reduction 26*, 1–6.

Government of Zimbabwe. (2010). *Multiple Indicator Monitoring Survey (MIMS)*, Zimbabwe National Statistical Agency, Belgravia, Harare.

Hoogendoorn, G., Letsatsi, N., Malleka, T., & Booyens, I. (2019). Tourist and resident perspectives of 'slum tourism': the case of the Vilakazi precinct, Soweto. *GeoJournal*, 1–17. doi:10.1007/s10708-019-10,016-2

Jalambi, R. (2016). After the hajj: Mecca residents grow hostile to changes in the holy city. The Guardian Online. Retrieved from http://www.theguardian.com/cities/2016/sep/14. mecca-hajj=pilgrim-tourism .

Ismael, H., & Baum, T. (2006). Urban tourism in developing countries. In the case of Melak (Malacca) City. Malaysia. *Anatolia 17* (20), 211–233.

Jamal, T., & Stronza, A. (2009). Collaboration theory and tourism practice in protected areas: Stakeholders, structuring and sustainability. *Journal of Sustainable Tourism, 17*(2), 169–189.

Khirfan, L. (2014). *World heritage, urban design and tourism: Three cities in the Middle East*. Farnham: Ashgate.

Kidane-Marian, T. (2015). Ethiopia: Opportunities and challenges of tourism development in the Addis Ababa upper Rift Valley Corridor. *Journal of Tourism and Hospitality 14*(4), 167.

Larson, L., & Poudyal, N.C. (2012). Developing sustainable tourism through adaptive resources management: A case study of Machu Picchu, Peru. *Journal of Sustainable Tourism 20*(7), 917–938.

Law, C. (1993). *Urban tourism: Attracting visitors to large cities*. London: Mansell.

Mackenzie, B.D.E., & Keith, A.K. (2009). Adaptive management in practice: Conservation of a threatened plant population. *Ecological Management and Restoration, 10*(sl), S129–Si135.

Maitland, R. (2006). How can we manage the tourist-historic city? Tourism strategy in Cambridge, UK, 1978–2003. *Tourism Management 27*(6), 1262–1273.

Manjengwa, J., Matema, C., & Tirivanhu, D. (2016). Understanding urban poverty in two high-density suburbs of Harare, Zimbabwe. *Development Southern Africa 33*(1), 23–38.

Maroyi, A. (2011). Protection of an archaeological site: A case study of Chiremba balancing rocks, Epworth, Harare, Zimbabwe. *Scientific Research and Essays, 6*(27). doi:10.5897/SRE11.724.

Mbaiwa, J., Toteng, E., & Moswete, N. (2007). Problems and prospects for the development of urban tourism in Gaborone and Maun, Botswana. *Development Southern Africa 24*(5), 725–740.

Miles, M., & Huberman, A. (1994). *Qualitative data analysis: An expanded source book*. Thousand Oaks, California: Sage.

Muchadenyika, D. (2015). Slum upgrading and inclusive municipal governance in Harare, Zimbabwe: New perspectives for the urban poor. *Habitat International 48,* 1–10.

Muchadenyika, D., & William, J.J. (2017). Politics and the practice of planning: The case of Zimbabwean cities. *Cities 63,* 33–40.

Mukoroverwa, M., & Chiutsi, S. (2018). Prospects and challenges of Positioning Harare as an urban Township tourism destination, *African Journal of Hospitality Tourism and Leisure 7*(4), 1–11.

Naumov, N. (2014). Heritage tourism in Urban Areas – Contemporary complexities. *IIluminare 12*(1), Indiana University, 67–75.

Nisbett, M. (2017). Empowering the empowered? Slum tourism and the depoliticisation of poverty. *Geoforum 85,* 37–45.

Novy, J., & Colomb, C. (2017). Urban tourism and its discontents: An introduction. In C. Colomb and J. Novy, (Eds.), *Protest and resistance in the tourist city*, 1–30.

Orbasli, A. (2000). *Tourists in historic towns*. London: E & FN Spon.

Page, S.J. (1995). *Urban tourism*. London: Routledge.

Page, S., & Hall, M. (2003). *Managing urban tourism*. Harlow: Pearson.

Park, H.Y. (2014). *Heritage tourism*. London: Routledge.

Plummer, R., & Fennell, D. (2009). Managing protected areas for sustainable tourism: prospects for adaptive co-management. *Journal of Sustainable Tourism 17*(2), 149–168.

Rist, L., Campbell, B.M., & Frost, P. (2012). Adaptive management: where are we now? *Environmental Conservation* 1–14.

Rogerson, J., & Rogerson, C. (2014). Urban Tourism research: recent progress and current paradoxes. *Tourism Management 32,* 1–15.

Saarien, J. (2014). Critical sustainability: setting the limits to growth and responsibility in tourism. *Sustainability 6,* 1–17.

Selby, M. (2004). Consuming the city: conceptualising and researching urban tourist knowledge. *Tourism Geographies 6*(2), 186–207.

Spirou, C. (2010). *Urban tourism and urban change: Cities in a global economy (The metropolis and modern life)* (1st ed). London: Routledge.

Tawodzera, G. (2012). Urban household survival and resilience to food insecurity in crisis conditions: the case of Epworth in Harare, Zimbabwe. *Journal of Hunger and Environmental Nutrition 7*(2/3), 293–320.

Timothy, D.J. (2011). *Cultural heritage and tourism: An introduction.* Bristol: Channel View Books.

UNWTO, (2018). World Tourism Organisation and United Nations Development Programme, 2017. Tourism and the sustainable development goals- journey to 2030, UNWTO, Madrid, doi:0.1811197789284419401.

Vumbunu, T., & Manyanhaire, I.O. (2010). Tourist arrivals at Chiremba balancing rocks in Epworth, Zimbabwe. *Journal of Sustainable Development in Africa 12*(8), 240–253.

Walters, C.J. (1986). *Adaptive management of renewable resources.* New York, NY: Macmillan.

ZEC, (2013). Constituency boundary. 2013 Harmonised elections results. www.zec.org.zw/pages/delimitationreports.

Zhou, Z. (2014). Marketing destination Zimbabwe during and post the 2000–2008 political and economic crises. *Journal of Tourism Management Research 1*(1), 14–26.

Zimstats (2013). Population census national report 2012. Retrieved from https://www.zimstat.co.zw/wp-content/uploads/publications/population/population/census-2012-national-report.pdf.

16 Prospects and challenges of sustainable urban tourism in Windhoek

Poverty, inequality and urban risks linkages

Erisher Woyo

16.1 Intoduction

Tourism provides both developmental challenges and opportunities for most sub-Saharan African (SSA) countries (Musavengane et al., 2019; Woyo & Slabbert, 2019). Key opportunities, as articulated in most national policies, include job creation and the generation of foreign currency revenue. As a result, tourism in SSA – specifically, in southern Africa – has become a critical tool for economic development (Siakwah et al., 2020; Woyo & Woyo, 2019). The developmental focus of tourism in southern African countries (including Namibia) has been dominated by rural communities, leading to urban areas being neglected, despite also being home to impoverished people (Fraser et al., 2017). Based on this argument, tourism development as a policy option has not yet been fully embraced in urban settings.

Urban tourism is "a type of tourism activity that takes place in an urban space encompassing a broad and heterogeneous range of cultural, architectural, technological, social and natural experiences and products for leisure and business" (United Nations World Tourism Organisation [UNWTO], 2019). Despite a significant body of literature focusing on what makes tourism sustainable, the notion of sustainable urban tourism appears to be under-researched (Timur & Getz, 2008). Discourse on urban tourism tends to be rather simplistic, more precisely in respect of the way sustainable development goals (SDGs) are integrated without paying due attention to the risks associated with a developmental approach. Furthermore, sustainable development challenges often focus more on the natural environment and protected areas, even though increasing numbers of people now live in urban areas.

This chapter is aimed at discussing the prospects and challenges of sustainable urban tourism development in Windhoek, the capital of Namibia, as a means of achieving the United Nations' 2030 SDGs 1 and 10 (United Nations [UN], 2015). The SDG 1, "no poverty", is concerned with eliminating poverty in communities in all its forms, while SDG 10 focuses on reducing inequality. Specifically, this chapter investigates the extent to which sustainable tourism development is capable of meeting the needs of contemporary citizens without jeopardising the tourism needs of future generations in the city of Windhoek. This discussion highlights the degree to which urban tourism has enabled Windhoek in particular, and Namibia in general, to achieve the SDGs (specifically, goals 1 and 10). The discussion also focuses on the risks that might emanate from pursuing a developmental approach to urban tourism in the context of this city. A systematic literature review and document analysis were employed to establish both the challenges and prospects associated with urban tourism in Windhoek. This was also done to identify the risks posed by the established challenges and prospects of sustainable tourism development in that city.

It is imperative for research – specifically in SSA, where poverty and social polarisation are worryingly high – to reflect on the prospects and challenges associated with developing urban tourism. The data thus obtained could prove helpful when formulating sustainable development strategies aimed at helping countries across Africa (Durokifa & Ijeoma, 2018) to meet the SDGs by 2030. Although a growing stream of research focuses on pro-poor tourism (PPT) in urban settings throughout SSA (Musavengane et al., 2019, 2020), there is a general lack of empirical evidence concerning the development of sustainable urban tourism, the reduction of poverty and inequity, and the mitigation of existing urban risks. The aim here is to contribute to the current discourse on tourism, poverty and inequality reduction. The author further seeks to provide practitioners and policymakers alike with comprehensive information on the prospects and likely challenges of developing urban tourism in a sustained manner while mitigating the possible concomitant risks. These aspects are crucial when formulating developmental policies aimed at countering social bias and poverty among the urban inhabitants of emergent economies.

The remainder of the chapter is organised as follows: the next section investigates the links between tourism, poverty and inequality reduction. The methods of research and study context are covered in the subsequent section. Thereafter, the prospects and challenges of developing sustainable urban tourism in Windhoek are outlined, before the chapter concludes with a consideration of several ways in which to develop urban tourism in a more sustainable manner in Windhoek.

16.2 The links between tourism, poverty and inequality reduction

Five years ago, the UN launched 17 SDGs aimed at providing a new system of indicators for sustainable development for application by all industry sectors across all nations (UN, 2015). This undertaking was, however, criticised for representing a mere rehash of the failed millennium development goals (MDGs) (Durokifa & Ijeoma, 2018). Despite these criticisms, in 2015, the 2030 Agenda for Sustainable Development was adopted by 195 member states, including Namibia. The agenda is a shared blueprint aimed at fostering peace and prosperity for people and the planet, now and into the future (UN, 2015). Key to this optimistic yet ambitious message is the recognition that member states need to work to end poverty (Dhahri & Omri, 2020) and other deprivations that go hand-in-hand with strategies aimed at improving citizens' health and education. These goals are pursued with a view of reducing inequity and spurring economic growth without neglecting the challenges of climate change and the preservation of our oceans and forests (UN, 2015).

In discussing the role of urban tourism in achieving SDGs 1 and 10, let us focus on the first, which entails working to eradicate poverty (UN, 2015). Sen (2001: 87) defines poverty as the "deprivation of basic capabilities", which is caused by receiving or having an inadequate income. A low income often equates to an "impoverished life" (Sen, 2001: 87) and subjects the poor to numerous risks. For that reason, a "lack of income is [deemed] the underlying cause of poverty" (Njoya & Seetaram, 2017: 513). Globally, the eradication of poverty, specifically in urban areas, is a critical concern (Panori et al., 2019). Poverty in cities, which is recognised as a complex construct (Panori et al., 2019), has the potential to undermine sustainable development and degenerate into urban risks. Amongst the risks emanating from poverty are gender-based violence and prostitution (Hunter, 2007; Magadi, 2016; Rodrigo & Rajapakse, 2010), and theft or burglary (Musavengane et al., 2020).

Globally speaking, the levels of extreme poverty are declining at a slower pace (UN, 2019). This suggests that UN member countries, including Namibia, may not be on track to achieve a world with less than 3% extreme poverty by 2030: in fact, in 2018, 8% of the world's workers and their dependents lived in extreme poverty (UN, 2019). The situation is reported to be dire in SSA, and thus requires evidence-based interventions. According to the UN (2019), 42% of the population in SSA continues to subsist in conditions of extreme poverty. Inequality, as measured by the Gini coefficient (which often reveals structured and recurring patterns regarding the unequal distribution of goods, wealth, opportunities, rewards and punishments), comes into play due to the unequal opportunities and statuses that exist within a group or society (more on this later). The UN (2019) concedes that social imbalances within and among nations remains a significant concern, which implies that progress towards reducing these discrepancies is also slow. Given rising inequality globally (UN, 2019), sustainable interventions are needed to reduce urban risks and build resilient cities.

Tourism, because of its significant contribution to national economies, is a sector which is critical in helping economies to achieve SDGs 1 and 10 through employment creation and income generation. This sector therefore has a direct impact on efforts to achieve the aforementioned (and other) SDGs.

16.3 Fundamentals of urban risk, tourism development and resilience in SSA

Tourism development is a policy option for many developing countries (Woyo & Slabbert, 2019) due to its economic contribution, which is considered to be transformational (Musavengane et al., 2020). Such a contribution is both direct and indirect (Lee & Chang, 2008). As a result, tourism plays a crucial role in the development of other sectors, as well as in the economic growth and infrastructure development of any destination (Ahmad et al., 2019; Musavengane et al., 2020). Due to its labour-intensive nature, a strong tourism industry is imperative in filling the vacuum of unemployment (Ahmad et al., 2019), which underscores how significant tourism development is. In turn, employment creation is a critical element in dealing with the dual scourges of poverty and inequality.

Tourism is a significant contributor to Namibia's gross domestic product (GDP) (Woyo & Amadhila, 2018). In 2015, Namibian tourism contributed N\$5.2 billion (approximately US\$346 million)[1] and 44 700 jobs (Ministry of Environment and Tourism (MET), 2016). In 2016, there was an improvement in the contribution that this sector made, as it contributed 10.5% (N\$16.7 billion; US\$1.1 billion) to the overall GDP and created 101 000 jobs – that represents 14.9% of the country's total employment (Namibia Tourism Board [NTB], 2017). In 2017, the NTB projected that, in 2020, tourism would contribute N\$26.4 billion (US\$1.7 billion) to the overall GDP and create 123 000 jobs. Such estimates show that developing sustainable urban tourism could be a workable policy option, especially for a city such as Windhoek.

An emerging stream of literature from SSA warns, however, that developing urban tourism could pose certain risks (Musavengane et al., 2019, 2020; Satterthwaite, 2017). According to the extant literature, urban risk is measured in terms of environmental hazards, poor local governance, unequal societies, social constraints and overstretched resources (which include infrastructure and superstructure) (Musavengane et al., 2019, 2020; Satterthwaite, 2017), as well as inadequate service provision (Musavengane et al., 2020). While tourism is pursued with good intentions, it must be balanced with a comprehensive understanding of the urban risks involved (Musavengane et al., 2020). The development of sustainable urban tourism is a more challenging process, primarily when the aim is to fight poverty and inequality among urban residents while working to minimise urban risks.

The variety of pressures being exerted on urban areas include "limited economic opportunities, inequalities, congestion, social vices, sanitation challenges and poor governance" (Musavengane et al., 2020). Research shows that tourism could be a panacea for some of these challenges and risks (Boakye et al., 2013; Musavengane et al., 2020; UNDP, 2015). As these issues remain largely unaddressed in debates centring around Windhoek, Namibia, unpacking possible treats associated with expanding urban tourism in this context is vital for developing strategies aimed at managing urban risks and making Windhoek a resilient African city.

16.4 Study context and methods

The Republic of Namibia, which is located in southern Africa, has a population of 2.5 million people (Namibia Statistics Agency [NSA], 2017). The country has a GDP of approximately US\$15 billion (International Monetary Fund [IMF], 2019; Bank of Namibia [BON], 2020) and a per capita annual income of US\$6 013 (IMF, 2019). Based on these statistics, Namibia is classified as a middle-income country (Central Bureau of Statistics [CBS], 2009). Despite its status, Namibia is an unequal-income country with a Gini coefficient of 0.63 (World Bank, 2019). Unemployment is high, with more than half of its citizens living in abject poverty (Humavindu & Stage, 2013). Though the country's economy is primarily supported by agriculture and mining, tourism is a significant contributor to its GDP – Namibia receives slightly more than a million arrivals per annum (Woyo & Amadhila, 2018).

Windhoek, the bustling capital city, is the gateway to major tourist attractions in the country. Following Namibia's independence from South Africa in 1990, Windhoek has become a significant tourist destination, together with the coastal towns of Walvis Bay and Swakopmund. Close to 1.6 million tourists visit the capital annually, while an average of 300 000 visitors have been recorded for Walvis Bay and Swakopmund (MET, 2019). Formerly known as South-West Africa (an erstwhile territory of Germany, before being placed under South African administration in 1915), the country of Namibia and the city of Windhoek in particular are famous among German tourists, who constitute 17% of the total number of visitors to these shores (MET, 2016: 6) – by far the largest long-haul market of tourists to the country (Atkinson, 2016). Other significant international source markets include the United Kingdom, Italy and France, while regional markets are dominated by tourists from South Africa, Botswana, Zambia and Zimbabwe. Windhoek is home to key attractions, including a craft centre, the NamibRand Nature Reserve and the Christuskirche.

Windhoek, which represents an intersection of African and European cultures (predominantly of German origin), is known for the friendliness of its people. The city has been declared one of the cleanest capitals in Africa (Nyanchama, 2020). Visitors might be surprised that the city, which is considered to be part of 'deepest Africa', offers all modern amenities that conform to some of the world's highest standards. These include hotels, banks, post offices, gyms, libraries, museums, car-hire companies, health facilities, airlines and estate agencies. The literature is, however, limited in terms of outlining any of the prospects or challenges confronting urban tourism development as a tool for dealing with poverty and various manifestations of inequality, as well as the possible risks associated with developing urban tourism in Windhoek in particular.

There is a need to apply the PPT approach to cities so that tourism can deliver more net benefits to the poor (Musavengane et al., 2019). This will be crucial in ensuring the resilience of a city such as Windhoek, as it fights extreme poverty and social polarisation in a way that minimises urban risk. Although policymakers consider tourism in Namibia to be a critical tool for socioeconomic development, community-based tourism is the most pursued strategy used to ensure the active participation of local communities (Saarinen, 2010). Since studies on sustainable urban tourism in SSA are limited, the hope is that the findings presented here will help Namibia to craft guidelines aimed at enhancing sustainable urban tourism development as a means of dealing with, and achieving, SDGs 1 and 10, while addressing the risks associated with urban tourism in Windhoek.

A qualitative approach involving document analysis was employed to investigate the challenges and prospects of urban tourism development – both its risks and potential ways of building resilience. Document analysis is generally valued for its inexpensive and unobtrusive nature, and for following a systematic procedure that involves the researcher evaluating and reviewing texts (both print and electronic/online versions) (Bowen, 2009). In this instance, data were collected from government documents, civil-society publications and research articles covering aspects of tourism, poverty and inequality (see Table 16.1). The identified documents were examined and interpreted to elicit meaning and gain

Table 16.1 Documents Reviewed and Analysed

Title	Source
Namibia domestic tourism expenditure 2015	Ministry of Environment and Tourism (2016)
Poverty and deprivation in Namibia	NPC (2015)
Update on Sustainable Development Goal indicators	Namibia Statistics Agency (NSA) (2017)
Local tourism awareness: community views in Katutura and King Nehale conservancy, Namibia	Saarinen (2010)
World Bank reports for Namibia	World Bank (2019)
Informal settlements in Namibia: their nature and growth, exploring ways to make Namibian urban development more socially just and inclusive	Weber and Mendelsohn (2017)
Tourists statistical reports	Ministry of Environment and Tourism (MET) (2016); MET (2019)
Tourism-led Poverty Reduction Programme	ITC (2009)
Preliminary national accounts, 2000–2008	CBS (2009)
Economic outlook update	BON (2020)
Poverty, unemployment and inequality in Namibia: TEMTI Series of economic perspectives on global sustainability	Jauch (2012)
Poverty and inequality in Namibia: An overview	Schmidt (2009)

Source: Author.

an understanding of the opportunities as well as the obstacles involved in urban tourism development that seeks to reduce poverty and inequality – this assisted the author in expanding his empirical knowledge (Corbin & Strauss, 2008).

The process of analysing various texts involved 3 significant aspects: skimming, reading and interpreting. Skimming was done to identify the main ideas and determine their suitability for further review and analysis. This was achieved by reading abstracts, perusing charts and tables, and studying the introductions, followed by reading the first and last sentences only of each paragraph. Documents that resonated with the topic under study were subsequently read and interpreted. Data were analysed iteratively, using both content and thematic analysis. In using content analysis, data were organised into the categories dealing with tourism development, poverty and inequality, as these related to the research questions. To guide this undertaking, the following research questions were formulated:

1. What are the prospects of developing urban tourism in Windhoek?
2. What are the challenges of developing urban tourism in Windhoek?
3. How much progress has been made regarding SDGs 1 and 10?
4. What are the possible risks of developing urban tourism in Windhoek?
5. How can resilience be ensured?

Data were also analysed using thematic analysis, which entails doing pattern recognition within the data (Bowen 2009). A more careful, focused rereading followed the skimming and review of the data. The data were carefully reviewed, analysed and ordered in line with the identified research questions. Therefore, the data were analysed based on prospects for tourism development; the challenges confronting urban tourism development; the concomitant risks; and the resilience of the sector. These themes were conceptually derived from the literature to form the categories for data analysis.

16.5 Findings

16.5.1 The prospects and challenges of urban tourism development in Windhoek

From the literature review, several critical challenges emerged in regards the development of sustainable urban tourism in Windhoek – challenges that hinder the meaningful achievement of SDGs 1 and 10. In conjunction with urban risks, such issues could be detrimental to the resilience of the city as a whole. The identified concerns include a lack of PPT policy for the city, the imperfect measurement of tourism's contribution to poverty reduction, inadequate employment creation and the continued unequal distribution of the resources inherited from the colonial era. Urban risks to the promotion of urban tourism in Windhoek include increased exposure to unhealthy environments (e.g. waste or sewage in the streets, and unhealthy environments where food is prepared and sold), gender-based violence, drug abuse, revenue 'leakages' and high crime rates.

In the capital, there is nonetheless the potential for tourism to contribute meaningfully towards the achievement of SDGs 1 and 10 through the development of township tourism and related aspects. Such developments may help to manage urban risks and make tourism in Windhoek more resilient. These aspects are discussed in detail below.

16.5.1.1 Prospects for urban tourism development

Regardless of the challenges discussed earlier, Windhoek has been a significant tourist destination in the country and offers marked opportunities for further development. By marketing the slum areas of Windhoek and developing innovative tourist attractions such as pop-up cultural spaces, ruin bars in derelict buildings and creative events such as carnivals, the city has the potential to develop and enhance its tourism offering. A boost in tourism will contribute significantly towards poverty alleviation and the reduction of all forms of social imbalance. However, this approach requires strategic interventions aimed at minimising the high crime rates associated with African townships (Musavengane et al., 2020), as well as the poorer health outcomes of inhabitants. These prospects are presented in Figure 16.1.

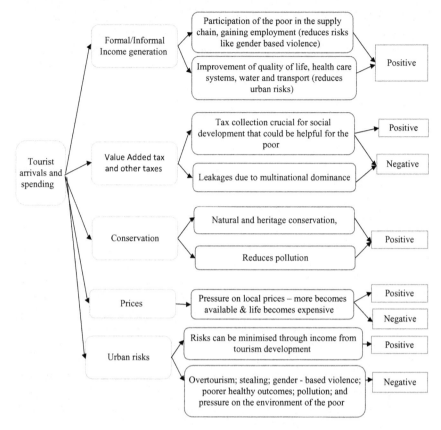

Figure 16.1 Prospects and challenges of urban tourism and the poor in Windhoek.
Source: Author.

Since the country's independence from South Africa in 1990, tourism has been growing and most travellers to the country have been visiting Windhoek. Tourism in the capital generates revenue through entrance fees to nature reserves, accommodation, restaurants and other activities. Though tourism revenue is created through urban development, risks are associated with revenue leakages due to the continued dominance of multinationals in the industry. The biggest spenders amongst day-trippers are business travellers (N$1 598, approximately US$106), followed by those visiting the city for shopping purposes (N$1 229; US$81.90). Holiday-makers spend an average of N$1 042 (US$69.47). The majority of overnight trippers are motivated to travel for shopping and spend N$736 per night, while business and holiday travellers spend N$325 (US$21.67) and N$254 per night (US$16.93), respectively (see Table 16.2).

The implementation of an urban tourism development strategy in Windhoek has the potential to benefit the poor through revenue generation, tax collection (Blake et al., 2008), conservation efforts and sociocultural attractions (see Figure 16.1). In so doing, the poor might receive an income from both their formal and informal participation in the tourism supply chain: income through formal means

Table 16.2 Number of Trips and Spending

	Day trips	Overnight trips	Total
Trips (millions)	2.05	3.74	5.79
Spending/person/day or night (N$)	993	220	N/A
Total spending (N$, billions)	2.04	4.26	6.3

Source: Ministry of Environment and Tourism (2016).

include being employed by tourism and hospitality establishments, while informal income is earned by selling items to visiting tourists. This means of revenue generation is critical in managing urban risks such as prostitution and crime, as people's livelihoods are improved. Urban tourism development is helpful in terms of expanding the tax base of Namibia's local and national governments. The revenue accrued from tourism is vital, with the city using it to improve the social infrastructure (Yu et al. 2019). Such improvements are crucial for ensuring the resilience of the city and for managing urban pressures on critical infrastructure such as schools.

Social grants have been instrumental in alleviating the challenges of extreme poverty over the past 30 years, but more could be achieved with the further development of urban tourism that prioritises the poor.

Revenue generated from developing urban tourism can be used to improve social infrastructure, advance education and promote gender equality (International Trade Centre [ICT] 2009). Windhoek currently faces the challenge of providing decent accommodation to its residents. Since the majority of its inhabitants live in shacks (National Planning Commission [NPC] 2015), the prospect of developing tourism will be beneficial in helping local government to address this perennial challenge and minimise urban risks related to the unhealthy environments that characterise life in a shack. Thus, a deliberate pursuit of sustainable urban tourism development, built on a PPT approach, could help Namibia achieve several SDGs, including poverty reduction, the combatting of inequality, the achievement of gender equality and the provision of quality education. The various SDGs are intrinsically linked and show some degree of inseparability when it comes to the element of sustainability. For instance, SDG 1 is linked to other goals such as those related to health (SDG 3), water and sanitation (SDG 6), energy (SDG 7), climate (SDG 13) and reducing inequality (SDG 10). Thus, it can be argued that reducing inequality (SDG 10) is critical for reinforcing progress towards poverty eradication (SDG 1). Therefore, the PPT approach – if integrated into sustainable urban tourism in Windhoek – would help to achieve many other goals, apart from SDGs 1 and 10.

Windhoek is a popular destination that boasts numerous natural and historical attractions, and these require a considered conservation approach to ensure sustainability. Bringing more people to such attractions will enhance the revenue the city generates and will help to minimise urban risks such as petty crime (e.g. stealing). Conservation is a critical aspect of sustainable urban tourism development, and increased numbers of tourists might result in environmental risks such

Table 16.3 Tourists' Motivations for Visiting

Motivation	%
Leisure/holiday	13.6
Shopping	17.1
Visiting friends and/or relatives	23.6
Weddings	9.9
Business and/or conferencing	15.9
Medical	11.2
Other	8.7
Total	**100**

Source: Ministry of Environment and Tourism (2016).

as pollution and carrying capacities being exceeded – issues that could have a lasting impact on biodiversity. Certainly, urban tourism development – if implemented in Windhoek – will benefit the poor, as it will increase the broader provision of goods and services, given that the city also attracts many tourists for business and shopping (Table 16.3). Tourism development, on the one hand, generates increased demand for local products that are generally supplied by locals, suggesting that the income of Windhoek residents will receive a boost. On the other hand, it makes goods and services expensive for many, and thus defeats progress towards poverty eradication and attempts to reduce inequality by forcing people to resort to perpetual urban risks such as crime (theft) and prostitution.

Understanding tourist motivations is crucial for any successful tourism establishment (Woyo & Slabbert, 2019). Urban tourism development will help the poor by creating a need for more accommodation, thereby generating further direct and indirect employment opportunities in the building and housing sectors. This will also afford opportunities for the poor to further participate in the tourism supply chain by offering authentic, township-based accommodation. Furthermore, the pursuit of an urban tourism development strategy in Windhoek will offer residents sociocultural opportunities that create spaces for intercultural communication (see Figure 16.1). However, urban tourism development also has the potential to dilute cultures due to the promotion of tourism that best suits tourists' cultures and lifestyles. The introduction of Western culture, for instance, has the potential to facilitate individualism within host townships, where collectivism would otherwise be highly appreciated and encouraged.

Windhoek's townships can also be developed and marketed as part of efforts to establish sustainable urban tourism. This will provide the city with increased opportunities for employment and income generation, if the PPT is pursued across urban areas. Local townships include Hakahana (predominantly consisting of shack dwellings), Wanaheda, Katutura and Otjomuise. Wanaheda and Katutura have *kapana* sites, where many patrons congregate to eat braaied meat and other traditional dishes. Tourists might appreciate experiencing everyday township life firsthand. To pursue this avenue, all critical role-players must be brought into the development equation, so that the poor realise the benefits of urban tourism development, and the tourists are granted an opportunity to appreciate Namibia's townships and their original features.

16.5.1.2 Progress made and remaining challenges in urban tourism development

Namibia's political stability and sound economic management have, in the past few years, helped with poverty reduction, mainly through social grants. These grants are financed by revenue generated from diverse sectors of the economy, including tourism. Albeit that tourism is a significant contributor to the country's GDP (Woyo & Amadhila, 2018) – a fact that should be celebrated – tourism development has not meaningfully translated into job creation. This perpetuates poverty-related urban risks such as theft and violence against women. Socio-economic inequalities, inherited from the apartheid system, persist. The city of Windhoek has a sizeable population that dwells in shacks, and township tours are already heavily marketed by tourism industry role-players. Despite this, revenue generation from tourism has not translated into decent accommodation for the population, which suggests weak coordination between the industry and gov-ernment, and a genuine need to tackle poverty. The Namibia Statistics Agency (NSA) (2017) reports that close to 1 million Namibians live in shacks, at least 327 000 of them in the city of Windhoek (Weber & Mendelsohn, 2017). While this offers the prospect of developing tourism in urban slums as part of the city's PPT approach, the shacks distort the city's urban planning efforts because they are increasing in number: townships such as Otjomuise are expanding, creating high-risk zones that are unsafe for tourists due to increased crime and unhealthy conditions.

Post-independence Namibia has made notable progress in terms of poverty reduction. The data presented in Table 16.4 show that the number of people living in poverty reduced by half, from 69.3% in 1993-1994 to 28.7% in 2009-2010. Poverty was further reduced to 17.4% in 2015-2016, while in 2018, a total of 15.5% of the population was recorded as living in poverty (World Bank, 2019). This achievement was most likely made possible through a reliance on govern-ment social grants, which are funded from revenue derived from the tourism sec-tor, amongst others. Therefore, developing urban tourism in Windhoek is critical, as it will generate much-needed revenue that could be used to uplift the poor. Currently, there is no promotion of tourism in a manner that is effective at the city level, which implies a failure to reduce the levels of inequality that exist in the capital (as suggested by its high Gini coefficient) (see Table 16.4). The Gini coef-ficient, which measures inequality in society, ranges from zero (perfect equality) to one (perfect inequality): last year, Namibia scored 0.59 (World Bank, 2019). Urban areas are generally associated with economic development and greater prosperity, yet instances of inequity and severe deprivation among poor urban communities in Windhoek show that tourism has not done enough to help this country move towards achieving SDG 10. Due to the inseparability of SDGs and the complexity of poverty in urban settings (Panori et al., 2019), it can also be argued that tourism has done little to help the country achieve SDG 1.

Table 16.4 Poverty Rates for Namibia and Gini Coefficients

Share of poor individuals (%)	1993-2004	2003-2004	2009-2010	2014-2016	2018
Urban areas	69.30%	38.00%	28.70%	17.40%	15.50%
Rural areas	69.00%	40.00%	38.80%	30.00%	32.00%
Gini coefficient	0.701	0.68	0.604	0.58	0.59

Source: Adapted from Schmidt (2009), Jauch (2012) and World Bank (2019).

Table 16.5 Poverty Headcount Rate per Constituency in Windhoek (2001–2011) (upper-bound poverty line)

Constituency	2001	Rank	2011	Rank	Change
Katutura Central	6.2	1	4.0	5	−2.2
Tobias Hainyeko	4.8	2	9.6	1	4.8
Katutura East	4.5	3	4.1	4	−0.4
Samora Machel	3.3	4	4.3	3	0.9
Soweto (now John Pandeni)	2.9	5	2.1	7	−0.8
Khomasdal North	1.6	6	2.4	6	0.7
Moses Garoeb	1.4	7	8.4	2	7
Windhoek West	0.5	8	0.4	8	−0.2
Windhoek East	0.2	9	0.1	9	−0.1

Source: National Planning Commission (2016).

Windhoek, the commercial hub of the country, has a population of 342 141, which accounts for about 16.2% of the total population in Namibia (NSA, 2017). The city has 9 constituencies and is a net recipient of migrants from other parts of the country due to its strong economic pull, as well as the push factors (poverty and unemployment) present in rural areas. Table 16.5 indicates mixed results concerning a reduction in the incidence of poverty in the city per constituency, especially as 4 of the 9 constituencies registered a rise in poverty levels. Notably, 5 constituencies registered a decline in the poverty headcount rate over the 2001–2011 period (National Planning Commission, 2016).

Katutura Central, which registered the most significant decline in incidences of poverty (see Table 16.5), could benefit more from the promotion of township tours. The development and promotion of urban tourism must also be extended to other parts of the city where poverty remains high, including Tobias Hainyeko, Moses Garoeb and Samora Machel. Notwithstanding the relatively low poverty levels, wide variations exist among the 9 urban constituencies in this region, which are characterised by informal settlements. Those settlements offer opportunities for the development of sustainable urban tourism, and policymakers would do well to integrate their residents into the development processes that they envisage.

While there is virtually no poverty in the Windhoek East constituency (0.1% incidence), in Tobias Hainyeko the figure stands at 10%, and in Moses Garoeb, at 8%. Overall, as the National Planning Commission (2016) reports, there was a 1% increase in poverty in Windhoek over the 2001–2011 period, meaning that 7 230 more people were living in poverty than in 2001. This implies that the tourism development efforts in use might not be sufficiently pro-poor in terms of governance or development, and in working to end poverty in all its forms.

Unemployment in Namibia was estimated to afflict 52% of the labour force in 2008 (Humavindu & Stage, 2013). Currently, most people survive on less than US$2 a day (World Bank, 2019), which suggests that tourism does not generate sufficient employment at present. With growing unemployment, urban risks are likely to be exacerbated. Though tourism in Windhoek could be promising (see Table 16.2 and Figure 16.1) in terms of revenue generation, the development of urban tourism is likely to face several challenges, particularly in the face of COVID-19. Inequality amongst urban residents in Windhoek is higher than that in rural areas (Table 16.4), despite government's generous spending on social programmes (World Bank, 2019). This perpetuates inequalities caused by historical imbalances in terms of access to the means of creating wealth, including access to tourism resources. Tourism in postcolonial Windhoek is generally dominated by foreign multinational corporations and the elite. Amongst the inhabitants, women – who tend to be less educated than men – mostly head households comprising large families, including the elderly and children (World Bank, 2019), a situation that hampers efforts to alleviate poverty and reduce the economic marginalisation of certain communities. Previous studies note that "tourism is an exploitative form of neo-colonialism" (Britton, 1982; Brohman, 1996). Continued inequitable socioeconomic and spatial development in Windhoek corroborates the arguments put forward by Milne (1997) about a vicious cycle of dependency being created. The means of wealth continue to be in the hands of the elite, with tourism organisations in Namibia mostly comprising multinationals owned by non-locals. Notably, arguments around neocolonial exploitation do not identify which strategies could or should be used to secure more significant tourism benefits (Scheyvens & Momsen, 2008). It is therefore sensible that the notion of PPT be applied to urban areas as a resilience-building strategy. This must, however, be done in a manner that promotes sound governance systems in respect of any pro-poor undertakings aimed at benefitting the intended groups (Musavengane et al., 2019) and combatting the risks associated with urban living.

16.6 Conclusion and recommendations

This chapter examined the sustainable urban tourism development trajectory in Windhoek and the urban risks that could emanate from the process of addressing poverty and inequality. Slow progress has been made in respect of alleviating poverty and eradicating social imbalances. The path of using sustainable urban tourism development in Windhoek as a tool for achieving SDG 1 could encounter obstacles, but might also deliver benefits. The city faces critical challenges, such as continued inequality, which compounds urban risks such as gender-based violence and theft. The key benefits of tourism development would include employment creation, revenue generation and conservation. Although sustainable urban tourism development has the potential to affect the city's economy positively, urban risks should be better anticipated and require scientific and strategic management on the part of role-players such as the Ministry of Environment and Tourism, the management of the city of Windhoek and tourism establishments. For example, petty crime and domestic violence require the city's stakeholders (police, law-enforcement agencies, legislators) to make a coordinated effort in dealing with these vices. Despite the contribution of tourism to the GDP, poverty and uneven income distribution remain critical concerns in the Windhoek metropole.

Further research is required to quantitatively measure the links between urban tourism, attempts to bring an end to poverty and efforts to reduce various manifestations of inequality. Also, it is recommended that government and tourism agencies pursue urban tourism development with the poor in mind. This could be critical in helping the city to reduce poverty and inequality, given the interrelationships between the SGDs.

This chapter has offered a conceptual model of how sustainable urban tourism can deliver sustained benefits to the residents of Windhoek (and similar cities) in order to improve the wealth of communities while advancing equality and mitigating urban risks. The continued high poverty levels and levels of social inequality show that while policymakers understand full-well that tourism is essential to the economy, there is no similar appreciation of how to use this sector to combat deprivation and social inequality. Thus, development practitioners and policymakers must develop practical and inclusive interventions that promote PPT in a much more meaningful sense, if SDGs 1 and 10 are to be achieved in a manner that minimises urban risks and promotes the resilience of urban areas.

Note

1 The United States dollar (USD) to Namibian dollar (NAD) at the time of writing was US$1 = NAD$15. This conversion rate applies to all monetary figures in the chapter.

References

Ahmad, F., Draz, M.U., Su, L. & Rauf, A. (2019). Taking the bad with the good: the nexus between tourism and environmental degradation in the lower middle-income Southeast Asian economies. *Journal of Cleaner Production, 233*, 1240–1249.

Atkinson, D. (2016). Is South Africa's Great Karoo region becoming a tourism destination? *Journal of Arid Environments, 127*, 199–210.

Bank of Namibia (BON). (2020). *Economic outlook update.* Windhoek: Bank of Namibia.

Blake, A., Arbache, J. S., Sinclair, M. T. & Teles, V. (2008). Tourism and poverty relief. *Annals of Tourism Research, 35*(1), 107–126.

Boakye, K.A., Otibo, F. & Frempong, F. (2013). Assessing Ghana's contemporary tourism development experience. *Journal of Global Initiatives, 8*(1), 133–154.

Bowen, G.A. (2009). Document analysis as a qualitative research method. *Qualitative Research Journal, 9*(2), 27–40.

Britton, S.G. (1982). The political economy of tourism in the third world. *Annals of Tourism Research, 9*(3), 331–358.

Brohman, J. (1996). New directions in tourism for the third world. *Annals of Tourism Research, 23*(1), 48–70.

Central Bureau of Statistics (CBS). (2009). *Preliminary national accounts, 2000–2008.* Windhoek: Government of the Republic of Namibia.

Corbin, J. & Strauss, A. (2008). *Basics of qualitative research: techniques and procedures for developing grounded theory* (3rd edition). Thousand Oaks, CA: Sage.

Dhahri, S. & Omri, A. (2020). Foreign capital towards SDGs 1 & 2 – ending poverty and hunger: the role of agricultural production. *Structural Change and Economic Dynamics, 53,* 208–221.

Durokifa, A.A. & Ijeoma, E.C. (2018). Neocolonialism and millennium development goals (MDGs) in Africa: a blend of an old wine in a new bottle. *African Journal of Science, Technology, Innovation and Development, 10*(3), 355–366.

Fraser, A., Leck, H., Parnell, S. & Pelling, M. (2017). Africa's urban risk and resilience. *International Journal of Disaster Reduction, 26,* 1–6.

Humavindu, M.N. & Stage, J. (2013). Key sectors of the Namibian economy. *Economic Structures, 2*(1). Doi: 10.1186/2193-2409-2-1.

Hunter, M. (2007). The changing political economy of sex in South Africa: the significance of unemployment and inequalities to the scale of Aids pandemic. *Social Science & Medicine, 64*(3), 689–700.

International Monetary Fund (IMF). (2019). *World economic outlook database, October 2019.* New York: IMF.

International Trade Centre (ICT). (2009). *Tourism-led Poverty Reduction Programme (TPRP): programme proposal.* Geneva: ITC. http://www.intracen.org/exporters/tourism/

Jauch, H. (2012). *Poverty, unemployment and inequality in Namibia. TEMTI series of economic perspectives on global sustainability.* EP 02–2013, TEMTI–CEESP/IUCN. https://www.iucn.org/downloads/temti_ep_02_2013.pdf

Lee, C. & Chang, C. (2008). Tourism development and economic growth: a closer look at panels. *Tourism Management, 28,* 180–192.

Magadi, M.A. (2016). Understanding the urban–rural disparity in HIV and poverty nexus: the case of Kenya. *Journal of Public Health, 39*(3), 63–72.

Milne, S. (1997). Tourism, dependency and South Pacific microstates: beyond the vicious cycle?, in: D.G. Lockhart & D. Drakakis-Smith (Eds), *Island tourism: trends and prospects* (pp. 281–301). London: Printer.

Ministry of Environment and Tourism. (2016). *Namibia domestic tourism expenditure survey.* Windhoek: Government of the Republic of Namibia.

Ministry of Environment and Tourism. (2019). *Tourists statistical report.* Windhoek: Government of the Republic of Namibia.

Ministry of Environment and Tourism (MET). (2016). *Tourists statistical report.* Windhoek: Government of the Republic of Namibia.

Musavengane, R., Siakwah, P. & Leonard, L. (2019). Does the 'poor' matter in pro-poor-driven sub-Saharan African cities? Towards progressive and inclusive pro-poor tourism. *International Journal of Tourism Cities, 5*(3), 392–411.

Musavengane, R., Siakwah, P. & Leonard, L. (2020). The nexus between tourism and urban risk: towards inclusive, safe, resilient and sustainable outdoor tourism in African cities. *Journal of Outdoor Recreation and Tourism, 29,* 100254.

Namibia Statistics Agency (NSA). (2017). *Namibia Inter-censal Demographic Survey (NIDS): 2016 report.* Windhoek: NSA.

Namibia Tourism Board (NTB). (2017). *Namibia tourism satellite account* (5th edition). Windhoek: NTB.

National Planning Commission. (2016). *Namibia poverty mapping.* Windhoek: Government of the Republic of Namibia.

National Planning Commission. (2019). *Update on sustainable development goal indicators.* Windhoek: Government of the Republic of Namibia.

National Planning Commission (NPC). (2015). *Poverty and deprivation in Namibia.* Windhoek: Government of the Republic of Namibia.

Njoya, E.T. & Seetaram, N. (2017). Tourism contribution to poverty alleviation in Kenya: a dynamic computable general equilibrium analysis. *Journal of Travel Research, 57*(4), 513–524.

Nyanchama, V. (2020). *Top 15 cleanest cities in Africa 2020.* https://www.tuko.co.ke/342455-top-15-cleanest-cities-africa-2020.html

Panori, A., Mora, L. & Reid, A. (2019). Five decades of research on urban poverty: main research communities, core knowledge producers and emerging thematic areas. *Journal of Cleaner Production, 237*, 117850.

Rodrigo, C. & Rajapakse, S. (2010). HIV, poverty and women. *International Health, 2*(1), 9–16.

Saarinen, J. (2010). Local tourism awareness: community views in Katutura and King Nehale Conservancy, Namibia. *Development Southern Africa, 27*(5), 713–724.

Satterthwaite, D. (2017). The impact of urban development on risk in sub-Saharan Africa's cities, with a focus on small and intermediate urban centres. *International Journal of Disaster Risk Reduction, 26*, 16–23.

Scheyvens, R. & Momsen, J.H. (2008). Tourism and poverty reduction: issues for small island states. *Tourism Geographies, 10*(1), 22–41.

Schmidt, M. (2009). *Poverty and inequality in Namibia: an overview.* Windhoek: Institute for Public Policy Research.

Sen, A. (2001). *Development as freedom.* Oxford: Oxford University Press.

Siakwah, P., Musavengane, R. & Leonard, L. (2020) Tourism governance and attainment of the sustainable development goals in Africa. *Tourism Planning & Development*, 17:4, 355–383, DOI: 10.1080/21568316.2019.1600160.

Timur, S. & Getz, D. (2008). A network perspective on managing stakeholders for sustainable urban tourism. *International Journal of Contemporary Hospitality Management, 20*(4), 445–461.

United Nations. (2015). *Transforming our world: the 2030 Agenda for sustainable development.* New York: UN.

United Nations (UN). (2019). *Report of the secretary-general on SDG progress, 2019* (special edition). New York: UN.

United Nations World Tourism Organisation (UNWTO) (2019). *Urban tourism.* http://marketintelligence.unwto.org

Weber, B. & Mendelsohn, J. (2017). *Informal settlements in Namibia: their nature and growth. Exploring ways to make Namibian urban development more socially just and inclusive.* Windhoek: Development Workshop Namibia.

World Bank. (2019). *The World Bank in Namibia.* Geneva: World Bank.

Woyo, E. & Amadhila, E. (2018). Desert tourists experiences in Namibia: a netnographic approach. *African Journal of Hospitality, Tourism and Leisure, 7*(3), 1–20.

Woyo, E. & Slabbert, E. (2019). Cross-border destination marketing of attractions between borders: the case of Victoria Falls. *Journal of Hospitality and Tourism Insights, 2*(2), 145–165.

Woyo, E. & Woyo, E. (2019). Towards the development of cultural tourism as an alternative for tourism growth in Northern Zimbabwe. *Journal of Cultural Heritage Management and Sustainable Development, 9*(1), 74–92.

Yu, L., Wang, G. & Marcouiller, D.W. (2019). A scientometric review of pro-poor tourism research: visualisation and analysis. *Tourism Management Perspectives, 30*, 75–88.

17 Conclusion

Navigating urban tourism amidst environmental, political and social risks

Regis Musavengane, Llewellyn Leonard, and Pius Siakwah

17.1 Snapshot

The discussion on the progress towards sustainable African cities has been growing. The African region has unique histories and distinctive social, economic and political dynamics. In this regard, a dialogue on the risks and challenges facing urban tourism in the sub-Saharan African (SSA) region has been provided in this volume. It fills a scholarship gap concerning urban tourism within the SSA context. While scholarship still largely regards Africa as a rural continent (although it is one of the fastest urbanising regions in the world) with limited and fairly insignificant megacities compared with Asia, the Americas and Europe, Africa, and in particular SSA, is changing rapidly (Dietz, 2018).

The chapters in this volume revealed the linkages between urban risks and urban tourism. Furthermore, the possible trajectories to follow to achieve sustainable urban tourism in SSA cities and how urban tourism spaces can potentially become resilient and inclusive were highlighted. As emphasised in previous research, understanding the link between urban risk and tourism can help mitigate the negative effects of urban risks pertaining to tourism operations through good governance practices (Musavengane et al., 2020). Unfortunately, urban risk and resilience have often not been linked to tourism. As we have indicated previously, the foundations of tourism resilience lie in the acknowledgement that social and environmental issues form an intertwined social-ecological entity and that tourism resilience complements sustainability, with the urban tourism environment continuously experiencing change (Cheer & Lew, 2017). In this concluding chapter, the future of urban tourism in SSA is navigated through themes focusing on urban environmental, political and social risks. Unplanned urban growth contributes to these risks (Asian Development Bank, 2013), hence the need for effective planning to mitigate (and alleviate) risks that affect tourism development (Fraser et al., 2017). It is within this context that this volume explored the 4 main themes: urban tourism and environmental pollution risks; peace through tourism, battlefields and war risks; tourism, climate change and flood risks; and inclusive urban tourism and enclaves.

The first theme (urban tourism and environmental pollution risks) explored the linkages between urban tourism and pollution and the implications of that for sustainability. It focused on urban tourism and environmental pollution risks. As such, the relevant chapters examined the extent to which tourism contributes to urban pollution. Apart from the usual discussions on the impacts of tourism on the environment, the chapters included a positive perspective by looking at how pollution could contribute to positive tourism. Filep et al. (2016) defined positive tourism as:

> broadly, a study of hedonic and eudaimonic human well-being and condi-
> tions (or various circumstances) for flourishing as they relate to individual
> tourists, members of host communities and tourism workers in diverse sec-
> tors of the tourism industry (p. 10).

The chapters consequently explored how vulnerable communities affected by urban pollution use tourism to address the environmental and socioeconomic impacts of neoliberal development strategies (Musavengane et al., 2019). For example, Leonard and Nunkoo (Chapter 2) demonstrated that toxic tourism has the potential to not only expand our understanding of how capitalist develop- ment intersects with and impacts on urban spaces, but also of how toxic tours have the potential to address urban environmental risks and create a collective discursive platform for possible improvement of governance operations. Toxic tours are a 'new' form of tourism that seeks to enlighten the world about the social, economic and environmental challenges facing communities located closer to polluting corporations. Africa, as a developing continent, continues to attract investors, and most of them prefer operating in urban areas. Most often, they emit toxic material in urban water bodies and wetlands, thereby threatening the livelihoods of both local communities and fauna. Toxic tourism has the potential to promote inclusive tourism by promoting the inclusion of local communities in urban development and planning and, through that, to address environmental injustices. Toxic tours can draw attention to environ- mental injustices, which can result in improved regulations and laws to address urban risks. The authors also showed that such tours can be effective strategies for environmental justice efforts by germinating discursive spaces and bringing together the cultures of tourists and residents – including issues of how resi- dents challenge, and are challenged by, capitalist frameworks. In Africa, the voice of the marginalised has been deemed unpopular by the capitalists and has, consequently, remained unheard in the development process. This weakens democratic processes concerning resource use and impact. The authors noted that toxic tourism can also provide invaluable lessons for other nonchemical sites exposed to environmental injustices, such as townships in South Africa (and slums globally).

In spite of the existence of environmental challenges, there has recently been a revival in general awareness and appreciation of responsible and sustainable practices among tourism organisations in Africa (Dube & Nhamo, 2020; Khonje et al., 2019; Musavengane, 2019). In their study, Nchinto and Mwale (Chap- ter 3) established that some of the larger entities, mainly those belonging to multinational chains, have waste reduction, reuse or recycling mechanisms in place. However, small tourism businesses in the SSA region have yet to achieve full sustainability. Nchinto and Mwale noted that, compared with multinational hotels, smaller hospitality entities in Livingstone, Zambia, lack similar waste management mechanisms, hence the call to strengthen linkages among the various tourism stakeholders to create viable systems for the reduction or elimination of 'wicked' environmental challenges in African urban spaces that will result in a reduction of the urban risks hindering tourism development. Sustainability guarantees the future of organisations and secures the livelihoods of many, thereby reducing poverty (United Nations sustainable development goal [SDG] number 1) that will, in turn, lead to the attainment of the SDG 11 (sustainable cities and communities) (Siakwah et al., 2020). But the pivotal challenge of the poor who need income for survival being surrounded by organisations that emit waste into essential commodity sources and threaten their livelihoods and means of earning income remains. Therefore, a balance has to be struck through good environmental and corporate governance practices to ensure sustainable business practices among urban tourism organisations.

Waste pollution is often associated with overcrowding, overpopulation and unplanned urbanisation (Kubanza et al., 2016; Musavengane et al., 2020). In Chapter 4, Siakwah demonstrated that due to exponential urbanisation in Ghana, social services provision such as waste management is overwhelmed and outstripped. As a result, promoting tourism as part of a broad development strategy by the government has been challenged. Siakwah raised questions about tourism promotion and a dirty environment; top-down policies on waste collection and citizen ownership concerning the urban waste drive; media education; and informal waste practices to de-plasticise Ghana's environment. Similarly, Leonard and Dladla (Chapter 5), in their study on the densely populated Alexandra Township in Johannesburg, South Africa, revealed that overcrowding has had a negative impact on the running of tourism businesses in that it contributes to the lack of sanitation facilities and the illegal dumping of waste. Although there are concerted efforts by some tourism safari companies to reduce the amount of pollution drastically by adopting responsible and sustainable tourism practices in South Africa, Botswana, Mozambique and Tanzania, such efforts remain fragmented, uncoordinated and inadequate (Dube et al., 2020). In the light of this, it can be concluded that attaining sustainable waste/pollution management in SSA depends on an effective legal and institutional framework; good governance; and citizenship participation. Furthermore, a coherent and synergistic approach by governments and the private sector is required to address development challenges in overcrowded urban communities to contribute to sustainable tourism development. There is also a need for residents to take greater ownership of and have more control over the environment to conserve and protect it from misuse or exploitation.

The second theme (peace through tourism, battlefields and war risks) examined unequal and unsustainable tourism development resulting in conflict and divisions within SSA urban cities, but, at the same time, opportunities for peace-building among people and nations. The applicable chapters highlighted the complexities of violence, xenophobia, urban conflict, peace-building, inclusion and the risks of urban tourism development in Africa. Conventionally, urban tourism thrives within political, social, cultural and environmental spaces that are conducive for visitors. Those spaces should be devoid of conflict, crime and environmental challenges, but this is not the reality in many SSA cities. However, it is a reality that tourism can test existing values, social norms, traditions and behaviour, and that can lead to positions of conflict where resistance or violence can unfold, sparked by the nature of cultural identity; social and economic power relations; legal and moral rights; and management responsibilities (Robinson & Boniface, 1998). Maharaj (Chapter 6) highlighted that although the hosting of the 2010 FIFA World Cup by South Africa advanced the country's tourism industry and showcased the ability of the destination to host mega events, personal safety, security and xenophobia are some of the weaknesses and risks in South Africa that can hinder urban tourism development. Criminality manifests in xenophobic acts in low-income areas and regarding tourism. Whereas a vast majority of tourists to South Africa, and many African countries, come from neighbouring countries, xenophobia has affected the neighbourhoods where migrant populations from the region have settled. Xenophobia has had a negative impact on the perception of South Africa as a tourist destination, which has resulted in a decrease in tourist arrivals. Maharaj's contribution drew attention to acts of xenophobia and criminality against migrants and provided an interesting case study of how a destination seeking to benefit from tourism has to undertake concurrent crisis management in a violent and xenophobic environment.

Despite xenophobia's implications for urban tourism development, peace remains the cornerstone of tourism and, as such, is essential to social growth and development (Wohlmuther & Wintersteiner, 2014). To this end, Musavengane (Chapter 7) concluded that urban areas have unique abilities to promote peace through tourism by their iconic places and buildings of historical significance. The author looked at Harare in Zimbabwe to trace and identify opportunities and routes to promote peace tourism amidst continued election-related conflicts. Promoting peace through urban tourism is inspired by the United Nation's SDG that focuses on peace, justice and strong institutions. Critical elements for promoting peace through tourism include human rights and the rule of law; peace museums; peace music concerts; and liberation routes. Similarly, Etambakonga (Chapter 8) highlighted peace-building and inclusion tourism in the Democratic Republic of Congo (DRC) by exploring tourism's contribution to peace-building efforts in post-conflict regions or spaces. Looking at Goma in the DRC, the challenges facing responsible tourism and local tourism activities that support peace-building efforts and social inclusion were examined. A broader discussion followed on how the budding urban tourism industry develops and its resilience amidst security risks, conflicts and violence in urban spaces. The conclusion was that tourism as a driving force can contribute to building peace among social actors for more sustainable urban tourism despite social conflicts in urban tourism environments. However, political will and good governance practices are required for the building of peaceful and resilient cities and inclusive urban tourism development, and to secure the unity of all Africa within a pan-African context. In 2005, Nelson Mandela stated (cited in O'Connell, 2017): "Well, people respond in accordance to how you relate to them. If you approach them on the basis of violence, that's how they'll react. But if you say we want peace, we want stability, we can then do a lot of things that will contribute towards the progress of our society." This serves as the basis for how African governments should build resilient cities if sustainable urban tourism is to be effective. Good governance will require recognition of and mediation concerning different societal interests (across class, race and national lines), and will also require an understanding of the historical, cultural and social context of society (Costantinos, 2014).

The third theme (tourism, climate change and flood risks) examined the connection between African cities, climate change and urban tourism risk. Evidence suggests that urban tourism in small and big cities has been disrupted severely in the past couple of years, raising questions about the sustainability of urban tourism in Africa. The contributions explored climate change impacts on African tourism businesses and how the latter adapt to a changing environment. The relationship between such businesses and tourism preparedness, their collaboration with government, policy implications and proactive tourism behaviours were also considered. There is strong evidence that climate change is altering the nature of environments globally (Environmental Defence Fund, 2020) and that the impact of climate change on SSA will be severe. Furthermore, indications are that it will increase the rate of rural–urban migration and add to urban (tourism) risks (Serdeczny et al., 2016). Ebhuoma and Leonard (Chapter 9) examined the factors influencing tourism accommodations' lack of preparedness for flooding in Lagos, Nigeria. They noted that the absence of effective adaptation strategies to combat extreme weather events has consequences for small- and medium-sized tourism accommodation businesses. The authors suggested that the absence of a better understanding of flood risks and decreased human and financial capital will undermine preparation for flooding. The same applies to other African cities. Unless there is government financial support and rewards for businesses that implement flood preparedness measures, and the information from disaster management agencies about early weather warnings is used, the situation for tourism businesses will remain dire. On the other hand, Van Staden (Chapter 10) explored policy interventions aimed at climate change impacts and adaptation strategies. The study provided a unique comparison between the coastal tourism hot spots in Mombasa, Kenya, and Cape Town, South Africa – both cities that are highly vulnerable to climate change. Although there were early shifts towards climate change adaptation in Cape Town through policy integration and mainstreaming, it was not the case in Mombasa, where the city's ability to adapt to climate change has been weakened by limited risk-based understanding of climate change. As such, its tourism sector is not protected by climate change adaptation policies. However, both cities face policy gaps, including the prominence of market-led adaptation rather than community-based adaptation, which influences the effectiveness of their climate change adaptation ability and disables sustainable tourism urban development. This provides critical lessons for African countries looking to strengthen policy interventions for climate change and adaptation, and for coastal tourism.

Moving to West Africa and combining climate impacts on tourism and policy, Atanga and Tichaawa (Chapter 11) examined the risk of floods impacting tourism in the coastal city of Accra in Ghana. With limited research on this subject from this region, the authors demonstrated that flood disasters have the potential to affect lives, tourist attractions and businesses directly and indirectly with the likelihood of flooding causing socioeconomic loss and environmental damage, the latter more so concerning the ramifications across the tourism value chain. The impact of floods on tourism thus needs special attention through flood risk management, and the study contributes to such policies and practices. It also provides direction for future research in the field. Linked to proactive behaviours to address climate change impacts, Donkor and Mearns (Chapter 12) explored the nexus of climate change and urban tourism in South Africa and how urban tourism operators in tourism hot spots are managing climate-induced challenges while exploiting opportunities. Urban tourist operators in Cape Town seem well-placed to be leaders in novel niches in the tourism sector, introducing features that can cause clients to become environmentally conscious while co-developing interventions and shaping related policy. The study contributes to the debate, addressing the insufficiency of current global responses to environmental challenges and the need for 'transformative changes' to restore and protect nature and enhance sustainable development. More research on proactive tourism operators is needed to move towards safeguarding the environment and adopting and encouraging appropriate lifestyle changes. From the contributions emanating from this theme, one can conclude that the repercussions of climate change will be felt by tourism businesses in various ways, as well as across natural tourism resources and the human arrangements that derive livelihoods from tourism throughout SSA. If climate change on urban tourism environments is to be addressed, cooperation between government, private and civil-society sectors is required to explore ways of designing appropriate policies and mechanisms that are context-specific for resilience and to safeguard tourism resources and people's livelihoods. Because of Africa's reliance on the tourism industry, mitigating, harmonious and practical solutions are needed (Sifolo & Henama, 2017). This is particularly important for countries in SSA where global environmental change due to climate impacts will be felt most severely by the vulnerable who lack adequate resources (Ahmed et al., 2009; Serdeczny et al., 2016). Ultimately, all stakeholders from government, the private sector and civil society will be required to be proactive, by taking the lead in their domains and working collectively across sectors towards improved cooperation and effective governance for sustainable urban tourism.

The fourth theme (inclusive urban tourism and enclaves) explored inclusive, sustainable urban tourism and ways to enhance local, sustainable tourism development. It highlighted that although tourism is a fast-growing sector that contributes towards livelihoods, it can exclude certain sectors of the population, such as vulnerable groups and informal settlements in urban spaces. To this end, Khumalo (Chapter 13) focused on the connection between informal settlements and urban tourism risk, and examined human settlements and tourism development in Kenya, where the city of Nairobi has a proliferation of informal settlements. The chapter unpacked the risks that emanate from informal settlements in urban spaces, and the socioeconomic and political factors that exacerbate the risks and undermine efforts to address settlement informality in Kenya. It, furthermore, identified prospects and practical strategies for better human settlement development that will curb threats to tourism, such as poor hygiene, crime and poor infrastructure, to support tourism and other development possibilities. Taking inclusive, sustainable tourism further, Dyssel (Chapter 14) examined conservation tourism challenges and opportunities on the Cape Flats, an area comprised of coloured ghettoes, black townships and shantytowns, in South Africa. The chapter showed how nature reserves in this area are impacted by the prevailing challenging socioeconomic conditions in the surrounding communities and the safety concerns and conservation apathy that go hand in hand with that. It was suggested that the challenges manifesting on the Cape Flats could be turned into opportunities as conservation tourism enablers. Thus, an appreciation of a city's conservation assets, including its neglected and less-favourable conservation spaces, can assist in reexamining urban risk and resilience concerns that can then be addressed to eliminate the risk of such concerns impacting negatively on further tourism development.

Similarly, Zhou (Chapter 15) addressed the less-viewed heritage tourism sites in precarious urban spaces, focusing on the Chiremba balancing rocks (CBRs) in Harare. Heritage tourism at the CBRs has been compromised by rapid, creeping urbanisation threatening the natural heritage tourism site's long-term viability and its pristine and authentic status. The study focused on resilience, inclusivity and challenges as they relate to urban heritage tourism at the heritage site and raised concerns about the non-inclusive nature of heritage tourism at the CBRs where local communities have been pushed to the periphery of the heritage tourism value chain. The study proposed that a multitier approach is required to reinvigorate tourism at the heritage site. Moving to Namibia, Woyo (Chapter 16) examined the prospects and challenges of sustainable urban tourism in Windhoek and explored the poverty, inequality and urban risk linkages. Woyo's contribution examined the extent to which urban tourism development might enable the city to arrive at zero poverty and reduce inequality. Progress towards alleviating poverty and eradicating social imbalances such as continued inequality has been slow. The conclusion was that although sustainable urban tourism development has the potential to boost the city's economy, urban risks should be better anticipated and require scientific and strategic management on the part of government and tourism establishments. The needs of the poor must also be incorporated to reduce poverty and inequality. Overall, this theme emphasises that excluding the poor from tourism development practices and development strategies poses a risk for the sustainability of tourism development and, in essence, the building of resilient cities.

17.2 The future of sustainable urban tourism in sub-Saharan Africa

Overall, the contributions in this volume make it clear that the promotion of sustainable urban tourism does indeed have the potential to mitigate urban poverty and urbanisation-related risks while including both national citizens and foreign nationals. Unfortunately, lack of good governance practices and political will to create the collective platforms to inform urban tourism development strategies has worked against securing the necessary gains required to move towards sustainable urban tourism in SSA cities and towns and for cities to become more resilient and inclusive in nature. Current SSA governance strategies must not exclude the poor from urban tourism development, but must instead harness and seize the collective cosmopolitan opportunities and skills within urban tourism design strategies boldly. While it is understood that neoliberal tourism development in the urban space mainly displays exclusionary tendencies often in opposition to wider social benefits (Pavlović & Knežević, 2017), this volume shows that such tendencies create urban risks and do not work in favour of democracy and for the benefit of all people and the environment.

Good governance approaches should be inclusive of non-state stakeholders in decision-making (Marissing, 2005; Rogers & Hall, 2003) and emphasise state accountability and transparency (McNutt & Rayner, 2010), while not relying on technocratic and bureaucratic processes to manage developmental and policy processes (Leonard, 2009). Of importance is that local governance remains a key driver of city resilience through funding and the integration of local actors and knowledge systems. This includes awareness among, investment in and the building of safe spaces by local actors and institutions through the promotion and consolidation of city governance (Amaratunga et al., 2016). As highlighted in the volume, good governance can increase urban resilience and the ability of cities to avert a range of urban tourism shocks and stressors. Considering the contribution of this volume, urban tourism scholarship may benefit from more robust, integrated resilience thinking on tourism linked to good governance. It would be an effective strategy for realising some important SDGs of the United Nations, such as SDG 11: "Making cities and human settlements inclusive, safe, resilient and sustainable". In practical terms, researchers embracing the work on urban risk, tourism and resilience would need to:

1. Appreciate that SSA tourism spaces are unique, and should not always be compared with other regions (the development trajectories are not similar).
2. Where possible, encourage collaboration among scholars from different subregions on the continent. This will provide more informed African perspectives and, at the same time, an appreciation that African countries are unique and should not be treated a as single nation. Africa is a collection of countries, and there is a need for Africans to learn from one another as they largely share similar backgrounds, urban risks and tourism resources.
3. Frame research questions that aim to discuss sustainability risks in African urban areas constructively, while celebrating success and notwithstanding failures.

Furthermore, to achieve Africa's Agenda 2063: The Africa We Want, it is important to synchronise the urban risk nexus and economic development of Africa's urban spaces. The Agenda 2063 blueprint aims for Africa to be the "global powerhouse of the future" (African Union Commission, 2015). Specifically, aspiration 3 of Agenda 2063 envisages an Africa of good governance, democracy, respect for human rights, justice and the rule of law. These elements are key in attaining sustainable urban tourism destinations, and almost all chapters in this volume addressed at least one element of aspiration 3. It will be interesting for scholars to look into linkages between Agenda 2063, the SDGs and urban tourism in Africa. In addition, the volume strengthens the works of the Common Future Report of 1987, the Rio Declaration of 1992 and the MDGs for 2000–2015. In the same vein, the volume adds weight to the Sendai Framework for Disaster Risk Reduction 2015–2030. The Framework covers 4 priorities for risk reduction: (i) understanding disaster risk; (ii) strengthening disaster risk governance to manage disaster risk; (iii) investing in disaster reduction for resilience; and (iv) enhancing disaster preparedness and response (United Nations Office for Disaster Risk Reduction [UNDRR], 2015). It will now be up to African leaders to engage in good governance practices to ensure resilient African urban spaces, and for civil society to hold African leaders accountable, when necessary.

References

African Union Commission. (2015). *Agenda 2063: The Africa we want*. https://au.int/en/agenda2063/overview

Ahmed, S.A., Diffenbaugh, N.S. & Hertel, T.W. (2009). Climate volatility deepens poverty vulnerability in developing countries. *Environmental Research Letters 4*(3). doi:10.1088/1748-9326/4/3/034004

Amaratunga, D., Haigh, R., & Hettige, S. (2016). The role of accountability within disaster risk governance. In N. Domingo, & S. Wilkinson (Eds.), *Proceedings of the 6th International conference on building resilience: Building resilience to address the unexpected* (pp. 688–698). Auckland: Massey University.

Asian Development Bank (2013). *Moving from risk to resilience*. Pacific Studies Series. http://hdl.handle.net/11540/801

Cheer, J. & Lew, A. (2017). Sustainable tourism development: towards resilience in tourism. *Interactions 45*(1), 10–15.

Costantinos, B. (2014). *Unleashing Africa's resilience: Pan-Africanist renaissance in a new African century*. Morrisville, North Carolina: Lulu Press.

Dietz, T. (2018). Online representation of sustainable city initiatives in Africa: how inclusive? *International Development Policy 10*, 139–161.

Dube, K. & Nhamo, G. (2020). Greenhouse gas emissions and sustainability in Victoria Falls: Focus on hotels, tour operators and related attractions. *African Geographical Review*. https:doi.org/10.1080/19376812.2020.1777437

Dube, K., Nhamo, G. & Mearns, K. (2020). Beyond's Response to the twin challenges of pollution and climate change in the context of SDGs. In: Nhamo, G., Odularu G., Mjimba, V. (Eds.), *Scaling up SDGs implementation* (pp. 87–98). Sustainable Development Goals Series. Springer, Cham. https://doi.org/10.1007/978-3-030-33,216-7_6

Environmental Defence Fund. (2020). *How climate change plunders the planet*. https://www.edf.org/climate/how-climate-change-plunders-planet

Filep, S., Laing, J., & Csikszentmihalyi, M. (Eds.). (2016). *Positive tourism* (1st ed.). Routledge. https://doi.org/10.4324/9781315707129

Fraser, A., Leck, H., Parnell, S. & Pelling, M. (2017). Africa's urban risk and resilience. *International Journal of Disaster Risk Reduction 26*, 1–6.

Khonje, L., Simatele, M.D., & Musavengane, R. (2019). A critical review of common methodological approaches in environmental sustainability practices within the Hotel Sector: In pursuit of a befitting synthesis. *e-Review ofTourism Research 16*(5), 400–433.

Kubanza, N.S., Das, D.K. & Simatele, D. (2016). Some happy, others sad: Exploring environmental justice in solid waste management in Kinshasa, The Democratic Republic of Congo, *Local Environment 22*(5), 595–620. https://doi.org/10.1080/13549839.201 6.1242120

Leonard, L. (2009). *"Civil society reflexiveness in an industrial risk society."* PhD dissertation, University of London (Kings College), London, United Kingdom.

Marissing, V.E. (2005). *Citizen participation in the Netherlands Motives to involve citizens in planning processes. Paper presented at the ENHR conference "Housing: New Challenges and Innovations in Tomorrow's Cities"*, Reykjavik, Iceland, 29 June–3 July.

McNutt, K. & Rayner, J. (2010). *Valuing metaphor: A constructive account of reflexive governance in policy networks. Paper presented at the 5th International Conference on Interpretive Policy Analysis, SciencesPo*, Grenoble, 23–25 June.

Musavengane, R. (2019). Small hotels and responsible tourism practice: hoteliers' perspectives. *Journal of Cleaner Production 220*, 786–799. https://doi.org/10.1016/j.jclepro.2019.02.143

Musavengane, R., Siakwah, P. & Leonard, L. (2019). "Does the poor matter" in pro-poor driven sub-Saharan African cities? towards progressive and inclusive pro-poor tourism. *International Journal of Tourism Cities 5*(3), 392–411. https://doi.org/10.1108/IJTC-05-2019-0057

Musavengane, R., Siakwah, P. & Leonard, L. (2020). The nexus between tourism and urban risk: Towards inclusive, safe, resilient and sustainable outdoor tourism in African cities. *Journal of Outdoor Recreation and Tourism 29*(100254), 1–13. https://doi.org/10.1016/j.jort.2019.100254

O'Connell, C. Who is Nelson Mandela? A reader's digest exclusive interview. *Readers digest*, 29 June 2017. https://www.rd.com/list/who-is-nelson-mandela-a-readers-digest-exclusive-interview/

Pavlović, D. & Knežević, M. (2017). Is contemporary tourism only a neoliberal manipulation? *Acta Economica Et Turistica 3*(1): 59–66. https://doi.org/10.1515/aet-2017-0007

Robinson, M. & Boniface, P. (Eds.). (1998). *Tourism and cultural conflicts.* CABI Publishing, Oxon, New York.

Rogers, P. & Hall, W. (2003). Effective water governance. *TEC background papers (7).* Elanders Novum, Stockholm.

Serdeczny, O., Adams, S., Baarsch, F., Coumou, D., Robinson, A., Hare, W., Schaeffer, M., Perrette, M. & Reinhard, J. (2016). Climate change impacts in Sub-Saharan Africa: from physical changes to their social repercussions. *Regional Environmental Change 17*, 1585–1600 (2017). https://doi.org/10.1007/s10113-015-0910-2

Siakwah, P., Musavengane, R. & Leonard, L. (2020) Tourism governance and attainment of the sustainable development goals in Africa. *Tourism Planning & Development*, 17:4, 355–383, DOI: 10.1080/21568316.2019.1600160.

Sifolo, P. & Henama, U. (2017). Implications of climate change for tourism in Africa, *GeoJournal of Tourism and Geosites 2*(20), 191–198.

United Nations Office for Disaster Risk Reduction [UNDRR]. (2015). *Sendai framework for disaster risk reduction 2015–2030.* https://www.undrr.org/publication/sendai-framework-disaster-risk-reduction-2015-2030

Wohlmuther, C. & Wintersteiner, W. (Eds.). (2014). *International handbook of tourism and peace. Centre for peace research and peace education of the Klagenfurt University/ Austria in cooperation with World Tourism Organization (UNWTO).* Drava Print.

Index

Page numbers in *italic* indicate figures. Page numbers in **bold** indicate tables.

Printed in the United States
By Bookmasters